the Guy can't Cook

Cinda Chavich

the Guy can't Cook

over 350 fabulous no-fail recipes a Guy can't be without

illustrations by Kirsten Horel

whitecap

Edited by Nicole de Montbrun and Nadine Boyd
Proofread by Viola Funk
Design by Roberta Batchelor
Typeset by Jesse Marchand
Illustrations by Kirsten Horel

Printed and bound in Canada

LIBRARY AND ARCHIVES CANADA CATALOGUING IN PUBLICATION

Chavich, Cinda
The Guy can't cook : over 350 fabulous no-fail recipes a Guy can't be
without / Cinda Chavich.

Includes index.
ISBN 978-1-55285-841-7
ISBN 1-55285-841-3

1. Quick and easy Cookery. I. Title.

TX833.5.C468 2007   641.5'12   C2006-904981-5

The publisher acknowledges the financial support of the Government of Canada through the Book
Publishing Industry Development Program (BPIDP) and the Province of British Columbia through the Book
Publishing Tax Credit.

Important: Some of the recipes in this book call for the use of raw eggs. Pregnant women, the elderly, young
children and anyone with a compromised immune system are advised against the consumption of raw
eggs. You may wish to consider the use of pasteurized eggs. www.aeborg/safety provides updated
information on eggs and food safety.

Contents

Intro 7

Sustenance 22

Decadence 168

Observance 334

The Toolman 484

Mix and Match Menus 490

Guy Glossary 494

Index 517

Intro

There was a time, long long ago and far far away, when guys never lifted a cooking pot. Being a Guy meant bringing home the bacon, and finding a girl to fry it up in the pan. But those days, my manly friends, are ancient history.

Real men not only eat quiche (and eggplant and risotto), they know how it's made. And when pressed, they can google around, find a recipe, and deliver it to the table. This is what most modern girls expect. There has never been a more macho time to pick up that pot and dazzle your friends with your knife skills. The chefs of the world are the new rock stars, unassuming guys who become the sexy center of attention when they step behind a stove. You too can generate that kind of heat with a few drop-dead recipes in your back pocket, a dash of wine, and food savvy conversation to toss around at the next dinner party.

The Guy never expected he would learn to cook. He hooked up with a woman who made cooking (and writing about it) a career. So, except for the odd breakfast and burger, he pretty much had it made when it came to the sustenance side of the basic necessities equation.

But then times changed, everyone got busier, and his partner and cook was often away on business trips. Furthermore, it started to get competitive around the campfire during his Guy-bonding ski and hiking weekends. That was it: he had to learn his way around a recipe. It was a matter of both self-preservation and -esteem. He needed to know which fork to use at the best restaurants, and how to find that gem on the wine list. He wanted to know what to buy at the grocery store, and how not to ruin that slab of beef tenderloin he'd maxed out the credit card to purchase. So herein lie the secrets of The Guy's incredible journey into the world of real food.

In college it was Kraft Dinner and taco kits. Today it's pasta with aged cheddar and quesadillas on the grill. He still likes sandwiches and stews, but he now gets his bread from the artisan baker down the street and his bacon from the butcher who smokes it from scratch.

He's begged and borrowed his culinary knowledge from the tv chefs he's met. He's learned the tricks to smoking a pork butt from a champion and how to pick the finest artisan cheeses from his local cheesemonger. The Girl—and the other guys—are impressed by The Guy's new food knowledge. And The Guy is eating much better.

This book won't make you as cute as Jamie Oliver or as funny as Emeril, but you'll be able to crank out a fast dinner on Tuesday before their cooking shows are even over. If your kids—or your own stomach—are screaming for sustenance, you'll learn how to turn a few eggs or a chicken breast into instant comfort. And when duty calls, you can show up at the potluck/party/barbecue/holiday dinner with a dish that will make your mother proud. Never mind that special someone who will be hanging on your every word after you present your perfectly romantic steak dinner for two.

So don't panic, put on your whites, and get ready to learn what those chef guys already know: cooking isn't brain surgery. But it's creative, challenging, and it can make you as sexy and addictive as chocolate mousse.

Cook On!

Garbage In, Garbage Out

When it comes to cooking, The Guy's mantra comes directly from his career in computing—what you put in is what you get out.

You've heard those uber-chef guys drone on about eating seasonally and buying ingredients locally. This isn't just some trendy restaurant sales shtick — they're actually sharing their best secret weapon.

Start with fresh, just-picked food straight from your local farmer, artisan baker, or butcher. These people care about quality and flavor first, and this gives you an instant edge over the other guy. Decide what to serve based on what's in season, then your menus will shine with simple ripe and exotic flavors. Forget strawberry shortcake in January, make a pecan or apple pie. Spend the extra money on a really delicious raw milk, artisan cheese, and a freshly baked baguette and you don't need to cook a thing. Just slice and serve.

Enjoy the simple pleasures of foods made with personal passion, not manufactured in a factory. You'll not only impress your friends, you might just make a difference to a farm family and help save the environment. At the very least, you'll have a fascinating little story to tell about the provenance of the free-range turkey you're carving.

So don't torture yourself in the kitchen trying to work wonders with substandard ingredients or dodgy equipment. Think about that new snowboard or bike you just bought and how having the right stuff instantly enhances your performance.

It's exactly the same when you're performing behind the stove. You wouldn't put watered-down gas in your car or head up Everest with bargain-basement boots. Treat your body and your kitchen with the same care and respect.

The Guy can't stress this point strongly enough. Start with top-quality, tasty ingredients and your meals will rise to a new level of quality and flavor, while saving you time and energy. Embrace simplicity—a bowl of perfectly ripe peaches, a creamy pudding made with pure chocolate—and authenticity.

While there's nothing wrong with a basic meat and potatoes meal, if you're doing Thai curry, you'll need to get yourself to an Asian grocery store to create authentic flavors.

Don't be intimidated by trying something new. Take it slow. Many ethnic cuisines have wonderful ingredients and convenient products that can cross over into other areas of your cooking. The Guy wouldn't be caught dead, for example, without a jar of Asian chili paste (sambal oelek) in the fridge, next to the Italian basil pesto, Thai curry paste, and Indian coriander chutney. The latter is a jar of puréed fresh cilantro, perfectly handy whenever you need a jolt of fresh coriander in a curry, chicken and tortilla soup, or guacamole.

A bit of sour cream or mayo with a dollop of curry paste makes an instant veggie dip. And a can of coconut milk can morph a basic stir-fry into an exotic Southeast Asian curry. A well-stocked pantry is essential when you're busy and need to improvise a fast soup or pasta dish.

Don't be a slave to a recipe—if it says lemon juice, try orange juice or wine vinegar. Apple juice can stand in for white wine, and Camembert for brie.

To keep your cooking creative and fresh, buy that gigantic bag of fresh peppers at the farmers' market in August and start looking for new ways to use them. Soon you'll have discovered the secrets to roasting peppers, canning salsa, and creating a classic Cajun étouffée.

Remember, good ingredients and the proper tools make cooking exponentially easier and a lot more fun. Saving a few pennies per pound is a false economy—spend more and you'll save time cooking, enjoy your meals more, and keep your body, the local economy, and the environment in better shape.

The Guy hates to preach but if there's one true thing he's learned in the food world it's this—eat locally and seasonally as often as possible, and you'll always eat better.

Tricks from the Commercial Kitchen—Culinary Guyville

Guys have long reigned in commercial chefdom (a reality that The Girl and The Guy have always considered strangely ironic). But most pro chefs—of whatever gender — rely on clever short cuts and essential pantry ingredients to take their cuisine into gourmet territory.

Peer into any top restaurant walk-in cooler and you'll find the shelves stacked with top-quality ingredients. These tasty, essential tricks of the trade are artisan cheeses, heirloom vegetables, fresh or dried wild mushrooms, bunches of fresh herbs and tiny micro greens, and kitchen-created concoctions like caramelized onions, fig jam, homemade stocks, fresh herb pestos, roasted garlic, reduced balsamic vinegar, and fresh salsas.

These are the little touches that take an average sandwich, pizza, or piece of grilled protein beyond the ordinary. A drizzle of this, a tiny quenelle of that, and soon your everyday plate is seriously chic. So take a cue from the guys in the commercial kitchen brigade—be prepared in the pantry!

Pantry 101

The best defense is a good offense or, as every boy scout knows, "be prepared."

That means stocking your pantry and refrigerator with the kind of products that will make your meals taste great, even if you only have the time and energy for a cheese omelet.

Make sure you have good free-range eggs and some real Parmesan cheese, and your omelet will be delicious (and finished faster than you can nuke a frozen entrée).

I know, I know, this list looks daunting. But don't panic. Once you find the good Asian grocery store and a decent Italian market in your area you will make sure you have these convenient products in your kitchen at all times. They're some of the secret weapons that good cooks and chefs use to trick you into thinking they've been slaving all day.

Cheese

Parmigiano Reggiano (a grating of good-quality Parmesan will save any pasta dish); creamy logs of goat cheese (it can be frozen); feta cheese; mozzarella and provolone (grating cheeses for pizza), havarti, cheddar, and Gouda (sliceable cheeses for sandwiches — buy them pre-sliced for convenience).

Fats/Oils

Olive oil, regular and EVO (extra virgin olive oil); canola oil; sesame oil; and unsalted butter.

Vinegars

Red and white wine vinegar; Chinese rice vinegar; balsamic vinegar; and apple cider vinegar.

Seasonings

Sea salt, whole black peppercorns (and a decent pepper mill), whole dried chilies, dried basil, thyme leaves, cinnamon, mustard seeds, whole nutmeg, fennel seed, oregano, granulated garlic, chili powder, sweet Hungarian paprika and smoked Spanish paprika, cumin (whole seed and ground), juniper berries (pick them off the shrubs in the yard), allspice berries (Jamaican food necessity), coriander (seeds and ground), white pepper, turmeric, saffron threads, cloves.

Olives

Hit the olive bar at your Italian grocery store for some kalamatas, some nice big green olives and even some that have been marinated and flavored with herbs and spices (all make instant appetizers). Get a few cans of anchovy-stuffed olives, and a jar of air-cured black olives (they last forever and make great additions to pasta sauces like puttanesca, pizza, or tapenade, pages 21, 289).

Bottles and Jars

Dijon mustard, Asian chili paste (sambal oelek), mayonnaise, curry paste (Thai and Indian), smoky barbecue sauce, mirin (Japanese rice wine), salsa, one good-quality bottled salad dressing, capers, wasabi, pesto, red currant jelly, apricot jam, marmalade, and maple syrup.

Canned Goods

Low-sodium chicken and beef broth (re-sealable Tetra Paks are handy); whole and chopped Roma tomatoes; sundried tomatoes packed in oil; artichoke hearts (packed in water, not oil); black, red, and white beans; vegetarian refried beans; kernel corn; tomato paste; cans of plain tomato sauce (check labels for no added fats); chickpeas; chipotle chilies in adobo; sweetened condensed milk; light coconut milk; canned salmon, tuna, clams, smoked oysters, and anchovy fillets.

Frozen Goodies

Smoked salmon, nuts (toasted hazelnuts, almonds, pecans, walnuts, pine nuts), thick Greek-style whole wheat pita bread (for instant pizza crusts), sliced air-dried salami, whole wheat tortilla shells for wraps, goat cheese, fresh Italian sausages, peas, orange juice concentrate, gourmet ice cream or frozen yogurt, puff pastry.

Fresh Essentials Year-Round

Wholegrain bread, large free-range eggs, milk, unsalted butter, cooking onions, green onions, garlic, ginger, tomatoes, English cucumbers, mixed salad greens, romaine lettuce, red and yellow bell peppers, baking and boiling potatoes (white and red), celery, carrots, mushrooms, plain yogurt, sour cream, selection of cheeses, fruits (like oranges, lemons, limes, apples, bananas, and grapefruit), fresh herbs (like rosemary, thyme, Italian parsley, and cilantro—store them upright in a jar, stems in a bit of water, and loosely cover the leaves with a plastic bag).

Dry Goods and Other Stuff

Maple syrup, good coffee, loose-leaf teas, Tetra Paks of real orange juice, a variety of long and short dried pasta (fettuccine, rotini, penne, spaghetti, orzo, couscous, egg noodles, Asian rice noodles), tahini (sesame paste), natural peanut butter (no added sugar or hydrogenated fats), honey, real vanilla extract, bittersweet chocolate, raisins, dried apricots and cranberries, good quality biscotti, water biscuits/crackers/flatbreads, flour (unbleached, whole wheat, and rye), sugar (granulated, brown, and icing sugar), oats (large flake, and steel cut), cornmeal, rice (basmati, arborio, brown, and sushi rice), pearl barley, green lentils, popping corn, and corn chips (in case all else fails).

Seasonal Fruits and Vegetables

Buy seasonal local fruits and vegetables whenever possible. Farmers' markets, u-pick farms, organic grocers, and gourmet shops are all good sources for top-quality local produce. Do your homework and find out who are the local growers and what's in season when. Then stick to it. Some vegetables to try when they're in season locally or when they look especially fresh in the market include: asparagus, baby artichokes, leeks, wild mushrooms, peas, carrots, green and yellow beans, baby bok choy, corn on the cob, summer squash, new potatoes, beets, kohlrabi, jicama, winter greens like Swiss chard and collard greens, Italian broccoli rabe, cabbage, cauliflower, mung bean sprouts, tomatillos, eggplant, fennel bulbs, sweet and hot peppers, sweet potatoes, rutabagas, parsnips, and winter squash. Seasonal fruits include blueberries, peaches, apricots, red ox heart plums, pears, rhubarb, strawberries, blood oranges, mangoes, pineapple, quince, clementines, kumquats, watermelon, and pomegranates.

Meat/Fish

Find a great butcher or make friends with an organic farmer. If you frequent the farmers' markets in your town or city in the summer, you'll likely find someone selling great beef, pastured chicken, or amazing lamb. Make an effort to buy locally from good producers and you will be rewarded with the best meals (and the easiest cooking). Always have good double-smoked bacon and pancetta in the fridge. Fresh sausage is another essential. Once you find that great local source of fresh Italian sausages, Spanish chorizo, and German bratwurst, you will have more essential ingredients in your arsenal. Ditto for a fishmonger. Find someone you trust to provide fresh, high-quality, and sustainably caught fish. And always buy in season.

The 10 Essential Sauces
(Don't Leave the Market Without Them)

Asian Chili Paste (a.k.a. Sambal Oelek)

Comes in a jar, keeps for months in the fridge and torques up any dish when you need a hit of pure heat. With this sauce in the fridge, you can get rid of all other bottled hot sauces. Use it in pasta sauces, barbecue sauces, rubs, soups, salad dressings, and dips. A Chinese chili bean sauce is good to have on hand, too.

Basil Pesto

You can make your own for special dishes, but it's always good to have a jar of basil pesto in the fridge. It adds that kick of fresh herbal flavor to any soup or sauce. It's the perfect base to slather on pita breads for instant appetizer pizzas, or to toss with plain pasta for a pasta salad. If you make your own pesto during the height of summer herb season, you can portion it in ice cube trays and freeze it—a cube finishes any soup or stew with a shot of fresh summer flavor.

Coriander Chutney

The Indian version of basil pesto, this condiment is a purée of fresh cilantro and chilies. Add it to curries, Mexican guacamole, salsas, bean dishes, or tortilla soup whenever you need a hit of fresh cilantro and there's none in the fridge.

Light and Dark Soy Sauce

The dark tamari made with 100 percent soy beans is essential for stir-fry sauces but the light stuff is nicer for dipping sushi. Look for the words "naturally brewed" on the label. Indonesian soy sauce (kecap manis) is sweet and thick as molasses—perfect for glazing grilled meats.

Oyster, Hoisin, and Black Bean Sauces

 This trilogy of Chinese sauces will get you through dumpling dips, duck quesadillas (or Peking duck) and all kinds of stir-fries.

Wasabi and Horseradish

Whether it's pre-mixed in a tube or powdered in a can, you need wasabi for Japanese food, and regular horseradish for roast beef. Mix with either a good-quality commercial mayo for an excellent dipping/sandwich sauce, or thin it with buttermilk for salad dressings.

Sundried Tomato Paste or Pesto

Make it yourself or buy it. A bit of sundried tomato purée is an intense jolt of tomato flavor—nature's perfect balance of sweetness and acidity that brightens almost any dish.

Worcestershire Sauce

An old English classic concoction of sweet, sour, and umami (the meaty, glutamate flavor that comes from the anchovies in the sauce). It works well as a rub over steak, and is essential in a spicy Caesar. A splash of the simpler Thai fermented fish sauce (a.k.a. nuoc nam) lifts almost any soup or sauce—you won't even taste it but your palate will notice an appreciable improvement.

Mayonnaise

Sure, a purist makes his own mayonnaise from scratch (The Guy has seen chefs do this, for sure) but the best store-bought mayo is fine and should always be in your fridge. Taste them—The Guy always goes for Hellmann's, and the "light" version is just as tasty as the full-fat one. Mayo is the base for many sauces and dips.

Mustard

The classic is Dijon, but there are so many interesting mustards out there to try, you should make sure to have at least something smooth and something grainy in your fridge. Yellow ballpark mustard is the kind to slather over pork or chicken for the smoker (the high level of sugar seals the meat) but a dab of Dijon is the emulsifier you need to bind the oil and vinegar in a vinaigrette.

Chefs' Secret Weapons

The Guy has discovered that the best restaurant chefs stay prepared with a few homemade goodies that add layers of flavor to their cooking. There are many such specialties in individual arsenals—from fig jam, to herbal vinegars, to signature spice mixtures. But The Guy has learned that almost every top chef has the following three secret weapons in the fridge at all times: caramelized onions, roasted garlic, reduced balsamic vinegar. Learn the secret of these three simple things, and everything you make will taste exponentially better. No lie.

Caramelized Onions

The Guy is absolutely addicted to onions, and once they've been slowly cooked down into a sweet brown mass (caramelized) you can pile them onto, or fold them into, almost anything—with spectacular results. Make caramelized onions in advance and keep them in a jar in the refrigerator for several days. Or make them an hour before your guests arrive and your house will have that mouth-watering sautéed onion smell, the one that crosses all cultures and age groups on the "gotta-have-that" scale.

For starters, The Guy can't have a burger without a mass of golden brown onions on top. Serve onions that have been caramelized in good olive oil with baguette slices, and you have a simple and addictive appetizer. Use them on flatbread, scatter them over pizzas, fold them into omelets, or add them to a simply dressed pasta along with black olives and cherry tomatoes. For traditional onion soup, add them to beef broth flavored with sherry. Pile them onto grilled sausage sandwiches, or chop them up for dips and frittatas. A simple caramelized onion is at home at a picnic or a top-drawer cocktail party. Make some now and when you run out, make more.

3 large onions, peeled and thinly sliced
   (white, red, and/or yellow)
¼ cup (60 mL) extra virgin olive oil

1 tsp (5 mL) sugar
1 tsp (5 mL) balsamic vinegar

1 Heat the oil in a sauté pan over medium-low heat. Add the onions and stir until they are coated with the oil. Cover the pan and sweat the onions for 5 minutes. Remove the cover and sauté until the onions begin to turn golden—if they are browning or burning, the heat is too high. Continue to cook until the onions are very soft and jammy, with a nice golden color. Stir the sugar and vinegar together, then add to the pan. Cook until the liquid is gone. Pile into a bowl and serve warm with bread, or put them in a container and refrigerate until you're ready to use them.

Roasted Garlic

This is another item in The Guy's arsenal of great food tricks—so simple, yet so effective. After less than an hour in the oven, the aggressive garlic is reduced to a melting mass of sweet, nutty, garlicky flavor. Make lots of roasted garlic and add it to mashed potatoes, salad dressings, soups, and pasta sauces. Or just squeeze it out of the dried roasted skins and slather it on French bread for an easy appetizer. Here's how to do it.

3 heads of garlic   3 tsp (15 mL) extra virgin olive oil

1 Preheat the oven to 350°F (180°C). With a sharp knife, cut off the top ¼ inch (the pointy part) of each whole head of garlic. You should be able to see the tops of the exposed cloves. Set each head of garlic on a piece of foil, and drizzle with 1 tsp (5 mL) of the olive oil. Loosely gather the foil around the head of garlic so it will hold in the oil—but don't seal the garlic completely. Place the garlic packages in the oven and roast for 45 minutes. Remove the garlic, unwrap, and cool slightly. Squeeze the roasted garlic out of the papery husk—it should be reduced to a creamy, sweet, caramel-colored paste. Roasted garlic will keep in a sealed container in the refrigerator for 2 weeks. Have it on hand and ready to use at all times.

Reduced Balsamic Vinegar

If you are a rich man, invest in a bottle of the real *balsamico tradizionale*—that super-expensive Italian condiment aged for decades in small wooden barrels until it becomes a sweet, syrupy elixir beyond compare. The Guy is still nursing the bottle he hauled back from Modena on one of his whirlwind food tours.

But when you're not serving the Queen, you can create a perfectly good syrupy drizzle from a bottle of basic balsamic. The trick is reduction—boiling your balsamic until it's thick and rich. It's up to you how much money you spend on the original bottle of vinegar. The Guy has had success with bottles from the local big-box store, but be aware that reducing concentrates both the fine and faulty flavors.

Use this yummy stuff to finish salads, especially composed salads that cry out for a bit of plate decoration. Drizzle it over grilled fish or veggies, or add it to any tomato sauce or soup.

1 Pour a whole bottle of balsamic vinegar into a stainless steel pot and bring it to a boil. Boil until it's reduced to ¼ of its original volume (if you start with 2 cups/500 mL, boil it down to ½ cup/125 mL). Do this on a day when you can open the windows, as boiling vinegar puts a sharp aroma into the air. Rebottle the vinegar and refrigerate. If you put it into a plastic squeeze bottle with a small tip, you can artfully drip and drizzle it onto plates like a real chef.

Added Artillery

Roasted Peppers

Colorful red, orange, and yellow bell peppers are expensive most of the year, but in the fall, when a bumper crop is available, you can buy big bags of fresh peppers for a song. Buy them, roast them, and freeze them. You'll have wonderful appetizers all year long.

Start with thick-fleshed sweet bell peppers. Preheat the barbecue or broiler to high. Place the whole peppers directly on the grill, or under the broiler, and roast until all sides are browned and beginning to char. Make sure the peppers don't burn too badly, but don't worry if the skins begin to blacken. When the peppers are blackened on all sides, remove from the heat and place in a covered bowl or closed paper bag to cool. This allows the peppers to steam. When cool enough to handle, peel off the charred skin and remove and discard the seeds and membranes. Tear or slice into long, thin strips.

The peppers can then be bagged in freezer bags and frozen. Use on pizzas, in pasta sauces, on sandwiches or marinated with garlic and basil for appetizers.

1 To serve marinated roasted peppers, mix 2 cups (500 mL) of thawed pepper strips with 3 tablespoons (45 mL) extra virgin olive oil, one clove of pressed or minced garlic, 3 tsp (15 mL) of balsamic vinegar, salt, pepper, and a few fresh basil leaves, minced. Let the marinated peppers stand at least 1 hour for the flavors to meld, or cover and refrigerate for up to 2 days. Serve with sliced baguette.

RED
PEPPER

Fig Paste

Many chefs have discovered the power of pairing a dab of sweet-and-sour flavor with strong cheeses or salty meats. This jammy concoction of sweet figs, honey, and balsamic vinegar is just that kind of condiment. It's perfect on a cracker with a bit of Stilton or scattered over a Gorgonzola and prosciutto pizza. Try wrapping a bit up with some strong blue cheese in a prosciutto packet. It keeps for a long time in a jar in the fridge, and makes a great gourmet gift.

1 cup (250 mL) dried Mission figs
  (stems removed)
¼ cup (60 mL) water
1 cup (250 mL) ruby port
½ cup (125 mL) balsamic vinegar

¼ cup (60 mL) liquid honey
2 cloves garlic, minced
1 tsp (5 mL) mixed peppercorns (pink, white,
  and black), coarsely crushed

1 Put the figs in a bowl with the water, cover, and microwave for a minute. Set aside to cool, then finely chop the figs.

2 In a non-reactive saucepan, combine the port, balsamic vinegar, honey, and garlic. Bring to a boil. Stir over high heat and boil vigorously until it is reduced by half (that is, until half the liquid has boiled away).

3 Stir in the chopped figs and peppercorns. Reduce the heat to low and simmer until it boils down to a thick, jam-like consistency, about 20-30 minutes. Put the preserves into small jars and refrigerate. Makes about 1 cup (250 mL).

Herb Oils

Anytime you make a dish with fresh herbs and want to torque the presentation into gourmet territory, think about a drizzle of herbal oil (either on the food, or artfully around the plate). Basil and cilantro work particularly well, but you can also use Italian parsley, chives, or a combination of other green stuff to create a brilliant green infusion. Chefs do this all the time—you should too.

1 cup (250 mL) fresh herbs (basil, cilantro, Italian parsley, watercress, etc.)

¾ cup (175 mL) extra virgin olive oil
½ tsp (2 mL) sea salt

1 Bring a saucepan of water to a boil. Plunge the herbs in the boiling water, then drain immediately, and immerse in ice water to chill and stop them from cooking further. This shocks the herbs and keeps their color bright. Drain the herbs well, squeezing them dry in a paper towel.

2 Blend the herbs, oil, and salt in a blender or food processor until smooth. The herb oil may be kept in a bottle in the fridge for a week or two. Strain for longer storage—infused oils will keep for several months. Makes 1 cup (250 mL).

Oven-Roasted Tomatoes

These chewy, oven-roasted tomatoes are perfect to use on sandwiches (they never get soggy), pizzas, or to toss into fast pasta combinations.

2 pounds (1 kg) Roma tomatoes (quartered) or grape tomatoes (halved)
⅓ cup (75 mL) extra virgin olive oil
2 tsp (10 mL) sea salt

1 tsp (5 mL) each: chopped fresh thyme, oregano, and rosemary
3 cloves garlic, peeled and halved
¼ tsp (1 mL) freshly ground black pepper

1 Preheat the oven to 225°F (105°C). Combine the ingredients in a bowl and toss to mix. Spread on a non-stick baking sheet, lined with parchment, and bake for 3 hours, until the tomatoes are dark and dehydrated (but still chewy). Cool to room temperature. Place tomatoes and remaining oil mixture in a covered container. Refrigerate for up to 1 week.

Tapenade

This is one of those easy spreads that anyone can make to have on hand for impromptu creations. Buy a jar of air-cured black olives and soon you'll have something wonderful in the refrigerator. Spread tapenade on your sandwiches or crostini toast appetizers, add to vinaigrettes and tomato sauces, dollop on pizzas (see The Pizza Party page 178), or stuff a boned leg of lamb.

1 cup (250 mL) dry-cured black olives (or green
   for green olive tapenade)
2 cloves garlic, pressed or minced
1 anchovy or 1 tsp (5 mL) fish sauce (optional)
1 tsp (5 mL) finely grated lemon zest

2 tsp (10 mL) fresh lemon juice
¼ cup (60 mL) good-quality olive oil
pinch of freshly ground black pepper and
   cayenne, or to taste

1 Put the olives on a cutting board. Place the flat side of your chef's knife over the olives and press down. This will split the olives so you can easily pick out the pits.

2 Chop the olives finely by hand, or use a food processor to chop. Add the remaining ingredients and whirl them together (or mix in a bowl). Make sure your tapenade stays a little chunky. Put it in a jar and refrigerate. Makes ¾ cup (175 mL). Keeps refrigerated for several weeks.

FISH
Sauce

OLIVES

Sustenance

**Easy everyday meals that will keep you going
without boring you**

Between Bread

A man cannot live on bread alone, but a sandwich, now that's a different story

The Guy could live on sandwiches. Like Dagwood before him, there's not much he can't imagine sandwiched between two slices of bread—the perfect fast and portable nosh.

Whether it's a knife-and-fork steak sandwich, a meaty pulled pork sandwich off the smoker, or a quick turkey sandwich for lunch, the key to a good sandwich is simple: great fillings and even greater bread.

The Guy loves the sourdough loaves shot with fresh rosemary and apples from his local artisan baker, and he always has big ciabatta buns in the freezer for an impromptu panini. A good baguette, cut into 4-inch (10-cm) lengths, is perfect for steak sandwiches or Italian sausages. A thick, Greek-style pita bread is easy to split and fill with grilled chicken, roasted peppers, and feta cheese. And a basic multigrain loaf is like a navy blazer — it goes with everything. From peanut butter and jelly to bacon and tomatoes, multigrain is your match.

The Guy likes to have the good stuff on hand for his late night sandwich-making forays. Make a few things like Caramelized Onions (see page 16) in advance and always have lean cold cuts, imported cheeses, and a sauce, or "slather", on the shelf to make your sandwiches memorable.

Sure, you can survive on plain cheese sandwiches, but these classic combinations make sandwiches that can stand in for supper (with a crisp green salad on the side). These are man-wiches!

Bistro Ham and Cheese

In a French café, a ham and cheese usually means Croque Monsieur—a cross between a ham and cheese sandwich and French toast. This makes the perfect breakfast or lunch on the run if you serve it cold. It's a classic. Swap the ham for chicken and it's a Monte Cristo.

8 slices French bread
2 Tbsp (30 mL) Dijon mustard
8 slices Swiss cheese
12 thin slices lean, smoked ham
3 Tbsp (45 mL) mayonnaise

3 eggs, beaten
¼ cup (60 mL) milk or cream
¼ tsp (1 mL) salt
2 Tbsp (30 mL) butter
2 Tbsp (30 mL) olive oil

1 Spread four slices of bread with mustard and place on the counter. Top each with a slice of cheese, three slices of ham, and another slice of cheese. Slather each of the remaining four slices of bread with mayonnaise and set on top, pressing down slightly, to make four sandwiches.

2 In a bowl, whisk together the egg, milk, and salt. Pour into a wide, shallow dish, large enough to hold a sandwich.

3 In a large, non-stick skillet, heat half of the butter and oil together over medium heat. When the pan is hot, dip each side of one sandwich into the egg mixture. Shake off any excess and place in the hot pan. Fry until browned on both sides, about 5 minutes per side. Repeat with the remaining sandwiches, then slice them on the diagonal to serve. Serves 4.

Toasted Canadian Bacon BLT

Canadian back bacon and aged white cheddar make this the king of BLTs.

8 slices whole wheat bread
½ cup (125 mL) mayonnaise
1 Tbsp (15 mL) Dijon mustard
8 thick slices double-smoked Canadian back
 bacon (or use a good double-smoked side
 bacon, cooked until nicely rendered but not
 super crispy)

8 to 12 thick tomato slices
salt and freshly ground black pepper
8 slices aged white cheddar cheese
thickly shredded romaine lettuce leaves

1 Toast the bread. Combine the mayonnaise and mustard, and lightly spread on one side of each slice of toast.

2 Preheat the broiler. Place four of the toast slices on a baking sheet. Arrange a layer of bacon on each piece of toast and top with a tomato slice. Season with salt and pepper and top with cheese.

3 Slide the open-faced sandwiches under the broiler, about 4 inches (10 cm) away from the element, and broil until the cheese is melted—this will only take a minute or two. Watch carefully that the bread doesn't burn.

4 Top each sandwich with a handful of shredded romaine, a drizzle of mustard and mayo, and the remaining toast slices. Cut diagonally, in halves or quarters, and skewer each piece with a toothpick. Arrange the sandwiches on individual plates with two triangles standing up (pointy parts facing skyward), and the other two lying along each side like wings. Serve warm. Serves 4.

Classic Clubhouse

These days there's nothing classic about the clubhouse—The Guy's seen the stacked, three-tiered sandwich stuffed with everything from shrimp salad to pancetta and garlic aioli. The classic club is the trilogy of turkey, ham, and bacon with lettuce, cheese, and tomato.

6 thick slices wholegrain bread
3 Tbsp (45 mL) mayonnaise
lettuce
1 tomato, sliced
4 slices roasted turkey breast (or chicken)

6 strips bacon, fried until crisp
4 slices black forest ham
4 slices old cheddar cheese
2 tsp (10 mL) grainy mustard

1 Toast the bread and slather each piece with mayonnaise.

2 Lay two slices of toast on the cutting board and top each with some lettuce, tomato, the sliced turkey and bacon. Top each with another slice of toast. Top that with more sliced tomato, the sliced ham and cheese, a drizzle of mustard, then more lettuce and the last piece of toast. Press down lightly.

3 Cut each sandwich into quarters, on the diagonal, and use toothpicks to hold each stack together.

4 Arrange on plates with two triangles standing up (pointy parts facing skyward), and the other two lying along each side like wings. Serves 2.

WISE GUY:
If you buy (or keep) your mayonnaise in a squeeze bottle, it's easy to drizzle over any sandwich.

The Meaty Italian

A crusty bun stacked with authentic Italian cold cuts, hot pickled peppers, and warm provolone cheese—that's amore!

6 crusty triangular ciabatta buns, sliced in half horizontally
6 Tbsp (90 mL) red pepper and eggplant vegetable spread (sold in jars in Italian markets)
6 Tbsp (90 mL) basil pesto
thinly sliced Italian cold cuts (spicy, dry-cured capicollo, mortadella, Italian ham, or prosciutto)

2 roasted red bell peppers, torn into strips (jarred are fine)
¼ cup (60 mL) sliced pickled hot peppers
6 to 10 thin slices provolone cheese
2 Roma tomatoes, thinly sliced
salt and freshly ground black pepper
shredded romaine lettuce
6 Tbsp (90 mL) lemon pepper aioli (see page 38)

1 Spread the buns generously with vegetable spread on one side, pesto on the other. Preheat the broiler.

2 Arrange the vegetable spread halves on a baking sheet and top each with a combination of deli meats, roasted peppers, pickled peppers, and cheese.

3 Broil until the cheese is just melted, then remove from the oven and top with sliced tomatoes. Season with salt and pepper. Add a layer of shredded lettuce, and drizzle with lemon pepper aioli. Cover with the top half of the bun (the pesto-side). Serve warm. Serves 6.

WISE GUY: The local Italian supermarket is a gold mine for guys who like their sandwiches loaded with delicious stuff. You'll never go back to basic supermarket sandwich meats after you try authentic hot capicollo, imported prosciutto, provolone cheese, jars of roasted red peppers, pesto, and red pepper vegetable spread. The latter is great on almost any sandwich and can be added to tomato or cream sauce for pasta. (Italian markets are also a good place to find great crusty breads and buns.)

Toasted Reuben on Rye

So who the heck was that Reuben guy anyways? One legend has it he was the Reuben of Reuben's Deli in New York who slapped together the first Reuben to feed a starving silent-film starlet. Another says he was a grocer in Nebraska. Whoever he was, Reuben was a guy who knew the power of a pickle—or at least a pile of soured cabbage—to compliment the richness of your basic corned beef and cheese sandwich. This sandwich gives you a mouthful of flavors in every bite—everything from salty to rich and acidic. There's even a little nutty sweetness in that cheese. It's a fast and fab supper any time.

4 slices rye bread
4 Tbsp (60 mL) mayonnaise
½ lb (250 g) Montreal smoked meat, corned
   beef, or pastrami

⅓ cup (75 mL) sauerkraut, drained
8 slices Swiss or Gruyère cheese
2 Tbsp (30 mL) melted butter, divided

1 Spread each slice of bread with mayonnaise. On two of the slices, place a piece of cheese. Top with a thick layer of sauerkraut, then meat, then another piece of cheese, and then the remaining bread. Press down to seal the sandwiches.

2 Heat a non-stick frying pan over medium heat and add 2 tsp (10 mL) of the butter.

3 When the butter begins to bubble, place the sandwiches in the pan. Brush the other side of the sandwiches with melted butter. Cook the sandwiches about 3 to 4 minutes per side, until brown and crispy. Add a little more butter when you turn them over. The meat should be heated through and the cheese melted to hold the sandwiches together. Slice each sandwich in half and serve with Perfect Potato Salad (see page 410). Serves 2.

Wrap and Roll

This may be The Guy's favorite solution to fast, everyday dining: wrap yesterday's leftovers in an envelope of fresh pita bread. The trick to this simple sandwich is in the quality of the leftovers, the pita bread, and the sauces—and of course the sandwich rolling technique to keep everything inside.

For each sandwich

one 8- x 10-inch (20- x 25-cm) wholegrain pita
   bread, very fresh
½ cup (125 mL) chopped or sliced romaine lettuce
1 small tomato, chopped or sliced
6 thin slices English cucumber
protein of choice (cooked and sliced leftover
   steak, chicken, grilled fish, falafels)

sauce of choice (mayonnaise, plain or flavored
   with chili paste, pesto, horseradish, etc.)
spread of choice (hummus, refried beans,
   cream cheese)
other leftovers (curries, mashed potatoes, cubed
   baked potatoes, rice)

1 Keep the pita bread whole but cut halfway around the circumference (using your kitchen shears) so that you can open the pita like a pouch with two "flaps." Stuff the pouch with your favorite fillings and leftovers, starting with chopped lettuce, tomato, and cucumber. Top with either cooked meat, poultry, or fish (sliced or chopped), a leftover curry dish, whatever. Drizzle the filling with a bit of mustard mayo or other sauce (even creamy salad dressing) then get ready to roll.

2 Here's the trick to rolling the ideal wrap: tuck one of the "flaps" inside the pita, folding it over and around the filling. Tuck it in to completely to enclose whatever's inside. Tightly roll the pita with the other flap on the outside. This keeps everything tidy and secure while you eat. Serves 1.

TUCK TOP FLAP
INSIDE POUCH
AROUND FILLING

AND ROLL
SANDWICH UP

Falafel Sandwich

The Guy buys pre-cooked falafels (chickpea patties) and fresh pita bread at the local Middle Eastern deli. He keeps them in the freezer for those days when a fat falafel sandwich is all that fits. You can reheat the falafels in the microwave, or if you like to keep them crispy, in a conventional oven. This is also a great combo when you have leftover roast lamb or grilled chicken.

Tahini Sauce
2 cloves garlic, minced
1 tsp (5 mL) salt
1 cup (250 mL) tahini
1 tsp (5 mL) paprika
¼ cup (60 mL) freshly squeezed lemon juice
¼ cup (60 mL) water

4 large (10-inch) wholegrain pita breads
16 falafels
2 large tomatoes, seeded and chopped
4 Tbsp (60 mL) sliced hot pickled peppers
12 thin slices English cucumber
1 cup (250 mL) shredded romaine lettuce

1 To make the tahini sauce, whirl together the garlic, salt, tahini, paprika, lemon juice, and water in a blender or food processor until smooth. Refrigerate until ready to use.

2 Keep the pita bread whole but cut halfway around the circumference (using your kitchen shears) to create a pouch with two "flaps." If you want to serve the sandwiches warm, microwave or bake the falafels until hot, then squeeze them slightly to break them open. Arrange four warm falafels in each of the pita pockets. Top with some chopped tomato, pickled peppers, sliced cucumber, and lettuce. Drizzle in a little tahini sauce.

3 Tuck one "flap" of bread inside the pouch and around the filling, then roll the entire sandwich up, with the other flap on the outside. This should keep most of the drippy stuff inside. But for even tidier eating, wrap the base of each sandwich in waxed paper. Eat immediately. Serves 4.

Meatball Subs

This is a sloppy sandwich for a hungry guy. You can pre-cook the meatballs, then refrigerate or freeze them so you can make these meaty subs whenever the craving strikes.

Meatballs

½ lb (250 g) each: lean ground beef and
    ground pork
½ cup (125 mL) dry bread or melba toast
    crumbs
2 cloves garlic, minced

Sauce

1 Tbsp (15 mL) olive oil
½ red bell pepper, seeded and sliced very thinly
1 medium onion, slivered
1½ cups (375 mL) tomato sauce with basil
    (look for a low-sugar brand)

1 egg
½ tsp (2 mL) freshly ground black pepper
½ tsp (2 mL) dried basil
¾ cup (175 mL) freshly grated Parmigiano
    Reggiano or Romano cheese

four 6-inch (15-cm) long panini buns
½ cup (125 mL) shredded mozzarella cheese
    (or a mixture of Italian cheeses)

1 Preheat the oven to 400°F (200°C).

2 Combine the ground beef, breadcrumbs, garlic, egg, pepper, basil, and Parmigiano Reggiano or Romano cheese and mix well with your hands. Shape into 1½-inch (4-cm) meatballs and arrange in a single layer on a non-stick baking sheet. Bake for about 12 to 15 minutes or until the meatballs are nicely browned. Drain the excess fat and set the meatballs aside.

3 To make the sauce, heat the olive oil in a non-stick sauté pan over medium-high. Add the red pepper and onion and cook for 5 minutes, until the onions wilt and start to brown. Stir in the tomato sauce and reserved meatballs and bring to a boil. Cover the pan, reduce the heat to low, and simmer for 5 minutes. Uncover and simmer for about 2 minutes or until the sauce is nicely thickened. Spoon the meatball mixture into the buns, topping each sandwich with a little shredded mozzarella cheese. Serve immediately. Serves 4.

WISE GUY:

The Guy also loves to serve these meatballs on top of spaghetti, all covered with cheese. Just use the whole jar of tomato sauce to simmer the meatballs (you can include the red pepper and onion, too), add 2 to 3 Tbsp (30 to 45 mL) chopped fresh basil and toss it with cooked spaghetti or linguine. Grate some fresh Parmesan cheese on top and you're done!

The PBB Kingwich

In deference to The Guy of all Guys, here's a toasted version of The King's favorite fried peanut butter and banana sandwich—with his signature bacon bits—for those days when you're feeling eccentric or reclusive. Thank you, thank you very much.

8 slices white bread
2 to 3 Tbsp (30 to 45 mL) softened butter
½ cup (125 mL) natural peanut butter

1 mashed banana
4 slices bacon, fried until crispy (optional)
liquid honey, in a squeeze bottle

1 Butter the bread slices on one side and place on your work surface, buttered-side down. Slather each slice with peanut butter. Top four of the slices with mashed banana, crumbled bacon, and a drizzle of honey. Top with the remaining bread, buttered-side out.

2 Heat a large non-stick frying pan over medium heat and cook the sandwiches on both sides until browned and toasted, about 3 to 4 minutes per side. Cool each sandwich slightly before cutting in half diagonally. Serves 4.

Grilled Panini Sandwiches
The Guy's Four Favorite Panini Combos

The panini is the modern generation of the grilled cheese—a version of that pan-fried gooey cheese sandwich of old, with the addition of all kinds of other tasty fillings and unique cheeses.

You can buy a panini press (or a convertible waffle iron) to make your sandwiches, or you can cook them in a heavy, non-stick frying pan and press the sandwiches with a spatula as you brown on each side. Choose your bread carefully—The Guy thinks the best panini is made using a fairly thin flatbread or focaccia that crisps quickly under pressure. What goes inside is up to you—just make sure the fillings aren't too thick, and that there's a layer of melted cheese to hold it all together.

Eggplant and Mushroom Melt

Grilled eggplant slices and portobello mushrooms give these vegetarian panini sandwiches a unique "meaty" character.

four 4- x 5-inch (10- x 12-cm) pieces focaccia
bread, sliced horizontally
three 5-inch (12-cm) portobello mushrooms
1 medium Asian eggplant

extra virgin olive oil for brushing
salt and freshly ground black pepper
artichoke and olive cheese spread (see page 36)
12 fresh basil leaves

1 Slice the focaccia in half horizontally (lightly press one hand over the bread while slicing with a serrated knife held parallel to the cutting board).

2 To clean the mushrooms, brush and scrape away the dark gills on the undersides with a spoon. Cut the eggplant lengthwise into ¼-inch (6-mm) slices. Heat the grill.

3 Brush the whole mushrooms and eggplant slices with olive oil and season with salt and pepper. Grill over medium-high heat for about 5 minutes, flipping the vegetables until golden on both sides.

4 Cool, and slice the mushrooms into ¼-inch (6-mm) slivers. Cut the eggplant to fit the bread.

5 To make sandwiches, spread each sandwich with about 3 Tbsp (45 mL) of the artichoke spread. Top each sandwich with sliced mushrooms, grilled eggplant, and 2 basil leaves. Top with remaining focaccia and press together. Grill in a panini press until toasted and melted. Cut in half diagonally to serve. Serves 4.

Black Olive, Roasted Pepper, Tomato, and Jack

four 4- x 5-inch (10- x 12-cm) pieces focaccia
    bread, sliced horizontally
8 Tbsp (120 mL) olive tapenade (see page 21)
2 roasted red or yellow bell peppers, peeled,
    seeded, and cut into strips

1 large Roma tomato, thinly sliced
8 thin slices Monterey Jack cheese (choose
    Monterey Jack with jalapeño for a spicier
    sandwich)

1 Slice the focaccia in half horizontally (lightly press one hand over the bread while slicing with a serrated knife held parallel to the cutting board). Spread ½ of each sandwich with the tapenade.

2 Top with the roasted peppers, sliced tomatoes, and cheese. Top with the remaining bread and press down.

3 Grill the sandwiches in an oiled panini press until crisp and melted. Cut each square in half diagonally to serve. Serves 4.

Ham, Tomato, and Asiago Cheese

four 4- x 5-inch (10- x 12-cm) pieces focaccia
    bread, sliced horizontally
4 Tbsp (60 mL) mayonnaise
2 Roma tomatoes, thinly sliced
1 cup (250 mL) thinly sliced or grated Asiago
    cheese

8 thin slices imported spicy capicollo ham (or
    prosciutto)
¼ cup (60 mL) Italian parsley leaves

1 Slice the focaccia in half horizontally (lightly press one hand over the bread while slicing with a serrated knife held parallel to the cutting board). Spread both halves of each slice with mayonnaise.

2 Top ½ of each sandwich with sliced tomatoes, sliced cheese, ham, a little parsley, then a little more cheese. Top with the remaining bread and press down.

3 Grill in an oiled panini press until crisp and melted. Cut each square in half diagonally to serve. Serves 4.

Artichoke and Olive Cheese Spread

Not only is this spread delicious when cold, if you slather it onto a panini before it gets heated on the grill, the cheese will melt into a warm, scrumptious filler. Also great for making "artichoke toast" appetizers—just slather on French bread and broil until bubbly.

¼ cup (60 mL) anchovy-stuffed green olives, drained

¾ cup (175 mL) softened cream cheese or Boursin

¼ cup (60 mL) light mayonnaise

4 cloves roasted garlic

1 can artichoke hearts, squeezed to drain well

1 cup (250 mL) grated Parmigiano Reggiano

1 In a food processor, purée the olives. Add the cream cheese, mayonnaise, and garlic and process until smooth. Add the artichokes and pulse (the spread should remain chunky). Stir in the cheese and chill. Makes 2 cups.

Smoked Turkey and Avocado with Mozzarella

four 4-inch (10-cm) squares focaccia bread, about 1 inch (2.5 cm) thick, sliced horizontally

1 firm, ripe avocado, peeled and sliced (rinse the avocado in cold water after slicing to prevent from browning)

4 oz (125 g) thinly sliced smoked turkey

4 oz (125 g) shredded mozzarella

2 Tbsp (30 mL) Dijon mustard

1 Slice the focaccia in half horizontally (lightly press one hand over the bread while slicing with a serrated knife held parallel to the cutting board). Spread both halves of focaccia with mustard.

2 Top one ½ of each sandwich with sliced turkey, avocado slices, and 1 oz (30 g) of the shredded cheese. Place the remaining bread on top and press down.

3 Grill the sandwiches in an oiled panini press until crisp and melted. Cut each square in half diagonally to serve. Serves 4.

The Aiolis
(a.k.a. Mayonnaise Sauces for Sandwiches)

These days, every sauce with a mayonnaise base is labeled aioli—a kind of homemade mayo traditionally made with garlic, egg yolks, and olive oil in the south of France.

Purists will make their aioli from scratch as they do in Provence—crushing fresh garlic with a mortar and pestle to form a purée, then adding salt and an egg yolk or two, and drizzling in extra virgin olive oil—all while whisking madly to form a flavorful emulsion.

But with a jar of good quality commercial mayonnaise (The Guy is partial to Hellmann's brand; even the low-fat version tastes pretty close to homemade mayo), and a little creative combining, you can make an interesting "aioli" in the blender or food processor almost instantly. Aiolis can stand in for regular mayo on a sandwich, be served alongside any kind of grilled or fried meat, poultry, or fish, or even be thinned with a little milk, buttermilk, or plain yogurt for salad dressing. Perfect for dipping, too.

 Horseradish Aioli

Combine ½ cup (125 mL) mayonnaise with 1 clove minced garlic and 2 Tbsp (30 mL) prepared horseradish. Whisk together in a bowl or whirl until smooth in a food processor or blender. Serve with roast beef (hot or in sandwiches) or alongside steak.

 Mustard Aioli

Combine ½ cup (125 mL) mayonnaise with 1 clove of minced garlic and 2 to 3 Tbsp (30 to 45 mL) Dijon mustard (you can vary this sauce by using sweet honey mustard, hot mustard, or grainy mustard). Whisk together in a bowl or whirl until smooth in a food processor or blender. Serve with beef, pork, chicken, or fish—even makes a nice dipping sauce for raw vegetables.

 Pesto Aioli

Combine ½ cup (125 mL) mayonnaise with 1 clove minced garlic and 2 to 3 Tbsp basil pesto. Whisk together in a bowl or whirl until smooth in a food processor or blender. Good with fish, tomato sandwiches or tossed with pasta for the base of a pasta salad.

Chipotle Aioli

Combine ½ cup (125 mL) mayonnaise with 1 clove minced garlic, 1 tsp lime juice, and 1 to 2 chipotle chilies in adobo sauce (they come in a can). Whirl until smooth in a food processor or blender and stir in 1 Tbsp (15 mL) minced cilantro (optional). This addictive sauce is great to drizzle over grilled chicken or onto a chicken/tomato/avocado tortilla wrap. You can also serve it with beef fajitas or toss it with cold cooked potatoes and green onions for a southwestern salad.

 Walnut Pesto Aioli

Toast ½ cup (125 mL) walnuts in a dry non-stick pan over medium heat until fragrant. Cool and pulse in a food processor until finely ground. Add ½ cup (125 mL) mayonnaise, 1 clove minced garlic, 3 Tbsp (45 mL) extra virgin olive oil, and 1 Tbsp (15 mL) chopped fresh basil. Whirl until smooth. Lovely with steamed vegetables or lean, white fish like sole or cod.

 Ranch Sauce

Combine ½ cup (125 mL) mayonnaise with ¼ cup (60 mL) spicy tomato salsa (homemade or commercial) and whirl until smooth in a food processor or blender. Stir in 1 Tbsp (15 mL) minced cilantro and/or green onion for a little texture. Thin with buttermilk to make a great salad dressing for mixed greens.

 Wasabi Mayo

So simple yet so addictive. Whisk together 1 cup (250 mL) mayonnaise with 3 to 4 Tbsp (45 to 60 mL) wasabi paste (from a tube). Good on grilled chicken sandwiches or slathered on a piece of salmon.

 Lemon Pepper Aioli

In a blender, whirl 1 cup (250 mL) mayonnaise with 3 cloves roasted garlic, 2 Tbsp (30 mL) extra virgin olive oil, 1 Tbsp (15 mL) each of Dijon mustard and finely grated lemon zest, and 2 tsp (10 mL) of crushed mixed black, white, and pink peppercorns. Serve with grilled salmon or tuna. Or you can fold it into a niçoise-style tuna sandwich with chopped hard-boiled eggs, artichokes, and black olives.

 Roasted Garlic Aioli

In a blender, whirl 1 cup (250 mL) mayonnaise with 1 Tbsp (15 mL) of Dijon mustard and a whole head of roasted garlic, the sweet, nutty purée squeezed out of the cloves' papery skins after roasting (see page 17 for instructions on roasting garlic). Season to taste with salt and freshly ground white pepper. Serve with beef, pork, or chicken, or drizzle over steamed vegetables as they do in France. It's even good to use when you're making potato salad.

onion
carrot
chop
simmer
tomato

Souped Up

The Guy likes to make a big pot of soup and then sup on it all week long. Not only is a bowl of soup the perfect foil for a sandwich (The Guy's everyday fallback position), it's also a healthy meal in itself and easy for busy guys to reheat whenever hunger strikes.

Stock Options

While there are acceptable commercial stocks and broths available for everyday cooking, when The Guy has his own homemade stock in the freezer—it's like money in the bank. Not only does homemade stock bring any soup or sauce up a notch, it's also invaluable to have a bowl or two of this folk medicine on hand when you're feeling under the weather. Any good restaurant has a chef devoted to making fresh stocks from scratch—and you can too. Always save the bones from a roasted chicken or turkey for stock, and buy meaty beef soup bones or shank when you see them at the supermarket. When you have a day at home, start the stock in the morning and let it slowly simmer for several hours. Once all of the good stuff is leached from the vegetables and meats, stick your stock in the freezer for a rainy day. Stock couldn't be easier to make, and will help keep both your body, and your bank account, healthy.

3 lb (1.5 kg) soup bones (chicken or turkey carcass, veal or beef bones including some shank meat)
1 Tbsp (15 mL) olive oil
1 large onion, peeled
2 large carrots
1 medium parsnip

2 stalks celery
1-inch (2.5-cm) chunk of fresh ginger
1 small jalapeño pepper (optional)
½ tsp (2 mL) black peppercorns
2 bay leaves
salt to taste

1 The Guy likes his soup stock dark and rich (a.k.a. brown stock), so he always browns the bones first. The meatier the bones, the better the soup—so throw in a turkey drumstick if you can, and always include at least some meat when making beef stock (bones alone don't cut it.)

2 Unless you're starting with the carcass from a roasted chicken or turkey, put your uncooked bones into a big (and I mean BIG) heavy pot with the olive oil. Turn the heat to high and cook, stirring often, until the meaty bits are nicely browned.

3 Meanwhile, coarsely chop the vegetables. You'll be straining them out later, so don't waste time making perfect, pretty cubes.

4 When the meat is nice and brown, add the chopped veggies and stir for 10 minutes or until they start to brown.

5 Add cold water, a few cups at a time, letting the water come to a boil before adding additional water. Skim off any scum that rises to the surface (a slotted skimmer spoon works well for this). This not only gets rid of most of the crud (which makes your finished stock cloudy), it gets the pot boiling faster.

6 When you've filled up the whole pot with water and it's boiling nicely, toss in the chili pepper, peppercorns, and bay leaf. Reduce the heat to low and let the soup simmer, uncovered, for about 3 to 4 hours. The longer you simmer, the more concentrated and flavorful the broth. You want to keep the heat low, so the stock barely bubbles—this is another chef's trick to keep it nice and clear.

7 When the stock is ready, line a sieve with cheesecloth (or just use a fine metal sieve) and strain the soup into a heatproof glass bowl or a big glass measuring cup. Let the stock cool for a few minutes—the fat will rise to the surface (you'll see the clear layer). Skim the fat with a metal spoon or by dragging a paper towel lightly over the surface. You don't need to remove all the fat (as The Guy's grandmother used to say, the soup should have "eyes"), but if you want to get rid of every last bit, chill the soup in the refrigerator overnight and just scoop off the congealed fat the next day.

8 Once the stock is as concentrated as you like it, season with salt to taste. Some chefs reduce their stocks until they're very, very thick and syrupy—this is called *glace de viande*, a gelatinous mass that keeps well in the refrigerator or freezer and can be used as the base of a demi-glace or rich wine sauce for roasts and steaks.

9 Your homemade stock is the best base for everything from basic barley or noodle soups, to big bowls of Vietnamese pho, and French onion soup. Or you can just pour it into a mug, nuke it for about a minute, and sip it when you're sick. Take the time to make stock and you won't regret it—it's always a good investment.

WISE GUY: For a light stock (in both color and flavor), don't brown the bones, just rinse them quickly in boiling water, and use raw, unbrowned vegetables, too. While meat and poultry stocks need to cook for several hours to release optimum flavors, when you're making fish stock (a.k.a. fish fumet) you only want to simmer it briefly. Start with a sautéed onion and add a pound of white fish bones (cod, halibut, snapper, or shells from shrimp or lobsters), a cup of white wine, a few peppercorns, and aromatics like celery, a sprig of parsley and thyme, and a bay leaf. Cover with cold water, bring to a boil, and simmer for 20 to 30 minutes, then strain.

Southwest Turkey and Corn Soup

This is the soup to make after the holidays, when there's that bit of roast turkey (or chicken) left over in the fridge that you're not sure what to do with. The Guy serves this soup garnished with crumbled corn chips, but if you want to make it look chic for a party, slice some corn tortillas into thin strips, fry them in oil until crispy, then pile them onto the center of each bowl of soup.

1 Tbsp (15 mL) canola oil
1 onion, minced
2 cloves garlic, minced
3 stalks celery, minced
1 red bell pepper, finely diced
2 carrots, finely diced
2 tsp (10 mL) dried oregano
1 tsp (5 mL) ground cumin
1 tsp (5 mL) chili paste
4 cups (1 L) chicken broth

1 can (7.5 oz/213 mL) tomato sauce
1 jalapeño chili pepper, seeded and minced
2 cups (500 mL) canned or frozen corn
2 cups (500 mL) chopped roasted turkey
  (or chicken)
2 Tbsp (30 mL) freshly squeezed lime juice
salt, freshly ground black pepper, and chili
  paste, to taste
crushed tortilla chips (or fried corn tortilla
  strips) for garnish

1 Heat the oil in a large soup pot and sauté the onion and garlic over medium heat for 5 minutes. Add the celery, pepper, and carrots; cook for 5 minutes more.

2 Stir in the oregano, cumin and chili paste, and cook for 1 minute before adding the broth, tomato sauce, and jalapeño. Bring the soup to a boil over high heat, then reduce the heat to low and simmer for 10 minutes.

3 Stir in the corn and chopped turkey and continue to simmer for 15 to 20 minutes or until the vegetables are tender. Add the lime juice and season to taste with salt, pepper, and extra chili paste.

4 Serve in shallow bowls, with a few corn tortilla chips crushed on top. Serves 4 to 6.

Manly Mulligatawny Soup

This is a soup with both English and Indian roots. It's spicy and exotic, but rather comfortable and familiar, too. Enjoy it as a full meal, or as the start to a grand Indian feast.

¾ cup (175 mL) long-grain basmati rice

one 398-mL can light coconut milk, divided

1 cup (250 mL) water

½ tsp (2 mL) salt

2 Tbsp (30 mL) canola oil

4 cloves garlic, minced

1 medium onion, finely chopped

2 chicken breast halves, cut into ¼-inch
  (5-mm) cubes

1 Granny Smith apple, peeled and cut into
  ¼-inch (5-mm) cubes

1 Tbsp (15 mL) hot Indian curry paste
  (or to taste)

4 cups (1 L) chicken broth

½ cup (125 mL) heavy cream

2 green onions, chopped

1 To make the rice, in a medium pot, combine the rice, ½ cup (125 mL) of the coconut milk, water, and salt. Bring to a boil over medium high heat. Cover and reduce the heat to low. Simmer for 20 minutes or until the rice is tender.

2 To make the soup, in a medium saucepan, heat the olive oil over high heat and sauté the garlic and onions for 5 to 10 minutes or until just soft. Add the chicken and apples and cook until the chicken is almost cooked through, about 5 minutes.

3 Stir in the curry paste, coating the chicken and apples, and cook for 1 minute or until the paste is very fragrant. Add the broth, cream, and remaining coconut milk, and bring to a boil. Reduce the heat to medium low and simmer for 10 minutes to slightly thicken.

4 Stir in the cooked coconut rice and green onions and heat through. For a special presentation, pile portions of the coconut rice in the center of each shallow soup plate, then ladle the creamy chicken soup around the edge of the rice. Serves 4 to 6.

Szechuan Pork Noodle Soup

At a hotel The Guy visited in Kunming, China, the breakfast of choice was noodles in steamy chicken soup with spicy ground pork—a.k.a. Over the Bridge Noodles. Made to order and garnished with everything from salty Yunnan ham and spicy pork in chili oil, to fresh bean sprouts with chopped green onions and slivers of cooked chicken, it's a build-your-own kind of meal. Set out all of the toppings so that diners can garnish their soup as they like. Black vinegar mixed with soy is a popular condiment in southern China (you'll find everything you need at an Asian foods market).

For a vegetarian soup, try making the sauce with ground soy protein instead of pork. A satisfying meal any time of the day.

Spicy Pork in Chili Sauce
2 Tbsp (30 mL) canola oil
½ lb (250g) lean ground pork
½ cup (125 mL) minced shallots
3 cloves garlic, minced
1 Tbsp (15 mL) brown sugar
2 Tbsp (30 mL) soy sauce
2 Tbsp (30 mL) minced ginger
3 to 4 Tbsp (45 to 60 mL) Asian chili paste (or 3 minced fresh red chilies)

1 Tbsp (15 mL) crunchy natural peanut butter or sesame paste
2 tsp (10 mL) dark Chinese vinegar or freshly squeezed lemon juice
6 to 8 cups (1.5 to 2 L) chicken broth
¾ lb (375 g) thin rice vermicelli or fresh Chinese egg noodles (if rice noodles are dry, soak in hot water for 15 minutes and drain)

Toppings
fresh bean sprouts
chopped green onions
shredded cooked chicken

slivered Yunnan ham or prosciutto
fresh pea shoots
black vinegar and soy sauce

1 In a wok, heat the oil over medium high heat. Add the ground pork, shallots, and garlic. Cook until the meat starts to brown. Add the sugar, soy sauce, ginger, and chili paste. Cook for 3 to 4 minutes, then stir in the peanut butter and vinegar. Remove from the heat and set aside.

2 In a large pot, bring the chicken broth to a boil. Set out all of the toppings in small bowls on the table.

WISE GUY:

If the spicy pork isn't spicy enough for your taste, add some extra chili paste or chili oil (alternatively, cook the ground pork with a commercial Szechuan soup paste, found in jars in Asian food markets).

3 Bring a large pot of water to a boil and add the noodles. After about 1 minute, test the noodles to make sure they're tender, then drain and evenly distribute the noodles among four large soup bowls. Fill each bowl ¾ full with the chicken broth. Let your guests choose their own toppings—a spoonful of the spicy pork goes on last to give the soup its unique fiery flavor. Pass the black vinegar and soy sauce for seasoning. Serves 4.

Spicy Chickpea and Sausage Soup

Use any kind of smoked pork sausage in this simple soup with Spanish roots—The Guy likes to start with garlicky ham sausage or spicy chorizo to add instant flavor.

2 Tbsp (30 mL) olive oil

1 large onion, chopped

2 cloves garlic, minced

½ lb (250 g) smoked garlic ham sausage or chorizo, chopped

1 Tbsp (15 mL) chili powder

½ tsp (2 mL) ground cumin

½ tsp (2 mL) freshly ground black pepper

1 tsp (5 mL) dried oregano leaves, crumbled

1 to 2 tsp (5 to 10 mL) chili paste

one 14-oz (398-mL) can whole Roma tomatoes, crushed

3 cups (750 mL) beef broth

½ cup (125 mL) tomato sauce

2 Tbsp (30 mL) brown sugar

two 14-oz (398-mL) cans chickpeas, drained and rinsed

1 In a large soup pot, heat the olive oil over medium-high heat. Sauté the onion and garlic for 10 minutes or until the onions begin to brown. Stir in the sausage and cook for 5 minutes longer.

2 Add the chili powder, cumin, pepper, oregano, and chili paste and stir to combine. Add the tomatoes, broth, tomato sauce, brown sugar, and chickpeas. Bring to a boil. Cover, reduce heat to low, and simmer for 30 minutes. Serves 8.

Satay Beef Soup

This is The Guy's favorite Vietnamese noodle soup, a recipe plucked from his neighbourhood noodle house. If you slice the beef paper thin, when it's partially frozen, it cooks right in the bowl with the steaming broth. Look for packages of flat rice noodles and jars of commercial satay sauce at Asian grocery stores and big urban supermarkets. You can also substitute cooked chicken or shrimp for the beef.

one 10-oz (284-mL) can beef or chicken broth, diluted with 1 can of water
4 to 5 Tbsp (60 to 75 mL) satay sauce (buy a commercial brand with no MSG)
½ cup (125 mL) water mixed with 1 Tbsp (15 mL) cornstarch
2 tsp (10 mL) granulated sugar
1 tsp (5 mL) salt
2 cups (500 mL) flat rice noodles or instant ramen noodles

¼ lb (125 g) eye of round steak, cut into paper-thin slices (this is easiest to do when the meat is slightly frozen)
2 tsp (10 mL) each: chopped fresh cilantro and green onions
1 cup (250 mL) fresh bean sprouts
2 large sprigs of fresh Vietnamese or Thai basil
1 lime, quartered

1 In a saucepan, bring the broth and water to a boil and add satay sauce. Stir in the water/cornstarch solution and return to a boil, stirring constantly. Reduce the heat to low to keep the soup at a simmer.

2 Place the rice noodles into a large, heatproof bowl and cover with boiling water. Let the noodles stand for 10 minutes to soften. Try a noodle to make sure it's cooked—if not, add more boiling water or simmer for a few seconds to soften. Drain.

3 Divide the hot drained noodles and sliced raw beef between two large soup bowls. Ladle the boiling soup into the bowls (the hot soup will cook the beef to medium rare on contact if it is cut thinly enough). You can also add the slices of beef to the soup just before removing it from the heat but make sure you don't overcook—the beef should remain rare.

4 Sprinkle each bowl of soup with some of the chopped cilantro and green onions. Serve the fresh bean sprouts, basil, and limes alongside the soup to add at the table. Serves 2.

Pasta e Fagioli

This chunky bean soup—a.k.a. pasta fazool—is pure comfort and dead easy to make with simple supermarket ingredients. It's one of those soups that eats like a stew. Mucho manly.

2 stalks celery, finely chopped
1 medium onion, finely chopped
6 slices Italian bacon (pancetta) or back bacon, diced
¼ cup (60 mL) extra virgin olive oil
2 large Roma tomatoes, seeded and diced (or a 7 ½-oz/213-mL can tomato sauce)
4 cups (1 L) chicken broth
one 19-oz (540-mL) can white cannellini beans, rinsed and drained

2 cloves garlic, finely chopped
2 tsp (10 mL) finely chopped fresh rosemary (discard the stems)
¾ cup (175 mL) small pasta (orzo, or Israeli couscous)
salt and freshly ground black pepper
freshly grated Parmigiano Reggiano cheese
chopped fresh basil

1 Finely chop the celery and onion in a food processor. In a large soup pot, heat the chopped bacon, celery, onion, and olive oil over medium heat and cook until the bacon fat is rendered. Add the tomatoes and sauté for 2 minutes or until the tomatoes break down a little. Stir in the broth, beans, garlic, and rosemary. Bring to a boil. Reduce the heat to low and cover. Simmer for 45 minutes.

2 Add the pasta and simmer for 10 minutes or until the pasta is just tender (al dente). Taste the soup and season with salt and pepper if necessary.

3 Top each serving with some freshly grated Parmesan cheese and chopped basil. Serves 6.

Chicken, Shrimp, and Sausage Gumbo

Every Cajun cook makes gumbo—and every gumbo is unique. Classic versions are loaded with shrimp, sausage, chicken, and even wild game ('gator anyone?). The Guy likes this simplified combo of chicken, shrimp, spicy sausage, and sweet peppers. Beer—the secret ingredient in this gumbo—is the perfect beverage to consume with it, too.

2 tsp (10 mL) each salt and garlic powder
1 tsp (5 mL) dried thyme
1 tsp (5 mL) cayenne
2 lb (1 kg) boneless, skinless chicken thighs
½ cup (125 mL) all-purpose flour
¼ cup (60 mL) olive oil, divided
1 large onion, chopped
2 stalks celery, chopped
3 cloves garlic, chopped
1 yellow bell pepper, seeded and chopped
1 red bell pepper, seeded and chopped
one 4-oz (125-g) spicy sausage, cubed

one 14-oz (398-mL) can tomatoes, puréed in a
    food processor or blender
one 12-oz (355-mL) bottle dark beer
1 cup (250 mL) chicken broth or water
1 Tbsp (15 mL) Worcestershire sauce
salt and black pepper
2 bay leaves
2 tsp (10 mL) ground marjoram
1 lb (450 g) large shrimp, peeled and deveined
salt and freshly ground black pepper
steamed long-grain rice for six

1 In a small bowl, mix together the salt, garlic powder, thyme, and cayenne. Set aside.

2 Cut the chicken into 2-inch (5-cm) chunks and place in a bowl. Rub the chicken pieces with 2 tsp (10 mL) of the spice mixture. Set the chicken in the refrigerator to marinate for 20 minutes.

3 Put the remaining spice mixture and the flour into a large, zippered plastic bag. When the chicken pieces have marinated, add them to the bag, seal, and shake to coat well with the seasoned flour.

4 In a large heavy pot or Dutch oven, heat half of the oil over medium-high heat. Remove the chicken from the bag, reserving the flour, and sauté the chicken pieces in batches until nicely browned. Remove the chicken from the pan and set aside.

5 Reduce the heat to medium-low and add the remaining 2 Tbsp (30 mL) of the olive oil to the pan. Add the reserved spiced flour to the oil and stir to form a creamy paste or roux (add a little more oil if the mixture seems too dry). Cook the roux over medium heat, stirring frequently, until it turns the color of peanut butter. Stir carefully, roux is very hot and can burn your skin.

6 Add the onions, celery, garlic, bell peppers, and sausage to the pan. Keep the heat fairly high, and sauté, stirring occasionally, for 5 minutes. Add the puréed tomatoes, beer, Worcestershire, bay leaves, marjoram, and reserved chicken to the pot.

7 Bring to a boil over medium-high heat, then reduce heat to low and cover. Simmer for 45 to 60 minutes until the chicken is tender.

8 Add the shrimp, cover the pot and simmer for 5 minutes or until the shrimp curl and turn pink. Season to taste with salt and pepper. Mound some steamed rice in each of six individual soup plates and ladle the gumbo around the rice. Serves 6.

Ham and Split Pea Soup

This version of pea soup is a bit chunkier than most, owing to the addition of barley and baby peas. Definitely a keeper in The Guy's hearty soup repertoire.

1 Tbsp (15 mL) butter
1 Tbsp (15 mL) olive oil
1 onion, minced
1 clove garlic, minced
1 large carrot, diced
1 sprig fresh thyme, leaves only
1 cup (250 mL) dried green split peas

¾ cup (175 mL) chopped cooked ham or
    back bacon
3 cups (750 mL) chicken broth
1 cup (250 mL) dry white wine
½ cup (125 mL) pearl barley
½ cup (125 mL) frozen baby peas
salt and freshly ground black pepper

1 In a large soup pot, heat the butter and olive oil over medium heat. Sauté the onion and garlic until softened, about 10 minutes.

2 Stir in the carrot, thyme, split peas, ham, chicken broth, and wine. Bring to a boil. Cover, reduce the heat to low, and simmer for 1 hour.

3 Add the barley and frozen peas and continue to simmer for 30 to 45 minutes or until the soup is thick. Season to taste with salt and pepper. Serves 4.

Beef and Barley Soup

This old-fashioned recipe comes from The Guy's grandmother. It's one of those comforting combinations that makes the best of simple and inexpensive ingredients. You can also add a shredded parsnip if you have one.

2 lb (1 kg) beef shank, bone in

1 Tbsp (15 mL) canola oil

10 cups (2.5 L) water

2 tsp (10 mL) salt

1 tsp (5 mL) black peppercorns

1 large onion, minced

3 stalks celery, minced

2 cups (500 mL) finely grated carrots

⅔ cup (150 mL) pearl barley

salt and freshly ground black pepper

1 Tbsp (15 mL) minced fresh parsley

1 Soak the beef shanks in cold water for 15 minutes, then rinse and drain.

2 In a large soup pot, heat the oil over medium high heat, and sear the meat. The beef should be nicely browned on all sides—this will add color and flavor to the finished soup.

3 Add the water, salt, and peppercorns, and bring to a boil. Skim off any scum that rises to the surface. Reduce the heat to low, and simmer for 2 hours.

4 After 2 hours, remove the meat from the pot. Separate the meat from the bone and discard bone. Finely chop the meat by hand and set aside. Strain the broth through a fine sieve and return to the soup pot.

5 Add the chopped meat, minced onion, and celery to the broth. Simmer for 30 minutes. Add the grated carrot and barley. Simmer for another 30 minutes, until the barley is tender. Season the soup with salt and pepper to taste. Stir in the parsley just before serving. Serves 6.

WISE GUY: To make this into a vegetarian mushroom and barley soup, skip the broth-making steps and start with 6 to 8 cups (1.5 to 2 L) vegetable broth (homemade or prepared) seasoned with 1 Tbsp (15 mL) soy sauce and a couple of cloves of garlic. Add a large portobello mushroom (scrape out the gills and chop it fine) with the remaining vegetables to stand in for the meat—it makes a stick-to-your-ribs vegetarian meal.

Manhattan Clam Chowder

Creamy New England–style clam chowder may be the classic, but The Guy thinks there's something sexier about the Manhattan version—just like its namesake. But if you must have your clam chowder creamy (and don't mind the extra calories), stir in some heavy cream at the end. Divine, dahling!

2 thick pieces smoky bacon, finely chopped
1 large onion, finely chopped
2 stalks celery, finely chopped
1 Tbsp (15 mL) all-purpose flour
3 cups (750 mL) water or chicken broth
one 14-oz (398-mL) can tomatoes, chopped
1 large carrot, grated or finely chopped
2 cups (500 mL) peeled and cubed potatoes

1 tsp (5 mL) dried thyme
2 bay leaves
pinch cayenne pepper
two 14-oz (375 mL) cans baby clams,
   including juice
½ to 1 cup (125 to 250 mL) whipping cream
   (optional)
salt and freshly ground black pepper

1 In a large soup pot over medium-high heat, fry the bacon until it begins to crisp. Add the onion and celery, and cook for 5 minutes or until the vegetables soften and start to brown. Stir in the flour. Slowly stir in the water, then add the tomatoes, carrots, potatoes, thyme, bay leaves, and cayenne. Bring to a boil, cover, and reduce the heat to low. Simmer for 20 minutes.

2 Discard the bay leaves. Stir in the clams and their juice and heat to a boil. Reduce heat to low and stir in the cream, if using. Simmer for 10 more minutes. Season to taste with salt and pepper before serving. Serves 6 to 8.

My Minestrone

While it's not completely traditional, The Guy's minestrone soup is a hearty version of the classic, using wholegrains instead of the usual small pasta. This soup is delicious garnished with a handful of freshly grated Parmesan cheese. (When you finish a piece of Parmigiano Reggiano, save the "heels," or rinds, and add them to the soup pot for real Italian flavor.)

3 Tbsp (45 mL) extra virgin olive oil
1 large onion, chopped
1 cup (250 mL) chopped cooked ham (or substitute 4 to 5 slices double-smoked bacon, chopped)
1 cup (250 mL) peeled and diced carrots
2 cups (500 mL) peeled and diced potatoes
2 cloves garlic, minced
1 cup (250 mL) chopped celery
4 large tomatoes, chopped (fresh or canned)
6 cups (1.5 L) chicken broth
1 ham bone, or chunks of Parmesan cheese rind (optional, but either will add an extra layer of flavor to your soup)
1 bay leaf
½ cup (125 mL) pot barley or brown rice
1 can (about 1½ cups/625 mL) cooked white beans, rinsed well and drained
1 cup (250 mL) frozen peas, thawed
2 to 3 Tbsp (30 to 45 mL) pesto, or to taste
salt and freshly ground black pepper
hot pepper sauce or chili paste to taste
freshly grated Parmigiano Reggiano cheese

1 Heat the oil in a large soup pot over medium high heat. Add the onion and sauté for 5 to 10 minutes, or until it begins to brown. If you're using bacon instead of ham, add it now and cook until the fat is rendered before adding the other ingredients. Or add the ham, then the carrots, potatoes, garlic, and celery. Cook and stir the vegetables for another 10 minutes or until they are aromatic and begin to soften.

2 Add the chopped tomatoes (if using canned tomatoes simply squeeze them slowly through your fingers into the pot to break them up). Cook and stir for about 5 minutes. Add the chicken broth and ham bone or cheese rind, if using. Bring to a boil. Cover the pot, reduce the heat to low, and simmer for 30 minutes.

3 Fish out the ham bone or cheese rind and discard. Stir in the barley and increase the heat to medium. Cover and simmer for 30 to 40 minutes or until the barley is tender. Stir in the thawed peas and heat through for 5 minutes. Stir in the pesto, season with salt, pepper, and hot sauce to taste. Serve with a bowl of freshly grated Parmesan cheese on the side for topping individual bowls of soup. Serves 8.

Breakfasts of Champions

Any guy who wants to get the girl must make breakfast, and do it well.

Give her a nice breakfast—the morning after the night before, and weekend mornings thereafter—and she'll find you irresistible forever.

Breakfast should be part of your daily routine. On this subject, The Guy takes his mother's advice to heart—you'll look better and feel better (maybe even make more money) if you eat your brekkie. Here are some ideas to get your day revved up a notch, and get you started with a full tank.

All About Eggs

Since The Guy has always prided himself as "The Breakfast Guy," he does know a thing or two about eggs.

First and foremost, eggs are good for you. While an egg does contain a lot of cholesterol, most current medical wisdom says it's not the cholesterol in foods like eggs and shrimp that is cause for concern, but rather the cholesterol your body makes from eating high-fat foods. Granted, the egg yolk (the source of that cholesterol) is also where the fat lies, but in the scheme of things, the amount of fat in the average large egg makes it a low-fat food. And there's a lot of other good nutrition in that convenient little package, from vitamins and protein to nine essential amino acids—something most of your other typical breakfast foods can't claim.

So eat a couple of eggs for breakfast on Sundays and don't sweat it. Or, if you really want to watch your intake of fat and calories, substitute two egg whites when a recipe calls for one egg (if it calls for two eggs, use one whole egg and two egg whites). Also, eggs are the tie that binds a multitude of dishes—from cakes and soufflés, to custards, bread puddings, fritters, and frittatas. You just can't cook without eggs in the fridge. So make sure you get your money's worth. Buy fresh farm eggs, from hens that range free and eat an organic vegetarian diet. You'll be rewarded with eggs that look and taste far better than the ubiquitous supermarket egg. The deep yellow yolks stand tall in the pan, and served straight up on toast, you won't find a nicer egg to eat.

Cooking Eggs

Obviously, guys eat eggs because they're easy to cook. Scrambled, boiled, poached, or pan-fried, cooking eggs is the first thing any good short-order cook learns how to do—and you can, too.

 Boiled

Remove eggs from the refrigerator 30 minutes before breakfast to warm them up to room temperature. Put the eggs in a pot and cover them with cold water. Turn the heat under the pot to high. When the water just begins to simmer and steam (not really boil), reduce the heat to keep it just barely bubbling and start timing. For soft-cooked eggs, simmer for 2 to 3 minutes; for medium-cooked eggs (cooked whites and runny yolks), simmer for 4 minutes; for hard-cooked eggs, simmer for 10 to 15 minutes. To make peeling hard-boiled eggs easier, plunge the cooked eggs immediately into ice water to chill, cracking the shells lightly to let water seep in. When they're fully chilled, roll the boiled eggs around lightly on the counter to loosen the membrane under the shell and peel.

The other way to boil eggs is called "coddling"—boiling the water first, then lowering the eggs carefully into the water and turning off the heat. Let the eggs remain in the covered pan for 6, 10, or 30 minutes, depending on the desired degree of doneness (soft, medium, or hard). Easy.

 **Scrambled**

The secret to good scrambled eggs is quitting while you're ahead.

In a small bowl, lightly whisk your eggs with salt, pepper, and 1 to 2 Tbsp (15 to 30 mL) of cream (or milk). Melt some butter in a non-stick pan over medium heat. Add the eggs and stir them around with a fork, scraping up the cooked bits from the bottom of the pan. Stop stirring while the eggs are still a bit runny (or creamy) on top. Cover the pan, remove it from the heat, and let the eggs cook in the retained heat for 5 minutes (this is the time to throw some minced green onions and finely grated cheese on top). If you overcook scrambled eggs, they're dry and grainy, so just don't.

 Fried

Unless you're frying bacon first (and have a bit of bacon fat left in the pan), fry eggs in a non-stick skillet with a little butter over medium-low heat. Cook until the whites of the eggs are firm, but the yolks remain soft—shake the pan to see how soft the egg is in the center. As they finish cooking, put the lid on for one minute. Serve the eggs on top of buttered toast.

 Poached

See poaching instructions in Eggs Bennie recipe (see page 59).

The Perfect Omelet

Any breakfast chef knows how to make a perfectly filled and folded omelet, and you should, too. (It's all in the wrist action.)

2 large eggs
1 Tbsp (15 mL) milk

salt and freshly ground black pepper to taste
1 Tbsp (15 mL) butter

1 In a bowl, whisk together the eggs, milk, salt, and pepper. Melt the butter over medium heat in a non-stick 7- to 8-inch (18- to 20-cm) sauté pan with flared sides (this kind of small non-stick pan is an essential part of your tool kit).

2 Pour the egg mixture into the pan and slightly reduce the heat. As the edges begin to set, lift with a spatula and push into the center of the pan. Scramble up the middle a bit, allowing the liquid egg to run around the edge of the pan and underneath the cooked bits. Cook for three or four minutes, shaking the pan to keep the omelet from sticking. When the omelet is light golden on the bottom, and still a little wet on top, it's done (the runny stuff will finish cooking once it's folded).

3 While it's still in the pan, fill the omelet down the center, at a right angle to the handle, with warm, precooked ingredients (sausage, smoked salmon, roasted peppers, caramelized onions, sautéed mushrooms, leftover chicken curry, crabmeat, etc.) and/or cheese (grated Swiss or cheddar, herbed cream cheese, blue cheese, etc.). Then slide the omelet away from you, onto a warm plate and flip the handle up to fold the omelet onto itself as it exits the pan. That's it. Serves 1.

Bacon, Eggs, and Home Fries

The Guy's specialty is Sunday morning breakfast, and that often means traditional pan-fried eggs on grainy toast, with a couple of slices of double-smoked bacon and a pile of home-fried potatoes on the side. Always boil or bake an extra few potatoes on Saturday night so there are cold potatoes in the fridge to fry in the morning. And don't forget to buy the best thick-cut, smoked bacon from a good butcher, artisan bread, and organic, grain-fed eggs for the ultimate bacon-and-egg breakfast. It's the ingredients that will make this simple combo sublime.

4 thick slices double-smoked bacon
1 cup (250 mL) sliced boiled potato (start with small, firm potatoes like fingerlings or baby potatoes in their skins)
1 green onion, finely chopped

4 organic eggs
1 Tbsp (15 mL) butter (optional)
2 slices multigrain or sourdough bread, toasted and buttered

1 In a non-stick sauté pan, cook the bacon over medium heat until the fat is rendered and the bacon is crisp. Remove the bacon from the pan and keep warm.

2 Drain all but 2 Tbsp (30 mL) of bacon fat from the pan (add butter if there is not enough fat). Add the sliced potatoes and season with salt and pepper. Sauté until browned on both sides. Stir in the green onion and cook for 1 minute, just to wilt. Remove the potatoes from the pan and keep warm (push them to one side of the pan if there's enough room to cook the eggs).

3 Break the eggs into the hot pan and reduce the heat to medium-low. Season with salt and pepper and cover the pan. Watch them carefully and check after a couple of minutes—when the whites are cooked and the yolks begin to look opaque, remove the eggs from the heat immediately. Shaking the pan to jiggle the yolks also gives you a good clue as to when they are cooked to your liking. The Guy likes his eggs when the whites are cooked but the yolks are still runny. Serve two eggs on top of each slice of toast with potatoes and bacon on the side. Serves 2.

Breakfast Bacon and Egg Sub

This is a hearty sandwich to start the day. The Guy likes to use a crusty Italian bun for these subs—the interior is soft enough to cradle the scrambled eggs and the firm crust helps to hold the ingredients inside. If you can find a wholegrain panini bun, all the better.

2 individual Italian sandwich buns (a.k.a. panini)
4 large eggs
2 Tbsp (30 mL) milk or cream
salt and freshly ground black pepper
4 tsp (20 mL) softened butter, divided
2 thick slices Canadian bacon, cooked and
   chopped

1 green onion, chopped
½ cup (125 mL) baby spinach leaves
¼ cup (60 mL) spicy tomato salsa
4 slices medium or aged cheddar cheese

1 Split the buns in half lengthwise and lightly butter both pieces using half the butter, and set aside.

2 In a medium bowl, beat the eggs with the milk, salt, and pepper. Melt the remaining 2 tsp (10 mL) of butter in a non-stick skillet. Add the eggs and cook over medium-low heat. Don't stir—push the eggs around the pan with a spatula until they start to set—and don't overcook (the mixture should remain slightly wet). Remove the pan from the heat and fold in the cooked bacon and green onions.

3 Layer one side of each bun with spinach leaves, and spoon the scrambled eggs overtop, dividing the eggs evenly between the two sandwiches. Top each sandwich with 2 Tbsp (30 mL) of the salsa and two slices of cheese.

4 Set the sandwiches on a baking sheet and broil for 1 to 2 minutes or until the cheese is melted. Close the buns and serve. Serves 2.

> **WISE GUY:**
>
> For a spicy Tex-Mex sub (or tortilla) filling, omit the bacon and spinach, and instead fold in some cooked spicy chorizo sausage. Top with extra spicy salsa, sour cream, and jalapeño Jack cheese.

Eggs Bennie

This is the ultimate brunch dish—whether you're serving breakfast on Christmas morning or Mother's Day, Eggs Benedict is always a hit. Make the hollandaise quickly in the blender from scratch, or use one of the imported European mixes.

4 English muffins
8 slices Canadian bacon
8 eggs, at room temperature
1 Tbsp (15 mL) vinegar or freshly squeezed
   lemon juice

½ tsp (2 mL) salt
1 cup (250 mL) hollandaise sauce (from a mix
   or from scratch, see following recipe)
cayenne pepper
2 oranges, cut into wedges, to garnish

1 Cut the English muffins in half, then toast and lightly butter. Set aside.

2 To poach the eggs, make sure they've been out of the refrigerator for at least 30 minutes to warm up. Heat 2 inches of water in a large, non-stick skillet and add the vinegar (or lemon juice) and salt. Bring the water to a rolling boil. It's easiest to slide the eggs into the water (and keep them intact) if you break them into a cup or saucer first. Have all of the eggs ready (cracked and in saucers) so that you can get them all into the water at once. Tip the eggs into the boiling water then immediately cover the pan and turn off the heat. Poach the eggs for 3 minutes for soft yolks or 4 minutes for firmer yolks. Lift the poached eggs out of the water with a slotted spoon. Drain well, and serve (or immediately put them into a bowl of ice water and store in the refrigerator to reheat later with a fast dip in boiling water—a restaurant chefs' trick).

3 When ready to serve, microwave the back bacon for a minute or two, just to heat. Place two toasted muffin halves on each warm plate. Top each muffin with a piece of warm back bacon and a poached egg. Drizzle 3 Tbsp (45 mL) of hot hollandaise sauce over each egg and lightly dust with cayenne pepper. Garnish each plate with orange wedges and serve. Serves 4.

WISE GUY: You can up the ante on eggs benedict with creative additions to the sauce (try 1 Tbsp/15 mL of tomato paste for tomato hollandaise) or switch the protein (for example, instead of back bacon, use a layer of cold smoked salmon). Or lose the English muffin altogether and replace it with a hot crab cake (see Southern Crab Cakes page 304).

Blender Hollandaise

This is a sauce that's loaded with calories and fat so don't be dumping it over everything (it's tempting, I know). Keep it for special occasions. The Guy really only serves Eggs Bennie on Christmas morning or other significant holidays, which makes it all the more impressive. You can also afford a bit of hollandaise at the year's halfway mark. It's outstanding drizzled over lightly steamed spring asparagus.

3 egg yolks (tasty, dark orange, organic, grain-fed egg yolks)
2 Tbsp (30 mL) freshly squeezed lemon juice
pinch of cayenne pepper
¼ tsp (1 mL) salt
½ cup (125 mL) butter, melted

1 In a blender, combine the egg yolks, lemon juice, cayenne, and salt. Blend until smooth.

2 Heat the butter in a small saucepan, or in the microwave, until it's melted and hot, but not brown. With the blender running at high speed, remove the small center section of the lid and very slowly drizzle the hot butter into the eggs. By the time you've finished adding the butter, the sauce should be thick and emulsified, like mayonnaise. Keep the sauce warm in a stainless steel bowl set in warm water, or in a small Thermos. You can also reheat the sauce, if necessary, in a double boiler over hot, but not boiling, water, whisking constantly to keep the sauce from separating. Makes about 1 cup.

Apple Muesli

It's the prunes that add the extra oomph to this traditional Swiss mountain man breakfast. The Guy likes to make his muesli on the weekend and keep it in the refrigerator for a healthy start to every weekday.

1½ cups (375 mL) large-flake rolled oats (not instant) or rolled barley
1½ cups (375 mL) water
2 cups (500 mL) shredded unpeeled apple (about 2 apples)
1½ cups (375 mL) pitted prunes, chopped
2 Tbsp (30 mL) honey
2 Tbsp (30 mL) freshly squeezed lemon juice
½ tsp (2 mL) ground cinnamon
2 cups (500 mL) plain yogurt

Garnishes
chopped fresh fruit (such as blueberries, bananas, melons, pineapple, or grapes)
dried fruit (such as raisins, cranberries, or apricots)
nuts (such as pecans, walnuts, slivered almonds, sunflower seeds, or sesame seeds)

1 In a large bowl or covered container, combine the oats, water, shredded apple, prunes, honey, lemon juice, and cinnamon. Stir well, cover, and refrigerate overnight.

2 In the morning, stir in the yogurt. To serve, spoon an individual serving of muesli into a bowl and top with fresh fruit and nuts. Makes 8 servings.

Banana Raisin French Toast

Like a banana sandwich, this is an easy but healthy breakfast to make for two adults or a few hungry kids.

1 large banana
½ tsp (2 mL) ground cinnamon
4 slices wholegrain raisin bread
½ cup (175 mL) milk or half-and-half cream
2 large eggs

1 Tbsp (15 mL) granulated sugar
1 tsp (5 mL) pure vanilla extract
3 Tbsp (45 mL) butter
icing sugar and maple syrup

1 Preheat the oven to 350°F (180°C).

2 In a bowl, mash the banana with the cinnamon. Divide the banana mixture in half and spread evenly over two slices of the raisin bread. Top each with remaining bread and press lightly to seal.

3 Whisk together the milk (or cream), eggs, sugar, and vanilla in a shallow bowl. Soak both sides of the banana-filled sandwiches in the egg mixture.

4 Melt the butter in an ovenproof, non-stick frying pan over medium-high heat. Fry the French toast about 2 to 3 minutes per side or until golden. Place the pan into the oven for 10 minutes to finish cooking—this makes the French toast nice and puffy.

5 To serve, cut each piece in half diagonally, dust with icing sugar, and pass the maple syrup. Serves 2.

Cornmeal Hotcakes with Fresh Berries

The Guy likes to make these delicious hotcakes when fresh blueberries or raspberries are in season. By setting the berries on top of the cakes once they're in the pan, you avoid the usual problem of berries bleeding into your pancakes.

½ cup (125 mL) cornmeal
½ cup (125 mL) boiling water
½ cup (125 mL) all-purpose flour
1 Tbsp (15 mL) baking powder
1 Tbsp (15 mL) granulated sugar

¼ tsp (1 mL) salt
1 large egg
¼ cup (60 mL) melted butter
¼ cup (60 mL) milk or buttermilk
1 cup (250 mL) fresh berries

1 Preheat the oven to 200°F (95°C).

2 In a mixing bowl, combine the cornmeal and boiling water, and set aside for 10 minutes.

3 In another bowl, combine the flour, baking powder, sugar, and salt. In a measuring cup, whisk together the egg, melted butter, and milk (or buttermilk) until well blended. Add the dry ingredients to the cornmeal and stir with a fork to combine before adding the egg mixture. Continue stirring until everything is barely moistened (be careful not to overmix).

4 Heat a non-stick frying pan over medium-high and brush with a little oil or melted butter. Reduce the heat to medium and spoon the batter onto the pan, 3 Tbsp (45 mL) at a time, to make 3- to 4-inch hotcakes. Set a few berries on top of each hotcake. When you see bubbles rising and breaking on the top of the hotcakes, they're ready to turn over. Cook the second side for a couple of minutes, until nicely browned, and transfer to a plate. Keep the cooked hotcakes warm in the oven while you finish cooking the rest. Serve with maple syrup. Makes 10 to 12.

WISE GUY: Making pancakes isn't brain surgery but there are tricks to make sure they're light and fluffy. Buttermilk seems to make the best pancakes, but you can also "sour" a cup of regular milk with 1 to 2 tsp (5 to 10 mL) of lemon juice for similar results. And don't overmix the batter—like muffins, pancakes are best when the batter is a little lumpy. If you're using a lot of low-gluten flour (buckwheat or wholegrain flours) consider separating the eggs and beating the whites until stiff, then folding them into the batter (it's more work, but guarantees fluffier results).

Banana Pancakes

Make this batter the night before a big breakfast and store it, covered, in the refrigerator.

½ cup (125 mL) whole wheat flour
½ cup (125 mL) all-purpose flour
1½ tsp (7 mL) baking powder
½ tsp (2 mL) baking soda
¼ tsp (1 mL) ground cinnamon
2 Tbsp (30 mL) granulated sugar

pinch of salt
1 cup (250 mL) buttermilk or plain yogurt
2 Tbsp (30 mL) melted butter or canola oil
1 large egg
¾ cup (175 mL) mashed bananas
extra sliced bananas and maple syrup

1 Preheat the oven to 200°F (95°C).

2 In a large bowl, combine the flours, baking powder, baking soda, cinnamon, sugar, and salt.

3 In another bowl, whisk together the buttermilk (or yogurt), melted butter (or oil), egg, and mashed bananas.

4 Make a well in the center of the dry ingredients and add the banana mixture. Stir with a fork until everything is barely moistened.

5 Heat a non-stick frying pan over medium-high heat and brush with a little oil or melted butter. Reduce the heat to medium and spoon the batter onto the pan, using 2 to 3 Tbsp (30 to 45 mL) of batter for each 3- to 4-inch pancake. When you see bubbles rising and breaking all over the top of the pancakes, they're ready to turn over. Cook the second side for a couple of minutes, until nicely browned, and transfer to a plate. Keep the cooked pancakes warm in the oven while you finish cooking the rest. When ready to serve, top the pancakes with sliced bananas and maple syrup. Makes 12.

Buttermilk Biscuits

The Guy loves biscuits for breakfast. Eat these with ham and eggs, or for a more decadent treat, split them in half and fry them southern-style in butter until golden and crisp. The trick to fluffy biscuits is a light touch. Don't overwork the dough and your biscuits will retain that ethereal quality.

2 cups (500 mL) all-purpose flour
½ tsp (2 mL) salt
2 tsp (10 mL) baking powder

6 Tbsp (90 mL) cold butter, cut into cubes
¾ cup (175 mL) buttermilk
melted butter or light olive oil for brushing

1 Preheat the oven to 425°F (220°C).

2 In a large bowl, combine the flour, salt, and baking powder. Add the butter. Use a pastry blender or two knives to cut through the butter and flour until the butter is chopped into small bits no bigger than peas. You can also combine these ingredients in a food processor and pulse until just crumbly. Add the buttermilk and stir quickly with a fork until just combined. Turn the dough out onto a lightly floured surface, gather into a ball then gently knead—just a couple of times until the dough comes together. Lightly pat the dough into a circle about ¾ inch (2 cm) thick.

3 Using a lightly floured glass or biscuit cutter, cut the dough into 2½-inch (6-cm) rounds. Reshape and flatten any leftover pieces of dough and cut more biscuits—you should have twelve. Set the biscuits on an ungreased baking sheet and brush them lightly with melted butter or oil. Bake until golden, about 15 to 20 minutes. Transfer to a cooling rack. Makes 12 biscuits.

WISE GUY: For savory herb biscuits, add 3 to 4 Tbsp (45 to 60 mL) of chopped fresh herbs (parsley, rosemary, basil, or thyme) when you add the buttermilk.

For sweet biscuits to serve with strawberries for shortcake (or to use to top cobblers and other desserts), make the biscuits with sweet cream instead of buttermilk and add ⅓ cup (75 mL) of granulated or brown sugar to the dry ingredients. Brush the tops of the biscuits with melted butter and sprinkle with a little extra sugar before baking.

To make the sweet biscuits into chocolate shortcakes (awesome with ice cream and hot caramelized banana and pineapple toppings), add ¾ cup (175 mL) Dutch cocoa to the flour and toss in ½ cup (125 mL) chocolate chips. The possibilities are endless!

Savory Scones

These manly scones are loaded with savory stuff, from roasted red peppers and spinach to fresh herbs. The combinations are infinite—so get creative. They're great split, toasted, and topped with poached eggs, or simply to grab for a portable breakfast.

1 cup (250 mL) all-purpose flour
1 cup (250 mL) whole wheat flour
1½ tsp (7 mL) salt
2 Tbsp (30 mL) baking powder
½ cup (125 mL) unsalted butter, chilled and cut into cubes
½ to ¾ cup (125 to 175 mL) finely chopped savory stuff (roasted red pepper, caramelized onion, roasted garlic, finely chopped spinach, chopped steamed broccoli, crumbled bacon, slivered prosciutto, etc.)

1 green onion, minced
1 Tbsp (15 mL) chopped fresh herbs (dill, basil, oregano, or thyme)
1 cup (250 mL) shredded or crumbled cheese (aged cheddar, feta, Gruyère, Gouda, or blue cheese)
⅓ to ½ cup (75 to 125 mL) half-and-half cream or buttermilk
poppy seeds or sesame seeds

1 Preheat the oven to 350°F (180°C).

2 In a food processor, combine the flours, salt, baking powder, and butter. Pulse until the mixture resembles coarse crumbs, then transfer to a bowl.

3 Stir the savory vegetables and/or meat into the dry ingredients along with the green onion, herbs, and cheese. Add just enough cream to make a soft dough (the amount you add will depend on how wet the vegetable mixture is), and stir with a fork until the dough forms. Don't work the dough too much—the less you handle it, the flakier your scones will be. Turn the dough out onto a lightly floured surface and gently pat the dough into an 8-inch (20-cm) square about 1½ inches (4 cm) thick. Cut into four 4-inch (10-cm) squares. Slice each square crosswise to make 8 triangular scones. Set the scones on a baking sheet lined with parchment paper. Using a pastry brush, lightly brush the tops with extra cream. Sprinkle with seeds.

WISE GUY:

Think about complementary and classic combinations for the scones (red pepper with oregano and cheddar cheese; spinach with dill and feta; prosciutto with chopped olives, basil, and Parmesan; cooked and crumbled Italian sausage with caramelized onions; or just get creative).

4 Bake for 20 to 25 minutes or until golden. Transfer to a cooling rack for a short time. Serve warm, with butter. Makes 8 scones.

Almond Apricot Scones

This is another of The Guy's favorite snacks from the local coffeehouse. It makes a great breakfast on the run.

2 cups (500 mL) all-purpose or wholegrain
    pastry flour
½ tsp (2 mL) salt
¼ cup (60 mL) granulated sugar
2 tsp (10 mL) baking powder
1 tsp (5 mL) baking soda
6 Tbsp (90 mL) diced cold butter

¼ cup (60 mL) sliced almonds
½ cup (125 mL) slivered dried apricots
¾ cup (175 mL) buttermilk or plain yogurt
1 tsp (5 mL) almond extract or Amaretto liqueur
melted butter for brushing
granulated sugar

1 Preheat the oven to 400°F (200°C).

2 In a food processor, combine the flour, salt, sugar, baking powder, baking soda, and butter. Pulse just until the mixture resembles coarse crumbs.

3 Transfer to a large bowl and mix in the almonds and apricots. Add the buttermilk and almond extract and stir with a fork until the dough just begins to come together.

4 Turn the dough out onto a lightly floured surface and gently pat into a 6- x 9-inch (15- x 23-cm) rectangle about 1½ inches (4 cm) thick. Cut into six 3-inch (8-cm) squares, then slice each square crosswise to make 12 triangular scones.

5 Set the scones on a baking sheet lined with parchment paper. Using a pastry brush, lightly brush the tops with melted butter. Sprinkle with sugar. Bake for 15 to 20 minutes or until golden, then transfer to a cooling rack. Makes 12.

Cranberry Oat Scones

The trick to perfect biscuits or scones is a light touch—don't handle the dough too much or your scones will become heavy. This is a slightly sweet but healthy scone. The cranberries add color and a sweet-tart flavor.

2 cups (500 mL) all-purpose flour (or try using some whole wheat or barley flour)
¼ cup (60 mL) granulated sugar, divided
1 Tbsp (15 mL) baking powder
¾ tsp (4 mL) baking soda
½ tsp (2 mL) salt

¾ cup (175 mL) unsalted butter, chilled and cut into cubes
1 cup (250 mL) rolled oats
¾ cup (175 mL) dried cranberries
2 Tbsp (30 mL) finely grated orange zest
⅔ cup (150 mL) buttermilk

1 Preheat the oven to 425°F (220°C).

2 In a food processor, combine the flour, 3 Tbsp (45 mL) of the sugar, baking powder, baking soda, and salt. Add the butter and pulse until the butter is chopped into small pieces and the mixture is crumbly. Pour into a large bowl and stir in the oats and cranberries.

3 In another bowl, whisk together the orange zest and buttermilk and add to the dry ingredients. Stir quickly with a fork until the batter begins to cling together.

4 Turn the dough onto a lightly floured surface and gently pat into an 8-inch (20-cm) square about 1½ inches (4 cm) thick. Cut into four 4-inch (10-cm) squares, then slice each square crosswise to make 8 triangular scones. Set the triangles on a baking sheet lined with parchment paper. Using a pastry brush, lightly brush the tops with buttermilk and sprinkle with the remaining sugar.

5 Bake for 15 to 18 minutes or until golden, then transfer to a cooling rack. Makes 8.

The Global Diner

In The Guy's world the "diner" has taken on new meaning—morphing from the classic burger bar to encompass the French bistro, Italian trattoria, Greek taverna, and all things in between. It's the kind of simple, local fare we enjoy the world over, whether it's the Parisian beef steak with fries, a steamy bowl of mussels, or a crispy fish taco. It's global cooking, in short order.

Meat Loaf

For The Guy, ground beef means one of two things: meat loaf or hamburgers. The latter is really nothing more than a miniature version of the former, grilled instead of baked. But a good meat loaf should be firm and juicy enough to morph from a main course on day one to a sandwich filling on day two. In fact, The Guy has been known to make meat loaf just so he can have day-after meat loaf sandwiches (they're good hot or cold).

1½ lb (750 g) lean ground beef
½ lb (250 g) ground pork (optional—but it adds juiciness and flavor)
1 small onion, finely minced (about 1 cup/ 250 mL)
2 cloves garlic, minced

½ cup (125 mL) breadcrumbs or cracker crumbs
½ cup (125 mL) barbecue sauce or chili sauce, divided
1 large egg, lightly beaten
1 Tbsp (15 mL) Worcestershire sauce
salt and freshly ground black pepper

1 Preheat the oven to 350°F (180°C). Crumble the ground meat into a large bowl.

2 Use a food processor to mince the onion and garlic. Add to the meat.

3 Use the food processor to make the breadcrumbs (you'll need 1 or 2 slices of day-old bread, or about 15 crackers). Add the crumbs to the meat mixture. Stir in half the barbecue sauce, the egg, Worcestershire sauce, salt, and pepper. Use your hands to mix and knead until everything is evenly combined.

4 Lightly press the meat mixture into a loaf pan or form into an oval, football-shaped loaf on a baking sheet. Spread the remaining barbecue sauce over the top.

5 Bake at 350°F (180°C) for 45 to 60 minutes, until the meat loaf is well-browned on top and the internal temperature reaches 170°F (75°C).

6 Drain any excess fat and let the meat loaf rest for 10 minutes, then carve into thick slices.
Serves 6 to 8.

WISE GUY: For faster, individual meat loaves (the kind that kids love or that you can make in advance and freeze for quick single-serving suppers), divide the meat mixture into 8 large balls and press them into individual muffin tins. Brush with sauce and bake at 400°F (200°C) for about 25 minutes. Or make this mixture into meatballs and brown at 400°F (200°C) for 12 minutes.

Steak Frites

One of the best contributions from the Parisian bistro, or brasserie, to modern restaurant food everywhere is the basic pan-fried steak and fries or steak frites. And this combination of fried potatoes flecked with Parmesan and parsley is perhaps the best sidekick The Guy's steak has ever seen. A drizzle of truffle oil adds a totally alluring aroma.

Steak
2 strip loin or rib eye steaks
1 Tbsp (15 mL) Worcestershire sauce

salt and freshly ground black pepper
granulated garlic
1 Tbsp (15 mL) olive oil

Frites
4 large white potatoes
canola oil for frying
¼ cup (60 mL) finely shredded Parmesan
   cheese

¼ cup (60 mL) minced parsley
1 clove garlic, pressed in a garlic press or finely
   minced
sea salt

1 Rub the steaks on both sides with Worcestershire sauce, then sprinkle with salt, black pepper, and granulated garlic.

2 Cook the steaks when you're ready to finish the fries. Heat the oil in a heavy skillet (cast iron is ideal) over high heat and sear the steaks until nicely browned but still medium rare in the middle, about 4 minutes per side. Make sure you have the hood fan going as this can get smoky. (Alternately, grill the steak on a hot gas barbecue, directly over the heat, for 4 minutes per side.)

3 Peel the potatoes and use a mandoline slicer or a sharp knife to cut into very thin fries. Fill a bowl with ice water and add the potatoes, then refrigerate for at least 2 hours. Rinse again to remove any excess starch and spin in a salad spinner until completely dry.

4 Fill a deep pot or wok with 4 cups (1 L) of canola oil and heat to 235°F (160°C). Add the fries to the oil and blanch for 2 minutes. Drain the fries well and spread them on a sheet pan to cool quickly, then refrigerate until you're ready to serve.

5 Just before serving, heat the oil to 360°F (185°C) and cook the fries a second time, until very crisp and golden brown.

6 Drain the hot fries well, then place them in a big bowl. Toss with the Parmesan, parsley, garlic, and sea salt. Pile them on a plate with the steak and serve immediately. Serves 2.

Warm Bacon and Egg Spinach Salad

Here's a substantial spinach salad to sustain you when it's hot outside and a cold supper hits the spot—a main meal salad straight from the bistro menu.

1 lb (500 g) baby spinach
4 slices double-smoked bacon, chopped
1 Tbsp (15 mL) extra virgin olive oil
1 Tbsp (15 mL) grainy mustard
1 Tbsp (15 mL) red wine vinegar or freshly squeezed
  lemon juice

6 white mushrooms, washed and thinly sliced
4 eggs, hard boiled, peeled and quartered
  (see page 55)
2 green onions, chopped
freshly ground black pepper

1 Wash the spinach well. Place the spinach in a bowl.

2 In a skillet, cook the bacon over medium-high heat until crisp. Remove the bacon from the pan with a slotted spoon and set aside.

3 Add the olive oil, mustard, and vinegar to the pan and stir for one minute. Add the mushrooms to the pan and toss for 1 to 2 minutes.

4 Add contents of the pan to the spinach in the bowl and toss quickly—the spinach should slightly wilt. Add half of the reserved bacon and toss.

5 Arrange the spinach mixture on four individual plates. Surround each salad with egg wedges. Top with the reserved bacon and green onions. Season with pepper. Serves 4.

Oven-Fried Cod and Crispy Smashed Potatoes

Baking rather than frying makes this classic crispy fish and potato combo better on the arteries than the usual fish and chips—something The Guy likes to take into consideration for everyday dinners. Fluffy Japanese panko breadcrumbs make all the difference in the crispy crust. The potatoes can go in the oven first, then reduce the heat and bake the fish. Both are great with the spicy mayo.

Fish

4 cod loins (individual 5 oz/150 g portions)
⅓ cup (75 mL) low-fat mayonnaise
1 Tbsp (15 mL) Dijon mustard
¼ tsp (1 mL) garlic powder

½ to 1 tsp (2 to 5 mL) garlic chili paste (or to taste)
2 tsp (10 mL) freshly squeezed lemon or lime juice
salt and freshly ground black pepper
1 cup (250 mL) Japanese panko breadcrumbs

Potatoes

20 to 24 baby yellow potatoes, unpeeled

3 Tbsp (45 mL) extra virgin olive oil
coarse sea salt

1 Preheat the oven to 500°F (260°C).

2 Stab the potatoes with a fork and boil in salted water for about 15 minutes. Drain the potatoes and place in a shallow baking dish. Add the olive oil and toss to coat.

3 Press each potato with a fork until it is slightly flattened. Sprinkle the potatoes with sea salt and bake in the oven for 20 minutes, until crisp and golden.

4 In a bowl, combine the mayonnaise, mustard, garlic powder, chili paste, and lemon juice. Stir to combine. Season with salt and pepper. Divide the mayonnaise mixture in two, and reserve one half in the refrigerator.

5 Place the panko on a plate. Coat both sides of the fish pieces in the non-refrigerated half of the mayonnaise mixture, then dip them into the panko, pressing gently to cover the fillets entirely with crumbs.

6 For easy clean-up later, place the fish on a baking sheet lined with parchment paper. Reduce the oven heat to 400°F (200°C), place the fish in the oven, and continue to bake until the fish is crispy and golden brown, about 20 to 25 minutes. Serve the fish with the refrigerated spicy mayo, potato cakes, and Classic Coleslaw (see page 165). Serves 4.

Roasted Halibut Italian Style

The Guy loves this dish—fast and dead easy, with loads of gourmet cachet, too. Stir up a pot of Saffron Risotto (see page 203) or sauté some spinach to serve alongside. Pure and so simple.

1 Tbsp (15 mL) extra virgin olive oil
1 clove garlic, pressed
¼ cup (60 mL) pine nuts, ground
¼ cup (60 mL) finely grated Parmesan cheese

1½ lb (750 g) boneless, skinless halibut fillet, cut into four portions
¼ cup (60 mL) basil pesto
1 large tomato, thinly sliced
salt and freshly ground black pepper

1 Preheat the oven to 450°F (230°C).

2 In a small bowl, combine the olive oil, pressed garlic, pine nuts, and Parmesan cheese.

3 Arrange the fish on a shallow baking sheet that has been lined with parchment paper. Smear each portion of fish with 1 Tbsp (15 mL) of pesto and top with a couple of slices of tomato. Season with salt and pepper.

4 Press 2 Tbsp (30 mL) of the pine nut topping over each piece of fish.

5 Place the baking sheet into the preheated oven and roast for 10 minutes, until the fish is just cooked through and the nuts are brown. Serves 4.

Spicy Potato Crêpes

The dosa is the ultimate Indian wrap. The Guy became so enamored with the ethereal crêpes (a.k.a. masala dosa) he was served throughout southern India, he had to figure out how to cook them himself. But be warned, these dosas, filled with spicy potatoes, are highly addictive.

You can buy a prepared dosa mix (sort of like pancake mix) in most Indian grocery stores. Or make dosas from scratch, soaking and grinding urad dal (a small white split bean) and rice for the crepe batter. The Guy has discovered that a mixture of rice and chickpea flour (both easy to find at health food stores) with water, and a bit of yogurt makes an almost instant (and decent) substitute. If you can boil a potato and flip a pancake, you can make this simple dish any time. And this delicious gluten-free meal is the perfect way to impress a vegetarian girl for brunch.

Dosa Batter

1 cup (250 mL) chickpea flour (a.k.a. besan) or
    urad dal flour
1½ cups (375 mL) rice flour
½ cup (125 mL) all-purpose flour

½ tsp (2 mL) salt
¼ cup (60 mL) plain natural yogurt
2 to 3 cups (500 to 750 mL) water (enough to
    make the batter thick as heavy cream)
canola oil for cooking

Potato Filling

6 large potatoes, peeled and boiled
2 Tbsp (30 mL) canola oil
1 Tbsp (15 mL) butter
½ tsp (2 mL) whole cumin or fennel seeds
1 tsp (5 mL) black mustard seeds
1 large onion, finely chopped

1 tsp (5 mL) grated ginger
2 jalapeño or serrano chili peppers, seeded and
    minced
1 tsp (5 mL) turmeric
salt and freshly ground black pepper
2 Tbsp (30 mL) chopped fresh cilantro (or
    coriander chutney)

1 In a blender, combine the chickpea flour, rice flour, all-purpose flour, salt, yogurt, and about 2 cups of water. Whirl until smooth. Place in a bowl and cover loosely with plastic wrap. Set aside in a warm place for 8 to 12 hours (you want the batter to bubble and ferment slightly). Then refrigerate until you're ready to make the dosas—the batter will keep for two days.

2 To make the filling, heat the oil and butter in a large sauté pan over medium-high heat. When it's hot, add the cumin and mustard seeds. Stir while the seeds pop, for about 30 seconds. Add the chopped onion and cook over medium heat until golden brown. Add the ginger and minced peppers and cook 1 minute longer. Stir in the turmeric. Chop or lightly crush the warm potatoes and add them to the pan. They should remain chunky but slightly mashed. Mix the potatoes with the spices and cook for 10 minutes. Keep the filling warm while you make the dosas (or make it in advance and reheat in the microwave).

3 To make the dosas, heat a very large non-stick frying pan or griddle over medium heat and brush with a little oil. Water dropped on the surface should sizzle. The Guy hauled a heavy cast iron griddle all the way from Hyderabad and found that this, or a cast iron pan, results in the lightest pancakes. A non-stick pan will work, though, and the pancakes don't stick.

4 Use a ½-cup (125-mL) ladle to pour a portion of the batter into the center of the hot pan. Quickly swirl the pan to distribute the batter thinly over the entire surface. After a minute or two, the edges of the crepe will start to brown—brush edges of the pan around the pancake with a little more oil. The dosa should be crisp and golden brown on the bottom. Use a wide spatula to loosen the pancake, then flip and quickly cook the second side for one minute.

5 Fill the dosa with ¼ cup (60 mL) of the warm potato filling. Pile the filling down the center of the crepe, then fold each side over the filling and roll. Serve immediately with coconut or coriander chutney. Wipe the pan and brush it with oil before making another dosa. Rather than serve immediately, you can also stack the dosas and keep them warm in a 200°F (95°C) oven—but they will soften. The best dosas are eaten as soon as they're out of the pan, so plan to be standing by the stove. Makes about 12 dosas.

WISE GUY: The potato filling for these delicious dosas is also a perfect side dish with an ethnic-inspired main course like the Tandoori Lamb Skewers (see page 265). If making the crêpes is too much trouble, just wrap the spicy potato filling in a fresh flour tortilla, or stuff it inside a pita pocket.

Greco Shrimp

The Guy likes to serve these shrimp in individual casserole dishes with thick Greek pita bread (toasted and brushed with garlic butter) or a baguette for dipping. Sheep milk feta has more flavor than the more common supermarket variety—usually made with cow's milk.

2 medium onions, finely chopped
3 Tbsp (45 mL) minced garlic (about 3 large
   cloves)
¼ cup (60 mL) extra virgin olive oil
½ cup (125 mL) white wine
one 28-oz (796-mL) can Roma tomatoes

2 tsp (10 mL) chopped fresh oregano leaves,
   divided
1 Tbsp (15 mL) chopped fresh basil, divided
salt and freshly ground black pepper
1 lb (500 g) extra-large fresh shrimp, peeled and
   deveined
8 oz (200 g) sheep milk feta cheese, crumbled

1 In a sauté pan, heat the olive oil over medium-high heat and sauté the onions and garlic until fragrant and softened, about 5 to 10 minutes. Add the white wine and simmer for 2 to 3 minutes, to reduce the wine by half. Chop the tomatoes or squeeze them through your fingers, then add them to the pan.

2 Stir in half of the oregano, half of the basil, and season with salt and pepper. Bring to a boil and simmer for 5 minutes. Preheat the broiler.

3 When the sauce has slightly cooked down, transfer it to an ovenproof serving dish (or several individual dishes set out on a baking sheet to make moving them easier).

4 Stir the shrimp into the tomato sauce and sprinkle liberally with cheese. Place the dish under the preheated broiler and broil for 5 to 8 minutes, until the dish is bubbly and the shrimp are just cooked. Sprinkle with the reserved fresh oregano and basil and serve at once, with thick Greek pita bread (or baguette) on the side for dipping. Serves 4 as a main dish.

WISE GUY: When you're shopping for shrimp, look for the "count" on the package. Extra large shrimp (often called prawns) are 12 to 15 count—that is, you'll get 12 to 15 shrimp in every pound. Forty count, as you might imagine, are a lot smaller—40 shrimp per pound. Some shrimp will benefit from a soak in salt water at home to get rid of muddy flavors and firm them up. Nearly all medium- to large-sized shrimp are sold deveined—if they're not, you'll have to split them along the back (the outside curve) and pull out the black vein with the tip of a paring knife, then rinse each one under running water. It's a good idea to split extra-large prawns anyway—they'll cook more quickly and evenly.

Fish Tacos in a Blue Corn Crust with Fresh Tomato Salsa

Use the food processor to whirl up this easy coating for your favorite fish fillets and you'll be dining in no time. You can even use the food processor for the simple salsa.

1 cup (250 mL) blue corn chips (or substitute regular yellow chips)
¼ tsp (1 mL) cumin
¼ tsp (1 mL) chipotle chile powder or smoked paprika
2 Tbsp (30 mL) unbleached, all-purpose, barley, or whole wheat flour

Salsa
1 clove garlic, peeled
1 jalapeño pepper, seeds removed, quartered
2 Tbsp (30 mL) chopped cilantro

4 to 6 boneless and skinless white fish fillets (The Guy is partial to pickerel but sole works well)
¼ cup (60 mL) canola oil for frying
warm corn tortillas
shredded romaine lettuce

2 ripe Roma tomatoes, seeded and chopped
¼ cup (60 mL) chopped white onion
1 Tbsp (15 mL) freshly squeezed lime juice

1 Whirl the chips in the food processor until ground to fine crumbs. Add the cumin, chili powder, and flour. Pulse to combine, then place on a plate.

2 Roll the fish in the corn chip crumbs. Set aside on a plate.

3 Preheat the oven to 150°F (65°C). Heat the oil in a non-stick sauté pan over high heat. When the oil is very hot, add the fish. Cook quickly until the fish is crisp, about 2 minutes per side. Use tongs to turn the fish to keep the coating intact. Set the cooked fish on a paper towel–lined plate and place in the warm oven.

4 Meanwhile, rinse out the food processor and dry with a paper towel. Place the garlic and jalapeño in the processor and pulse until finely minced. Add the cilantro, and pulse to combine. Add the tomatoes, onion, and lime juice and whirl for a second or two to combine. Place the salsa in a bowl and set aside to allow flavors to meld (you can make this in advance and refrigerate it).

5 To serve, break the fried fish into chunks and wrap up in warm corn tortillas with salsa and shredded lettuce. You can also serve the the fish with steamed rice—just arrange the crispy fish fillets on a platter and spoon some salsa overtop. Serves 4.

Ginger Beef Salad

The Guy tasted this beefy salad in a swish hotel bar—it's an Asian version of the classic fried chicken salad, but with strips of crispy fried beef, tossed in a spicy Szechuan-style sauce. Perfect for those days when you're counting carbs.

Salad

4 cups (1 L) mixed greens
½ red bell pepper, cleaned and slivered
2 green onions, cut into 2-inch (5-cm) pieces
1 large carrot
1 tsp (5 mL) sesame oil
¾ lb (375 g) top beef sirloin steak

Sauce

¼ cup (60 mL) chicken stock
¼ cup (60 mL) soy sauce
2 Tbsp (30 mL) rice wine vinegar
¼ cup (60 mL) brown sugar
½ tsp (2 mL) sesame oil

1 egg, beaten
½ cup (125 mL) cornstarch
2 Tbsp (30 mL) all-purpose flour
⅔ cup (150 mL) water
3 Tbsp (45 mL) canola oil (plus extra for deep frying)

¼ tsp (1 mL) ground ginger
¼ tsp (1 mL) cayenne pepper
¼ tsp (1 mL) granulated garlic
2 tsp (10 mL) cornstarch mixed with 1 tsp (5 mL) cold water

1 Place the salad greens in a large bowl. Add the bell pepper. Slice each small section of green onion lengthwise to form slivers. Add to the bowl. Peel the carrot and either shred or cut diagonally into thin ovals, then cut each oval into matchstick julienne strips. Add to the bowl. Toss the salad, cover, and chill.

2 Trim all of the visible fat from the steak and cut the meat into long, thin fingers, about ¼ inch (5 mm) thick and 2 inches (5 cm) long.

3 In a bowl, whisk together the egg, cornstarch, flour, water, and oil. Add the meat strips to the bowl and mix with your hands until they are coated with batter.

4 In a wok or other deep pan, place 2 to 3 inches (5 to 8 cm) of canola oil and heat over medium-high heat until the oil reaches 380°F (190°C). Watch the oil carefully—don't walk away—this is how grease fires start. Keep the wok lid nearby as a precaution (to smother any flare-ups).

5 When the oil is hot, add the beef, a few pieces at a time, and fry in batches until golden brown, about 5 to 6 minutes. Remove from the oil with a slotted skimmer spoon, shake off excess oil, and place the beef on a paper towel–lined platter to drain. Finish cooking the meat and cool the oil.

6 In another clean wok or pot, combine all of the sauce ingredients and bring to a boil over medium heat. Boil for 1 minute, until the sauce is smoother and thick. Add the fried beef to this sauce and toss to coat. Set aside to cool slightly.

7 Toss the chilled salad mixture with a little sesame oil and divide between four individual salad bowls. Top each salad with some of the warm beef. Serve immediately. Serves 4.

Pork Cutlets Cubano

The Guy loves to rub whole tenderloins with spice mixtures for the grill (see Pork Tenderloin with Southern BBQ Rub, page 258), but he recently learned how easy it is to create tenderloin cutlets to sear in a skillet on the stovetop. Like chicken, you can marinate or season the pork pieces with almost any herbs and spices. Simply season, dust with flour, and pan-fry, then serve with a wedge of fresh lemon to squeeze overtop. For a simple Burgundian version, replace the peppers with 3 cups (750 mL) of sliced mushrooms (wild porcini, portobello, or brown) and use red wine instead of the white in the sauce.

2 pork tenderloins (about ¾ lb/375 g each)
salt and freshly ground black pepper
all-purpose or whole wheat flour for dusting
   (optional)
4 Tbsp (60 mL) olive oil, divided
2 Cubanelle or long Hungarian peppers, seeded
   and sliced
2 bell peppers (red and/or yellow), seeded
   and sliced

1 large red onion, slivered
2 cloves garlic, minced
½ cup (125 mL) white wine
1 Tbsp (15 mL) balsamic vinegar or sour orange
   juice (a bottled product available in Latin
   markets)
½ cup (125 mL) chicken stock
salt and freshly ground black pepper
chopped fresh parsley to garnish

1 Using a sharp, pointed knife, remove any silver skin on the outside of the tenderloin. Slip the tip of the knife under the skin at one end to release it, then lift the skin with one hand as you slice it away.

2 Once the meat is trimmed, cut each tenderloin into slices, each about 2 inches (5 cm) thick.

3 Lay the pieces of pork on a piece of plastic wrap, cut-side down. Cover with a second piece of plastic and, using a meat mallet or the back of your chef's knife, lightly pound the pieces to an even thickness of about ½ inch (1 cm).

4 To cook the cutlets, season with salt and pepper on both sides, and dredge lightly in flour, if desired. Heat half of the olive oil in a non-stick sauté pan over medium-high heat and when the oil is hot pan-fry the cutlets until just browned (about 2 minutes per side).

5 Remove the cutlets from the pan and set aside. Add the remaining oil to the pan and fry the peppers, onion, and garlic for about 10 minutes, until the vegetables begin to soften and brown. Sprinkle 1 Tbsp (15 mL) of flour over the vegetables and stir. Add the wine, vinegar, and stock. Bring to a boil, scraping up the browned bits from frying the meat. Return the cutlets to the pan and spoon some of the vegetables and sauce over them.

6 Cover the skillet, reduce heat to low, and braise for 20 minutes, until the pork is tender. Sprinkle with salt, pepper and parsley. Serves 4 to 6.

Penne with Chunky Ratatouille Sauce

This is The Guy's favorite sauce to concoct in the fall when the market is bursting with the harvest of fresh peppers, eggplants, and fennel. It's also a great sauce to make when you feel the need to be virtuous—or when there's a vegetarian coming to dinner. It makes the best base for a vegetarian Greek pastitsio (see Wise Guy, below). Don't skip the eggplant—it's the secret ingredient that gives this sauce its meaty texture.

3 cups (750 mL) peeled and diced eggplant
   (¼-inch/5-mm dice)
sea salt
½ cup (125 mL) extra virgin olive oil
1 medium onion, chopped
3 to 4 cloves garlic, minced
1 cup (250 mL) diced zucchini (¼-inch/
   5-mm dice)
1½ cups (375 mL) finely chopped fennel bulb
1 cup (250 mL) diced red bell pepper
   (¼-inch/5-mm dice)

½ cup (125 mL) dry white wine
one 28-oz (796-mL) can tomatoes, puréed
1 tsp (5 mL) dried oregano
1 tsp (5 mL) dried basil
¼ cup (60 mL) tomato paste
1 tsp (5 mL) sugar
½ tsp (2 mL) hot chili pepper paste
   (or cayenne)
salt and freshly ground black pepper

1 Place the eggplant into a colander and salt generously. Set aside for 30 minutes to drain in the sink—the bitter brown juices will rise to the surface. Rinse under cold running water, then squeeze the eggplant in your hands to remove all of the excess water.

2 In a large sauté pan, heat the olive oil over medium high heat and sauté the onion until tender. Add the garlic and cook for 1 minute. Stir in the eggplant and sauté until the eggplant and onions begin to brown, about 5 to 10 minutes.

3 Add a little more olive oil along with the zucchini, fennel, and bell pepper. Cook for 10 minutes, until the vegetables are tender and fragrant. Add the wine and simmer until some of the liquid has evaporated, about 3 minutes. Then stir in the tomatoes, oregano, basil, tomato paste, and sugar. Cover the pan, reduce the heat to medium-low, and simmer for 30 minutes. Season to taste with chili paste, salt, and pepper. Simmer uncovered for 5 minutes to thicken. Makes 5 to 6 cups (enough for a pound of pasta).

WISE GUY: This sauce is also perfect for making pastitsio—a Greek macaroni casserole reminiscent of lasagna but easier to make. Simply cook 1 lb (500 g) of short pasta (macaroni, penne, or gemeli) and toss with the sauce. In a large oiled baking dish, layer half of the pasta and sauce, 1 cup (250 mL) of crumbled feta cheese, and the remaining pasta. Make a cheesy white sauce by melting 3 Tbsp (45 mL) of butter with 3 Tbsp (45 mL) of flour, then whisking in 1½ cups (375 mL) of milk and a pinch of salt. Stir over medium heat until thick. Cool the sauce and whisk in 2 beaten eggs and another 1 cup (250 mL) of feta cheese. Pour the sauce over the pasta and bake at 350°F (180°C) for 60 minutes. Serves 4 to 6.

Thai-Style Coconut Curry Noodle Soup

Curry paste (either Thai or Indian) is the secret ingredient for speedy and exotic soups like this one. Buy a jar and keep it in the fridge to use whenever you need a blast of flavor. Since you'll need to use a whole can of coconut milk, you might as well make this meal-sized soup for two or three of your friends, too. And it's more fun (and faster) with at least one helper in the kitchen to chop and shred.

4 cups (1 L) chicken stock
1 skinless, boneless chicken breast (or 2 cups/500 mL leftover cooked chicken)
2 Tbsp (30 mL) Thai red curry paste or 1 Tbsp (15 mL) Indian curry paste
one 13.5-oz. (400-mL) can light coconut milk

½ lb (250 g) medium shrimp, peeled and deveined
2 to 3 packages instant soup noodles (discard the seasoning)
salt and freshly ground black pepper
handful of fresh cilantro or mint leaves

Toppings
handful of green stuff (slivered spinach, cabbage, bok choy, etc.)
1 medium carrot, peeled and shredded
2 green onions, chopped

1 In a large saucepan, heat the stock to a rolling boil over medium-high heat. Add the chicken breast and poach for 10 minutes, then remove and cool (eliminate this step if you have leftover cooked chicken).

> **WISE GUY:**
> The Guy has recently learned how easy it is to cook authentic-tasting Thai food with a bit of red or green curry paste—both come in resealable tubs and keep in the fridge for months, so he can scoop out some Southeast Asian flavor whenever the mood strikes. Find curry pastes at Asian grocery stores along with canned coconut milk, fresh herbs, and greens for this speedy soup.

2 Slice the cooked chicken into thin, bite-sized pieces. Divide among four large soup bowls.

3 Add the curry paste to the stock and bring back to a boil. Stir in the coconut milk and shrimp. Simmer for 1 minute. Add the noodles and stir for 1 to 2 minutes, until they are tender. Season the broth with the salt and pepper to taste. Divide the cilantro or mint leaves among the bowls.

4 Ladle the hot soup over the chicken and herbs. Ensure each serving gets an equal portion of noodles and shrimp (use tongs or chopsticks to make picking up the noodles easier).

5 Top each bowl with some green stuff, shredded carrot, and green onion. Serve immediately. Serves 4 as part of an Asian meal, or 2 for lunch.

Risotto-Stuffed Red Peppers

When you're a guy, you like your vegetables stuffed with something substantial—this cheesy combo is like a meaty risotto. It works wonderfully in thick-sided halves of sweet red and yellow peppers, but is equally yummy inside small squash, mini pumpkins, or hollowed-out Japanese eggplants. These stuffed peppers are perfectly portable and easy to reheat in a microwave. Vegetarians can substitute soy protein or a big can of lightly mashed chickpeas for the ground meat.

1 lb (500 g) fresh mild or spicy Italian sausages

2 cups (500 mL) short-grain arborio or other Italian risotto rice

1½ cups (375 mL) grated Italian cheese mix (or half mozzarella and half Parmesan)

3 Tbsp (45 mL) chopped Italian parsley

2 cloves garlic, minced

½ tsp (2 mL) salt

½ tsp (2 mL) freshly ground black pepper

4 large eggs, lightly beaten

½ to ¾ cup (125 to 175 mL) dry breadcrumbs

8 large red or yellow bell peppers, halved, seeds and ribs removed

2 Tbsp (30 mL) extra virgin olive oil

tomato sauce (canned is fine) and grated Parmigiano Reggiano cheese

1 Slice the sausage casings lengthwise to release the sausage meat. In a sauté pan, crumble the sausage and cook over medium heat until nicely browned. Break it up with a fork as it cooks. Drain the excess fat and dicard. Set the sausage aside in a large bowl.

2 In a saucepan, bring 4 cups (1 L) of salted water to a boil. Add the rice, cover, and reduce the heat to low. Simmer for about 20 minutes until the water is absorbed and the rice is tender. Remove from the heat and let stand, covered, for 10 minutes to steam. Add the rice to the bowl with the cooked sausage. Stir to combine and cool.

3 Stir in the cheese, parsley, garlic, salt, pepper, and eggs. Combine with your hands until well-mixed, then add just enough breadcrumbs to bind the mixture.

4 Place the red pepper halves on a plate, cut-side up, and sprinkle lightly with salt. Press the stuffing firmly into the peppers, mounding slightly.

5 Heat the olive oil in a large, non-stick pan over medium heat and cook the peppers, skin-side down, for 5 to 7 minutes. Flip so the filling side is down and cook for another 8 to10 minutes until the tops are nicely browned and the filling is cooked through.

6 Serve immediately, or refrigerate and reheat later. These peppers also freeze well. Serve with a little warm tomato sauce and grated Parmigiano Reggiano over top of each stuffed pepper. Serves 8 to 12.

Hot Chicks

Chicken again? Roast chicken was once reserved for Sunday dinner, but these days chicken is ubiquitous. That's probably because chicken is easy to cook and very versatile. It's available everywhere in convenient boneless, skinless parts, and is often the quickest protein to get onto the table. But that doesn't mean you must be bored by chicken—discover why it's popular around the world with these simple chicken supper solutions.

Chicken Stew Provençal

This is a classic Mediterranean-style stew—chicken pieces cooked low and slow in herbed tomato sauce. It's a cheap and cheerful everyday meal, but can also stand in nicely as a casual weekend dinner for friends when it's paired with fresh pasta or polenta. It's also a dish that reheats well and tastes even better the second day. Use boneless chicken thighs—they're juicier than breasts in braised dishes like this.

2 lb (1 kg) boneless, skinless chicken thighs, quartered

salt and freshly ground black pepper

3 Tbsp (45 mL) extra virgin olive oil, divided

3 slices smoky bacon or slivered ham

1 onion, chopped

1 large red bell pepper, seeded and diced

4 cloves garlic, minced

½ cup (125 mL) dry white or red wine

2 cups (500 mL) canned whole tomatoes, chopped

1 tsp (5 mL) minced fresh oregano (or ½ tsp/ 2 mL dried)

1 tsp (5 mL) minced fresh thyme (or ½ tsp/ 2 mL dried)

1 bay leaf

2 Tbsp (30 mL) minced fresh basil leaves

½ cup (125 mL) pitted black niçoise or kalamata olives

one 12-oz (375-mL) can artichoke hearts, drained and chopped

½ tsp (2 mL) Asian chili paste (or hot sauce to taste)

1 Season the chicken with salt and pepper. Heat 1 Tbsp (15 mL) of the oil in a large non-stick pan and sauté the chicken and bacon over medium heat for 7 to 10 minutes, turning occasionally, until the chicken is nicely browned. Transfer the chicken and bacon to a plate and set aside.

2 Add the remaining 2 Tbsp (30 mL) of the olive oil to the pan and sauté the onion, bell pepper, and garlic for 5 minutes. Stir in the wine and simmer for 1 minute, stirring and scraping up any browned bits from the bottom of the pan. Add the tomatoes, oregano, thyme, bay leaf, salt, and pepper.

3 Return the chicken and bacon to the pan and bring to a boil. Cover the pan, reduce the heat to low, and simmer for 45 minutes or until the chicken is tender. Remove the lid and simmer for 10 minutes or until the sauce is reduced and thickened. Season to taste with chili paste. Stir in the olives and artichokes, and heat through.

4 Serve immediately or cool and refrigerate, then reheat to serve. Serve the chicken stew spooned over pasta, gnocchi or soft polenta (see page 161), and sprinkled with fresh basil. Serves 4.

Fast-Fix Chicken Cutlets

The Guy learned early that boneless chicken breasts cook almost instantly when you slice them into thin cutlets. These crisp cutlets are great for a quick supper and are endlessly adaptable. You can use them in sandwiches (try Italian panini rolls with lettuce, mustard mayonnaise, and grilled red peppers or tomatoes). Top your cutlets with fresh tomato and avocado salsa, or tomato and basil bruschetta from the deli. Try a drizzle of your favorite spicy mango chutney, or cut your crispy cutlets into strips and pile on a Caesar salad for a simple summer supper. A speedy sauce (see Wise Guy at right) can quickly turn these everyday cutlets into the main event at an impromptu dinner party.

4 boneless, skinless chicken breasts
salt and freshly ground black pepper

all-purpose flour
2 Tbsp (30 mL) olive or canola oil for frying

1 Preheat the oven to 200°F (95°C).

2 With a large chef's knife, slice each chicken breast horizontally into two slices, each about ½ inch (1 cm) thick. (The easiest way to do this is to lay each breast on the cutting board and press one hand lightly over the chicken as you slice through the center of the meat parallel to the cutting board.) Cover each slice with waxed paper or plastic wrap and use either a meat mallet or the back of a heavy knife blade to pound the chicken to a uniform ¼-inch (5-mm) thickness.

3 Season both sides of the chicken cutlets with salt and pepper. Place about ¼ cup (60 mL) of flour on a dinner plate and, if you choose, season it with dried herbs like thyme, oregano, and/or basil. Dip the cutlets into the flour and coat both sides. Shake off any excess flour.

4 Heat a large, non-stick sauté pan over medium-high heat. When the pan is hot, add the oil. Heat the oil for a minute, then add the cutlets to the pan and fry in batches until they are golden brown—about 2 to 3 minutes per side. Keep the cutlets warm in the preheated oven while you cook the rest. Makes 8 cutlets. Serves 4 to 6.

When company's coming (or just drops by), make your cutlets fancier with a speedy sauce. Just arrange the browned cutlets on a warm serving platter, pour the sauce overtop, and garnish with a handful of chopped Italian parsley or other fresh herbs.

Sauces to make

● Fry a couple of finely chopped shallots or a little onion in the same pan in which you cooked the chicken. Splash ½ cup (125 mL) of white wine or vermouth into the pan and scrape up the browned stuff on the bottom. Boil until the liquid is reduced and the pan's almost dry, then remove the pan from the heat. Whisk in 1 to 2 Tbsp (15 to 30 mL) of cold butter and add 1 tsp (5 mL) of chopped basil.

● For a classic Marsala sauce, add a handful of sliced mushrooms to the pan with 1 tsp (5 mL) minced garlic. Sauté until tender. Whisk in 1 tsp (5 mL) of tomato paste and 1 cup (250 mL) of sweet Marsala wine. Boil until reduced and thickened. Whisk in 2 Tbsp (30 mL) of cold butter.

● For a creamy mushroom sauce, add 1 cup (250 mL) of sliced mushrooms to the pan with 1 tsp (5 mL) of minced garlic and sauté until tender. Stir in ¼ cup (60 mL) white wine and boil until nearly dry. Stir in ¼ cup (60 mL) each of chicken stock and cream. Simmer until thick.

● For a honey mustard sauce, add a couple of chopped shallots and one clove of minced garlic to the pan. Sauté for 2 minutes. Stir in ¼ cup (60 mL) white wine and boil until almost dry. Stir in ½ cup (125 mL) of chicken broth, 2 Tbsp (30 mL) of grainy mustard, and a heaping 1 tsp (5 mL) of honey. Simmer with a pinch of fresh thyme leaves until reduced to a nice glaze.

● Lemon chicken? Sauté a couple of minced shallots in the pan, then add ½ cup (125 mL) of chicken broth, 1 Tbsp (15 mL) of balsamic vinegar, and ½ lemon, sliced. Stir and boil for 5 minutes, then remove from the heat and whisk in 2 Tbsp (30 mL) of cold butter and a good grinding of black pepper.

● For baked Chicken Parmesan, add a handful of chopped onion, garlic, and mushrooms to the pan. Splash in a little wine, stir it around, and pour in a small tin of tomato sauce. Simmer for 5 minutes. Place the cutlets in a shallow baking pan, top with the mushroom sauce and a few large handfuls of grated Parmesan cheese. Bake at 400°F (200°C) until bubbly and brown.

All-Dressed Chicken Breasts

Why wait for the holidays to enjoy your favorite poultry and stuffing? With the requisite mashed potatoes, Brussels sprouts, and cranberries on the side, this simple combo makes a perfectly delicious holiday meal when you can't face cooking a whole bird. If you can't find boneless chicken breasts with the skin attached, buy whole breasts on the bone, and debone at home. Or use boneless, skinless breasts and brush the chicken with melted butter or olive oil before and during baking.

Stuffing

2 Tbsp (30 mL) butter
1 cup (125 mL) chopped onion
1 stalk celery, chopped
4 cups (1 L) crusty wholegrain or sourdough
    bread cubes

½ tsp (2 mL) dried sage
½ tsp (2 mL) dried thyme
½ tsp (2 mL) celery salt
freshly ground black pepper
1 egg, lightly beaten with ¼ cup (60 mL) cream

Orange Sage Sauce

2 Tbsp (30 mL) butter
¼ cup (60 mL) minced shallots or onions
1 tsp (5 mL) crumbled dried sage leaves
    (or 1 Tbsp/15 mL minced fresh sage)

½ cup (125 mL) freshly squeezed orange juice
1 cup (250 mL) chicken broth
1 Tbsp (15 mL) cornstarch mixed with 1 tsp
    (5 mL) water
salt and freshly ground pepper

4 large boneless chicken breasts, skin on

hot paprika or cayenne

1 For the stuffing, melt the butter in a sauté pan over medium heat and sauté the onions and celery until soft, about 10 minutes. Place the bread cubes in a large bowl and pour the sautéed vegetables overtop, stirring to mix well. Sprinkle with sage, thyme, celery salt, and pepper. Add the egg mixture and stir to combine. Set aside.

2 For the sauce, melt the butter and sauté the shallots over medium heat for 10 minutes or until lightly browned. Add the orange juice and chicken broth to the pan and bring to a boil. Whisk in the cornstarch mixture and simmer until the sauce is reduced and nicely thickened. Season with salt and pepper to taste. Set aside and keep warm.

3 Preheat the oven to 400°F (200°C). Lay the breasts on your work surface, skin-side down. Cover with plastic wrap and use a meat mallet to pound each breast to an even thickness.

4 Divide the stuffing into four equal portions and mold each into a large ball. Place a ball of stuffing in the center of each flattened breast. Bring the ends of the chicken up and around to wrap the stuffing with meat, then invert each bundle, tucking the ends underneath and making sure the skin is pulled tightly around the outside. Place the stuffed breasts in a roasting pan, seam-side down, and dust with paprika. (If you're making this with skinless chicken breasts, make sure you brush the meat with melted butter or olive oil to keep it moist.)

5 Cover the pan with foil and roast in the preheated oven for 15 minutes. Uncover and roast 15 minutes longer to brown the skin. Remove from the oven and let the meat rest for 5 to 10 minutes before serving. Slice and serve drizzled with warm orange sauce. Serves 4.

Sesame Chicken Nuggets

For a fast meal, top a Chinese Chopped Salad (see page 408) with these sweet and spicy chicken bites, or serve them alongside a pile of rice and stir-fried veggies. For cocktail time, just pass these tasty morsels with toothpicks.

Marinade

1 tsp (5 mL) sesame oil
1 Tbsp (15 mL) liquid honey
2 Tbsp (30 mL) freshly squeezed orange juice
1 Tbsp (15 mL) soy sauce

2 Tbsp (30 mL) freshly squeezed lemon juice (about ½ a lemon)
1 tsp (5 mL) minced fresh garlic
2 tsp (10 mL) peeled and minced fresh ginger
½ tsp (2 mL) Asian chili paste

Nuggets

1½ lb (750 g) boneless, skinless chicken breasts or thighs, cut into 1-inch (2.5-cm) chunks

1 cup (250 mL) toasted sesame seeds

1 In a blender, combine the sesame oil, honey, orange juice, soy sauce, lemon juice, garlic, ginger, and chili paste. Blend until smooth. Place the chicken in a zippered plastic bag and add the marinade. Seal and refrigerate for 2 hours.

2 Preheat the oven to 350°F (180°C). To cook the chicken nuggets, roll the marinated chicken pieces in sesame seeds to coat all sides. Line a baking sheet with foil (to help with clean-up) and place the chicken in a single layer. Bake for 45 minutes or until golden and crisp. Serves 4 to 6.

Hungarian Chicken and Dumplings in Creamy Paprika Sauce

When The Guy was in college, he often ate in a tiny Hungarian restaurant—the paprika chicken, peppery goulash, and homemade dumplings sustained him through many lean times. While he has since made several Hungarian friends who don't remember their paprika-infused daily dinners quite so fondly, The Guy created an updated version of this classic dish in their honor. Serve it over wide egg noodles, gnocchi, or when you have the time, tiny homemade potato dumplings. Cucumber Salad (see page 165) is a traditional side dish.

8 skinless, boneless chicken breasts and/or
   thighs (about 3 lb/1.5 kg)
salt and freshly ground black pepper
1 Tbsp (15 mL) extra virgin olive oil
1 large yellow onion, minced
2 bell peppers, sliced (1 red and 1 yellow)
1 Tbsp (15 mL) sweet Hungarian paprika
1 tsp (5 mL) dried thyme

1 Tbsp (15 mL) apple cider vinegar
½ cup (125 mL) dry white wine
one 12-oz (385-mL) can chicken broth, undiluted
2 Tbsp (30 mL) tomato paste
½ cup (125 mL) sour cream or heavy cream
2 Tbsp (30 mL) Dijon mustard
chopped Italian parsley to garnish

Dumplings
1 cup (250 mL) cold mashed potatoes
2 cups (500 mL) all-purpose flour
½ tsp (2 mL) salt

1 Tbsp (15 mL) butter, melted
1 egg
¾ to 1 cup (175 to 250 mL) warm water

1 Cut the chicken into cubes or strips and season with salt and pepper.

2 Heat the oil in a large sauté pan over medium-high heat and sear the chicken until it begins to brown. Remove from the pan and set aside.

3 In the same pan, sauté the onion and peppers over medium heat for 5 minutes or until they start to brown. Stir in the thyme and paprika and cook for one minute or until fragrant. Add the vinegar and wine and bring to a boil. Cook for 5 minutes or until the liquid has reduced by half. Whisk in the broth and tomato paste, and simmer for 2 minutes longer. Whisk in the cream and mustard and continue to simmer for 10 minutes or until the sauce is reduced to about 1 cup (250 mL), and is thick enough to coat the back of a spoon.

4 To make the dumplings, in a large bowl use your hands to mix together the mashed potatoes, flour, and salt until crumbly.

5 In a separate bowl, whisk together the melted butter, egg, and water. Make a well in the center of the potato mixture and add the egg mixture, gradually incorporating with a fork to form a smooth, soft dough. Meanwhile, bring a large pot of salted water to a rolling boil. Press about ¼ of the dough into a ¼-inch (5-mm) flat piece on your cutting board. With a wet knife, cut into small slivers and push them off the board into the boiling water (you can also press the dough through a spaetzle maker or through a colander with big holes). Simmer until the noodles float. Drain well before tossing with butter, salt, and pepper. Set aside on a warm platter. Repeat with remaining dough until all of the noodles are cooked.

6 Return the cooked chicken to the sauce, cover, and simmer for 5 minutes to heat through. Spoon the paprika chicken over the noodles. Sprinkle with chopped parsley before serving. Serves 8.

WISE GUY: Make sure you buy good quality Spanish or Hungarian paprika, especially for dishes like this which rely on paprika as the dominant seasoning. The flavor of the more expensive imported paprika is far superior to standard paprika: it is sweet and lacks the bitter aftertaste of some lesser brands. And make sure the paprika you buy is labeled "sweet" and not "hot." Hot paprika is good, but you can't use nearly as much.

Butter Chicken

This wonderfully rich and creamy dish is a northern Indian classic. A little goes a long way, especially when you serve it with fragrant basmati rice and steamed green beans or broccoli. Or plan to serve this chicken as part of an Indian meal. You'll need to marinate the chicken for several hours, so start preparing this dish the night before or early in the morning.

2 to 3 lb (1 to 1.5 kg) skinless, boneless chicken thighs
2 to 3 Tbsp (30 to 45 mL) tandoori paste

Butter Sauce
2-inch (5-cm) piece of ginger, peeled
4 large cloves garlic
1 small onion, chopped
½ cup (125 mL) butter, divided
one 28-oz (796-mL) can peeled Roma tomatoes, puréed in a blender
½ tsp (2 mL) salt
2 serrano or small jalapeño peppers, seeded and finely chopped
1 Tbsp (15 mL) minced ginger

½ cup (125 mL) plain yogurt
1 Tbsp (15 mL) freshly squeezed lemon juice
2 cloves garlic, minced

1 tsp (5 mL) sweet Hungarian or Spanish paprika
pinch of white pepper
½ tsp (2 mL) ground cumin
½ tsp (2 mL) ground coriander
½ tsp (2 mL) ground turmeric
3 Tbsp (45 mL) granulated sugar
¼ cup (60 mL) ground almonds
1 cup (250 mL) heavy cream
2 Tbsp (30 mL) chopped cilantro

1 In a large bowl or resealable plastic bag, combine the chicken pieces with the tandoori paste and stir to coat all sides of the chicken. Add the yogurt, lemon juice, and garlic. Stir to combine. Marinate the chicken for several hours, or overnight, in the refrigerator. Once marinated, grill the chicken over medium high heat for 20 minutes or bake at 400°F (200°C) for 30 minutes. Cool and set aside.

2 To make the sauce, combine and purée the whole piece of ginger, garlic, and onion with ¼ cup (60 mL) of water in a blender or food processor. Heat ¼ cup (60 mL) of the butter in a saucepan over medium heat until melted. Add the contents of the blender to the pan. Cook the paste until the liquid evaporates and the mixture thickens. Stir in the puréed tomatoes and salt. Cover and simmer for 15 minutes. Set aside.

3 In a separate saucepan, melt the remaining ¼ cup (60 mL) of butter over medium heat. Sauté the green chilies and minced ginger for a minute or two. Add the paprika, white pepper, cumin, coriander, and turmeric. Stir in the sugar and reserved tomato sauce. Bring to a boil and simmer for 10 minutes.

4 Meanwhile, chop the tandoori chicken into bite-sized pieces and add to the sauce. Stir the ground almonds and cream into the sauce, and simmer 5 minutes longer or until the mixture is thick and smooth. Pour the butter chicken into a small serving dish and garnish with cilantro. Serves 6.

CHILI PEPPERS

Chicken and Corn Tortilla Casserole

The only trick to this easy Tex-Mex casserole—sort of a spicy south-of-the-border chicken and corn lasagna—is using good-quality corn tortillas. Look for them in authentic Mexican or Latin American food markets where they are often made on site (if you don't live in a city with a large Hispanic population, the best tortillas may actually be the frozen ones). For a vegetarian version, substitute a large can of black beans (drained and rinsed) for the chicken. The Speedy Salsa also makes a great instant dip for corn chips—whip some up for your next party.

Speedy Salsa
one 14-oz (398-mL) can Roma tomatoes
one 4-oz (114-mL) can jalapeño chilies, drained
1 tsp (5 mL) minced or pressed garlic
½ medium white onion, chopped

1 tsp (5 mL) salt
1 tsp (5 mL) ground cumin
1 tsp (5 mL) dried oregano
1 tsp (5 mL) chili powder

recipe continued on next page

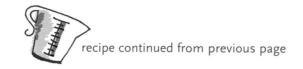recipe continued from previous page

Tortilla Casserole

1 Tbsp (15 mL) canola oil
1 red bell pepper, seeded and chopped
2 cups (500 mL) chopped onion
1½ lb (750 g) skinless, boneless chicken
    thighs, cubed
1 recipe Speedy Salsa or 2 cups (500 mL)
    commercial salsa

½ cup (125 mL) pitted black olives, chopped
1 to 2 Tbsp (15 to 30 mL) chopped cilantro
12 corn tortillas
2 cups (500 mL) shredded mozzarella, Monterey
    Jack, or medium cheddar cheese
sour cream, shredded lettuce, and chopped
    tomatoes for garnish

1 In a food processor or blender, combine the tomatoes, jalapeño, garlic, onion, salt, and spices. Pulse into a chunky purée. Taste the salsa. If it's not spicy enough for you, add hot sauce or Asian chili paste to taste.

2 Preheat the oven to 350°F (180°C).

3 Heat a sauté pan over medium heat and add the oil. Sauté the bell pepper, onion, and chopped chicken for 10 minutes or until the chicken is nicely browned. Add the salsa and simmer for 10 minutes. Remove the sauce from the heat and stir in the olives and cilantro.

4 Rub a large oblong or oval casserole dish with a little oil. Arrange 4 tortillas in the bottom of the dish, cutting one or two in half if necessary to fit the space. Top with ⅓ of the sauce and ⅓ of the shredded cheese. Add another layer of tortillas, sauce, and cheese, then repeat.

5 Cover the dish with foil, place in the oven and bake for 30 minutes. Remove the foil and bake 10 minutes longer or until the cheese is browned and bubbly. Remove from the oven and let the casserole stand for 10 minutes before cutting into portions. Serve sour cream, shredded lettuce, and chopped tomatoes on the side to garnish the casserole. Serves 4 to 6.

Chili and Beans

There may be no meal more macho than a pot of beans. Cowboy chili, pork and beans, thick bowls of black bean soup—all dishes for manly meals.

Whether he's having the guys over to watch the game or hauling his favorite dish to a potluck, good ol' chili and beans just seem to work. Herewith, the best of The Guy's bean cuisine.

Unadulterated Heirloom Beans

The Guy recently discovered the joys of heirloom beans. Like heirloom tomatoes (or other vegetables) these are the older, unusual varieties of dried shell beans, often found in specialty health food and ethnic markets, or through mail order sources. It's a revelation to cook heirloom beans—the flavor and texture go far beyond the black, white, and red varieties we all know, and each tastes completely different, even when prepared. Anyone can cook a pot of beans—it just takes time. Here's everything you need to know.

1 cup (250 mL) heirloom beans (look for
    varieties such as Vallarta, Rio Zappe, Flageolet,
    Eye of the Tiger, Yellow Indian Woman, etc.)
water
1 carrot

1 small onion
1 stalk celery
2 cloves garlic
1 Tbsp (15 mL) olive oil
salt and freshly ground black pepper

1 Place the beans in a pot and cover with water—the beans should be well-submerged, with about 1 to 2 inches (2.5 to 5 cm) of water showing above the beans. Soak from 4 hours to overnight.

2 Finely chop the carrot, onion, celery, and garlic with a knife or food processor.

3 In a large saucepan, heat the oil over medium-high heat. Add the minced vegetables; stir and sauté for 10 minutes or until fragrant (this is known as a mirepoix, and is the flavor base of many soups and sauces).

4 Add the beans, along with their soaking liquid, and enough water to cover them by about an inch. Bring to a boil over high heat, then turn the heat to low and let the beans simmer slowly. Keep them bubbling very slightly—it will take an hour or two before they're ready, depending on the type of bean, its age, and the altitude. Start tasting the beans after one hour to see how they're doing. At this time (but not before) you can season the beans with salt and pepper. Serves 4.

WISE GUY: It's fascinating to cook several different varieties of heirloom beans and taste their differences. The tiny mottled pink Red Nightfall stay firm and have a sweet flavor, while the bigger Tiger Eye turn from orange to brown before breaking down—their starch creates a lovely thick sauce (a.k.a. pot licker among bean aficionados).

If you want to season the beans after they're cooked, consider adding a chopped chipotle chili in adobo sauce and some chopped cilantro for a Latin meal. Or stir in fresh chopped herbs, like rosemary and thyme, a little garlic, and some butter or cream into a pot of tiny French Flageolets.

Spicy Black Bean Soup

Purists cook their beans from scratch, but black bean soup comes together quickly with a couple of cans of beans from the supermarket. Just remember to drain and rinse canned beans well to remove excess sodium. For a vegetarian version, just leave out the sausage.

2 Tbsp (30 mL) olive oil

1 large yellow onion, finely chopped

2 cloves garlic, finely chopped

1 stalk celery, finely chopped

2 Roma tomatoes, seeded and chopped

½ pound (225 g) spicy smoked sausage (like chorizo), cubed

1 chipotle chili pepper in adobo, chopped (or a jalapeño pepper, chopped)

2 tsp (10 mL) chili powder

½ tsp (2 mL) ground cumin

½ tsp (2 mL) oregano

½ tsp (2 mL) thyme

4 cups (a 900-mL Tetra Pack) chicken broth

two 14-oz (398-mL) cans black beans, rinsed and drained

2 tsp (10 mL) brown sugar

salt and freshly ground black pepper

hot sauce to taste

Garnish

⅓ cup (75 mL) sour cream

½ cup (125 mL) finely diced red pepper

¼ cup (60 mL) chopped green onion

1 In a large soup pot, heat the olive oil over medium-high heat and add the onion and garlic. Cook for 10 minutes, until the onion begins to brown. Stir in the celery, tomatoes, and sausage and cook for 10 minutes more. Stir in the chili pepper, chili powder, cumin, oregano, and thyme. Add the chicken broth and beans, and bring to a boil.

2 Reduce the heat to medium-low and simmer for 20 minutes, mashing some of the beans into the broth to thicken it. Season to taste with sugar, salt and pepper, and add more hot sauce if you like your soup spicier. Serve soup in individual bowls. Top with a spoonful of sour cream and a sprinkling of red pepper and green onion. Serves 6 to 8.

The Ultimate Bowl of Red

Here's The Guy's favorite Texas-style chili recipe. It's loaded with chunks of tender beef, sweet ancho chili peppers, and just enough bite to make it dangerous. While Texans will argue about whether or not it's right to add beans to chili, The Guy likes the way the glossy black beans taste and look in his bowl of red. Drag this recipe out when you're entering the neighborhood chili cook-off—you might just win the grand prize. And remember, chili is always best the second day, when all of the complex flavors have had a chance to get to know one another better. So make your award-winning pot the night before the contest.

2 large dried ancho chili peppers
2 lb (1 kg) beef round or chuck steak, cut into
   ¼-inch (5-mm) cubes
2 Tbsp (30 mL) olive oil
2 cups (500 mL) chopped onions
4 cloves garlic, chopped
1 Tbsp (15 mL) ground cumin
1 Tbsp (15 mL) dried oregano
one 28-oz (796-mL) can plum tomatoes

1 cup (250 mL) beef broth
¼ cup (60 mL) rye whisky
¼ cup (60 mL) tomato paste
1 Tbsp (15 mL) brown sugar
2 cups (500 mL) cooked black or pinto beans
   (drained and rinsed well, if canned; or
   cooked from scratch if you want to win the
   chili cook-off)
2 tsp (10 mL) hot Asian chili paste (or to taste)

1 Break open the ancho chili peppers and remove and discard the stems and seeds. Place the chilies in a heatproof bowl and cover with 1 cup (250 mL) of boiling water. Let them soak for about 20 minutes or until they're soft, then scoop them out of the water and transfer to a food processor or blender. Add a bit of the soaking water and process until the chilies are finely chopped. Add the rest of the soaking water and let the machine run until the chilies are completely puréed. Set aside.

2 In a Dutch oven or a large, heavy-bottomed pot, heat the oil over medium high heat and brown the beef in batches, removing it with a slotted spoon and setting it aside in a bowl as it's cooked. Don't overcrowd the pot or the meat won't brown nicely (not a disaster, but you'll miss out on the prize-winning layer of caramelized beef flavor).

3 Once all the beef has been browned, reduce the heat to medium-low and add the onions and garlic to the pot. Cook for 10 minutes, stirring occasionally, until the onions are light brown.

4 Return the browned beef to the pot and stir in the cumin and oregano. Add the ancho chili purée and stir to combine.

it) and whirl until the tomatoes are chopped (this will also get every last bit of the anchos out of the processor and into your chili). Pour this tomato mixture into the pot and bring to a boil.

6 Reduce the heat to low, partially cover the pot, and simmer for 1 to 2 hours or until the meat is very tender.

7 Stir in the tomato paste, brown sugar, and the cooked, drained beans. Simmer, uncovered, for another 15 to 20 minutes or until the chili has thickened nicely. Season to taste with Asian chili paste, salt, and pepper. Serves 6 to 8.

WISE GUY:

While this chili is perfectly good straight up, some guys like to gild the lily with toppings like sour cream, shredded cheese, chopped tomatoes, and avocados. You might want to use these extras if you're rolling your chili in flour tortillas. Otherwise, it's nice with a little rice.

Speedy Red Bean and Sausage Chili

The Guy likes to substitute his favorite fresh Italian sausage in sauces and other dishes that call for ground meat. A good quality spicy sausage (all meat, no fat or fillers) will give you an instant pre-spiced base for chili, meat sauce, and other similar concoctions.

1 lb (500 g) fresh Italian sausage (half mild and half spicy)
2 medium yellow onions, chopped
3 cloves garlic, minced
2 Tbsp (30 mL) chili powder
1 tsp (15 mL) ground cumin
1 tsp (15 mL) dried oregano
1 cup (250 mL) beef broth

2 cups (500 mL) tomato sauce
¼ cup (60 mL) maple syrup
1 Tbsp (15 mL) dry mustard
1 Tbsp (15 mL) Worcestershire sauce
one 19-oz (540-mL) can red or pinto beans, rinsed and drained
3 Tbsp (45 mL) cornmeal

1 Slice the sausages lengthwise. Remove the sausage meat from the casings and crumble into a pot. Heat the sausage over medium-high heat and stir until it browns (if the sausage is super lean, like The Guy's favorite brand, you might need to add a touch of olive oil to prevent the meat from sticking).

2 When the sausage is nicely browned, add the onions and continue to cook for 10 minutes or until the onions begin to color. Add the garlic, chili powder, cumin, and oregano and stir for another minute.

3 Add the broth and scrape up any browned bits from the bottom of the pan while you stir. Stir in the tomato sauce, maple syrup, mustard, Worcestershire sauce, and beans. Bring the chili to a boil. Reduce the heat to low, cover the pot, and simmer for 30 minutes. Remove the lid, stir in the cornmeal and continue to simmer for 5 minutes or until the chili is nicely thickened. Serves 6.

Pork and Beans

Sure, you can crack open a can but who really knows where that pork came from? (if you can find it, that is). This version of beans, with big chunks of tender pork in a sweet and slightly spicy tomato and molasses sauce, is the ultimate version of that campfire classic. It's easy to make and very yummy with some creamy mashed potatoes and salad on the side.

1 lb (450 g) lean pork loin chops
1 Tbsp (15 mL) olive oil
1 medium yellow onion or 4 fat shallots, minced
1 clove garlic, minced
½ cup (125 mL) cold coffee, chicken broth, or water
1 cup (250 mL) V-8 juice or plain tomato juice
¼ cup (60 mL) maple syrup

2 Tbsp (30 mL) molasses
2 tsp (10 mL) dry mustard
1 canned chipotle chili, minced (or 1 tsp/5 mL Asian chili sauce)
two 14-oz (398-mL) cans white (navy) beans, rinsed well and drained
salt and freshly ground black pepper

1 Trim all of the visible fat from the pork and cut into small ½-inch (1-cm) cubes. Heat the oil in a heavy saucepan or Dutch oven over medium-high heat and cook the pork in batches until it's browned on all sides. Don't overcrowd the pot or the pork won't brown nicely. Remove the pork from the pan.

2 Add the minced onion and garlic to the pan and cook for 5 minutes or until soft. Stir in the cold coffee, broth, or water. As you stir, scrape up any browned bits from the bottom of the pan. Add the tomato juice, maple syrup, molasses, dry mustard, and chili. Bring to a boil.

3 Place the beans in a strainer and rinse well under running water to remove all of the thick liquid (it's loaded with sodium and guys don't need that). Stir the beans into the pot along with the reserved pork. Season to taste with salt and pepper and bring the mixture back to a boil. Reduce the heat to low, cover the pot, and simmer for 1 hour. You can also transfer the beans to a covered casserole dish or bean pot and bake them in the oven for 1 hour at 250°F (120°C). Serves 4.

WISE GUY: The last time The Guy made this dish, there was no tomato juice in the house. You can improvise with diluted tomato sauce—even diluted ketchup will do in a pinch. If you're a purist, cook 1 cup (250 mL) of white beans from scratch. Just cover with lots of water and boil for 1 hour, then drain, fill the pot full of cold water again and add a few cloves of garlic and some herbs. Simmer for 1 hour and drain well. This should leave you with about 3 cups (750 mL) of cooked beans—the perfect amount for this dish.

Vegetarian Chili

This is a great way to get the kids to eat their veggies—somehow they forget they're eating zucchini when it's in a pot of chili. Make a big batch of this addictive and low-fat chili in late summer, when all the ingredients are fresh.

⅓ cup (75 mL) extra virgin olive oil
1 lb (500 g) zucchini, cut into small cubes
1 large yellow onion, chopped
4 cloves garlic, minced
1 large red bell pepper, chopped
two 28-oz (796-mL) cans tomatoes with juice
3 large ripe Roma tomatoes, chopped
2 Tbsp (30 mL) chili powder
2 tsp (10 mL) ground cumin
1 Tbsp (15 mL) dried basil
1 Tbsp (15 mL) dried oregano
1 tsp (5 mL) freshly ground black pepper

1 tsp (5 mL) salt
1 tsp (5 mL) fennel seeds
2 Tbsp (30 mL) dried parsley
one 19-oz (540-mL) can red kidney beans, rinsed
    and drained (about 2 cups/500 mL)
one 14-oz (398-mL) can chickpeas, rinsed and
    drained (about 1½ cups/375 mL)
2 Tbsp (30 mL) chopped fresh dill
1 Tbsp (15 mL) freshly sqeezed lemon juice
1 tsp (5 mL) sugar
hot sauce to taste (optional)

1 In a large Dutch oven or heavy-bottomed pot, heat the oil over medium-high heat. Add the zucchini, onion, garlic, and red peppers. Stir-fry until the vegetables begin to soften.

2 Add the canned tomatoes to the pot, squeezing each tomato carefully through your fingers to break it apart (it's faster than chopping). Stir in the fresh tomatoes, chili powder, cumin, basil, oregano, pepper, salt, fennel, and parsley. Bring to a boil. Reduce the heat to medium-low and simmer uncovered, stirring often, for 30 minutes. (This is one recipe in which dried herbs work well. Don't cut back on the herbs or oil—it may seem like a lot but, without the meat, this chili needs a lot of seasoning.)

3 Stir in the beans, chickpeas, dill, lemon juice, and sugar. Cook for 15 minutes longer. If desired, spice up the chili with hot sauce to taste. Serves 8.

Moo Goo Guy

A wok on the wild side with The Guy's favorite Asian eats—from spicy Szechuan noodles to a killer chicken and broccoli in garlic sauce. You can combine the following dishes to create a Chinese banquet or choose any of them for a weekday dinner, Chinese style. Just start a pot of fluffy basmati rice before you start stir-frying and dinner will be done in less than an hour.

The Basic Stir-Fry

Stir-frying is a technique that every Guy needs to learn. No matter what kind of vegetables or meat you have in the refrigerator, you can create a tasty stir-fry. Pick up the pantry ingredients at your supermarket or Asian grocery (ginger, oyster sauce, soy sauce, hoisin sauce, hot chili paste, and sesame oil), and you will always be ready to create an almost instant, and authentic, Asian meal. Remember, the stir-fry is more about chopping than cooking, and anyone can cut up a carrot. The only trick is to have everything chopped, measured, and ready to go into the pan before you start cooking.

This is The Guy's basic weekday stir-fry recipe—protein and vegetables, cooked quickly with garlic, ginger, and simple sauces, then served over rice or noodles equals a healthy and speedy, one-dish dinner.

½ to 1 lb (250 to 500 g) lean meat (chicken, beef, pork, shrimp), cut into thin slices
2 Tbsp (30 mL) canola oil
1 Tbsp (15 mL) minced ginger

2 cloves garlic, minced
4 to 6 cups (1 to 1.5 L) diced or sliced vegetables (red peppers, onions, carrots, zucchini, green beans, pea pods, broccoli, bok choy, asparagus, mushrooms, etc.)

Sauce
½ cup (125 mL) broth (chicken or beef)
2 to 3 Tbsp (30 to 45 mL) oyster sauce (or half oyster and half soy sauce)
2 tsp (2 mL) granulated sugar

½ tsp (2 mL) hot Asian chili paste
1 Tbsp (15 mL) cornstarch mi xed with 1 Tbsp (15 mL) water (a.k.a. cornstarch solution)
½ tsp (2 mL) sesame oil

1 Before stir-frying, make the rice (see page 516). Marinate the meat in a splash of soy sauce for a minute or two, if you like. Chop all of the vegetables. Measure and combine all of the sauce ingredients.

2 Place a wok over medium-high heat for 30 seconds and drizzle 1 Tbsp (15 mL) of the canola oil around the top of the wok so it falls down the sides. Add the meat to the hot wok and stir-fry until it begins to brown (do this in batches to ensure that the meat sizzles and browns quickly—if it starts to stew and lose liquid, the wok isn't hot enough or there's too much meat in the pan). Remove the meat from the wok as it's browned and set aside. (Use the same method for cooking shrimp—just toss in the hot wok for a minute or two until they turn pink, then remove).

3 Add the remaining canola oil to the wok, along with the ginger and garlic. Stir for a minute, just until the garlic sizzles, but make sure it doesn't burn. Add the vegetables and stir-fry, tossing for 5 to 8 minutes, or until the vegetables start to wilt and brown. Add a splash of water to the wok, cover, and steam for 2 to 3 minutes to finish cooking the veggies. If you're combining slower-cooking vegetables (carrots, broccoli, and cauliflower) with faster-cooking vegetables (asparagus, bok choy, and greens), add them in two batches (greens take only a few minutes to cook). Just remember to cut all the vegetables about the same size for even cooking.

4 Meanwhile, in a large measuring cup or bowl, stir together the broth, oyster sauce, sugar, and chili paste. Add to the wok and bring to a boil. Slowly add the cornstarch solution and continue to stir until the sauce is clear and nicely thickened. Return the meat to the pan and toss to heat through. Add a splash of water or broth if the sauce seems too thick. Drizzle with sesame oil and serve immediately over rice or Asian noodles. Serves 4.

Shrimp with Asparagus and Cashew Nuts

This is a simple stir-fry to make in the spring, when fresh asparagus is available. You can buy peeled frozen raw shrimp. Just don't get the pre-cooked kind.

1 lb (500 g) large shrimp, peeled and deveined
2 Tbsp (30 mL) canola oil, divided
¼ cup (60 mL) oyster sauce
1 tsp (5 mL) fish sauce
1 Tbsp (15 mL) vinegar
1 tsp (5 mL) Asian chili paste

1 tsp (5 mL) cornstarch mixed with 1 tsp (5 mL) water
12 stalks of asparagus, cut into 2-inch pieces
½ red bell pepper, slivered
1 small onion, slivered
¼ cup (60 mL) toasted cashews

1 In a wok or large sauté pan, heat half the oil over medium-high heat. Add the shrimp and cook just until it turns pink. Remove from the pan and set aside.

2 In a small bowl, combine the oyster sauce, fish sauce, vinegar, and chili paste. Make the cornstarch solution by combining the cornstarch and water.

3 Add the remaining oil to the hot pan and add the asparagus, red pepper, and onion. Stir-fry over medium-high heat for 5 minutes or until the vegetables are tender and begin to brown. Add the sauce mixture and cook for 1 minute. Add the cornstarch solution and stir until the sauce bubbles and thickens (add a splash of water or broth if it seems too thick). Return the shrimp to the wok and toss to heat through. Stir in the cashews and serve immediately. Serves 4.

Mu Shu Duck

Mu shu may refer to ground or chopped pork, chicken, or duck combined with mushrooms and vegetables, then wrapped up in thin Peking pancakes with a little hoisin sauce. You can also wrap your mu shu in flour tortillas or butter lettuce leaves (or simply serve the filling over brown rice). But wrapping and rolling is half the fun!

½ cup (125 mL) dried, sliced shiitake
    mushrooms
½ cup (125 cup) water
1 Tbsp (15 mL) vegetable oil
3 cloves garlic, minced
2 stalks celery, finely chopped
1 large carrot, finely chopped
1 cup (250 mL) boneless chopped, roasted duck
    meat (from the Chinese barbecue house or Asian
    supermarket)
3 green onions, chopped
½ cup (125 mL) chopped water chestnuts or
    jicama

1 cup (250 mL) shredded cabbage or bean
    sprouts
2 eggs, beaten
1 tsp (5 mL) sesame oil
⅓ cup (75 mL) chicken broth
3 Tbsp (45 mL) hoisin sauce
1 tsp (5 mL) cornstarch
salt
10 to 12 frozen Peking pancakes, thawed (sold
    in packages in the freezer section of Asian
    supermarkets)

1 In a heatproof bowl or glass measuring cup, combine the dried mushrooms and water. Microwave for 1 minute. Remove and let stand for 10 minutes to soften. Drain well, then squeeze out excess moisture.

2 Heat a sauté pan or wok over medium-high heat. Add the oil, then the garlic, celery, carrot, duck, green onions, water chestnuts, and cabbage. Increase the heat to high and stir-fry for 3 to 5 minutes or until the vegetables have softened. Push the vegetables to one side of the pan and add the beaten eggs. Stir to scramble, then toss the egg with the rest of the ingredients in the wok.

3 Meanwhile, in a small bowl, whisk together the sesame oil, broth, hoisin sauce, and cornstarch. Add the sauce mixture to the wok and continue to cook for 1 minute or until the sauce is thick and clear. Remove from the heat immediately. Transfer the filling to a serving bowl and season with salt to taste.

4 Heat the pancakes according to package directions and serve alongside the mu shu. Guests spoon 2 to 3 Tbsp (30 to 45 mL) of the filling onto each pancake—then wrap, roll, and eat. Serves 4.

HOISIN AND
BLACK BEAN Sauce

WISE GUY: Any leftover mu shu filling makes great soup for one or two. Heat 3 cups (750 mL) of chicken broth to boiling, add ½ cup (125 mL) fine egg noodles, and cook until almost tender. Stir in ½ cup leftover mu shu filling and heat 1 minute longer. Season to taste with a bit of soy sauce and sesame oil.

Spicy Chinese Noodles with Szechuan Sauce

Speedy, simple, and just like the bowls at the local noodle house. This is a vegetarian version of a fast, Chinese-style pasta dish, but you can also add any cooked protein you like—try fried and slivered tofu, chicken, beef, barbecued pork, or shrimp. You can find chili bean paste, a spicy sauce available in jars, in Chinese grocery stores or in the Asian section of most supermarkets.

½ lb (250 g) fresh Shanghai or Japanese ramen
   noodles, cooked
1 tsp (5 mL) sesame oil
1 large clove garlic, pressed in a garlic press
1 slice ginger, minced
1 large carrot, shredded
3 baby bok choy, shredded

1 yellow bell pepper, seeded and shredded
2 Tbsp (30 mL) vegetable oil
5 Tbsp (75 mL) soy sauce
1 Tbsp (15 mL) chili bean paste
1 tsp (5 mL) granulated sugar
1 green onion, slivered

1 Cook the noodles in a large pot of boiling, salted water according to the package directions. Drain, then toss with sesame oil. Set aside.

2 lace a wok over medium-high heat for 30 seconds, then drizzle in the oil. Add the ginger and garlic to the hot wok. Cook for 30 seconds then add the carrot, bok choy, and bell pepper. Stir-fry for 5 minutes or until the greens are wilted and the peppers begin to brown.

3 Add the soy sauce to the pan and stir in the chili bean paste and sugar. Stir in the cooked noodles and toss with the rest of the ingredients to combine. Heat through for 1 minute, top with green onions, and serve immediately. Serves 2 to 3.

Egg Foo Yong

There's something so comforting about this easy and old-fashioned Cantonese menu item. It's one of those childhood foods that always arrived at the door in perfect condition from the little Chinese takeout joint down the street (unlike the sometimes soggy egg rolls and chicken balls). Who knows if it's even authentic—but egg foo yong is one Asian dish anyone can make, even without a wok. Eat it straight up or slap it between two slices of brown toast and you've got an Asian twist on a classic Denver (a.k.a. Western) sandwich.

1 clove garlic, minced
1 Tbsp (15 mL) minced fresh ginger
3 cups (750 mL) fresh bean sprouts
4 green onions, finely chopped
1 medium carrot, peeled and grated
6 eggs, beaten

1 tsp (5 mL) soy sauce
½ tsp (2 mL) salt
1 cup (250 mL) minced cooked ham or small
   cooked shrimp
canola oil for frying

Sauce
¾ cup (175 mL) chicken broth
1 Tbsp (15 mL) soy sauce

½ tsp (2 mL) granulated sugar
2 tsp (10 mL) cornstarch

1 In a large bowl, combine the garlic, ginger, bean sprouts, green onions, and carrot. Stir in the eggs, soy sauce and salt to combine well. Fold in the ham or shrimp.

2 Heat a little oil in a large, non-stick frying pan over medium-high heat. When the oil is hot, ladle the vegetable mixture into the pan to make several 3-inch (8-cm) pancakes. If the liquid egg runs out beyond the vegetables while cooking, push it back into the omelet with the spatula to keep the edges even.

3 Cook until brown on one side, about 3 to 4 minutes, then flip over to brown the other side. Place on a heatproof plate and keep warm in a 200°F (95°C) oven until all the pancakes are cooked.

4 For the sauce, combine the broth, soy sauce, sugar, and cornstarch in a bowl, then pour into the hot pan. Stir the sauce until it bubbles and is clear and thick, about 3 minutes.

5 Arrange the egg foo yong on a serving platter and pour the sauce overtop before serving. Serves 4.

WISE GUY: Crispy fresh bean sprouts can quickly turn slimy in the fridge, but here's a trick: place your sprouts in a plastic container, fill with cold water, and refrigerate. They'll stay crunchy and fresh for several days.

Special Fried Rice

When you make rice, make extra so you can make fried rice with the leftovers. You can add almost anything to your fried rice—from barbecue pork, to shrimp, ham, chicken, bell peppers, or frozen peas (this is what most Chinese restaurants call their everything-but-the-kitchen-sink "Special Fried Rice"). The Guy likes the following version, with slivers of baby bok choy, mushrooms, and chicken. Be creative and use what you have in the fridge—make it special with leftovers, just remember the garlic, egg, and soy sauce (fried rice essentials).

2 cups (500 mL) baby bok choy
1 cup (250 mL) fresh shiitake or other brown
    mushrooms
3 Tbsp (45 mL) canola oil
1 Tbsp (15 mL) minced garlic
3 to 4 cups (750 mL-1 L) leftover cooked rice,
    cold

½ lb (250 g) cooked chicken, roast pork, or
    turkey, chopped into small cubes
2 eggs, lightly beaten with 1 tsp (5 mL) sesame
    oil
2 Tbsp (30 mL) light soy sauce
1 Tbsp (15 mL) oyster sauce or hoisin sauce
2 green onions, chopped

1 Separate the leaves and clean the bok choy well (it can be gritty), then sliver. Rinse the mushrooms quickly to remove debris, trim the stems and cut into slivers. Have all of the other ingredients chopped and measured, ready to add to the wok.

2 Place a wok over high heat for 30 seconds, then drizzle with the oil. Immediately add the garlic and stir-fry for 1 minute. Turn the heat down slightly and add the rice, spreading it evenly over the surface of the pan. Stir-fry the rice for 1 to 2 minutes, then add the bok choy and mushrooms. Cook for 3 to 5 minutes longer, stirring, until the vegetables begin to wilt and give up some liquid. Add the chicken and stir to combine.

3 Push the rice mixture to one side of the pan and add the beaten eggs, stirring to lightly scramble before mixing into the rice. In a small bowl, whisk together the soy and oyster sauce and drizzle over the stir-fried rice. Toss to combine. Add the green onions and serve immediately. Serves 4.

Velvet Chicken with Broccoli and Peppers in Garlic Sauce

Marinating thin slices of chicken in egg white and cornstarch is a Chinese chef's trick to make it velvety and tender. If you can find tender stems of Chinese broccoli or broccolini (a leafy, tender broccoli), try it in this simple dish.

Sauce

2 tsp (10 mL) Chinese rice vinegar (or white wine vinegar)

½–1 tsp (2-5 mL) Asian chili paste (optional, omit for a milder dish)

1 cup (250 mL) chicken broth

½ tsp (2 mL) salt

Cornstarch solution: 2 tsp (10 mL) cornstarch mixed with 1 Tbsp (15 mL) water

In Advance

¾ lb (375 g) skinless, boneless chicken breasts, about 2 breasts

1 egg white

½ tsp (2 mL) salt or 1 tsp (5 mL) light soy sauce

freshly ground black pepper

1 tsp (5 mL) canola oil

1 Tbsp (15 mL) cornstarch

1 lb (500 g) broccoli, peeled and cut into florets, stems sliced diagonally

To Finish

3 Tbsp (45 mL) canola oil

1 Tbsp (15 mL) minced garlic

3 green onions, chopped

1 red bell pepper, seeded and diced

½ tsp (2 mL) sesame oil

1 To make the sauce, in a medium bowl, combine the vinegar, chili paste (if using), broth, and salt. In a separate bowl, mix together the 2 tsp (10 mL) cornstarch and water. Set aside.

2 Cut the chicken breasts in half lengthwise, then slice on a 45-degree angle into paper-thin slices. It helps if the chicken is slightly frozen.

3 In a medium bowl, whisk together the egg white, salt, pepper, 1 tsp canola oil, and 1 Tbsp (15 mL) cornstarch. Add the chicken and stir to thoroughly coat the meat in the marinade. Set aside in the refrigerator for several hours to tenderize.

4 Blanch the broccoli in 3 cups (750 mL) of boiling water just until it turns bright green, about 1 to 2 minutes. Immediately remove from the pot and plunge into a bath of ice water to stop the cooking process. Drain and set aside.

5 When you're ready to cook the dish, place a wok over high heat for 30 seconds and drizzle in 2 Tbsp (30 mL) of canola oil. Add the chicken to the wok and stir-fry for 2 to 3 minutes or just until the meat is white throughout. Remove the chicken from the wok and set aside.

6 Drizzle the remaining 1 Tbsp (15 mL) of canola oil into the hot wok and wait 30 seconds for it to heat up. Add the garlic and green onions and stir-fry for 10 seconds. Add the red pepper and the reserved broccoli and stir-fry for 1 to 2 minutes. Add a little water if the mixture is sticking.

7 Add the broth mixture and bring to a boil. Stir and scrape up any browned bits. Drizzle in the cornstarch solution and continue stirring until the sauce is thick and clear. Return the cooked chicken to the wok, stir to heat through for 1 to 2 minutes. Drizzle with sesame oil. Serve immediately. Serves 4.

Kung Pao Pork

This popular spicy dish has made its way from southwestern China to many Canadian Chinese restaurant menus. You can use regular roasted peanuts in this dish, but for authenticity use the small, unsalted peanuts sold in bags in Chinatown.

1 lb (500 g) pork tenderloin (or boneless
    chicken), cut in 1-inch (2.5-cm) cubes
1 Tbsp (15 mL) soy sauce

½ tsp (2 mL) Asian chili paste
1 tsp (5 mL) cornstarch

Sauce
1 cup (250 mL) chicken stock
2 Tbsp (30 mL) Chinese black bean sauce
1 Tbsp (15 mL) soy sauce

1 Tbsp (15 mL) brown sugar
1 tsp (5 mL) Asian chili paste
1 Tbsp (15 mL) cornstarch

2 Tbsp (30 mL) canola oil, divided
1 small onion, slivered
2 tsp (10 mL) ginger, minced
2 cloves garlic, minced
1 small dried red chili pepper, crumbled
1 red or yellow bell pepper, diced into ½-inch
    (2.5-cm) cubes

½ cup (125 mL) snow peas or frozen baby
    peas, thawed
2 green onions, cut into 1-inch (2.5-cm) lengths
⅓ cup (75 mL) roasted unsalted peanuts

1 Marinate the pork in the soy sauce, chili paste, and 1 tsp (5 mL) cornstarch for 30 minutes in the refrigerator.

2 Meanwhile, make the sauce. In a small bowl, combine the stock, black bean sauce, soy sauce, brown sugar, chili paste, and 1 Tbsp (15 mL) cornstarch. Set aside.

3 Heat a wok over high heat for 30 seconds before adding 1 Tbsp (15 mL) of the oil. Add the pork to the hot wok and stir-fry for 2 to 3 minutes or until it's no longer pink. Remove the pork and set aside.

4 Add the remaining oil to the wok. Add the onion, ginger, garlic, dried chili pepper, bell pepper, and snow peas. Stir-fry for 1 minute. Add the reserved sauce and bring to a boil.

5 Return the pork to the wok. Bring to a boil and heat through. Stir in the peanuts and serve immediately over rice or noodles. Serves 4.

BABY BURGER • OVEN FRIES

SUMMER CAMP SUNDAES

Daddy Duty

There are times when guys need to cook for the little guys. Kids like food that's small, portable, simple, and easy to eat. Anything mini is good. Nothing weird, spicy, or exotic. When it comes to cooking for kids, the more basic, the better. So here are some simple family-style suppers designed for the kids—or the kid in you.

Cheesy Potato Skins

You can use any kind of cheese in this easy after-school snack—most kids prefer mild cheddar but you can dress up this dish for adults with aged Friulano or feta cheese.

6 large white potatoes (Burbank or Idaho)
2 Tbsp (30 mL) butter, melted
2 green onions, finely chopped
3 slices double-smoked bacon, cut into slivers

8 oz (230 g) cheddar cheese, shredded (or
   Friulano, Gruyère, or feta)
freshly ground black pepper

1 Scrub the potatoes well and poke all over with a fork (this will allow steam to escape while baking and prevent the potatoes from bursting).

2 Bake the potatoes in a 400°F (200°C) oven until cooked through and crisp on the outside, about 45 to 50 minutes. Use a fork or a metal skewer to test the potatoes—the flesh should yield easily. Cool the potatoes and cut them lengthwise into 4 or 6 wedges, depending on the size of the potatoes.

3 Using a small spoon, scoop out most of the flesh to form boat-shaped shells, leaving only about ¼ to ½ inch (5 mm to 1 cm) potato lining. (You can use the excess potato to make mashed potatoes or to thicken soup.)

4 Increase the oven temperature to 450°F (230°C). Set the skins on a baking sheet and brush the inner sides with melted butter. Place the baking sheet in the oven for 5 minutes or until the skins have browned.

5 Meanwhile, in a small sauté pan, cook the bacon until crisp. Drain and discard the bacon fat. Set the bacon aside.

6 To finish, season the browned potato skins with a light grinding of black pepper. Top with shredded cheese, green onions, and bacon. Return skins to the oven and bake for 5 minutes longer or until the cheese is melted and bubbly. Serves 6.

Stuffed Potato Supper

Kids like things that come in neat little packages. You can make these stuffed spuds in advance so they're ready to be popped into the microwave whenever the kids return from school or soccer practice. You can substitute ingredients based on what your kids like to eat and what's in the fridge. Leftover steamed broccoli and cheddar, for example, can easily stand in for the spinach, feta, and dill.

two 7.5-oz (213-mL) cans wild sockeye salmon
4 baking potatoes
2 Tbsp (30 mL) butter
1 cup (250 mL) chopped fresh spinach
1 cup (250 mL) crumbled feta cheese

½ cup (125 mL) grated mozzarella cheese
2 green onions, chopped
1 Tbsp (30 mL) chopped fresh dill (optional)
salt and freshly ground black pepper to taste

1 Preheat oven to 400°F (200°C).

2 Drain the salmon and use a fork to break it into chunks. Discard any skin and bones.

3 Scrub the potatoes well and pierce with a fork all over to allow steam to escape. Bake the potatoes for 45 to 60 minutes or until soft—the potatoes should yield to pressure when squeezed.

4 Cut the potatoes in half, lengthwise. Use a spoon to carefully scoop the flesh into a medium bowl, leaving the baked shells intact.

5 Mash the potato flesh with butter and stir in the spinach, cheese, green onions, dill, salt, and pepper. Fold in the salmon. Pile the mixture back into the potato skins and place the stuffed potatoes on a baking sheet. Bake for 15 to 20 minutes, until hot and bubbly. Serves 4.

Tex-Mex Fingers and Oven Fries

Sure, you can buy frozen chicken fingers, but these are so much tastier. The Guy took The Girl's chicken finger recipe and added his own yummy twist—a kind of cowboy creation based on his favorite junk food: the cheesy Dorito corn chip. If your kids will eat vegetables, double the avocado aioli dipping sauce and use it to lightly dress a chopped romaine, avocado, and tomato salad to serve on the side.

Fries
4 large russet potatoes, unpeeled

6 Tbsp (90 mL) olive oil
2 tsp (10 mL) coarse sea salt

Chicken Fingers
2 to 3 boneless, skinless chicken breast halves
1 large egg
¼ cup (60 mL) buttermilk or plain yogurt
1 tsp (5 mL) mustard

2 to 3 cups (500 to 750 mL) tortilla chip crumbs
    (about 8 oz—The Guy likes the Doritos nacho
    cheese flavor, but you can choose your own
    favorite corn chips)

Avocado Aioli Dipping Sauce
½ cup (125 mL) mayonnaise

1 whole Haas avocado, peeled and cubed
1 clove garlic, minced

1 Preheat the oven to 450°F (230°C).

2 Scrub the potatoes well and cut them into wedges. Place in a bowl and cover with hot tap water. Soak for 10 minutes, then drain well. Spread on paper towels and press with additional towels to dry. Return the potatoes to the bowl, add the olive oil, and toss to coat.

3 Sprinkle the sea salt over a heavy, non-stick baking sheet and spread the potatoes across the sheet in a single layer. Cover the pan with foil and bake for 5 minutes in the preheated oven. Remove the foil and lower the heat to 400°F (200°C). Bake for another 35 to 45 minutes. Turn the wedges with a spatula partway through the baking time.

4 Meanwhile, combine the egg, buttermilk, and mustard in a bowl. Use a sharp knife to cut the chicken lengthwise into thin strips (about four to five strips per breast). Add the chicken to the egg mixture and toss to coat. Cover and refrigerate for 30 minutes.

5 In a food processor, whirl the tortilla chips to create fine crumbs. Pour the crumbs onto a plate and clean the food processor. Add the mayonnaise, avocado, and garlic to the processor and whirl until smooth. Transfer the mayonnaise-avocado mixture to a bowl; cover and refrigerate.

6 Using tongs, pick up a piece of chicken, shake off any excess liquid, and roll it in the tortilla crumbs to coat all sides. Place the battered chicken on a rack, set over a baking sheet, for 10 minutes to allow the coating to set. Repeat with remaining chicken strips. Place the chicken strips, still on the rack on the baking sheet, in the oven alongside the fries during the last 15 minutes of the fries cooking. Bake for 15 minutes or just until the coating on the chicken strips begins to brown.

7 Serve the chicken strips and chips with the avocado aioli for dipping, reserving 3 Tbsp (45 mL) to lightly dress a side salad of chopped romaine hearts, cubed Roma tomatoes, and avocado. Serves 4.

Baby Burgers

There's a big push to use lean ground beef, but when making burgers, regular ground beef gives juicier results. Try it in these mini, kid-sized burgers.

1 lb (500 g) medium ground beef
1 large egg, beaten
1 small yellow onion, finely chopped
¼ cup (60 mL) dry breadcrumbs or cracker crumbs
2 cloves garlic, minced
2 Tbsp (30 mL) barbecue sauce

¼ tsp (1 mL) salt
¼ tsp (1 mL) freshly ground black pepper
small buns (look for 2- to 3-inch dinner rolls or biscuits), toasted
cherry tomatoes, sliced
baby lettuce leaves
ketchup, mustard, and relish

1 In a large bowl, combine the ground beef, egg, onion, breadcrumbs, garlic, barbecue sauce, salt, and pepper. Mix lightly and, using your hands, shape into 12 to 14 small patties that will fit into your buns.

2 Grill, broil, or pan-fry using medium-high heat for 4 minutes per side, until a digital rapid-read thermometer, inserted sideways into center of each patty, reads at least 160°F (70°C). Serve burger patties on toasted buns and top with sliced cherry tomato and baby lettuce. Add ketchup, mustard, and relish as desired. Serves 4.

Sweet and Sour Chicken

A Chinese restaurant classic—this simple sweet and sour chicken is a bit spicy, but kids love it. And you can substitute any vegetables (try broccoli or snow peas) for the bell peppers and water chestnuts. Make a pot of white rice and stir in some butter just before serving.

1 lb (500 g) skinless and boneless chicken breasts, cut into 1-inch (2.5-cm) chunks
1 egg white

½ tsp (2 mL) salt
¼ cup (60 mL) cornstarch
¼ cup (60 mL) canola oil

Sweet and Sour Sauce
1 ½-inch (4-cm) piece ginger, minced
1 clove garlic, minced
½ red or yellow bell pepper, seeded and diced
½ cup (125 mL) sliced water chestnuts (canned is fine)
¼ cup (60 mL) packed brown sugar
½ cup (125 mL) chicken stock

2 Tbsp (30 mL) white vinegar
1 tsp (5 mL) light soy sauce
¼ to ½ tsp (1 to 2 mL) crushed dried chilies
1 Tbsp (15 mL) cornstarch mixed with 1 tsp (5 mL) water
2 green onions, cut into 1-inch (2.5-cm) lengths, then slivered

1 Toss the chicken with the egg white and salt. Set in the refrigerator to marinate for 15 minutes.

2 Pour the cornstarch into a bag and add the marinated chicken in batches. Toss to lightly coat.

3 Heat the canola oil in a wok or sauté pan over medium-high heat. Quickly fry the chicken, in batches, until nicely browned on all sides. (Add more oil if you need to for subsequent batches.) Remove the chicken and set aside to drain on a plate lined with paper towels.

4 In the same pan, add the ginger, garlic, red pepper, and water chestnuts. Stir-fry over high heat for 2 minutes. Add the sugar, chicken stock, vinegar, soy sauce, and chilies. Bring to a boil. Cook for 1 minute, then add the cornstarch solution. Stir and simmer for 1 minute more to thicken the sauce. Return the chicken to the sauce, stir in the green onions, and heat through for 2 minutes. Serve immediately with lots of fluffy rice. Serves 4.

Mac and Cheese

When The Guy graduated from university, he left boxed mac and cheese behind in the dorm—but he still craves cheesy macaroni. Now he makes it from scratch—a simple white sauce (a.k.a. bechamel) flavored with whatever cheese is on hand. On a weeknight, it's great to scoop the mac and cheese right out of the pot and into soup plates, but if you're serving guests, bake your mac with a crispy topping. For a more virtuous (but equally silky) sauce, try using one 13-oz (385-mL) can of evaporated milk instead of whole milk and cream—it makes a low-fat, yet amazingly creamy, macaroni. Kids like it, too.

3 cups (750 mL) macaroni or cavatappi (Italian
    spiral macaroni)
2 Tbsp (30 mL) butter
1 heaping Tbsp (20 mL) all-purpose flour
1 cup (250 mL) milk
½ cup (125 mL) whipping cream
½ tsp (2 mL) Dijon mustard

2 to 3 drops hot pepper sauce
2 cups (500 mL) grated aged cheddar (or
    substitute 1 cup/250 mL of Monterey Jack,
    Swiss, pecorino romano, or Parmesan for 1
    cup/250 mL of the cheddar)
salt and freshly ground black pepper

1 Bring a big pot of salted water to a rolling boil and cook the pasta for 8 to 10 minutes or until al dente (tender but still firm to the bite). Drain and set aside.

2 To make the sauce, melt the butter in a saucepan over medium-high heat. Whisk in the flour and cook for 1 to 2 minutes or until the flour begins to color. Slowly add the milk and cream, whisking until the sauce is smooth and bubbly. Whisk in the mustard and hot sauce. Remove the pan from the heat, add the cheese, and stir until just melted. Season with salt and pepper.

3 Add the pasta to the sauce and heat through for 1 minute on medium-low heat (be careful not to overheat or the cheese may separate). Serve immediately. Serves 2 to 4.

WISE GUY: If you double this recipe for company (i.e. use 1 lb/500 g of pasta and cheese), you can present it with a crispy topping in a 3- to 4-quart gratin dish. Mix 1 cup (250 mL) breadcrumbs with 2 Tbsp (30 mL) melted butter, salt, and pepper. Sprinkle over the casserole, then broil for 3 to 5 minutes or until the top is golden. Alternatively, top your mac with extra shredded cheese and brown under the broiler.

If you want to dress up your mac, stir in some steamed broccoli, sliced spinach, chopped roasted red pepper, or green onion. You can even add a scoop of fresh tomato salsa from the deli.

Chicken Chili Wraps

This is an easy after-work idea for boneless, skinless chicken breasts or thighs. Spiced, baked, topped with fresh tomato and avocado salsa, then wrapped in a whole-wheat tortilla with brown rice, this is the perfect meal to take along when you're running late for the kid's hockey game or dance class. On less frantic days, when you can all sit down at the table to eat, just top the chicken with salsa and serve rice on the side.

1 Tbsp (15 mL) olive oil
2 Tbsp (30 mL) freshly squeezed lime or lemon
    juice
1 clove garlic, smashed and finely minced
1 tsp (5 mL) ground cumin
1 tsp (5 mL) paprika

1 tsp (5 mL) oregano
1 tsp (5 mL) chili powder
¼ tsp (1 mL) cayenne pepper (to taste, or omit
    if your kids dislike the spice)
4 skinless, boneless chicken breasts
    (or 1 lb/500 g boneless thighs)

Salsa
1 cup (250 mL) seeded and diced Roma
    tomatoes (about 3 tomatoes)
1 avocado, peeled and chopped
juice of half a lime

¼ cup (60 mL) chopped fresh cilantro
pinch of salt and cumin
1 Tbsp (15 mL) minced jalapeño pepper
whole wheat tortillas
2 cups (500 mL) cooked brown rice

1 To make the rub, combine the oil, lemon or lime juice, garlic, spices, and cayenne pepper in a small bowl. Slather the rub over the chicken on all sides and set aside in the refrigerator for 10 minutes.

2 Preheat the oven to 375°F (190°C). Arrange the chicken in a single layer on a non-stick baking sheet. (Line the sheet with foil or parchment to reduce clean-up time.) Bake, uncovered, for 25 to 35 minutes or until the juices run clear when pierced. Be careful not to overcook the chicken—25 minutes should suffice for a ¼-lb (125-g) breast. Remember, chicken breasts can dry out easily, but while thighs tend to be more forgiving, they are also higher in fat.

3 Meanwhile, combine the chopped tomato, avocado, lime juice, cilantro, salt, and cumin in a bowl. Set the salsa aside at room temperature while the chicken cooks.

4 Slice the chicken and roll it up in flour tortillas with the salsa and rice. Serves 4.

Dad's Gooey Spare Ribs

The Guy loved these simple spare ribs when he was kid. This is the perfect recipe for using the less expensive pork side ribs (save the expensive baby backs for the barbecue). If you want to spice them up (and your kids can take the heat) add 1 tsp (5 mL) of Asian chili paste—and put on a pot of fluffy basmati rice to soak up the sauce.

2 Tbsp (30 mL) soy sauce
3 Tbsp (45 mL) honey
2 Tbsp (30 mL) hoisin sauce
1 Tbsp (15 mL) white vinegar
2 tsp (10 mL) minced ginger
2 tsp (10 mL) minced garlic
⅔ cup (150 mL) ketchup

½ cup (125 mL) water
1 Tbsp (15 mL) Worcestershire sauce
salt and freshly ground black pepper
2½ lb (2.25 kg) pork side ribs, cut into 2-inch
   (5-cm) portions
1 large yellow onion, finely chopped

1 In a medium bowl, whisk together the soy sauce, honey, hoisin sauce, vinegar, ginger, garlic, ketchup, water, Worcestershire sauce, salt, and pepper.

2 Cut the ribs between every second or third bone to make smaller portions. Place the ribs in a Dutch oven and sauté over medium-high heat for 10 to 15 minutes or until nicely browned. Drain off any excess fat, then stir in the onion. Cook until the onion is soft, about 5 minutes.

3 Pour the sauce over the ribs and bring to a boil. Reduce the heat to medium-low, cover the pot, and simmer for 1 hour (the meat should be very tender and almost falling off the bone). Remove the lid and continue to cook for 10 to 15 minutes longer or until the sauce has thickened and the ribs are nicely glazed. Serve over rice. Serves 4.

Lemon Pudding Cake

The Guy loves it when he can surprise the kids—and this pudding-in-a-cake dessert does it. You don't need to do anything to create the magic that happens in the oven—the layers separate and you get a golden lemon cake layer on top with a saucy lemon pudding underneath. You'll need to buy two medium lemons to get enough fresh juice for this recipe. Easy to whip up together for a family dessert!

¼ cup (60 mL) unsalted butter, softened
1 cup (250 mL) granulated sugar
2 Tbsp (30 mL) lemon zest (the zest from about 1 lemon)

3 large eggs, separated
¼ cup (60 mL) all-purpose flour
1 cup (250 mL) milk
⅓ cup (75 mL) freshly squeezed lemon juice

1 Preheat the oven to 350°F (180°C). Butter an 8-inch (20-cm) square glass or ceramic baking dish.

2 In a mixing bowl, use an electric mixer to beat the butter and ¾ cup (175 mL) of the sugar until fluffy. Add the lemon rind and then the egg yolks, one at a time, beating well after each addition. Add the flour, alternating with the milk and lemon juice, and beat until the batter is smooth.

3 Wash the beaters. In another bowl, beat the egg whites with the electric mixer until foamy. Add the remaining ¼ cup (60 mL) of sugar, 1 Tbsp (15 mL) at a time, while you continue to beat. When the egg whites form stiff peaks, use a wooden spoon to mix ⅓ of the meringue into the lemon mixture. Fold in the rest, being careful not to overmix—the idea is to keep the batter fluffy.

4 Pour the batter into the prepared baking dish and place the dish in a larger baking pan. Transfer to the oven and add boiling water to the larger pan, filling until the water bath is about 1 inch (2.5 cm) deep. Bake for 35 to 45 minutes or until the cake's top is slightly browned and set, which means it should be firm to the touch.

5 Remove the pudding from the water bath and set it on a rack to cool for 20 minutes before serving. (This dessert can be served warm or chilled.) To serve, scoop the pudding into individual dessert dishes, making sure each serving includes some of the saucy stuff on the bottom of the baking dish. Serves 6.

WISE GUY: When you want to turn this comforting family dessert into something that'll wow your friends, just bake the batter in six individual ramekins for about 20 minutes. Call it Souffléed Lemon Pudding. Serve each dessert dusted with icing sugar, then artfully arrange a few fresh raspberries and a sprig of mint on top.

One, Two, Three Bite Brownies

This is your classic homestyle brownie—chewy, nutty, and addictive. You can make these in a regular 9- x 13-inch (3.5-L) baking pan (and cut them into three-bite pieces) or do as The Guy does and use a silicon mini-muffin pan. The brownies bake in half the time and pop out like little chocolate ice cubes!

1 cup (250 mL) unsalted butter
4 oz (115 g) unsweetened chocolate, chopped
2 cups (500 mL) granulated sugar
4 large eggs

1 tsp (5 mL) pure vanilla extract
1 cup (250 mL) all-purpose flour
½ tsp (2 mL) salt
1 cup (250 mL) walnuts or pecans, chopped

1 Lightly grease a 9- x 13-inch baking pan, or use a silicon mini-muffin pan. In a medium saucepan, heat the butter over low heat until it's half melted. Add the chocolate and stir until both are completely melted. Remove from heat and stir in the sugar. Beat in the eggs, one at a time, until the mixture is shiny. Stir in the vanilla, flour, salt, and chopped nuts.

2 Pour the batter into a prepared pan and bake at 350°F (180°C) for 30 minutes or until firm (about 15 minutes for mini muffins). A cake tester inserted in the middle of the pan should come out clean. Let cool completely in the pan before cutting into squares. Makes 36 to 42 pieces.

Summer Camp Sundaes

This gooey ice cream dessert is reminiscent of those campfire treats known as S'mores—the graham cracker, chocolate, and marshmallow concoctions most kids learn to make at summer camp. But you don't need a roaring fire, or even a backyard grill, to construct this easy summer sundae. You can still eat it in the backyard.

6 to 8 graham wafers, divided
1 cup (250 mL) chocolate fudge sauce (look for a
   brand without hydrogenated oil)

4 scoops chocolate chunk ice cream
½ cup (125 mL) marshmallow topping

1 Place a graham wafer into the bottom of four small cereal bowls. Crumble the remaining wafers (put them into a sealed zippered plastic bag and roll over them with a rolling pin) and reserve.

2 Spoon a little chocolate sauce into each bowl and follow with one scoop of ice cream.

3 Top each ice cream scoop with 3 Tbsp (45 mL) of the marshmallow topping. Drizzle with remaining chocolate sauce, sprinkle with the crumbled graham wafers, and serve immediately. Serves 4.

WISE GUY: You can make this treat marginally healthier by slicing a couple of bananas to scatter around in the bowl.

Real Guys Make Pot Pies

Real men may eat quiche, but The Guy prefers pie—savory pot pie—topped with all manner of creative carbs, from cornmeal biscuits to vegetable mashes.

There's a "pie man" at the local market in The Guy's hometown who makes individual pot pies from scratch, then delivers them to your door, frozen, with reheating instructions. The Guy figures this is a fine way to serve any of his favorite pot pies. Make them in a big casserole dish to serve a crowd or collect a few oven-proof, 1- to 2-cup (250- to 500-mL) bowls and make a bunch of individual pot pies on the weekend, then freeze them to enjoy on your own any time.

Classic Chicken Pot Pie with Dumplings

Without the cornmeal dumplings, this makes a great chicken stew. For individual pot pies, divide the stew among six ovenproof bowls, top with dumplings, and bake.

2 lb (1 kg) skinless, boneless chicken thighs, cut into large chunks
2 Tbsp (30 mL) canola oil
2 Tbsp (30 mL) butter
2 large yellow onions, peeled and finely chopped
1 Tbsp (15 mL) minced garlic
2 Tbsp (30 mL) all-purpose flour
4 medium carrots, cut into thick rounds
3 stalks of celery, chopped
1 large parsnip, peeled and cubed

one 10-oz (284-mL) can of condensed chicken broth, diluted with ½ can of water (about 1½ cups/375 mL in total)
½ cup (125 mL) dry white wine
1 bay leaf
1 cup (250 mL) frozen sweet baby peas, thawed
2 Tbsp (30 mL) chopped fresh parsley
¼ tsp (1 mL) dried thyme leaves
salt and freshly ground black pepper

Dumplings
¾ cup (175 mL) cornmeal
¾ cup (175 mL) all-purpose flour
1 Tbsp (15 mL) baking powder
½ tsp (2 mL) dried mustard

½ tsp (2 mL) salt
2 Tbsp (30 mL) butter, melted
1 large egg, beaten
½ cup (125 mL) milk

1 In a large, deep sauté pan or Dutch oven, heat the butter and oil over medium-high heat. Cook the chicken in batches until browned. Remove the chicken from the pan, and set aside.

2 Add the onions to the same pan and sauté for 5 to 10 minutes or until the onion has softened. Scrape up any browned bits left in the pan. Add the garlic and cook for 1 minute. Stir in the flour, then add the carrot, celery, parsnip, diluted chicken stock, wine, and bay leaf. Bring to a boil.

3 Return the cooked chicken and any accumulated juices to the pan. Bring to a boil, then reduce the heat to low, cover, and simmer for 45 minutes or until the chicken is very tender. If the sauce seems too thin, raise the heat and remove the lid to reduce the liquid. Stir in the baby peas, parsley, and thyme. Season with salt and pepper to taste. Transfer the stew into a baking dish.

4 Preheat the oven to 400°F (200°C).

5 Meanwhile, combine the dry ingredients for the dumplings in a small bowl. In a measuring cup, melt the butter in the microwave (it will take about 20 to 30 seconds), then stir in the egg and milk and beat lightly with a fork. Add the egg mixture to the dry ingredients. Stir quickly and only enough to combine.

6 Top the stew with large spoonfuls of the cornmeal dumplings. Bake for 20 to 30 minutes or until the dumplings are puffed and golden brown. Place the baking dish in the middle of the table and serve the pot pie family style. Serves 4 to 6.

WISE GUY: Another cool way to top individual pot pies is by draping a piece of pastry over top of the bowls before baking, and pressing lightly around the rim to seal. Use the pastry recipe off the box of lard or buy some frozen puff pastry sheets and roll them out into circles or squares.

Picadillo Pot Pie

This is the perfect solution for that ubiquitous pound of ground—a kind of South American pot pie inspired by The Guy's favorite empanada filling. Vegetarian guys can substitute a big can of black beans (rinse and drain them well) for the meat.

2 Tbsp (30 mL) extra virgin olive oil
1 large yellow onion, finely chopped
3 cloves garlic, minced
1 large red or yellow bell pepper, chopped
1 lb (500 g) lean ground beef (or substitute
    ground lamb or turkey)
1 Tbsp (15 mL) ground cumin
½ tsp (2 mL) crushed dried red chili pepper or
    ¼ tsp (1 mL) cayenne pepper
2 tsp (10 mL) chili powder
2 cups (500 mL) plain tomato sauce,
    homemade or from a can

2 Tbsp (30 mL) freshly squeezed lime juice or
    wine vinegar
1 Tbsp (15 mL) unsweetened cocoa powder
one 13-oz (398-mL) can sliced black olives,
    drained
one 12-oz (341mL) can sweet corn
¼ cup (60 mL) raisins
2 Tbsp (30 mL) Worcestershire sauce
¼ cup (60 mL) stone-ground cornmeal
salt and freshly ground black pepper

Topping
3 cups (750 mL) water
1 clove garlic, minced
2 Tbsp (30 mL) butter
1 cup (250 mL) stone-ground cornmeal

1 large egg, lightly beaten
2 tsp (10 mL) baking powder
1½ cups (375 mL) grated cheddar cheese, divided

1 To make the filling, heat the oil in a sauté pan over medium-high heat, add the onion, garlic, and bell pepper, and sauté for 10 minutes. Add the ground beef to the pan, breaking it up with a spoon, and cook until it's no longer pink. Stir in the cumin, dried crushed chili, and chili powder. Add the tomato sauce, lime juice, cocoa powder, olives, corn, raisins, and Worcestershire. Simmer, uncovered, for 10 minutes, then stir in the ¼ cup (60 mL) of cornmeal and cook for a couple of minutes, until thickened. Season with salt and pepper to taste. Sample your filling—add a little more cayenne or a bit of chili paste if you'd like it hotter. Pour the filling into a shallow casserole dish.

2 To make the topping, heat the water to a rolling boil in a saucepan, then add the minced garlic and butter. Use a whisk and stir constantly as you slowly pour the 1 cup (250 mL) of cornmeal into the boiling water (this will prevent lumps). Immediately reduce the heat to medium-low and cook, stirring, for 5 minutes more. Remove the pan from the heat and stir to cool slightly.

3 Meanwhile, in a small bowl, beat the egg with the baking powder. Quickly whisk this mixture into the cooked cornmeal, then fold in 1 cup (250 mL) of the grated cheese.

4 Pour the topping over the filling in the casserole dish, smoothing the top with the back of a spoon. Sprinkle the remaining cheese on top and bake at 350°F (180°C) for 45 to 55 minutes or until the top is set and lightly browned. Serves 6.

WISE GUY:

This filling can also be used to make yummy empanada-style pockets for portable lunches. See page 386 for The Guy's easy calzones (using frozen whole wheat bread dough) and add some grated cheddar cheese before sealing the pockets and baking. A great way to take your favorite beefy pot pie on a hike!

Cape Curried Pot Pie

When The Guy went to Cape Town in South Africa, he found a wonderful mélange of flavors reflecting local English, Dutch, Indian, and, of course, African traditions. This ground meat pie, known there as bobotie, is a sweet and spicy South African version of shepherd's pie. While it usually has a custard topping, The Guy likes this mixed-vegetable mash piled on top (a combination of colorful sweet potatoes with carrots and ginger). It makes an easy and exotic dish for a potluck party or a family dinner.

2 Tbsp (30 mL) curry powder

1 tsp (5 mL) ground ginger

1 tsp (5 mL) turmeric

1 tsp (5 mL) granulated sugar

¼ tsp (1 mL) cayenne pepper

1 tsp (5 mL) salt

½ tsp (2 mL) freshly ground black pepper

1 Tbsp (15 mL) extra virgin olive oil

2 medium yellow onions, chopped

1 green apple, peeled and chopped

1 lb (500 g) lean ground beef or lamb

1 Tbsp (15 mL) freshly squeezed lemon juice or
   white vinegar

⅓ cup (75 mL) raisins

2 Tbsp (30 mL) Worcestershire sauce

2 Tbsp (30 mL) ketchup or tomato paste

1 Tbsp (15 mL) honey

½ cup (125 mL) fresh breadcrumbs

1 egg, beaten

Topping

2 large Yukon Gold potatoes, peeled and cubed

2 large sweet potatoes, peeled and cubed

3 medium carrots, peeled and cubed

2 medium parsnips, peeled and cubed

¼ cup (60 mL) butter

1 medium onion, finely chopped

2 Tbsp (30 mL) minced fresh ginger

¼ cup (60 mL) cream or milk

salt and freshly ground black pepper

1 In a small bowl, combine the curry powder, ginger, turmeric, sugar, cayenne, salt, and pepper. In a non-stick sauté pan, heat the olive oil over medium high heat. Add the spice mixture and cook for 30 seconds or until fragrant (be careful not to burn the spices). Immediately add the onions and cook for 5 minutes, until they begin to color. Then stir in the chopped apple and sauté 3 minutes more.

2 Add the ground beef to the pan, breaking it up as it browns. When the meat is no longer pink and begins to brown, remove the pan from the heat. Stir in the lemon juice, raisins, Worcestershire, ketchup, honey, and breadcrumbs. Add the beaten egg and stir to bind the ingredients, then spread the meat mixture into a 9- x 13-inch (3.5-L) rectangular baking dish.

3 To make the topping, combine the potatoes, sweet potatoes, carrots, and parsnips in a saucepan. Cover with salted water and bring to a boil over high heat. Reduce the heat to low, cover, and simmer for about 20 minutes or until tender. Drain well and use a potato masher to mash the vegetables together.

4 While the vegetables are cooking, melt the butter in a sauté pan over medium heat. Add the onions and ginger and sauté until tender and starting to brown. Stir this mixture into the mashed vegetables along with the cream. Season to taste with salt and pepper.

5 Pile the topping over the filling and smooth. Bake at 350°F (180°C) for 45 minutes or until filling is hot and the topping is golden brown. Remove from the oven and let cool for 15 minutes before cutting into squares to serve. Serves 6 to 8.

Pork and Sweet Potato Pot Pie

This colorful pie has Latin American roots—with its tender chunks of pork, black beans, and cilantro. Comforting stuff from points south.

1 Tbsp (15 mL) extra virgin olive oil

2 lb (1 kg) boneless pork shoulder, trimmed of fat and cut into 2-inch chunks

1 large white onion, chopped

1 lb (500 g) sweet potatoes, peeled and cubed

2 Tbsp (30 mL) all-purpose flour

1 cup (250 mL) chicken stock, preferably homemade

½ cup (125 mL) white wine

¼ cup (60 mL) freshly squeezed orange juice

5 cloves garlic, minced

2 tsp (10 mL) ground cumin

½ tsp (2 mL) Asian chili paste

¼ tsp (1 mL) freshly ground black pepper

one 14-oz (398-mL) can black beans, rinsed and drained (or about 1½ cups/375 mL cooked black beans)

⅓ cup (75 mL) chopped cilantro

Biscuit Crust

½ cup (125 mL) all-purpose flour

½ cup (125 mL) whole wheat flour

½ tsp (2 mL) salt

1 tsp (5 mL) baking powder

2 Tbsp (30 mL) cold butter

1 cup (250 mL) grated white cheddar cheese

⅔ cup (175 mL) skim milk

paprika or cayenne pepper for dusting

1 In a large Dutch oven, heat the oil and sauté the pork chunks in batches over medium-high heat for 5 to 10 minutes, or until nicely browned on all sides. Remove the pork from the pan and set aside.

2 Add the onions and sweet potato to the pan and sauté for about 10 minutes or until they begin to brown and caramelize. Stir in the flour, then slowly add the stock and white wine, scraping up any browned bits on the bottom of the pan. Bring the mixture to a boil, then add the orange juice, garlic, cumin, chili paste, and pepper. Return the browned pork cubes to the pot, stir in the beans, then cover and turn the heat down to low. Simmer the stew for 1 hour. Stir occasionally to make sure it doesn't stick.

3 In the meantime, make the biscuit topping. Combine the flours, salt, and baking powder in a mixing bowl. Using a pastry blender or two table knives, cut in the cold butter until the mixture resembles coarse crumbs. Stir in the shredded cheese and enough of the milk to make a soft dough. (You can also quickly make the topping in the food processor or simply serve the pork stew over brown rice.)

4 Preheat the oven to 400°F (200°C). When the stew is cooked and the pork is tender, stir in the chopped cilantro. Pour the pork stew into a large oval baking dish that you can take to the table. Drop the biscuit mixture on top to rustically cover the meat. (Alternatively, make six smaller pot pies in individual baking dishes.) Bake for 25 to 30 minutes or until the biscuit topping is golden and the filling is bubbling. Dust with paprika or cayenne pepper before serving. Serves 6.

Tourtière

This is a Christmas Eve tradition in The Guy's house—serve pieces of this meaty pork and beef pie with sweet gherkins, pickled beets, or chutney to balance the richness. The filling in this recipe is enough for three 9-inch (23-cm) pies—exactly the amount of pastry you'll have if you follow the recipe on the box of shortening or lard. Don't give in to your fear of making pie crust, the recipe works! The pies can be filled and frozen unbaked—just thaw in the refrigerator before you're ready to bake.

Filling

2 cups (500 mL) finely chopped onion
3 cloves garlic, minced
1 cup (250 mL) minced celery and celery leaves
1 tsp (5 mL) extra virgin olive oil
2 lb (1 kg) ground pork
1 lb (500 g) lean ground beef
½ tsp (2 mL) dried savory
½ tsp (2 mL) ground sage

pinch ground cloves
pinch cinnamon
salt and freshly ground black pepper
1 cup (250 mL) water
3 cups (750 mL) hot, boiled potatoes, mashed
   or put through a ricer
½ cup (125 mL) chopped fresh parsley
pastry for three double-crust pies
1 egg yolk, beaten with 2 Tbsp (30 mL) milk

1 In a large sauté pan, heat the oil over medium heat. Sauté the chopped onion, garlic, and celery for 5 minutes or until softened. Crumble the ground pork and beef into the pan and stir until the meat is no longer pink. Drain any excess fat from the pan before adding the savory, sage, cloves, cinnamon, salt, pepper, and water. Cover the pan and simmer for 30 minutes. Stir in the mashed potatoes and parsley. Set aside to cool.

2 Make the pastry, following the instructions on the box of shortening or lard. Chill the pastry for 1 hour before rolling. Preheat the oven to 375°F (190°C). On a floured surface, roll the pastry into six thin rounds and line three 9-inch (23-cm) pie plates. Fill each pie shell with ⅓ of the cooled meat mixture and top with the remaining pastry, sealing and fluting the edges with your fingers to form a ruffled border. Cut small steam vents in the tops of the pies using the tip of a sharp knife. Brush the pies with the egg yolk glaze, and bake for 30 to 40 minutes, until golden brown. Cool for 20 minutes before cutting into wedges to serve. Makes three 9-inch (23-cm) meat pies.

Salmon Pot Pie

The Guy likes to top these individual pot pies with rustic peaks of creamy mashed potatoes—just dollop on with a spoon. But if you're feeling extra fancy, you can purée the potatoes and use a piping bag with a large tip to artfully pipe the potatoes over the filling. Makes a very chic pie.

¼ cup (60 mL) butter, divided
1 cup (250 mL) minced fresh mushrooms
2 cloves garlic, minced
1 medium yellow onion, minced
1 Tbsp (15 mL) all-purpose flour
½ cup (125 mL) white wine
1 cup (250 mL) fish stock (see page XX)
  or water
½ cup (125 mL) heavy cream or milk
¼ cup (60 mL) chopped fresh parsley

1 Tbsp (15 mL) chopped fresh thyme or dill
1 Tbsp (15 mL) freshly squeezed lemon juice
salt and freshly ground black pepper
2 lb (1 kg) Yukon Gold or other yellow-fleshed
  potatoes, boiled and mashed
3 Tbsp (45 mL) butter
¼ cup (60 mL) milk or cream
freshly ground black pepper
1½ lb (750 g) salmon fillet, skin and bones
  removed, cut into ½- to 1-inch cubes

1 In a medium saucepan, melt 2 Tbsp (30 mL) of the butter over medium heat and sauté the mushrooms and garlic for 10 minutes (until they are tender and most of the liquid has evaporated). Cool the mushroom mixture and divide among four individual, 2-cup (500-mL) ovenproof ramekins or one 6- to 8-cup baking dish (a straight-sided soufflé dish makes a nice pot pie).

2 Sauté the onion in the remaining butter for 10 minutes or until tender and golden. Stir in the flour and cook for 1 minute. Slowly whisk in the wine, stock or water, and ½ cup (125 mL) cream. Stir and simmer for 5 to 10 minutes until you have a thick, smooth sauce. Mix in the parsley, thyme (or dill), and lemon juice. Season with salt and pepper to taste.

3 Meanwhile, boil the potatoes in lots of salted water until tender, about 20 to 30 minutes. Drain the potatoes and mash with the butter, ¼ cup (60 mL) milk, and some black pepper. If you wish to pipe the potatoes over the pot pies, the mash needs to be very smooth. Otherwise, leave it a little chunky for texture.

4 Arrange the salmon chunks over the mushroom mixture in the baking dishes and pour the sauce overtop. Artfully top each pie with mashed potatoes. Bake in a 350°F (180°C) oven for 40 minutes or until the filling bubbles and the tops are golden. Serves 4.

WISE GUY:

For an elegant mixed seafood pot pie, instead of salmon, use ¾ lb (375 g) of a white fish such as cod or halibut (cubed), 1 lb (500 g) of medium shrimp, peeled and deveined, and ½ lb (250 g) sea scallops. Before baking, top the pot pies with rounds of frozen puff pastry.

Beefcake

There's no doubt The Guy's a committed carnivore, and when it comes to meat, beef is king. But there's more to beef than steak and burgers on the barbie. The Guy likes to include roast beef, braising steaks, and even beefy short ribs in his repertoire—manly things to make any time.

Weekday Roast Beef

The Guy usually saves roasting the big joint of beef for the weekend, when there's time to relax and guests to serve. But when he wants to do a quick roast for roast beef sandwiches, nothing beats this simple and inexpensive, little boneless roast. Start with an eye of the round or boneless top sirloin roast, rub with spices, and roast it in 45 minutes flat.

one 2 lb (1 kg) eye of the round boneless roast (or substitute a small top round roast)
1 Tbsp (15 mL) extra virgin olive oil
1 tsp (5 mL) Worcestershire sauce
1 Tbsp (15 mL) Dijon mustard

¼ tsp (1 mL) garlic powder
¼ tsp (1 mL) paprika
¼ tsp (1 mL) salt
½ tsp (2 mL) coarsely ground black pepper

1 Preheat the oven to 500°F (260°C). In a small bowl, combine the olive oil, Worcestershire, and Dijon. Rub this mixture over the entire roast. Sprinkle all sides with the garlic powder, paprika, salt, and black pepper. Press to adhere the spices to the roast.

2 Place the roast on a rack in a shallow roasting pan. Put it into the hot oven and set the timer for 10 minutes. When it rings, reduce the heat to 300°F (150°C) (don't open the oven) and continue to roast for 35 to 45 minutes. Remove the roast from the oven and let rest for at least 15 minutes before slicing thinly across the grain. The roast will be rare (which is great for cold roast beef sandwiches) but if you want to be sure, test it with an instant-read thermometer 5 minutes after you remove it from the oven (the internal temperature actually rises as the meat rests). The Guy likes to cook the roast to an internal temperature of 125 to 130°F (45 to 54°C)—no more or it will be tough. Slice it very thinly and serve warm in sandwiches, or refrigerate and slice for sandwiches when cold. A drizzle of Horseradish Aioli (see page 37) makes a roast beef sandwich to die for! Serves 6.

WISE GUY: For a magical mushroom-rubbed roast, follow the same instructions (above) but add 1 tsp (5 mL) of fresh, chopped thyme leaves and ¼ cup (60 mL) pulverized dried porcini, morel, or shiitake mushrooms to the rub (use a blender or clean electric spice grinder to process mushrooms to a powder). You can also make a quick mushroom sauce after you remove the meat from the roasting pan—just add 1 Tbsp (15 mL) of butter to the pan, stirring up the browned bits, then whisk in 1 Tbsp (15 mL) of flour. Cook over medium heat for a few seconds, then slowly add ¼ cup (60 mL) of red wine and 1 cup (250 mL) of water or stock. Add ¼ cup (60 mL) dried mushrooms, whole or crushed, and bring to a boil, then reduce the heat and simmer until the sauce is nicely thickened. Season with salt and pepper to taste, and serve it over thinly sliced roast beef, with garlic mashed potatoes (see page 156) and something green (like steamed broccoli, asparagus, or peas). Makes a speedy but chic roast beef dinner.

Hot Beef Sandwich with Caramelized Onions and Bubbly Blue Cheese

When there's roast beef or steak one day, The Guy uses the leftovers to make these big beefy sandwiches the next.

¼ cup (60 mL) crumbled blue cheese
½ cup (125 mL) softened cream cheese
1 Tbsp (15 mL) cream or milk
4 wholegrain individual baguettes or crusty buns
Horseradish Aioli (see page 37)

1 lb (500 g) thickly sliced cold roast beef or leftover flank steak
2 large red or white onions, sliced and caramelized (see page 16)
1 cup (250 mL) baby arugula or watercress leaves

1 In a medium bowl, combine the blue cheese, cream cheese, and cream. Mix until mostly smooth but still slightly chunky.

2 Preheat the broiler. Cut the buns in half. Spread one side with horseradish mayonnaise, the other with blue cheese spread (not too thick). Pile the beef over the mayonnaise side, top with lots of caramelized onions, and dot with a little more cheese mixture. Place under the broiler for a minute, until bubbly and hot. Top with arugula or watercress and drizzle with more horseradish mayo. Close, cut in half diagonally, and serve while warm. Serves 4.

Monster Beef Ribs

This is the real Flintstone-style feed—up to your ears in gigantic, sticky beef ribs. Don't confuse these with short ribs; these are the kind of big ribs that come from rib roasts. If you can't find them at the supermarket, ask your favorite butcher. Serve the ribs with baked potatoes, coleslaw, and lots of napkins. It's pre-history in the making.

1 Tbsp (15 mL) brown sugar
1 Tbsp (15 mL) paprika
1 Tbsp (15 mL) dry mustard

1 Tbsp (15 mL) black pepper
1 Tbsp (15 mL) granulated garlic
5 lb (2.2 kg) meaty beef side or back ribs

Sauce
1 Tbsp (15 mL) canola oil
1 medium yellow onion, minced
3 cloves garlic, minced
1½ cups (375 mL) ketchup
½ cup (125 mL) bottled chili sauce

½ cup (125 mL) strong brewed coffee
¼ cup (60 mL) brown sugar
¼ cup (60 mL) molasses
1 Tbsp (15 mL) Worcestershire sauce
2 tsp (10 mL) Asian chili paste or chipotle chili
    in adobo sauce

1 Combine the 1 Tbsp (15 mL) of brown sugar with the paprika, mustard, black pepper, and garlic. Rub over the entire ribs. Place the ribs in a large Dutch oven, and roast at 450°F (230°C) for 20 minutes.

2 Meanwhile, in a saucepan, heat the oil over medium heat. Sauté the onion and garlic for 5 minutes or until softened and fragrant. Add the ketchup, chili sauce, coffee, ¼ cup (60 mL) brown sugar, molasses, Worcestershire, and chili paste. Bring to a boil. Reduce the heat to medium-low and simmer for 15 minutes.

3 Remove the ribs from the oven, drain, and discard any excess fat. Pour the sauce over the ribs, cover the pot, and return it to the oven. Reduce the heat to 300°F (150°C) and cook for 1½ to 2 hours or until the meat is tender and almost falling off the bones.

4 Transfer the pot to the stovetop, remove the lid, and simmer, basting the ribs with the sauce until it is reduced and the ribs are well-glazed. Serves 4.

Beef and Beer Stew

Like wine, beer is more than a beverage: it's an integral ingredient in many soups, sauces, and stews (like this one). The Guy has his favorite microbrewed ale, which he uses in this and other beer-based concoctions, but you can use your own favorite dark ale. This stew is even better the next day, when the flavors have had a chance to meld and soften. Serve it, of course, with a pint.

2 Tbsp (30 mL) vegetable oil
2 lb (1 kg) round steak, cut into large cubes
2 large white onions, thinly sliced
3 cloves garlic, minced
2 to 3 Tbsp (30 to 45 mL) all-purpose flour
½ tsp (2 mL) salt
½ tsp (2 mL) freshly ground black pepper
1 tsp (5 mL) chopped fresh thyme leaves

1 bay leaf, crumbled
one 12-oz (375-mL) bottle dark beer
3 Tbsp (45 mL) dark brown sugar
2 Tbsp (30 mL) tomato paste
1 lb (500 g) baby potatoes, unpeeled and
   steamed
¼ cup (60 mL) chopped fresh parsley

1 Preheat the oven to 325°F (160°C).

2 In a Dutch oven, heat the oil over medium-high heat and sear the beef in batches until nicely browned on all sides. Don't be tempted to add all of the meat at once—it will cool the pan and the meat will stew instead of sear. Remove the beef from the pan as it's browned and set aside. When all the beef has been browned, add the onion and garlic to the pot. Reduce the heat to medium-low and cook for 15 to 20 minutes or until the onions are nicely browned. Return the beef to the pot. Stir the flour into the pan juices, and season with the salt, pepper, thyme, and bay leaf. Add the beer, sugar, and tomato paste and stir well. Increase the heat to medium-high and bring the stew to a boil. Cover the pot and transfer to the oven. Braise for 2 hours. Return to the pot to the stovetop and uncover. Simmer over medium heat until the stew is nicely thickened.

3 Stir in the steamed potatoes (or serve around the stew) and sprinkle with fresh parsley. Serves 6.

Chicken-Fried Steak

This is the poor man's answer to what to do with less-than-tender cuts of beef. Buy the pre-pounded "minute steak" from the supermarket or, if you'd rather, start with boneless round steak and tenderize it yourself by pounding it with a meat mallet (The Guy finds this can be a great stress reliever). Chicken-fried steak is traditionally served with a creamy gravy made from the pan drippings, but you can also serve it as a big cowboy-style sandwich, piled with lettuce, tomatoes, and spicy Chipotle Aioli (see page 38).

1½ cups (375 mL) all-purpose flour
1 tsp (5 mL) salt
1 tsp (5 mL) freshly ground black pepper
3 lb (1.5 kg) tenderized "minute steak", cut into
   6 portions
1 egg

¼ cup (60 mL) milk
¼ cup (60 mL) vegetable oil for frying
2 Tbsp (30 mL) all-purpose flour
2 cups (500 mL) milk or half-and-half cream
salt and freshly ground black pepper

1 Combine the 1½ cups (375 mL) of flour with the salt and pepper on a large plate. Toss the steaks with the flour to coat well on both sides. Pound the steaks with a meat mallet to incorporate the flour.

2 In a medium bowl, beat together the egg and milk. Using tongs, dip each steak in the egg mixture, shaking off any excess. Dredge both sides of the meat in the flour mixture again and set aside on a plate.

3 In a large, heavy-bottomed frying pan, heat ¼ inch (5 mm) of oil over medium-high heat. Test it with a drop of water—when the oil sizzles, it's hot enough. Add the breaded steaks to the pan and brown in batches, 1 to 2 minutes per side. Return all of the browned steaks to the pan and reduce the heat to medium. Add ¼ cup (60 mL) of water and cover. Cook for 8 minutes, until the meat is cooked through. Remove from the pan, place on a platter and and place into a warm oven while you make the gravy.

4 For the gravy, stir the flour into the pan, scraping up any browned bits from the bottom. Slowly add the milk or cream, and bring to a boil while stirring. Simmer until the gravy is thick and smooth. Season with salt and pepper and serve over the steaks. Serves 6.

Mahogany-Glazed Short Ribs

With a thick mahogany glaze, this recipe for braised beef has an exotic air about it, even though it's as easy to make as any stew. Look for meaty, boneless short ribs that have been trimmed of all visible fat. Five-spice powder is a Chinese spice blend—a mixture of dark, exotic spices like star anise, cloves, cinnamon, fennel seed, and Szechuan peppercorns.

1 Tbsp (15 mL) extra virgin olive oil
2 lb (1 kg) boneless beef short ribs
1 yellow onion, slivered
1 Tbsp (15 mL) minced fresh ginger
1 tsp (5 mL) minced garlic
1 tsp (5 mL) Asian chili paste

2 cups (500 mL) beef broth
1 cinnamon stick
1 tsp (5 mL) Chinese five-spice powder
2 Tbsp (30 mL) brown sugar
2 Tbsp (30 mL) soy sauce
2 green onions, cut into 1-inch (2.5-cm) slivers

1 In a deep Dutch oven, heat the oil over medium-high heat. Add the short ribs and cook in batches until they are browned well on all sides. Drain any excess fat and discard. Add the onion and cook together with the short ribs until the onion begins to brown.

2 Stir in the ginger, garlic, and chili paste and cook for 1 minute. Add the broth, cinnamon stick, five-spice powder, brown sugar, and soy sauce. Bring to a boil, cover and reduce the heat to medium-low. Simmer for 1 hour.

3 Remove the lid and simmer uncovered for 30 to 40 minutes longer, until the beef is very tender and the sauce is thickened. Transfer the ribs to a platter. Skim any excess fat from the surface of the sauce. Season the sauce with additional chili paste if you would like it spicier. Pour the sauce over the meat and scatter the green onion slivers over top. Serve with steamed basmati rice. Serves 4 to 6.

Swiss Steak

How this relates to fondue and chocolate—those Swiss staples—The Guy can't say. But this is a favorite recipe for inexpensive round steak and other tougher cuts of beef. To speed up preparation, you can use the already-tenderized minute steaks from the supermarket. Serve with noodles, polenta, or baked potatoes. This is the perfect dish to reheat for leftovers—it's even better the next day.

2 lb (1 kg) round steak, cut into ½-inch (1-cm) thick pieces

½ cup (125 mL) all-purpose flour, seasoned with salt and pepper

¼ cup (60 mL) bacon fat (or a combination of butter and olive oil)

½ cup (125 mL) chopped yellow onion

1 cup (250 mL) chopped green onion

⅓ cup (75 mL) chopped celery

¾ cup (175 mL) chopped red or yellow bell pepper

1 cup (250 mL) chopped fresh or canned tomatoes

½ cup (125 mL) water or beef broth

½ cup (125 mL) red wine

1 tsp (5 mL) salt

¼ tsp (1 mL) freshly ground black pepper

½ tsp (2 mL) dried thyme

1 bay leaf

1 tsp (5 mL) Asian chili paste

1 Tbsp (15 mL) Worcestershire sauce

2 Tbsp (30 mL) chopped fresh parsley

1 Cut the steak into 4 or 6 serving-sized pieces. Place the seasoned flour on a work surface and, using a meat mallet, pound the steaks on both sides into the flour until they are ¼ inch (5 mm) thick. Incorporate as much flour as the meat will absorb and reserve the excess.

2 In a Dutch oven or deep sauté pan, heat the bacon fat over medium-high heat and brown the meat well on both sides. Cook the steaks in batches—they'll brown better if you don't crowd the pan.

3 Add the remaining seasoned flour to the fat in the pan and stir to make a paste. Cook, stirring constantly, until the mixture turns brown (about the color of peanut butter). Add the onions, green onions, celery, and bell pepper. Cook for 5 minutes, then stir in the tomatoes, water or broth, and wine. Add the salt, pepper, thyme, bay leaf, chili paste, and Worcestershire. Bring to a boil and return the meat to the pan.

4 Reduce the heat to low, cover, and simmer for about 1½ hours (or transfer to the oven and bake for 2 hours in a 300°F/150°C oven). For the best flavor, make the steak the night before and reheat it. Sprinkle with parsley before serving. Serves 4 to 6.

The Italian Stallion

Pasta meals are perfect for weekdays, but you do get into that jar-of-tomato-sauce-and-spaghetti rut, don't you? The Guy believes there is a time for a jar of basic tomato sauce but you'd better be ready to "torque it up" with some fresh herbs and spices. Or better yet, get yourself to a good Italian market, pick up some authentic ingredients—good quality extra virgin olive oil, pure Italian sausage (free from fillers and additives), basil pesto, imported risotto rice, real Parmigiano Reggiano, and hard durum wheat pasta—and learn to make your favorite Italian food from scratch. You'll never be stuck with plain tomato sauce or mushy pasta again. Viva Italia!

Italian Sausage Sauce

The mamma of all meat sauces! Using real Italian sausage, from a reputable Italian grocer, will make your spaghetti sauce sing "O Solo Mio" or maybe even "New York, New York." The Guy uses Italian sausage meat (pulled out of its casings) like other people use hamburger meat—it's fresh ground meat that's already spiced, and it's perfect to season your sauces.

1 Tbsp (15 mL) extra virgin olive oil
1 yellow onion, minced
1 lb (500 g) sweet or hot Italian sausage
2 cloves garlic, pressed
hefty splash of red or white wine

one 28-oz (796-mL) can Roma tomatoes (or the equivalent amount of meatless spaghetti sauce)
½ tsp (2 mL) dried basil
½ tsp (2 mL) dried oregano

1 In a large sauté pan, heat the oil over medium-high heat and cook the onion for 5 to 10 minutes or until tender and just beginning to color.

2 Slice the sausage casings lengthwise, remove the sausage meat, and crumble into the pan. Discard the casings. Cook the meat until it's no longer pink and begins to brown. Stir in the garlic and sauté for 1 minute. Pour in the wine, and stir to get any browned bits up from the bottom of the pan.

3 Put the tomatoes (juice and all) into the blender or food processor to purée and add to the pan (or carefully squeeze tomatoes through your fingers and into the pan to break them up). Season with basil and oregano. Cover, reduce the heat to low, and simmer for 15 minutes. That's it. Make this sauce in advance and freeze it for fast weekday suppers. Makes 4 cups (1 L).

WISE GUY:

I know I told you how you can get your frustrations out by smashing cloves of garlic (see page 500), but you can also use a garlic press—a nifty tool for guys who don't like to get their hands dirty. Peel the clove, put it in the press, close the device and squeeze. Voilà! Perfect garlic purée that's great for smooth sauces and soups, or anytime a recipe calls for minced garlic. Your microplane grater (see page 487) makes a speedy mince, too.

This is the perfect sauce to—

🍅 Toss with short, chunky pasta like penne or gnocchi (see page 148). Top with lots of freshly grated Parmesan cheese.

🍅 Layer with shredded mozzarella, grated Parmesan, ricotta cheese, and cooked lasagna noodles for instant lasagna (bake at 350°F/180°C for 45 minutes).

🍅 Spread on top of a pizza shell or pita bread, then top with pre-shredded pizza cheese and whatever else is around (from pitted black olives to onions, ham sausage, or salami) for simple home-baked pizza pies.

🍅 Spread inside a crusty Italian bun or a chunk of French baguette with sliced mozzarella and roasted peppers, then grill for a warm Italian panini sandwich.

Basic Risotto

Risotto for every day? Roger that. Risotto is a classic comfort food, and something you can make when there's nothing in the cupboard but some rice and a can of chicken broth, and a heel of Parmesan in the fridge. It's fast food too—cooked in 20 minutes flat. Once you've got the basic risotto down, you can add anything else you have kicking around to spice it up—fresh chopped herbs, a little sausage or prosciutto, or cooked veggies like chopped tomatoes, peas, asparagus, or winter squash. Or kick it up for company with wild mushrooms and prawns. Just remember, the broth-to-rice ratio is four to one. Always start with some olive oil and butter, chopped onion, and a splash of white wine, and finish with a cup or two of freshly grated Parmesan cheese. Use hot broth, add it very slowly, and stir. That's it. Really. Just remember to serve it immediately. Risotto waits for no one.

4 cups (1 L) broth (vegetable or chicken, homemade if possible)
2 Tbsp (15 mL) extra virgin olive oil
2 Tbsp (15 mL) butter
1 cup (250 mL) minced yellow onion

1 clove garlic, minced
1 cup (250 mL) risotto rice (arborio, carnaroli, or vialone nano)
½ cup (125 mL) white wine
1 cup (250 mL) freshly grated Parmesan cheese

1 Bring the broth to a boil in a saucepan over high heat, then reduce the heat to low to keep the broth hot.

2 Meanwhile, in a wide, non-stick sauté pan, heat the oil and butter over medium-high heat. Add the onion and garlic and cook for 5 minutes until softened but not browned. Stir in the rice and cook for about a minute, until the rice is coated and shiny. Then add the wine, stirring until it is completely absorbed. (Pour yourself a glass, too. You'll be standing here for awhile.)

3 Now begin adding the hot broth, about ½ cup (125 mL) at a time. Stir the risotto with a wooden spoon until the broth is absorbed, then add another ½ cup (125 mL) of broth, stirring until it too is absorbed. Continue in this manner until the broth is used up and the rice is cooked al dente (toothsome and tender, but not mushy). Don't worry about stirring constantly or vigorously—the risotto will be fine even if you almost ignore it. But do remember to stir occasionally, and don't add the broth all at once. The more you stir, and the more attention you pay, the creamier the end result. You'll have to start tasting the rice before all of the broth is used up to determine when it's ready. The entire cooking process will take 20 to 25 minutes.

4 Stir in the Parmesan cheese and another 2 Tbsp (30 mL) of broth, then cover the pan and let the risotto rest for 2 minutes. Serve in wide and shallow bowls, and sprinkled with additional grated cheese. Serves 4.

WISE GUY: The Guy knows a Guy who is legendary for his perfectly al dente risotto. His secret? The best carnaroli risotto rice money can buy (imported from Italy and more than fifteen bucks a pound!)

Whatever rice you use for risotto, it must be a short-grain rice like arborio, the aforementioned carnaroli, or vialone nano (the latter makes the creamiest risotto). Risotto is all about releasing the starch from the rice and getting it into a creamy sauce that binds the whole dish together. It just won't work with long-grain or converted rice, so don't even attempt it.

Get to a good Italian grocery store, buy some good-quality rice and real Parmigiano Reggiano (Parmesan) cheese, and learn to make this simple dish. It's easy—really.

Extras

For wild mushroom risotto, sauté ½ cup (125 mL) fresh (or dry and rehydrated), sliced wild mushrooms (porcini, morel, chanterelle, or portobello) with the onion and garlic. For extra flavor, rehydrate dry mushrooms in white wine.

If you want to add other vegetables that require some cooking (like fresh asparagus, peas, cubed squash, or chopped spinach), add them to the rice after about 10 minutes of cooking.

If you have leftover roasted or grilled vegetables, add them with the cheese at the end. Or you can purée 1 cup (250 mL) of cooked veggies with 2 Tbsp (30 mL) of melted butter in the food processor (this works well with anything from steamed asparagus, to peas, spinach, carrots, roasted red peppers, or pumpkin). Stir the purée into the risotto at the end (the perfect way to add instant color).

Large, peeled and deveined prawns can be added halfway through the cooking time (around the 10-minute mark) or smaller shrimp can be halved lengthwise and stirred in at the end, just before the resting period. They will cook perfectly in the hot rice.

Minced fresh herbs (basil, thyme, parsley, or rosemary) can go in at the end, too.

Saffron gives the risotto an exotic flavor and gorgeous golden color—just crumble a few saffron threads into the hot broth before adding it to the rice.

Vary the cheese. Try stirring some aged Friulano, blue cheese, or even goat cheese into your risotto.

Homemade Potato Gnocchi

The Guy learned from chef Nick that gnocchi (a hearty, dumpling-like pasta) can be made quickly and efficiently by rolling the dough into thick, 1-inch (2.5-cm) sheets, then simply cutting it into long 1-inch wide strips (rather than rolling it into ropes). You can even use a special rolling pin to add the classic ridges to the dough before cutting it. The strips are simply cut into cubes, and squeezed between your fingers to give them a classic pillowy appearance. Make a bunch of these fluffy potato dumplings and set them on a lightly floured tray. To cook, add them carefully to a big pot of boiling, salted water, stir them gently, and wait for them to pop up to the surface. A classic sauce to toss with the hot gnocchi is basil pesto or smooth tomato sauce, cut with a little cream (see page 153), or creamy gorgonzola (blue cheese) sauce. Once you master these basic gnocchi recipes you can search out more exotic recipes that use ingredients like ricotta, puréed winter squash and spinach. If you're a Guy who likes his potatoes, you're gonna love gnocchi!

1 lb (500 g) white baking potatoes (about 4)   1 tsp (5 mL) salt
⅔ to 1 cup (150 to 250 mL) all-purpose flour

1 Puncture the potatoes with a fork and bake them at 400°F (200°C) for about 30 minutes or until soft. Cool slightly and cut them in half. Scoop the hot flesh into a large bowl and mash well, or put it through a ricer. Add the flour and salt and knead until the dough just comes together. If you knead the gnocchi too long, you risk incorporating too much flour, which equals heavy, not ethereal, dumplings. The dough should be just a bit sticky.

2 On a floured surface or large cutting board, roll or pat the dough into a rectangle, about 1 inch (2.5 cm) thick. Cut into 1-inch (2.5-cm) strips, then cut each strip into bite-sized, rectangular dumplings. Roll each dumpling lightly along the back of a fork (this is optional but gives the gnocchi its classic ridges) and press the ends in to plump and round the pieces. Place the dumplings on a lightly floured baking tray in a single layer. They can be stored in the refrigerator, lightly covered, for up to 24 hours, or cooked immediately.

3 To cook the gnocchi, bring a large pot of salted water to a boil. Add a few dumplings at a time, stir gently so the gnocchi don't stick together. Cook the gnocchi in batches. When the gnocchi float to the surface, boil them for another 30 seconds, then lift them out of the water using a slotted spoon. Toss with pesto, melted butter, and herbs—or your favorite sauce—and serve. Serves 4.

WISE GUY:

The secret to fluffy gnocchi is using the right potato—a dry Russet type potato is necessary; waxier red potatoes won't make good gnocchi. If you find that your gnocchi disintegrate in boiling water, you may not have used enough flour, or you may be boiling the water too vigorously. Gnocchi are simple peasant food, good simply tossed with olive oil and garlic; butter, fresh herbs, and freshly grated Parmesan cheese; or tomato or gorgonzola sauce. For the latter, just simmer some heavy cream with a little crumbled gorgonzola cheese, pour over the gnocchi, and toss with pepper and freshly grated Parmesan. Chopped fresh herbs, whether you use sage, basil, or oregano, are always good with gnocchi.

Simple Spinach and Ricotta Lasagna

All the ingredients you need for this speedy vegetarian lasagna are available at the supermarket, ready to combine after work for a fast supper. With a box of oven-ready lasagna noodles (that means you don't even have to boil them), a jar of tomato sauce, a bag of shredded Italian cheese mix, a tub of ricotta, and a box of frozen chopped spinach, this is assembly-line cooking at its best. Just chop an onion and pop the cork on your favorite Chianti. You can even make it in a disposable pan. That's amore!

1 box oven-ready lasagna noodles
   (9 to 12 noodles)
3 cups (750 mL) homemade tomato sauce (or one
   jar good quality tomato sauce), divided
2 Tbsp (30 mL) olive oil
1 medium yellow onion, chopped
1 clove garlic, minced
one 10-oz (300-mL) package chopped frozen
   spinach, thawed and squeezed to remove
   excess moisture

salt and freshly ground black pepper
1 large egg
pinch white pepper
pinch ground nutmeg
2 cups (500 mL) ricotta cheese
1½ cups (375 mL) shredded Italian cheese
   mixture (mozzarella and Parmesan), divided

1 Pour 1 cup (250 mL) of the tomato sauce into a rectangular 9- x 14-inch lasagna pan to cover the bottom. Place three or four lasagna noodles side by side, close together but not touching (the noodles will expand slightly as they cook).

2 In a sauté pan over medium-high heat, heat the olive oil and sauté the onion and garlic for 5 minutes or until the onion is soft and just beginning to brown. Stir in the chopped spinach and heat through, seasoning with salt and pepper to taste. Spread the cooked spinach mixture evenly over the noodles in the pan. Top with three or four more noodles, and 1 cup (250 mL) of the sauce.

3 In a bowl, beat the egg. Add the white pepper, nutmeg, ricotta cheese, and ½ cup (125 mL) of the Italian cheese mixture. Mix well and spread evenly over the noodles and sauce. Top with three or four additional noodles. Pour the remaining sauce over top and sprinkle evenly with remaining cheese.

4 Place in a 350°F (180°C) oven for 40 to 45 minutes or until the noodles are tender and the cheese is bubbling and lightly browned. Let the lasagna stand for 10 minutes to cool and set before cutting and serving. Serves 6.

Pasta Fresca

Take some fresh tomatoes, basil, olive oil, and a few shards of good Parmesan cheese. Toss it all together with hot, chunky pasta and you'll be eating before the fat lady sings. Add some capers for a shot of acidity—if you like that sort of thing. A dab of chili paste is good for guys who like to spice it up.

2 cups (500 mL) sweet, vine-ripened tomatoes
a handful of fresh, basil leaves, slivered
2 cloves garlic, minced
1 tsp (5 mL) top quality balsamic vinegar
  (balsamico)
¼ cup (60 mL) extra virgin olive oil

1 Tbsp (15 mL) capers (optional)
salt and freshly ground black pepper
¾ lb (375 g) short pasta (such as gemeli, rotini,
  or orechiette)
2 oz (50 g) Parmesan cheese, grated or slivered

1 The tomatoes must be really ripe and tasty for this dish—make it in the height of summer, with tomatoes fresh from the vine. Or use really good quality tomatoes from a can, drained and seeded.

2 Chop the tomatoes by hand into small pieces. In a large bowl, combine the tomatoes with the basil, garlic, balsamic, and olive oil. Stir in the capers, if using. Squish and mash everything around with a fork and set aside at room temperature to marry.

3 Cook the pasta in lots of boiling, salted water until it's cooked al dente (tender but still firm to the bite), about 8 to 12 minutes, depending on the size of the pasta you choose. Drain the pasta well and toss with the fresh tomato sauce while hot. Season with salt and pepper. Top with Parmesan cheese to serve. Serves 3 to 4.

WISE GUY: Turn this into a puttanesca sauce by adding some chopped black olives (the air-dried kind are more assertive), and a spoonful of spicy chili paste. Fast and easy, like its namesake.

Easy Eggplant Parmesan

Start with a fat purple eggplant, slice and sauté it, then layer it like lasagna noodles with cheese and a simple sauce (or your favorite bottled tomato sauce), and voilà! An easy and elegant vegetarian dinner for four. Just add a green salad.

Sauce

½ cup (125 mL) extra virgin olive oil, divided
2 cloves garlic, minced
1 small onion, minced
½ cup (125 mL) white wine
½ tsp (2 mL) hot chili paste
1 14-oz (385-mL) can plum tomatoes, crushed
½ tsp (2 mL) sugar
½ tsp (2 mL) salt

2 Tbsp (30 mL) chopped fresh basil (or 2 tsp/ 10 mL dried basil)
1½ lb (750 g) eggplant (about 1 large)
salt
½ cup (125 mL) flour, seasoned with ¼ tsp (1 mL) freshly ground black pepper
1¼ cup (310 mL) finely grated Parmesan cheese, divided
1 cup (250 mL) shredded mozzarella cheese

1 In a saucepan, heat ¼ cup (60 mL) of the olive oil over medium heat. Add the garlic and onion and cook together, stirring occasionally, until the onion is tender and begins to brown. Add the white wine and simmer for 5 minutes or until most of the liquid has cooked away. Stir in the chili paste and crushed tomatoes (crush them through your fingers into the pan or whirl them in a blender or food processor). Bring to a boil, then simmer for 15 minutes or until slightly thickened. Season with sugar and salt to taste, and stir in the basil. Set aside.

2 Meanwhile, slice the eggplant crosswise into ¼-inch (5-mm) rounds. Salt the eggplant on both sides and set in a colander in the sink for 20 minutes (this will draw out any bitter juices). Rinse the eggplant with water and press between paper towels to dry.

3 Spread the seasoned flour on a plate. Heat 2 Tbsp (30 mL) of the olive oil in a non-stick pan over medium-high heat. Dip the eggplant slices in the flour, shake off any excess, and place into the hot pan. Fry quickly, a few minutes per side, until nicely browned, then drain on paper towels.

EGGPLANT

4 In a bowl, combine the Parmesan and mozzarella cheeses.

5 To assemble, brush a shallow 9- x 14-inch (3.5 L) rectangular baking dish (or a 10-inch/25-cm round, shallow baking dish) with olive oil. Place a thin layer of tomato sauce in the bottom of the dish. Top with half the eggplant slices (overlap to fit), half the sauce, and half the cheese. Repeat the layers and bake at 350°F (180°C) for 30 to 40 minutes or until bubbly and lightly browned. Let stand for 10 minutes before cutting. Serves 4.

Baked Rigatoni with Spicy Sausage and Creamy Tomato Sauce

The spicy Italian sausage in this simple sauce is tempered by the cream, but it's still a zesty combination. Start with a good quality, lean Italian pork sausage—there should be little or no fat in the pan when you sauté the sausage. If there is, drain the fat before proceeding with the recipe, and buy a different brand next time. Serve a low-tannin red wine—a simple Chianti or Valpolicella—to match this rich and assertive sauce.

1 lb (500 g) spicy Italian sausages, casings removed, crumbled
4 garlic cloves, finely chopped
1 yellow or green bell pepper, cut into slivers
1 lb (500 g) cherry tomatoes, halved (or one 28-oz/796 mL can diced tomatoes)
1 cup (125 mL) chicken or beef broth

½ cup (125 mL) whipping cream
1 lb (500 g) rigatoni (or other short pasta like penne, cavatapi, or rotini)
1 cup (250 mL) freshly grated Parmesan cheese
1 cup (250 mL) grated mozzarella cheese
½ cup (125 mL) fresh basil leaves, slivered
freshly grated Parmesan cheese, for garnish

1 Heat a large saucepan over medium-high heat and add the crumbled sausage. Saute for 5 to 10 minutes or until it begins to brown. Add a splash of olive oil if the sausage is very lean. Add the garlic and bell pepper to the pan and sauté for 5 minutes. Stir in the cherry tomatoes and cook 1 minute longer. Add the broth and stir up any brown bits from the bottom of the pan. Bring to a boil and cook for 5 minutes or until the broth has reduced by half. Reduce heat to low and simmer. Slowly add the whipping cream and simmer until the sauce is thick enough to coat the back of a spoon.

2 Meanwhile, cook the pasta until al dente (tender but still firm to the bite). Drain and mix with the sauce. Stir in the basil.

3 Rub a 9- x 13-inch (3.5-L) baking dish with olive oil. Pour half of the pasta into the dish. Combine the two cheeses. Scatter half of the cheese mixture over the pasta, then fill the dish with the remaining pasta and top with the remaining cheese. Bake at 375°F (190°C) for 20 to 30 minutes or until the cheese is bubbly and browned on top. Serves 6.

Sideman

A guy is nothing without his "sideman," the one who adds that back-up riff to make everything harmonize and hang together.

So while The Guy likes to keep his cooking simple—a grilled chicken breast, steak, or pan-fried chop—it's often the stuff on the side that makes his meals sing.

When time is at a premium, his sides are frequently rice and green salad (the latter topped with a sliced tomato and/or cucumber and a splash of bottled dressing). But there are simple ways to improve your side dishes, even if it's only mashed potatoes and peas.

Herewith, a collection of The Guy's favorite sidekicks—inspired solutions to that ubiquitous question of what to serve on the side.

Perfect Mashed Potatoes

What makes the perfect mashed potatoes? The Guy has had advice on this topic from several pros. Here's what they recommend:

1 Start with the right kind of potato. Yellow-fleshed bintje and Yukon Gold potatoes are buttery in color and almost mash themselves when cooked. But any baking potato (i.e. Idaho) is good for mashing.

2 Steam your potatoes rather than boiling them so they won't get waterlogged when you mash them.

3 Some chefs insist on boiling potatoes whole in their "jackets" (skins) to keep them dry and fluffy, then peeling the boiled potatoes while they are still hot (you'll need an oven mitt), and then putting them through a ricer rather than mashing. A ricer makes the smoothest mash.

4 Never mash potatoes in a food processor—they just get gummy.

5 If your potatoes are new and the skins are thin, don't peel them at all. Just wash well, boil, and make a chunky mash.

6 When mashing potatoes, add the butter first and fully incorporate before adding cream or milk. Using warm cream or milk, rather than cold, makes creamier mashed potatoes.

7 Anything creamy adds richness to mashed potatoes. Use whipping cream or triple-cream mascarpone cheese for really decadent potatoes. Or cut the fat way back by using evaporated skim milk, quark cheese, plain yogurt, or puréed cottage cheese.

8 Think about flavoring your mashed spuds with cheddar cheese, Parmigiano Reggiano, blue cheese, or goat cheese. Or stir in a little horseradish or chopped herbs.

9 When you're on a diet, skip the butter and add just a touch of olive oil and skim milk, then season with roasted garlic. Mash with the skins for extra fiber and vitamins.

Garlic Mashed Potatoes

This is the starch The Guy serves with almost everything—creamy, golden-fleshed potatoes flecked with sweet, nutty, roasted garlic. If you don't have roasted garlic in your fridge (shame on you, it's one of The Guy's tricks of the trade), just add four whole peeled cloves to the potatoes while boiling and then mash the boiled garlic into the potato purée (not as good, but passable).

3 lb (1.5 kg) yellow-fleshed potatoes like Yukon Gold (about 6 medium-sized potatoes)
2 tsp (10 mL) salt
4 Tbsp (60 mL) butter

½ cup (125 mL) whipping cream (half-and-half or milk if you're more virtuous)
white pepper
1 head garlic, roasted (see page 17)

1 Peel the potatoes and cut each into 6 to 8 pieces. Put the potatoes in a large pot and cover with cold water. Add the salt and bring to a boil over high heat. Reduce the heat to medium, cover, and simmer for 15 to 20 minutes or until the potatoes are just tender.

2 Drain well, then return the pot of potatoes to the stove, shaking it to allow excess moisture to steam away. Mash the potatoes by hand with a masher or fork. Stir in the butter and cream. Season with white pepper to taste.

3 Squeeze the roasted garlic out of the papery skins right into the potatoes and stir well to combine. Serve immediately or place in a bowl, cover with plastic wrap, and chill. Reheat in the microwave before serving. Serves 6 to 8.

ROASTED GARLIC

WISE GUY:

Other root vegetables are delicious when mashed with potatoes. The Guy likes to add sweet potatoes, carrots, and parsnips to the pot and then mash with a mixture of chopped onions and ginger that have been sautéed together in butter (see "Topping" sub-recipe, page 130). Mmmmm.

Lemony Lentils

When you're grilling salmon, halibut, or even lamb chops, consider a side dish of simple French lentils (the tiny green or black ones), seasoned with lemon, herbs, and olive oil. You can also use brown lentils, but don't use red lentils—they disintegrate when cooked, so are best in soups or spreads.

1 cup (250 mL) French lentils
3 cups (750 mL) water
bouquet garnis (1 sprig thyme, 1 sprig rosemary, and 1 bay leaf tied together in a small muslin bag, or fill a tea ball with 1 tsp/5 mL dried thyme, 1 tsp/5 mL dried rosemary, and 1 bay leaf)
1 medium carrot, peeled and quartered
2 cloves garlic, peeled but left whole

Dressing
zest of 1 lemon
3 Tbsp (45 mL) freshly squeezed lemon juice (about 1 lemon)
1 Tbsp (15 mL) Dijon mustard
1 tsp (5 mL) salt
2 tsp (10 mL) chopped fresh thyme (or 1 tsp/ 5 mL dried thyme)
¼ cup (60 mL) extra virgin olive oil
freshly ground black pepper
3 green onions, chopped
¼ cup (60 mL) chopped roasted red pepper (from a jar is okay)

1 In a saucepan, combine the lentils, water, bouquet garni, carrot, and whole garlic cloves. Bring to a boil over high heat. Reduce heat to medium-low and simmer for 20 to 30 minutes or until the lentils are just tender but still firm. Drain the lentils and discard the bouquet garni, carrot, and garlic.

2 Use a microplane grater to remove the yellow zest from the lemon (or carefully peel it off with a vegetable peeler and mince until very fine). Combine the zest with the lemon juice, mustard, salt, and thyme. Slowly add the olive oil, whisking as you go, to emulsify and thicken the dressing. You can also combine everything except the oil in a blender, then add the oil slowly through the feed tube, with the machine running, until the dressing is emulsified. Season with pepper to taste.

3 Place the warm lentils in a bowl and toss with the dressing. Stir in the chopped roasted red pepper and the green onions. Serve the lentils warm as a base for grilled lamb or fish.
Serves 4 to 6.

A Great Green Salad

(with Three Speedy Dressings)

It's never been easier to toss together a green salad that goes with anything you're serving. The Guy likes to buy pre-washed mixed baby greens, mixed herb salad, and romaine hearts, and combine all three. A handful of watercress or pea shoots add crunch.

4 cups (1 L) mixed salad greens

2 tomatoes, seeded and chopped (or ½ cup/125 mL cherry tomatoes)

1 green onion, chopped

1 If you're not using pre-washed, bagged greens, wash the greens in a sink full of cold water and spin dry in a salad spinner. (If you're not using them immediately after washing, pack loosely in a plastic bag with a piece of paper towel, seal, and refrigerate for several hours or overnight—this will ensure your salad is crisp.)

2 Right before you're ready to serve the salad, toss everything together in a salad bowl and top with your favorite bottled dressing (just a small amount) or one of the following speedy combinations:

Buttermilk Ranch Dressing

This is a simple, old-fashioned combo—but still a winner.

½ cup (125 mL) buttermilk or plain yogurt

¼ cup (60 mL) bottled tomato salsa or bottled chili sauce

2 Tbsp (30 mL) mayonnaise

¼ tsp (1 mL) sugar

¼ tsp (1 mL) dillweed

¼ tsp (1 mL) dry mustard

salt and white pepper

1 Whirl all the ingredients in a blender or food processor until smooth and creamy. Transfer to a covered container and refrigerate for up to three days. Makes 1 cup (250 mL).

Creamy Miso Dressing

Added to any greens, this dressing makes an Asian-inspired salad.

½ cup (125 mL) mayonnaise
1 Tbsp (15 mL) dark miso
1 tsp (5 mL) minced ginger
1 tsp (5 mL) minced garlic

1 tsp (5 mL) sugar
1 tsp (5 mL) rice vinegar
1 tsp (5 mL) sesame oil

1 Whirl all the ingredients in a blender or food processor until creamy. Transfer to a covered container and refrigerate for up to three days. Makes ¾ cup (175 mL).

Green Goddess

A thicker dressing that's great on a chunky romaine or chopped salad, and perfect on potato salad.

⅔ cup (150 mL) mayonnaise
2 green onions, chopped
¼ cup (60 mL) fresh parsley and
   dill (or a mix of fresh herbs)

1 tsp (5 mL) Dijon mustard
1 tsp (5 mL) granulated sugar
salt and freshly ground black pepper
¼ cup (60 mL) extra virgin olive oil

1 Whirl all the ingredients in a blender or food processor until smooth and creamy. Transfer to a covered container and refrigerate for up to three days. Makes 1 cup (250 mL).

WISE GUY: Feel free to add anything to your green salad that's in the fridge, from chopped bell peppers and cucumbers to toasted pine nuts and Parmesan cheese. For a main event, top your salad with cubed leftover chicken, chickpeas, or sliced steak.

And remember, there's no reason to stick with one leafy green in your salad bowl. There's so much more than iceberg and romaine lettuce available at the supermarket—and when summer rolls around, the selection of green stuff is almost endless. Make sure you add something soft and simple (leaf or butter lettuce), something crunchy (slivered iceberg or romaine), something spicy (mustard greens, watercress, nasturtium leaves from your flower garden, or peppery arugula), and something unusual (pea shoots, beet greens, or fresh herbs such as basil or dill). Your salads will sing.

Rosti

The other favorite potato dish at The Guy's house is a big crispy potato pancake—also known as "rosti." Haul out the seasoned cast iron skillet for this simply addictive side.

2 Tbsp (30 mL) butter, melted
2 Tbsp (30 mL) extra virgin olive oil

4 large baking potatoes, peeled and shredded
    (use a hand grater, a mandoline, or the
    grating blade on your food processor)
salt and freshly ground black pepper

1 In a large, heavy, non-stick frying pan over medium heat, add the butter and olive oil. When the fat is hot and sizzling, add the potatoes and toss well to coat. Season with salt and pepper. Use a spatula to press the potatoes down into the pan to form a pancake.

2 Reduce the heat to low and cook for 30 to 40 minutes or until the potato cake is browned on the bottom.

3 To flip the pancake and cook the second side, place a plate over top of the frying pan (it must be larger than the pan) and invert the pancake onto the plate. Using the spatula, carefully slide it back into the pan. Cook the second side for about 20 minutes or until the bottom is browned and crisp. Remove from the pan, cut the pancake into wedges, and serve. Serves 4.

MANDOLINE

WISE GUY:

You can also make these rosti potatoes into individual pancakes (called latkes). Make them 2 to 3 inches in diameter and serve for breakfast. Or make them even smaller, top with sour cream and caviar, and serve them as an appetizer.

Creamy Polenta

This is the Mediterranean version of mashed potatoes—creamy cornmeal, flavored with cheese and herbs. Serve it as a base for a mushroom ragout, meat sauce, or lamb stew. Très Provençal!

5 cups (1.25 L) water or chicken broth
1 cup (250 mL) coarse ground cornmeal
1 tsp (5 mL) salt
1 Tbsp (15 mL) butter

3 Tbsp (45 mL) sour cream
2 oz (50 g) Parmesan cheese, grated
1 Tbsp (15 mL) chopped fresh rosemary, Italian
    parsley, or basil (optional)

1 In a large pot, bring the water or broth to a rolling boil over high heat. Add the salt and butter. Slowly add the cornmeal to the pot in a steady stream, whisking as you go to prevent lumps from forming. Stir for 5 more minutes, then reduce the heat to low and continue to cook for 10 to 15 minutes, stirring to make sure the cornmeal mixture doesn't stick to the pot.

2 When nicely thickened, remove the polenta from the heat and stir in the sour cream, Parmesan cheese, and fresh herbs. Serve immediately. Serves 4 to 6.

Mushroom Ragout

This is the kind of mushroom stuff you can use as a vegetarian dish over polenta, as a sauce over steak, or as a topping for crostini appetizers (see page 286).

2 Tbsp (30 mL) butter
1 cup (250 mL) minced yellow onion
2 cloves garlic, minced
2 lb (1 kg) assorted fresh mushrooms (oyster,
    shiitake, morel, chanterelle, etc.), thickly sliced

½ tsp (2 mL) salt
¼ tsp (1 mL) freshly ground black pepper
½ cup (125 mL) vegetable broth, chicken stock,
    or white wine
¼ cup (60 mL) cream

1 Melt the butter in a wide pan and sauté the onion and garlic until soft, about 5 minutes. Add the sliced mushrooms, salt, and pepper to the pan. Cook until the mushrooms give up their liquid and begin to soften.

2 Add the broth, stock, or wine and increase the heat. Simmer until the liquid in the pan is reduced by half. Stir in the cream and bring to a boil. Cook for 1 minute, until the ragout is thick.

Zucchini and Tomato Gratin

This is the kind of thing you might be served alongside your grilled lamb or fish, while lolling on the French Riviera. It takes that ubiquitous garden summer squash into another world.

½ cup (125 mL) Caramelized Onions (see page 16)
1 clove garlic, minced
1½ lb (800 g) zucchini, sliced into thin rounds
1 lb (500 g) Roma tomatoes, thinly sliced
2 Tbsp (30 mL) extra virgin olive oil

1 Tbsp (15 mL) minced fresh thyme or rosemary
 (discard the stems)
salt and freshly ground black pepper
½ cup (125 mL) freshly grated Parmesan
 cheese

1 Preheat the oven to 400°F (200°C).

2 In a shallow round gratin dish, spread the onions and scatter the garlic on top. Arrange the zucchini and tomato slices in alternating and overlapping concentric circles, beginning at the outside of the dish with a row of zuchinni, then a row of tomatoes, etc. Drizzle with the olive oil, season with salt and pepper, and strew the minced herbs over top. Sprinkle with cheese.

3 Bake in the preheated oven for 45 to 50 minutes or until nicely browned on top. Serve at room temperature. Serves 4.

Simply Sautéed Spinach

The Guy has learned from his chef buddies that baby spinach, quickly sautéed and lightly spiced, is the best thing to serve under or alongside almost any piece of protein. Start with a bag of pre-washed baby spinach and this side dish comes together almost instantly. The trick to great spinach is making sure it's not over-cooked—when it turns electric green, it's done.

1 Tbsp (15 mL) extra virgin olive oil
1 tsp (5 mL) butter
1 clove garlic, minced

4 cups (1 L) baby spinach
1 Tbsp (15 mL) freshly squeezed orange juice
salt and freshly ground black pepper

1 Heat the oil and butter in a large sauté pan over high heat. Add the garlic and spinach and toss quickly in the pan until it begins to wilt and turn bright green (about 1 minute). Stir in the orange juice and season with salt and pepper. Serve immediately. Serves 4.

Wilted Spinach with Rice

The Guy first encountered this dish in Greece, at a Lenten lunch in a Greek Orthodox monastery. The Greeks combine all kinds of wild and bitter greens in their spanakorizo, but this version uses a big bag of baby spinach. It's become a very popular side dish to all kinds of meals among The Guy's friends, whether they're serving Greek food or not.

1 lb (500 g) fresh, pre-washed baby spinach (or a mixture of baby spinach and winter greens such as chard, dandelion, mustard, and sorrel)

¼ cup (60 mL) extra virgin olive oil

1 large yellow onion, minced

2 cloves garlic, minced

½ cup (125 mL) white or brown basmati or other long-grain rice

½ cup (125 mL) water or vegetable broth

¼ cup (60 mL) minced fresh dill, divided

1 to 2 Tbsp (15 to 30 mL) freshly squeezed lemon juice (about ½ a lemon)

salt and freshly ground black pepper

pinch of crushed red chili peppers

1 Wash the spinach well and remove any tough stems. Shred the spinach and set aside.

2 Heat the olive oil in a heavy, deep pot and cook the onions over medium heat until soft and translucent. Add the garlic and cook for 1 minute longer, being careful not to burn the garlic.

3 Add the rice and stir to coat with oil. Cook for 2 minutes. Add the spinach and stir to combine. When the spinach is starting to wilt and cook down, add the water and half of the dill. Bring to a boil, cover, and reduce the heat to low. Steam until all of the liquid is absorbed, about 20 minutes—add a little more water if necessary.

4 When the rice is tender, stir in the lemon juice and remaining dill. Season with the salt, pepper, and crushed chilies. Before serving, drizzle with a little more olive oil. If desired, garnish with lemon slices, olives, and crumbled feta. Serves 4.

Corn-on-the-Cob

Everyone knows the best corn is corn still on the cob—ferried straight from the garden to the pot. This is because the sugar in fresh corn starts turning to starch the minute it's picked. So look for the freshest corn at the market, with crisp green husks and plump, juicy kernels. If you don't plan to eat the corn right away, blanch it (immerse in boiling water for 1 minute then immediately plunge in ice water to stop the cooking process), drain, seal in a bag, and refrigerate for up to three days (this stops the sugar-to-starch conversion). You can then cook it, like fresh corn.

You can boil, steam, grill, or even microwave corn. Here's how

 Boiled

Bring a large pot of water to a rolling boil. Add 1 tsp (5 mL) of salt and 1 tsp (5 mL) of sugar, then add the cobs. Return the water to a boil, then cover the pot and remove it from the heat. Let it stand for 5 to 10 minutes. Drain and serve immediately.

 Grilled

Pull back the husks, leaving them attached at the base of the cobs, and remove the corn silk. Pull the husks back up over the cobs and tie the ends with string. Fully immerse the cobs in a sink full of cold water for 10 minutes. Grill the soaked cobs for 15 to 20 minutes, until the husks are charred and the corn is steamed. This is a great way to cook corn over the campfire.

 Microwaved

Really, this works and is easy when you're cooking just a cob or two. Remove the husks and silk from the cobs. Wrap each cob individually in plastic wrap. Microwave on high for 3 to 5 minutes per cob. Remove plastic and serve.

 Creamed

Technically, this is corn-off-the-cob—something you have to take care of first. Remove the husks and silk from the cobs. Stand the cobs upright and use a sharp knife to remove the kernels, cutting from the top to the bottom. Do this inside a big bowl (so the corn doesn't fly all over the kitchen) and so that the sweet juice is captured (scrape the cobs to release all of the juice). For 4 cups (1 L) of kernels, sauté ¼ cup (60 mL) of onion in ¼ cup (60 mL) of butter until tender, then add the kernels, 3 Tbsp (45 mL) of maple syrup, and ⅓ cup (75 mL) of whipping cream. Bring to a boil and simmer until thick. Season with salt and pepper.

Cucumber Salad

The Guy grew up eating this easy salad alongside almost everything. Salt the cucumbers before you add the dressing to draw out excess moisture and keep the creamy sauce nice and thick.

1 long English cucumber, thinly sliced
sea salt
½ cup (125 mL) low-fat sour cream
   (or plain yogurt)
1 tsp (5 mL) white wine or rice vinegar

1 tsp (5 mL) granulated sugar
1 green onion, minced
1 Tbsp (15 mL) chopped fresh dill
freshly ground black pepper to taste

1 Place the cucumber slices in a colander and salt well on both sides. Set the colander in the sink and let the cucumbers drain for half an hour. Press the cucumber slices to release any additional juice, then rinse and squeeze dry with your hands.

2 In a salad bowl, whisk together the sour cream, vinegar, and sugar. Add the cucumber, green onion, and dill, and toss well. Season with pepper to taste. You can serve this immediately or chill for several hours. Serves 4.

Classic Coleslaw

The side dish for any barbecue—coleslaw is the perfect pairing for dishes like pulled pork sandwiches to grilled chicken—and an essential companion to fish and chips (see page 72).

1 ½-lb (750-g) head of cabbage, finely shredded
3 green onions, finely chopped
1 apple, shredded
1 carrot, shredded
½ cup (125 mL) fat-reduced mayonnaise
½ cup (125 mL) fat-free sour cream
1 Tbsp (15 mL) Dijon mustard

1 tsp (5 mL) granulated sugar
2 Tbsp (30 mL) cider vinegar
¼ tsp (1 mL) celery salt
1 Tbsp (15 mL) chopped fresh dill or 1 tsp
   (5 mL) dried dill
salt and freshly ground black pepper

1 In a large bowl, toss all the ingredients to thoroughly combine. Cover with plastic wrap and refrigerate for 1 hour or until ready to serve. Serves 8.

Pickled Asian Slaw

The Guy found a nifty gadget in Chinatown that shreds all kinds of firm vegetables—from daikon radishes and potatoes to carrots and rutabagas—into thin strands of vegetable spaghetti. Lightly pickled, with sushi vinegar and a splash of soy sauce, this slaw is perfect piled onto sandwiches or just served on the side. Once it's marinated, it keeps well in the refrigerator for days. Use a mandoline or large-holed grater to make strips or strands if you don't have the special gizmo, but look for one the next time you're at an Asian market (it's fun for making fluffy nests of deep-fried potatoes, too). You can use all three vegetables in this salad, or just choose one and triple the amount.

1 cup (250 mL) carrots, shredded or cut into
    fine matchsticks
1 cup (250 mL) rutabaga, shredded or cut into
    fine matchsticks
1 cup (250 mL) daikon radish, shredded or cut
    into fine matchsticks
2 Tbsp (30 mL) salt

2 Tbsp (30 mL) granulated sugar
¼ cup (60 mL) rice vinegar
1 Tbsp (15 mL) soy sauce
2 cups (250 mL) water
2 Tbsp (30 mL) chopped fresh cilantro
½ tsp (2 mL) sesame oil

1 Put the shredded vegetables in a colander and sprinkle with the salt. Place the colander in the sink and let the vegetables drain for one hour to remove excess moisture. After they have drained, rinse in cold water, then pat dry with paper towels (or spin in a salad spinner).

2 Transfer the vegetables to a bowl and combine with the sugar, vinegar, soy sauce, and water. Cover and refrigerate for at least 1 hour (or up to 3 days) to fully marinate. Drain and toss with the cilantro and sesame oil before serving. Makes 3 cups.

MANDOLINE

Sweet Potato Fries

Oven-baked sweet potato chips are great as a side dish with almost anything—healthy too, with their colorful carotenes.

2 large orange-fleshed sweet potatoes, peeled
2 Tbsp (30 mL) extra virgin olive oil

1 tsp (5 mL) coarse sea salt

1 Preheat the oven to 450°F (230°C).

2 Cut the potatoes lengthwise into long, fat chips. Place the chips in a bowl and toss with the olive oil. Line a baking sheet with parchment paper and arrange the potatoes in a single layer on the sheet. Sprinkle with salt.

3 Bake for 30 to 45 minutes, turning once, until the potatoes are crisp. Serves 4.

WISE GUY: If you don't mind the extra calories, try cutting the sweet potatoes into very thin ribbons (use a mandoline or a vegetable peeler) and quickly deep-fry for piles of sweet, crispy chips.

Sautéed Edamame Beans

Edamame are fresh, green soy beans—the kind they serve at the sushi bar for snacking with beer. You can buy frozen edamame, in the pod or shelled, at any Asian grocery store. Just pop the pods into the microwave with a bit of water to steam, then top with coarse sea salt. Pull the pods through your teeth to release the beans (toss the pod shells), or shell the beans and sauté for a shot of electric green color on the plate.

2 Tbsp (30 mL) extra virgin olive oil
1 clove garlic, minced
⅓ cup (75 mL) slivered shallots (about 2 to 3 shallots)
2 cups (500 mL) frozen and shelled edamame, thawed

1 Tbsp (15 mL) chopped fresh Italian parsley (or any fresh herb)
salt and freshly ground black pepper

1 In a sauté pan, heat the olive oil over medium heat. Add the garlic and shallots. Sauté for 3 to 5 minutes or until the shallots are softened and beginning to brown. Add the edamame beans and parsley. Toss to coat the beans with the herbs. Season with salt and pepper and serve. Serves 4.

Decadence

Are You (Suitably) Impressed?

There comes a time in every guy's life when he has to host a dinner that will impress someone who's really important. Whether it's the boss, the in-laws, or anyone else who needs to know what a fabulous, well-rounded, and classy guy you are, this is the meal to let them know.

Buy the best ingredients you can afford, pull out the fine, oversized white plates, make lots of lists, and be a Boy Scout (prep, prep, prep), and you'll sail through this dinner with flying colors. Who knew you were such a force behind the stove?

Root Vegetable Mash with Roasted Garlic and Onions

Here's a make-ahead side dish that hits all of The Guy's hot buttons. It combines his favorite "tricks of the trade"—including roasted garlic and caramelized onions (see page 16–17)—with veggies you can find in the supermarket any time. It's perfect alongside roast beef or a holiday turkey.

6 cups (1.5 L) chicken broth

2 lb (1 kg) potatoes, peeled and cubed

1 lb (500 g) orange-fleshed sweet potato, peeled and cubed

1 lb (500 g) rutabaga, peeled and cubed

1 lb (500 g) parsnips, peeled and cubed

1 sprig fresh thyme (or 1 tsp/5 mL dried)

1 whole head garlic, roasted (see Wise Guy tip)

½ cup (125 mL) butter, divided

¼ cup (60 mL) whipping cream or reserved cooking liquid

3 large onions, thinly sliced

salt and freshly ground black pepper

1 In a large pot, combine the broth, potatoes, sweet potato, rutabaga, parsnips, and thyme. Bring to a boil over medium-high heat. Reduce the heat to low and simmer, partially covered, for about 30 minutes or until everything is tender. Drain the vegetables, discard the sprig of thyme, and reserve the cooking liquid.

2 Squeeze the roasted garlic cloves out of their husks and into the vegetables. Add ¼ cup (60 mL) of the butter along with the cream and use a hand-held masher to mash everything together. Don't make the mash too smooth—The Guy likes to leave it a little chunky. Season with salt and pepper to taste.

3 Butter a shallow 9- x 13-inch (4-L) casserole dish and transfer the mashed vegetables to the dish. Meanwhile, in a heavy sauté pan, melt the remaining butter over medium heat and add the sliced onions. Cover the pan and cook the onions until they begin to sweat and soften. Remove the lid, reduce the heat to low, and cook the onions until they're caramelized (dark brown and jammy)—this will take 30 to 45 minutes. Mix half the caramelized onions into the mashed vegetables and spread the rest on top. (You can make the dish up to this point, then cover and refrigerate until you're ready to bake.)

4 Finish the casserole in a 350°F (180°C) oven, baking for 30 to 40 minutes or until it's nicely browned on top. Serves 8 to 10.

WISE GUY:

To roast a whole head of garlic, cut ¼ inch (5 mm) off the top of the head to expose the tips of the cloves, place the whole head on a piece of foil, drizzle with a wee bit of oil, wrap loosely and roast in a 350°F to 400°F (180°C to 200°C) oven for 45 minutes or until the garlic is soft—then squeeze the roasted garlic out of the papery husk and enjoy!

Roasted Beet and Watercress Salad with Gorgonzola Sauce

As all the best chefs know, when you really want to make a statement, stack the food. This composed salad course is basically a stacked mini-terrine of sliced, roasted beets and onions, glued together with a creamy blue cheese sauce. Chefs often use ring molds to keep their stacked creations corralled—you can use a biscuit cutter or small clean tin, with both ends removed. Look for a variety of red, pink, and yellow heirloom beets to make this composed salad stunning.

3 lb (1.5 kg) red, striped chiogga, or yellow beets, trimmed and halved
2 red onions, peeled and quartered
¼ cup (60 mL) extra virgin olive oil
1 tsp (5 mL) salt
½ tsp (2 mL) freshly ground black pepper

Gorgonzola sauce
1 Tbsp (15 mL) extra virgin olive oil
½ cup (125 mL) finely chopped or ground walnuts
1 tsp (5 mL) finely chopped fresh rosemary (leaves only, discard stems)

2 tsp (10 mL) reduced balsamic vinegar (see page xxx), plus extra for garnish
2 cups (500 mL) watercress leaves, stems removed, washed and spun dry (about 2 bunches)
½ cup (125 mL) toasted walnut halves

1 Tbsp (15 mL) balsamic vinegar
½ tsp (2 mL) salt
6 oz (175 g) soft gorgonzola cheese (or substitute garlic Boursin)
½ cup (125 mL) heavy cream

1 Preheat the oven to 425°F (220°C).

2 Arrange the beets and onions in a roasting pan. Drizzle with olive oil and season with salt and pepper. Roast for about 45 minutes, stirring occasionally, until the beets and onions are tender. Cool. Peel the beets and slice thinly into a bowl. Slice the onions and place in a separate bowl. Drizzle the reduced balsamic over both the beets and the onions, toss to coat, and set aside.

3 To make the gorgonzola sauce, heat the olive oil in a small skillet, add the chopped walnuts, and toast them for 2 minutes. Transfer the walnuts to a bowl to cool, then stir in the rosemary, balsamic, and salt. Meanwhile, combine the cheese and cream in a blender or food processor and whirl until smooth. Add to the walnut mixture and stir to combine.

4 To serve, place a small dab of gorgonzola sauce on the center of eight salad plates—just enough to secure your stacked beet salad. Top with some sliced beets, another dab of sauce, some red onions, a third dab of sauce, and more beets, forming a stack. To make this easier, use a ring mold (a small tin with both ends removed will work). Top each stack with a dollop of sauce and a tiny bouquet of watercress leaves. Arrange toasted walnut halves artfully around the edge of the plate, interspersed with drops of reduced balsamic vinegar. Serves 8.

Sautéed Oysters in Panko Crust

Panko is crisp Japanese breadcrumbs that make a particularly nice coating for fried seafood. Look for it at Asian markets. You can use pre-shucked oysters, sold in jars, for this dish. Serve with a tangy fresh fruit salsa or Wasabi Mayo (see page 38).

24 small fresh oysters, shucked
2 eggs
¼ cup (60 mL) water

2 cups (500 mL) panko (Japanese breadcrumbs)
   or other coarse dry breadcrumbs
salt and freshly ground black pepper
canola oil, for frying

1 Preheat the oven to 200°F (95°C).

2 Pat the oysters dry on paper towels and set aside. Beat together the egg and water in a small bowl and set aside. Combine the crumbs with salt and pepper on a plate. Using a fork, dip each oyster in the egg mixture, shaking off any excess liquid, then roll in the seasoned breadcrumbs to coat well. Set the coated oysters on a wire rack to dry for 30 minutes.

3 In a heavy skillet, heat ½ inch (1 cm) of oil to 375°F (190°C) and fry the oysters in batches until golden, about 2 minutes per side. Drain the oysters on a plate lined with paper towels and keep them warm in the preheated oven while you fry the remaining oysters.

4 Serve the oysters on individual plates, with a dollop of salsa or mayonnaise on the side. Serves 6 to 8 (3 to 4 oysters each).

WISE GUY: For a simple mango, apricot, or peach salsa, finely chop the peeled fruit and combine with minced red and green onion, a seeded and minced hot chili pepper, a bit of lime juice, chopped cilantro leaves, and salt and pepper to taste. You can keep the salsa in the refrigerator for up to 2 days.

Classic Prime Rib Roast

Prime rib roast (or standing rib, as it's sometimes called) is the ultimate beef roast—a top cut cooked on the bone for a dramatic presentation. Ask your butcher to "french" the rib bones, and order 1 lb (500 g) for every two people you plan to serve. You can also use this method for a whole beef tenderloin, which is equally impressive. Just remember that a tenderloin is leaner and will cook faster, so it may be ready after the first 20 to 30 minutes in the oven.

2 Tbsp (30 mL) Dijon mustard
2 Tbsp (30 mL) minced rosemary leaves
2 Tbsp (30 mL) thyme
2 Tbsp (30 mL) olive oil
6 cloves garlic, puréed in a garlic press
1 Tbsp (15 mL) Worcestershire sauce

one 6-lb (2.7-kg) prime rib roast (graded Prime or AAA)
¼ tsp (1 mL) salt
1 tsp (5 mL) coarsely cracked black peppercorns
4 to 5 Tbsp (60 to 75 mL) flour
1 cup (250 mL) red wine
1 cup (250 mL) beef stock

1 In a small bowl, combine the mustard, rosemary, thyme, olive oil, garlic, and Worcestershire sauce. Rub the meat with the mustard mixture on all sides, then season with the salt and cracked pepper. Set the roast aside at room temperature for 1 hour—you want it to reach room temperature before it goes into the oven.

2 Place the meat in a shallow roasting pan, fat-side up and bone-side down. Cook the roast in the oven at 450°F (230°C) for 20 minutes, then reduce the heat to 300°F (150°C) and continue to roast (about 10 to 15 minutes per lb) until desired doneness. Use an instant-read meat thermometer to guide you—for medium-rare, pull the roast out of the oven when the internal temperature hits 130°F to 140°F (55°C to 60°C); for well-done, take it out when the thermometer reads 155°F to 165°F (68°C to 74°C). The Guy urges you to serve this tender piece of meat at its optimal medium-rare stage but, if you must cook it well-done to please a picky but important guest, pull it at 155°F (68°C) max.

3 Place the roast on a platter and tent with foil to keep it warm while it rests for 10 to 15 minutes. This is a vital step for juicy beef—the juices will redistribute throughout the meat as the roast rests, and the internal temperature will actually rise about five degrees. If you have blood on the carving board when you start to slice, you've cut into it too soon.

4 Meanwhile, make some gravy with the pan juices. Set the roasting pan on the stove, over medium-high heat, and blend 2 Tbsp (30 mL) of flour into the drippings. Add enough of the remaining flour to soak up the pan juices and stir until smooth and brown. Slowly drizzle in the red wine and beef stock, whisking constantly to prevent any lumps, and bring the sauce to a boil. When the sauce is smooth, bubbling, and nicely thickened, season with salt and pepper to taste. Thin with extra wine or stock if necessary.

5 You can serve the roast in thick slabs on the bone (for big appetites) or create more elegant slices by first carving down along the ribs—to separate the meat from the bone in one piece—then slicing the meat at right angles to the bone. Serve with pan gravy. Serves 8 to 10.

YUMMY PLATE

French Apple Tart

The beauty of this upside-down apple pie is the fact that you can make it in advance, then simply reheat it on the stovetop and invert it onto a serving dish—warm, gooey, and ready for a scoop of French vanilla ice cream. A bistro classic in France (and a recipe shared with The Guy by a real Parisian chef), it's sure to be a show-stopper in your dining room. It's always good to end an impressive meal with an equally impressive dessert!

8 to 10 Golden Delicious apples
   (about 3 lb/1.5 kg)
½ cup (125 mL) unsalted butter

2 Tbsp (30 mL) honey
½ cup (125 mL) granulated sugar
1 sheet puff pastry dough (thawed if frozen)

1 Peel the apples, cut them in half lengthwise, and remove the cores. In a 10- to 12-inch (25- to 30-cm) non-stick, ovenproof skillet, melt the butter and honey together over medium heat. Spread the sugar evenly over the butter-honey mixture and arrange the apples, cut-side up, overtop, filling the pan. Cut any remaining apples into chunks and tuck in between the apple halves to fill in the gaps.

2 Increase the heat under the skillet to medium-high and cook until the butter and sugar form a deep, golden brown syrup that bubbles up around the edges of the apples. Once the sugar looks caramelized, turn the heat down to medium-low and continue to cook for about 45 minutes or until the apples are softened and collapsing. Cool the apples in the pan.

3 Preheat the oven to 400°F (200°C).

4 On a floured surface, roll the puff pastry into a circle slightly larger than the skillet. Fold the pastry in half (this makes it easier to pick up), lay it over the apples, then unfold it to completely to cover the skillet. Trim the pastry into a neat circle with a knife or kitchen shears, then press it down over the apples, using a spoon to tuck the edges in around the inside edges of the skillet.

5 Place the tart into the preheated oven and bake for 20 to 30 minutes or until the crust is golden brown. Cool the tart for one hour. (You can make the dessert up to this point one day ahead and chill.)

6 Before unmolding (especially if the tart has been chilled), place the skillet over medium-high heat for 2 to 3 minutes to soften the caramel. Place a pretty serving plate (one that's larger than your skillet) over the pan and in one deft move (and wearing oven mitts) flip the pan and plate over, and voilà! If any apples are left stuck to the skillet just slide them off with a spoon and replace them on top of the tart.

7 Bring the whole steamy tart to the table (for your guests to ogle), then cut it into wedges and serve with vanilla ice cream. Serves 6 to 8.

Construction Projects

You know what they say—"If you build it, they will come." So next time you want to gather the gang, think about a do-it-yourself (DIY) construction project in the kitchen. Whether you just build something while they watch (like The Guy's party paella) or get your guests into full-on DIY mode (think build-your-own pizza or roll-your-own sushi), it's the easiest way to make dinner for a crowd.

And it's interactive—the kind of dinner that gets people mixing, talking, and intimately involved with their food—which is what entertaining is all about.

Any cooking (or making components like seasoned sushi rice or pizza sauces) can be done in advance. You're the project manager and foreman, so make sure all of the essential ingredients and equipment are on site, then just sit back and supervise.

It's The Guy's favorite way to throw a dinner party. Some assembly required.

The Pizza Party

A party where everyone cooks their own food is a brilliant strategy for the reluctant cook—guests are responsible for their own choices, and the heat's off you. Pizza is a no-brainer—even guys relish building and baking their own pies—and when organized as an interactive group activity, making pizza can be a deliciously creative party mixer.

Get everyone chopping, cooking, and contributing—a pizza topping potluck always garners great ingredients. Then fire up the oven as hot as it will go, get the pizza stone sizzling, then send those pizzas flying from a pizza paddle into the oven (with a flourish) like your favorite TV chef. The Guy guarantees that your friends will be impressed.

Just make a couple of batches of pizza dough (or buy it from an Italian deli), then ask each guest to bring a topping and soon you'll be creating gourmet combinations like fresh figs and gorgonzola, prosciutto and wild mushrooms with fresh sage, or the best heirloom tomato, niçoise olive, and anchovy pizza in town. There is absolutely no recipe—you use what you like.

Hey, if hot chefs like Todd English and Wolfgang Puck can build careers on pizza, it can't hurt your reputation to become the pizza Guy in your gang.

The Crust

If you ever spend time out in the country, miles from the pizza delivery guy, like I do, knowing how to whip up a pizza from scratch is a lifesaver.

But there are easier ways, too. The fastest way to make a pizza at home is to start with a pre-baked bread pizza shell that you'll find at the local supermarket. It's nothing like a crust from scratch, but it's not a bad way to get your veggies and carbs. Dress it up with a slather of pesto (from a jar, of course), slivered red onions, mushrooms, green pepper, ham or Italian sausage, black olives, and the ubiquitous shredded three-cheese mix from the dairy case, and you have an instant after-work dinner that's kid-friendly and cheaper than takeout. A thick, Greek-style pita bread also makes a perfect crisp crust for an instant personal pizza any time.

But if you want authentic, thin crust Italian pizza (the kind The Guy finds is becoming extinct in fast food joints and replaced with fat, bready pies), take more time and make the dough from scratch. You can do this in your food processor, with a stand mixer, or even in the bread machine (possibly the only good use for this massive kitchen paper weight). It sounds complicated, but it's dead easy. Really.

This pizza dough recipe can be expanded to feed a crowd for a pizza party, or you can just make a couple of pizzas on a weeknight instead of ordering out. Go nuts at the local Italian deli picking out fancy cheeses and exquisite imported olives, or just open the refrigerator and see what kind of cheese, sliced sandwich meat, and other condiments in there just might work together. If you can't face the prospect of making pizza dough, you can usually buy it frozen at the local Italian deli or from any mom-and-pop pizza joint.

Pizza Dough

3 cups (750 mL) flour (try a combination of
    2 cups/500 mL all-purpose flour and 1 cup/
    250 mL whole wheat or barley flour, or add a
    little cornmeal)
2 tsp (10 mL) instant yeast

1 tsp (5 mL) salt
1 tsp (5 mL) granulated sugar
1 cup (250 mL) warm water (about 125°F/ 50°C)
2 Tbsp (30 mL) olive oil
cornmeal

1 In a food processor, combine the flour, yeast, and salt and whirl briefly. Dissolve the sugar in the warm water, and whisk in the olive oil. With the processor running, slowly add the liquid until the dough comes together in a ball. You can add up to ¼ cup (60 mL) more warm water if you need to—the dough should be smooth and soft, but not sticky. You can also mix the dough with an electric mixer or mix it by hand in a large bowl.

2 Knead the dough by hand on a lightly floured surface for about 10 minutes or until the dough is smooth and elastic (add a bit more flour if the dough becomes too sticky while kneading).

3 If you have a bread machine, use the dough cycle and just dump the ingredients into the machine. It's convenient and easy because it mixes the dough and gives it a warm place to rest until you're ready to roll out your pizza crusts. Once the dough is kneaded, you can refrigerate the dough or even freeze it—just bring it back to room temperature before proceeding.

4 To make the pizza, heat a pizza stone (or an inverted heavy baking sheet) on the lowest rack of your oven, at 500°F (260°C) for 30 minutes. (The Guy has even successfully used unglazed clay tiles from the hardware store, arranged tightly together on the bottom oven rack, to approximate the clay pizza stone.)

5 Divide the dough into 3 or 4 balls and roll or stretch each into 8-inch (20-cm) rounds—the thinner the better. On a wooden pizza peel (or a heavy piece of cardboard that's covered in foil—an old pizza box works) sprinkle some cornmeal (important so the dough will slide off later). Set the pizza crust on top and dress lightly with your favorite toppings. Lightly is the operative word here—too much topping makes soggy pizza.

6 Carefully slide the pizza from the peel, directly onto the preheated pizza stone or baking sheet in your oven and bake for 10 to 12 minutes or until the bottom is crisp and brown. Repeat with the additional pizzas.

7 Let the pizza rest on a cutting board for 2 minutes before cutting into wedges using your biggest chef's knife or a rotary pizza cutter. Serve immediately. Makes four 8-inch (20-cm) pizzas.

Pizza Sauce

There are some decent bottled tomato sauces on the market but it's easy to make your own pizzeria-style sauce from scratch.

one 14-oz (398-mL) can tomatoes
2 to 3 Tbsp (30 to 45 mL) tomato paste
2 Tbsp (30 mL) granulated sugar
¼ cup (60 mL) extra virgin olive oil
salt and freshly ground black pepper

1 tsp (5 mL) dried oregano
¼ cup (60 mL) freshly grated Parmigiano
    Reggiano cheese
¼ tsp (1 mL) Asian chili paste

1 Combine the tomatoes, tomato paste, sugar, oil, salt, pepper, oregano, cheese, and chili paste in a food processor. Whirl until smooth. Place in a covered container and refrigerate. The sauce will keep for up to 2 days. Makes 2¼ cups (550 mL).

The Toppings

When you're having an interactive pizza party, divide your guests into teams of two (it's more fun and social if couples don't work together). Then let the topping and baking of pies go on all evening while you sit in the kitchen, at the bar, or around the dining table, and comment on your cohorts' combinations. Set out the toppings—chopped, cooked, shredded, and ready to use—and let the games begin.

Anything goes, but at right are some tried-and-true combos:

WISE GUY:

Buy tomato paste in convenient tubes for those times when you only need 1 to 2 Tbsp (15 to 30 mL)—the tube can be resealed and kept almost indefinitely in the refrigerator. Use canned tomato paste for soups and sauces, and freeze any leftovers.

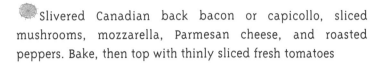Tomato sauce, sautéed mushrooms, sautéed onions, minced garlic, thinly sliced prosciutto, and fontina cheese

Slivered Canadian back bacon or capicollo, sliced mushrooms, mozzarella, Parmesan cheese, and roasted peppers. Bake, then top with thinly sliced fresh tomatoes

Basil pesto, thinly sliced Roma tomatoes, slivered onions, and mozzarella cheese

Slivered sun-dried tomatoes (packed in oil), artichoke hearts (drained well, if canned, and chopped), black olives, slivered fresh basil leaves, and grated, aged Friulano cheese

Tomato sauce, minced fresh basil, black pepper, and Parmesan cheese

Extra virgin olive oil, roasted garlic purée, grilled asparagus, caramelized onions, grated Provolone, and Asiago cheese

Tomato sauce, fresh mozzarella cheese, and anchovies

Pesto, Italian sausage (crumbled and cooked), chopped tomatoes, and Provolone or Friulano cheese

Pesto, chopped tomatoes, dry salami, black olives, and mozzarella cheese

Tomato sauce, thinly sliced prosciutto or spicy capocollo, slivered black olives, and fresh basil

Caramelized onions, sliced tomatoes, black olives, and anchovies

Sliced pears or figs marinated in balsamic vinegar, gorgonzola cheese, toasted walnuts or pine nuts, and shredded arugula (greens go on after baking)

Build-Your-Own Taco Party

The Guy learned in Texas that the secret to a perfect taco is a good homemade sauce. Start with dried chilies, a can of tomatoes, and a blender—that spicy, seasoned meat you stuff into these crispy shells will be downright addictive. Sure, you can slap together a fast taco with a supermarket "kit" or hit the drive-through window, but take the time to make this simple sauce, and you won't go back.

This is also a great way to get your family and friends to make their own meal. Kids (especially teenagers) love 'em, so it's the perfect solution for a family-style gathering. Don't forget to pass lots of paper napkins (or better yet, plan to eat outside on the deck!).

Meat filling

2 chipotle chili peppers in adobo sauce
   (canned)
1 cup (250 mL) canned tomatoes
¾ cup (175 mL) water or stock
2 Tbsp (30 mL) tomato paste
1 Tbsp (15 mL) granulated sugar

2 lb (1 kg) lean ground beef (or chicken)
2 Tbsp (30 mL) olive oil
2 large onions, finely chopped
3 to 4 cloves garlic, minced
4 tsp (20 mL) chili powder
½ tsp (2 mL) ground cumin
salt and freshly ground black pepper

Fixings

warm taco shells (or corn or flour tortillas)
shredded iceberg lettuce
grated medium cheddar cheese
chopped fresh tomatoes or fresh salsa

chopped fresh cilantro leaves
sliced black olives
sour cream
hot sauce
chopped avocados or guacamole

WISE GUY: For a really special taco party, start with flank steak that's been marinated for a few hours in a little olive oil, lime juice, garlic, salt, and pepper. Sear the marinated steak on the barbecue to medium-rare perfection, about 5 minutes per side over high heat. Rest the meat for 10 minutes before slicing thinly across the grain, then serve with the sauce (made without meat) and the other taco fixings.

You can also start with a 2-lb (1-kg) steak (instead of the ground beef) and chop it into tiny cubes to create an upscale meat sauce for Tex-Mex tacos.

1 In a blender, combine the chipotle chilies, tomatoes, water, tomato paste, and sugar. Whirl until smooth. Set this tomato sauce aside.

2 In a large sauté pan over medium-high heat, cook the ground meat, breaking it up with a fork, until it's nicely browned and caramelized. Add the onions and garlic to the pan and cook for 10 minutes, stirring occasionally, until the onions begin to brown. Stir in the chili powder and cumin and cook for 1 minute, until the spices are fragrant.

3 Add the reserved tomato sauce and bring to a boil. Adjust the seasoning with salt and pepper to taste. Reduce the heat to low and simmer the meat mixture, uncovered, for about 15 minutes or until the sauce is nicely thickened.

4 To warm the tacos or tortillas, wrap them loosely in foil and heat in a 200°F (95°C) oven for 15 minutes. Set out the spiced meat mixture in a small, covered casserole dish or bowl along with a basket of warm taco or tortilla shells, and the remainder of the fixings in separate bowls. Invite your guests to build their own tacos. Serves 8.

Roll-Your-Own Sushi

Sushi may be The Guy's favorite construction-project-style dinner party—there's really very little cooking involved. It's exotic and stylish, and the ultimate party mixer for a group. Just buy some very fresh, sushi-grade fish, steam a pot of short-grain sushi rice, chop up some vegetables, and your guests can dig in and wrap and roll their own dinner.

Make sure you tell your fishmonger that you're planning to serve raw fish—either buy sushi-grade fish from a reputable Japanese supplier or ask the fishmonger when (and where) the fish was caught. What you want is fish that's been scrupulously handled, whether it's fresh or frozen.

Even if you don't like raw fish, you can enjoy making and eating sushi. Plan to use cooked prawns, crabmeat, smoked salmon, and vegetables like cucumber, avocado, daikon radish, lettuce, shredded carrot, and bell pepper. Get creative and pass the wasabi!

Sushi Basics

Here's what you'll need for making sushi at home for 8 people:

steamed and seasoned sushi rice (about 6 cups/1.5 L of raw Japanese rice like Kokuho Rose)

20 sheets of yaki nori (toasted seaweed)

3 lb (1.5 kg) of fresh fish or shellfish (including salmon, tuna, snapper, scallops, prawns, octopus, etc.), cut into thin slices. 1 lb (500 g) of fish yields about 20 pieces of sushi

1 package imitation crab sticks

1 English cucumber, seeds removed but not peeled, cut into long, narrow strips

carrots, daikon radish, and green onion cut into fine strips

ripe Haas avocados, peeled, quartered, and sliced

cooked shiitake mushrooms and omelette strips (see pages 189)

roasted sesame seeds

4 oz (100 g) salmon or flying fish roe

tamari soy sauce

wasabi paste (Japanese horseradish), available premixed in tubes or in powder form to mix with water

bamboo sushi rolling mats

sliced pickled ginger (served as a condiment)

Types of Sushi

Every piece of sushi starts with seasoned rice and a dab of wasabi (the electric green Japanese horseradish that gives sushi its addictive quality). After that, let your imagination run wild. Start with the following combinations:

- crab and avocado
- fresh raw sliced tuna, salmon, or sea scallops
- egg strips, pickled gourd, shiitake mushrooms, and/or fish
- cucumber strips and toasted sesame seed
- tuna or salmon, tobiko roe, and lettuce
- carrot, cucumber, and green onion matchsticks
- grilled soy-marinated eel and cucumber
- smoked salmon, sesame seeds, carrot, cucumber, and red pepper matchsticks
- smoked salmon and capers

The Technique

There are several types of sushi—individual balls of rice topped with raw or cooked fish (nigiri); traditional rolls of rice, fish, and vegetables wrapped in nori then sliced (maki); and larger, hand-rolled cones of nori filled with rice, vegetables, and fish (temaki).

The first trick is making the rice—a short-grain Japanese rice that's rinsed, steamed, then seasoned with salt, sugar, and vinegar. You can buy pre-seasoned sushi vinegar but The Guy always likes his sushi better if he starts from scratch.

To make rolling easier, buy a bamboo rolling mat. The Guy learned to form sushi rolls with his sushi chef friend Tom. Here are some of his tricks:

Once the rice is cooked and seasoned, keep it well covered at room temperature (or just warm in a rice cooker). Cover the rice to prevent it from getting dry.

Nori needs to be sealed to keep it dry and crisp. If your nori is limp, toast the sheets of seaweed for 40 seconds in the microwave until crisp.

Wasabi loses its searing heat quickly when it's exposed to air. Buy it pre-mixed and sealed in a tube, or mix powdered wasabi with water just before you plan to use it.

Make sure you remove all the bones from raw fish before slicing it for sushi. For even pieces, trim fish fillets into 2- x ½-inch (5- x 1-cm) blocks, then use a sushi knife—the edge is specially ground to form the tapered cuts that drape perfectly over a mound of rice.

To cook prawns (jumbo shrimp) for sushi—and to keep them long and straight—skewer the unshelled prawns lengthwise on bamboo skewers before plunging them into boiling water. Chill in cold water before removing the skewers. Then shell, devein, and butterfly the prawns (cut them almost through and flatten like a book) for nigiri.

Start rolling by laying a piece of nori, shiny-side down, on a bamboo rolling mat—set the long side of the square of seaweed along the bottom edge of the mat. If you don't have a mat, improvise with a clean kitchen towel or flexible placemat. There are faint lines in the nori—make sure to roll parallel to them. For a small roll, use half a sheet (cut the sheet of nori in half with kitchen shears, following the lines). Use a whole sheet for a large futomaki roll.

Keep your hands wet while spreading the rice on the nori so it doesn't stick. Start with a sausage-shaped ball of rice (about 4 oz/100g for a small roll). Set the rice at the center of the nori and, with wet hands, press from side to side and down towards the bottom edge of the mat, leaving a ½-inch (1-cm) strip bare along the top edge.

Use your finger to smear a line of wasabi paste down the center of the rice and fill with strips of onion, cucumber, and small pieces of chopped raw fish.

Hold the filling in place with your index fingers, lift the bottom edge of the mat and roll the nori and rice up and over the filling, rolling away from you to form a log. Use the mat to compress the roll, then set it seam-side down to seal. Cover with plastic wrap.

To slice the maki rolls, remove the plastic wrap and use a wet, sharp knife to cut it into 1-inch (2.5-cm) pieces. You can also cut the rolls on a sharp diagonal for a more dramatic presentation.

Nigiri sushi requires some good knife skills to slice the fish into perfectly tapered pieces. Once you have your fish cut, form a small oval ball of rice the size of a walnut in your right hand, and, with your left hand, pick up a slice of raw fish, dab it with wasabi, then place the rice ball over the fish and press the piece into your left hand . Turn the ball over, and smooth the fish down over the rice.

Making a temaki cone is simple. Just use ½ sheet of nori, spread with rice along one corner, top with vegetables and fish, then roll into a cone shape.

Sushi Rice

This makes enough rice for 10 rolls. If you're having a party of 8 to 10 people, plan to make a double recipe of rice. Save time by buying seasoned sushi rice vinegar (the salt and sugar have already been added).

5 cups (1.25 L) short-grain Japanese rice
6 cups (1.5 L) water
½ cup (125 mL) Japanese rice vinegar

6 Tbsp (75 mL) granulated sugar
1 Tbsp (15 mL) salt

1 Put the rice in a bowl and rinse with cold water. Drain and re-wash the rice three times. Set the rice in a colander and leave it to drain for 30 minutes before cooking.

2 A rice cooker makes the best sushi rice but to make it on the stove top, use 1 part washed rice to 1.2 parts water. In a saucepan, combine the water and rice and bring to a boil over medium-high heat. Cover, reduce the heat to low, and cook for 20 minutes. Remove the pan from the heat and let it stand for 15 minutes to finish cooking.

3 Meanwhile, in a saucepan, combine the rice vinegar, sugar, and salt. Stir over medium heat until the sugar and salt have dissolved. Remove from heat and let cool. Place the hot rice in a large bowl and fluff. Slowly pour the vinegar mixture over the rice, folding the rice with a big spatula until all of the vinegar is absorbed and the rice is shiny. Cover tightly with plastic wrap and cool to room temperature. (Make sure the rice doesn't dry out.)

Braised Shiitake Mushrooms for Sushi

These are the sweet and savory mushrooms you find in the big rolls of futomaki—cook the mushrooms in advance and combine with strips of omelet and sesame seeds in rolls. These mushrooms are also delicious in a Japanese-style rice salad with a wasabi dressing.

12 dried shiitake mushrooms

2 Tbsp (30 mL) granulated sugar

2 Tbsp (30 m) Japanese soy sauce

2 Tbsp (30 mL) mirin (Japanese sweet rice wine)

1 Place the dried mushrooms in a bowl and cover with boiling water. Set the mushrooms aside to soak for 20 minutes. Remove the mushrooms from the water and squeeze dry. Cut off the woody stems and thinly slice the mushroom caps.

2 In a saucepan, combine the sugar, soy sauce, mirin, and sliced mushrooms. Bring to a boil over medium heat and simmer until most of the liquid has evaporated.

3 Remove from the heat and cool.

Japanese Omelet for Sushi

Sushi chefs often make rolls with strips of cooked egg inside, or top pieces of nigiri with thin squares of omelet, and strips of green onion. Here's how to make these easy omelets.

4 large eggs

2 Tbsp (30 mL) granulated sugar

2 tsp (10 mL) soy sauce

2 Tbsp (30 mL) sake or cooking wine

2 tsp (10 mL) vegetable oil

1 In a medium bowl, whisk together the eggs, sugar, soy sauce, and sake. In a 10-inch (25-cm), non-stick skillet, heat the oil over medium-low heat. Add ¼ of the egg mixture and tilt the pan so that it spreads evenly over the bottom of the skillet. Cook until the egg is set, then fold over and remove from the pan. Repeat with the remaining egg mixture. When the omelet is cool, slice into strips or squares for sushi.

A Party Paella

The Guy's buddy Dennis learned how to make paella in Spain where it's truly a man's meal—created outdoors over portable gas rings, in huge shallow paella pans, and including any kind of meat and seafood that's available.

Not exactly a construction project but something that's perfect for a potluck party, and a meal you can build together. Just ask your guests to bring along some kind of raw protein (from a favorite spicy sausage to chicken, prawns, scallops, or mussels) and it can all go into the collective paella pan.

In Spain, the paella ritual involves adding each ingredient in stages and to particular portions of the pan—more of a process than a recipe—but Dennis has developed his own technique that simplifies the making of paella. You don't have to do anything until your guests arrive (except make the sangria—see page xxx). Then you can build a paella together around the stove like they do in the Spanish countryside, and enjoy it communally right out of the pan. You won't believe how addictive this basic combination of seafood and creamy rice can be—just make sure you don't skip the saffron (it's the key flavoring ingredient), and use a good quality short-grain rice.

The Guy's paella pan is 13 ½ inches (34 cm) across—just large enough for this dish for four—but you can buy larger pans for bigger paellas.

¼ cup (60 mL) extra virgin olive oil

1 large red bell pepper, peeled and sliced

2 cups (500 mL) Valencia or short-grain pearl rice

6 cups (1.5 L) water

3 tsp (15 mL) salt, divided

1 lb (500 g) large sea scallops, halved

12 to 16 large shrimp, peeled and deveined

¾ cup (175 mL) frozen peas

½ tsp (2 mL) crushed saffron threads

lemon wedges to garnish

1 Pour the oil into the center of a wide, shallow paella pan or skillet. It should spread to cover ¾ of the base of the pan. Heat the oil over medium-high heat.

2 Slice the pepper into thick, lengthwise strips and arrange it around the outside edge of the pan, in a ring. Sprinkle the peppers with 1 tsp (5 mL) of the salt and let them sizzle. When the peppers are hot, add the rice to the center of the pan and stir it around in the oil. Add the water and remaining salt (Dennis says you should add salt just until you can taste it) and bring to a boil (the pan will be quite full). Simmer for 10 minutes. Add the scallops, shrimp, and peas. Reduce the heat to medium, keeping the mixture bubbling, and crumble in the saffron. Continue to simmer for about 10 to 15 minutes or until the water has been absorbed. You can reduce the heat slightly under the pan as the paella cooks, but never stir it, the rice should cook to a creamy mass and begin to brown on the bottom. When it looks like all of the water has been absorbed, use a spoon to check the middle of the pan. If a nice brown crust is beginning to form on the bottom of the pan, it's ready to serve.

3 Take the whole paella pan to the table and serve it family style, with lemons to squeeze over top. Serves 4 to 6.

WISE GUY:

If you want to include chicken, rabbit, or sausage in the paella, brown it in the olive oil before you add the rice and water. If you're adding mussels in the shell, just perch them artfully around in the bubbling pan during the last 10 minutes of cooking. They're done when they pop open.

Sharing Shabu Shabu

This is Japanese communal cooking at its best. Set an electric wok or wide clay fondue pot in the center of your coffee table, get lots of comfortable cushions, and invite your guests to sit on the floor to cook and eat together. Healthy and fresh, shabu shabu involves simmering vegetables and paper-thin pieces of meat or chicken in simple broth, which just gets tastier as the cooking progresses. Chopsticks for everyone are a must (a set for eating and another for cooking), along with individual bowls for dipping sauces and a small bowl for rice. At the end of the meal, when all of the cooking is complete, guests share the broth, sipped from small porcelain cups.

1 lb (500 g) beef tenderloin or strip loin
1 lb (500 g) skinless, boneless chicken breast
1 block medium tofu (about 8 oz/200 g),
     cut into ¾-inch (2-cm) cubes
8 fresh Chinese black mushrooms
     (or 1 large portobello), sliced
1 bunch asparagus, trimmed
6 green onions, cut into 2-inch (5-cm) pieces

4 to 6 baby bok choy or small Chinese
     cabbages, leaves separated and sliced
3 cups (750 mL) fresh bean sprouts
6 cups (1.5 L) beef or chicken broth
2 Tbsp (30 mL) soy sauce
1-inch (2.5-cm) piece of fresh ginger, crushed
8 cups (2 L) short-grain steamed rice

Sesame Dipping Sauce
2 Tbsp (30 mL) white miso
½ cup (125 mL) sesame paste (tahini) or
     ground sesame seeds

¼ cup (60 mL) soy sauce
¼ cup (60 mL) mayonnaise

1 Trim all of the visible fat from the beef. Put it in the freezer for 30 minutes to partially freeze; then, using a sharp knife, cut it across the grain into paper-thin strips. Arrange the slices on a platter in an attractive overlapping pattern. Cover with plastic wrap and refrigerate until dinner time.

2 Thinly slice the chicken and arrange on a separate platter. Cover and refrigerate. Make sure to wash up well (knives and cutting boards) between slicing the beef, chicken, and the vegetables to prevent any cross-contamination. This is important—you don't want to poison your guests!

3 On another platter, arrange the cubed tofu, sliced mushrooms, asparagus, green onions, bok choy, and bean sprouts. Cover and refrigerate.

4 To make the dipping sauce, in a medium bowl, whisk the miso, sesame paste, soy sauce, and mayonnaise together. Divide among 6 to 8 tiny dipping bowls, one for each guest.

5 In a medium saucepan, bring the broth, soy sauce, and ginger to a boil. Pour into a large, shallow cast iron or earthenware pot and set over a heat source (an electric or solid-fuel fondue pot) at the center of the table. Keep the stock at a low simmer.

6 To cook, guests pick up pieces of meat or chicken with their chopsticks and "swish" them through the broth for about 10 seconds, until lightly cooked, then dip into the sauce and eat. Don't drop the ingredients into the broth—they're too difficult to fish out. Vegetables and tofu are cooked the same way, with the meal progressing until all of the food has been cooked and consumed. Add more broth as necessary to keep the pot topped up. Serve individual bowls of steamed rice on the side, and finish the meal by serving the flavorful broth—a final clear soup, drunk like tea from small bowls. Serves 6 to 8.

WISE GUY:

The Japanese have lots of nifty little snacks you can pass to start your shabu shabu dinner. Try some electric green wasabi peas (green peas in a sweet wasabi glaze) or little soy-glazed Japanese rice crackers. A plate of cucumber or crab and avocado sushi rolls, from the local Japanese take-out, makes a good starter, too.

And don't forget to pour the sake (rice wine). Buy a good-quality sake and serve it cold in tiny cups. Or serve this party meal with champagne.

Dining à Deux

Two's company, as they say, and The Guy just loves the chance to order the "for two" selections on the fine-dining menu. But romance is just as easy to attain at home, especially when you can create the perfect meal to share with your significant other.

Feel free to double (or even triple) any of these decadent recipes for your next party of four or six.

Tenderloin for Two

Sometimes The Guy can't resist a juicy steak—and tenderloin is the perfect way to impress The Girl. Make the herb butter in advance and dollop it on the steak as it comes off the grill—a little extra is equally exquisite on a baked potato or as part of your favorite mash (see page 155 for instructions on cooking the perfect potato). Grill some asparagus to go alongside or just steam some in the microwave. Pour your favorite "beefy" Cabernet Sauvignon or Syrah, start a fire, and get ready for romance.

1 tsp (5 mL) minced garlic
1 Tbsp (15 mL) olive oil
two 6-oz (175-g) beef tenderloin steaks, about
    1½ inches (4 cm) thick

2 tsp (10 mL) Worcestershire sauce
freshly ground black pepper

Lemon Herb Steak Butter
2 Tbsp (30 mL) unsalted butter, softened
½ tsp (2 mL) finely grated lemon zest
1 clove garlic, minced or puréed in a garlic press

½ tsp (2 mL) salt or steak spice
2 tsp (10 mL) minced fresh Italian parsley or
    basil

1 Preheat the grill to medium-high.

2 In a small bowl, combine the garlic with the olive oil and pour over the steaks. Then drizzle and rub the steaks with Worcestershire and season liberally with pepper. Set aside at room temperature.

3 Combine the softened butter with the zest, garlic, salt, and herbs. Divide the herbed butter in two and either pipe or artfully dollop on a plate, or press into two tiny dipping sauce dishes. Freeze or chill while you cook the steak (the idea is to create individual "coins" of herbed butter that will melt over the steaks when you serve them).

4 Grill the steaks to rare or medium rare—about 5 minutes per side (see the "touch test", page 229). Transfer the steaks to individual serving plates and top each with a piece of herb butter. Serves 2.

WISE GUY: The classic "aphrodisiac" vegetable is the asparagus—long, slender spears to pick up with your hands and nibble from tip to base. (Yes, this is considered the proper way to consume asparagus, and how sexy is that?) You can cook asparagus quickly while you grill the steaks—just break off the tough bases of each spear (they snap easily at this point), toss with a little olive oil, lemon juice, salt, and pepper, then grill quickly until tender-crisp and lightly browned. Serve immediately, with a few shavings of aged Parmesan or Asiago on top.

Shellfish Stew for Two

Since you can do most of the prep in advance—and that leaves you to be completely spontaneous—this makes a romantic meal. Just heat the base and add the seafood, and it's ready when you are. Then there's the whole issue of eating a meal that's loaded with zinc, the secret to every guy's peak performance! Just buy a fresh baguette and some sweet, unsalted butter, and indulge.

This recipe doubles or triples easily if you're serving more than one couple. Feel free to vary the fish and seafood according to the season.

Base
1 Tbsp (15 mL) olive oil
1 small onion, peeled and slivered
1 clove garlic, minced
1 small fennel bulb, trimmed and slivered (or a
   mix of ½ cup/125 mL slivered celery, ¼
   tsp/1 mL fennel seeds, and a splash of
   Pernod)
1 large carrot, cut into 1-inch (2.5-cm) long juliennes
   (thin matchstick strips)

1 Tbsp (15 mL) all-purpose flour
4 cups (1 L) fish stock, clam juice, or water
1 cup (250 mL) white wine
1 cup (250 mL) canned Roma tomatoes, whirled
   in the blender until smooth
½ tsp (2 mL) saffron threads, crumbled
1 small dried chili, crumbled
¼ tsp (1 mL) finely grated orange zest
salt and freshly ground black pepper
¼ cup (60 mL) whipping cream (optional)

Fish and Seafood
½ lb (250 g) scallops or halibut
½ lb (250 g) prawns, peeled and deveined

½ lb (250 g) large mussels, debearded and
   scrubbed
chopped fresh Italian parsley, for garnish

1 Heat the oil in a large sauté pan over medium heat. Sauté the onion, garlic, fennel, and carrots together for 8 to 10 minutes. Add the flour and stir, then blend in the stock, wine, tomatoes, saffron, chili pepper, and orange zest. Bring to a boil over medium-high heat, then reduce heat to medium-low and simmer, covered, for 20 minutes. At this point, you can add the seafood to finish the dish or you can stop, chill the base overnight, and reheat it when you're ready to eat.

2 If the soup has been chilled, bring to a boil over medium-high heat in a large sauté pan or Dutch oven. (The Guy likes the chunky bits of vegetables in his seafood stew, but for a more elegant and smoother presentation, you can strain the base and discard the solids—or put it through a food mill to purée—before adding the seafood.)

3 When it's bubbling nicely, stir in the cream (if using) and add the scallops or halibut and cook for 2 minutes. Stir in the prawns and mussels, cover, and steam for 3 to 4 minutes longer. Discard any mussels that don't open. Ladle the stew into two wide soup bowls and sprinkle each with chopped parsley. Serve immediately with French bread on the side. Serves 2 as a main dish (or 4 as a starter).

WISE GUY:

When The Guy took The Girl to France, they enjoyed their seafood stew with rouille—a spicy red mayonnaise seasoned with paprika and garlic. Make a simpler version of rouille at home by blending ½ cup (125 mL) commercial mayonnaise with 2 to 3 cloves of chopped garlic in a blender and whirl until smooth. For authentic flavor, add ½ tsp (2 mL) Dijon mustard and, with the motor running, incorporate about ⅓ cup (75 mL) of tasty extra virgin olive oil. Add a big pinch of cayenne pepper and some Spanish paprika to make the sauce red and a little spicy. Cover and refrigerate for up to 2 days.

Pass the sauce with the bread, so diners can add a dollop to their fish stew.

Romantic Raclette for Two

Everyone loves melted cheese and raclette—that Swiss dish based on melted raclette cheese—is so easy, especially when you have one of the new electric raclette machines.

Anything that can be grilled can be cooked on the flat, non-stick surface of a modern raclette machine. Try sliced vegetables such as zucchini, red peppers, portobello mushrooms, and sweet potatoes, as well as seafood or lean meats such as steak, chicken breast, and pork tenderloin (sliced across the grain and/or marinated before cooking).

Classic raclette cheese accompaniments include gherkins and pickled onions, but barbecue sauce, soy sauce, salsa, and chutney also make an interesting contrast to the richness of the melted cheese. Make sure to serve a crisp, chilled white wine and a rich, fruity red wine. An easy dish to double when company comes, raclette is another favorite in The Guy's cook-your-own meal repertoire, but it also makes a stress-free meal for two.

6 oz (175 g) sirloin steak, sliced across the grain
6 sea scallops
6 large shrimp, peeled and deveined
sliced vegetables for grilling (white or green onions, bell peppers, zucchini, mushrooms, sweet potatoes, asparagus, etc.)
1 lb (500 g) baby potatoes, boiled in their skins and sliced

gherkins and pickled onions
salsa, soy sauce, chutney, or barbecue sauce for dipping
8 oz (225 g) raclette cheese (or try Gouda or aged cheddar), sliced into 1-oz (25-g) pieces or shredded

1 Season the raw meats and seafood with salt and pepper and set out on separate plates. Place the sliced vegetables on another plate to avoid cross-contamination with the raw meats. Dense vegetables—like sweet potatoes or squash—may benefit by partial steaming. Brush all vegetables with a little olive oil before grilling.

2 Set out the hot, boiled potatoes, pickles, sauces, and sliced cheese. Heat the raclette machine to medium-high and invite guests to cook. Meats and vegetables can be browned on the griddle while cheese is melted in the special trays below. Simply pour the melted cheese over the grilled food, consume, and continue cooking. Or, you may place a few slices of boiled potato or grilled bell pepper directly in the melting tray, top with shredded cheese, and broil below the element until brown and bubbling. Serves 2.

WISE GUY: Be imaginative. The raclette grill could be used for a fajita party, a build-your-own satay station, or for a quesadilla feast. Just gather 'round and let everyone else do the cooking.

Fettucine with Mussels and Cherry Tomatoes

Time to put some Edith Piaf on the stereo and serve up a simple but romantic bistro-style meal. Make sure to buy fresh linguine—homemade from an Italian deli or gourmet shop, if possible—or a good artisan-style egg pasta. Like this simple sauce, fresh pasta cooks up almost instantly. Pass a crispy baguette and some sweet butter, and don't forget the champagne, mon amour.

2 Tbsp (30 mL) olive oil
2 shallots, minced
2 cloves garlic, minced
½ cup (125 mL) white wine
1 cup (250 mL) grape tomatoes, quartered
2 Tbsp (30 mL) chopped fresh basil, divided
1 tsp (5 mL) finely grated lemon zest (use a
   microplane grater)

salt and freshly ground black pepper
¼ cup (60 mL) whipping cream
2 lb (1 kg) fresh blue mussels (scrubbed and
   debearded)
½ lb (250 g) fresh fettuccine

1 Bring a large pot of salted water to a boil.

2 In a large, deep saucepan or wok, heat the olive oil over high heat and sauté the shallots and garlic for 3 minutes, until soft and fragrant. Add the white wine, bring to a boil, and simmer until the wine is reduced by half.

3 Stir in the tomatoes, 1 Tbsp (15 mL) of the basil, lemon zest, salt, and pepper. Add the cream and simmer for 2 to 3 minutes. Add the mussels to the pan, cover, and shake for about 2 to 3 minutes or just until the shells pop open. Remove the pan from the heat and set aside, discarding any shells that haven't opened.

4 Meanwhile, add the pasta to the boiling water. Boil until the pasta is al dente—just a few minutes— then drain and return to the cooking pot. Pour the mussels and sauce over the cooked pasta in the pot and heat, tossing to combine, for 30 seconds to 1 minute (the pasta will soak up some of the sauce). Divide the pasta and sauce between two warm soup plates or pasta bowls, arranging the mussels overtop and around the dish. Sprinkle with the remaining basil and serve immediately. Serves 2.

Nut-Crusted Chicken Breasts Stuffed with Goat Cheese

This is a main course that looks gorgeous fanned out on individual plates. Stuff and bread the chicken in advance, then refrigerate until ready to cook. It's also a recipe that's easy to double or triple.

2 large skinless, boneless chicken breasts
2 oz (50 g) creamy fresh goat cheese
2 Tbsp (30 mL) cream cheese
1 egg yolk
2 green onions, chopped
½ red or yellow bell pepper, roasted, seeded, and chopped

¼ cup (60 mL) dry breadcrumbs
¼ cup (60 mL) finely ground almonds or pine nuts
salt and freshly ground black pepper
1 egg beaten with 2 Tbsp (30 mL) milk or cream
1 Tbsp (15 mL) olive oil

1 Preheat the oven to 350°F (180°C).

2 Lay the chicken breasts flat on a cutting board. Insert a small paring knife into the thickest part of each chicken breast. Holding your palm over the breast, wiggle the knife back and forth to form a pocket, keeping the entry to the pocket small.

3 In a small bowl, combine the goat cheese and cream cheese with a fork, then stir in the egg yolk, green onions, and roasted pepper. Using your fingers, stuff the chicken pockets with the cheese mixture. Press to close.

4 On a plate, combine the breadcrumbs, ground nuts, salt, and pepper. Whisk together the egg and milk or cream. Dip both sides of the stuffed chicken breasts in the egg mixture, then roll in the crumbs to coat on both sides.

5 Heat the olive oil in a heavy, non-stick ovenproof skillet over medium-high heat and brown the chicken quickly on both sides. Transfer the skillet to the oven and bake for 10 minutes or just until the chicken is cooked through. Remove from the oven and let rest for 5 to 10 minutes before slicing across the grain. Fan the sliced chicken over two warm plates and serve with garlic mashed potatoes (see page 156) and a green vegetable like asparagus or green beans. Serves 2.

Seared Scallops St. Jacques

Here's The Guy's updated version of an old steak house recipe—fat scallops sautéed until their sugars caramelize, then served with a potato purée and a drizzle of creamy white wine sauce.

Potatoes
2 medium potatoes
1 Tbsp (15 mL) unsalted butter

Sauce
1 Tbsp (15 mL) unsalted butter
1 Tbsp (15 mL) all-purpose flour
¼ cup (60 mL) dry white wine

Scallops
¾ lb (375 g) large sea scallops, patted dry
3 Tbsp (45 mL) olive oil

2 Tbsp (30 mL) whipping cream or sour cream
salt and freshly ground white pepper

½ cup (125 mL) fish stock, bottled clam nectar, or chicken stock
¼ cup (60 mL) whipping cream
salt and freshly ground white pepper

sea salt
minced Italian parsley for garnish

1 To make the potatoes, peel the potatoes and boil or steam them until tender. Put the cooked potatoes through a ricer or mash well (you want them creamy) with the butter and the whipping cream. Season to taste with salt and pepper and keep warm.

2 To make the sauce, melt the butter in a saucepan over medium heat and stir in the flour. Slowly add the white wine, whisking until thick. Add the stock and bring to a boil. Add the whipping cream and simmer until the sauce thickens, then season with salt and white pepper to taste. Keep warm.

3 To sear the scallops, heat the olive oil in a large, non-stick skillet over high until it begins to smoke (make sure the hood fan is turned on). Set the scallops in the hot skillet and sear. Don't move them for 2 to 3 minutes (you want the scallops to brown and caramelize). Then turn and sear the second side for 1 to 2 minutes more. Be careful not to overcook—the scallops should be almost raw in the middle.

4 To serve, place some of the creamy potatoes in the center of two dinner plates. Surround by seared scallops. Drizzle the scallops with the cream sauce and sprinkle with the minced Italian parsley. Serves 2.

Chicken Saltimbocca with Saffron Risotto

Prosciutto is the duct tape of the kitchen—wrap it around almost anything and make it better. The Guy learned this simple trick in Italy, where saltimbocca was invented to take any lean meat—from chicken breasts to seafood—into gourmet territory.

Try wrapping thick fish fillets, individual tenderloin steaks, or tiger prawns in paper-thin slices of this salt-cured ham before pan-frying or grilling. The results are always impressive.

4 thin slices lean prosciutto

2 boneless, skinless chicken breast halves, about
 5 to 6 oz (150 to 175 g) each

4 to 6 fresh sage leaves

2 Tbsp (30 mL) olive oil, divided

2 shallots, minced

1 clove garlic, minced

½ cup (125 mL) chicken broth

1 Tbsp (15 mL) cold butter

1 Place the prosciutto on your work surface, overlapping two slices slightly for each piece of chicken. Arrange a chicken breast on top of each piece of prosciutto and top each breast with 2 to 3 fresh sage leaves. Wrap the prosciutto around the chicken to enclose it—if the prosciutto is cut thinly it will adhere to itself, otherwise, use toothpicks to secure.

2 Heat 1 Tbsp (15 mL) of the oil in a non-stick sauté pan over medium-high heat. Place the wrapped chicken breasts in the pan, seam-side down, and sauté for 5 to 6 minutes per side, until lightly browned. Add the shallots and garlic to the pan and sauté for a few minutes, until starting to brown, then add the chicken broth. Bring to a boil and cover the pan. Simmer for 5 minutes, then remove the lid and cook for a few minutes longer, until the liquid is reduced by half.

3 Arrange the chicken on individual serving plates. Quickly whisk the butter into the sauce in the pan, then drizzle over each chicken breast. Serve with Saffron Risotto (see next page) or cream-spiked mashed potatoes and something green (a simple romaine salad, steamed broccoli, sautéed spinach with garlic, etc.). Serves 2.

Saffron Risotto

Alongside The Guy's prosciutto-wrapped chicken, this creamy, golden rice, shot through with vibrant green onions and sweet baby peas, is perfection (or you can add sautéed mushrooms and prawns to make it a main dish).

Get everything ready for the risotto before you start cooking the chicken and both will be finished in 20 minutes—ask your date to stir and you'll be in close and steamy quarters even before you score a hit with dinner. And remember to eat it immediately.

2 cups (500 mL) broth (vegetable or chicken, homemade if possible)
½ tsp (2 mL) crumbled saffron threads
1 Tbsp (15 mL) extra virgin olive oil
1 Tbsp (15 mL) butter
½ cup (125 mL) minced onion
1 clove garlic, minced

½ cup (125 mL) risotto rice (arborio, carnaroli, or vialone nano)
¼ cup (60 mL) white wine
½ cup (125 mL) frozen baby peas, thawed
½ cup (125 mL) freshly grated Parmesan cheese

1   In a saucepan, bring the broth to a boil over high heat. Reduce the heat to low and stir in the saffron. Keep warm.

2   Meanwhile, in a wide, non-stick sauté pan, heat the oil and butter together over medium-high heat. Add the onion and garlic and cook for 5 minutes or until softened, but not brown. Add the rice and stir for about 1 minute, until it's coated and shiny. Add the wine, stirring until it's completely absorbed.

3   Now, begin adding the hot broth, about ½ cup (125 mL) at a time. Stir the risotto with a wooden spoon until the broth is absorbed, then add another ladle of broth. Continue in this manner until the broth is used up and the rice is cooked al dente (tender but not mushy). Don't worry about stirring constantly or vigorously—the risotto will be fine even if you almost ignore it. But do stir it and don't add the broth all at once. The more you stir, and the more attention you pay, the creamier the end result. You'll have to start testing the risotto before all of the broth is used up to determine when it's ready. The entire process will take 20 to 25 minutes. Stir in the peas and ¼ cup (60 mL) of the cheese, plus a little more broth, cover the pan and let the risotto rest for 2 minutes. Sprinkle with the remaining cheese and serve alongside the chicken. Serves 2.

WISE GUY:

If you want great risotto you need great rice and Parmigiano Reggiano cheese. Risotto is a special, short-grain rice that's starchy and gets creamy when it's cooked with broth added incrementally, over time. Don't try this at home with long-grain or converted rice, or you'll never make risotto again.

Arborio is the easiest kind of risotto rice to find but it also makes the stiffest risotto. The Guy hates to be a risotto snob but, for a date, splurge on vialone nano rice (this starchy variety makes a particularly creamy risotto) or go nuts and get carnaroli, Italy's ritziest rice. You might pay more than $15 a pound, but for that really special date, don't risk gummy risotto—learn to be a risotto guru and you'll reap the rewards.

Vodka Prawns on Angel Hair Pasta

Start with big, fresh tiger prawns to make this simple but decadent dinner for two. If you have all the ingredients ready, and the pasta is precooked, it only takes about 10 minutes to finish this dish. Do what they do in Italian restaurants—cook and portion the pasta in advance then, just before serving, place it in a sieve and lower it into a big pot of boiling water for 30 seconds to reheat.

½ cup (125 mL) all-purpose flour
¾ lb (375 g) large tiger prawns, peeled and
  deveined (about 5 prawns per person)
2 Tbsp (30 mL) olive oil
1 Tbsp (15 mL) butter
1 Tbsp (15 mL) minced garlic
¼ cup (60 mL) finely chopped shallots or
  onions
¼ cup (60 mL) vodka

½ cup (125 mL) chicken broth
¾ cup (175 mL) diced or puréed canned
  tomatoes or tomato sauce
½ cup (125 mL) heavy cream
salt and freshly ground black pepper
1 Tbsp (15 mL) chopped fresh basil or basil
  pesto
½ lb (250 g) angel hair pasta
fresh basil, for garnish

1 Put the flour in a bag, add the prawns, and toss to lightly coat. Remove the prawns from the bag and shake off any excess flour. In a non-stick sauté pan, heat the oil and butter over high heat. When the fat is sizzling, add the prawns, browning lightly on both sides—this should only take a minute or two. Remove the prawns from the oil and drain on a plate lined with paper towels.

2 Add the garlic and shallots to the hot pan and cook for a couple of minutes, until softened. Add the vodka and cook together for 1 minute, then add the chicken broth and tomatoes and bring to a boil. Reduce the heat to medium and simmer for 5 to 10 minutes, until the liquid has reduced by half. Slowly stir in the cream and simmer for 3 minutes to thicken.

3 Meanwhile, bring a large pot of salted water to a boil, add the angel hair pasta and cook until al dente (about 5 minutes). Drain and return to the pot.

4 Season the sauce with salt and pepper to taste, and a pinch of sugar if needed, then stir in the fresh basil. Return the prawns to the sauce and toss to heat through for 1 minute. Pour the sauce over the hot, cooked pasta and toss together over medium heat for 30 seconds. Serve immediately in warmed pasta bowls, topped with a sprinkling of chopped basil. Serves 2.

Halibut with Squash Ribbons and Lemon Butter Sauce

This is a delicious fish dish to create quickly when the mood strikes. Serve it with basmati rice or baby potatoes on the side.

1 lemon

¾ lb (375 g) boneless halibut fillet, skin removed, cut across the grain on a diagonal, into 1-inch- (2.5-cm-) thick slices

salt and cayenne pepper

¼ cup (60 mL) all-purpose flour

Zucchini Ribbons

2 small, 6-inch (15-cm) zucchini

2 to 3 Tbsp (30 to 45 mL) olive oil

1 clove garlic, minced

½ cup (125 mL) white wine

2 Tbsp (30 mL) butter, cold

1 Tbsp (15 mL) minced fresh parsley

1 Tbsp (15 mL) unsalted butter

salt

1 Scrub the lemon well. Using a microplane grater, remove the zest from the lemon. Set the zest aside.

2 Cut the lemon in half, remove the seeds and use a citrus reamer to remove the juice (you should have about 3 to 4 Tbsp/45 to 60 mL). Set aside. To make the zucchini ribbons, wash the zucchini and remove the ends but don't peel. Using a vegetable peeler, slice the zucchini into long, lengthwise, paper-thin ribbons. Have all the sauce ingredients ready and measured before you begin cooking.

3 Put the fish slices on a plate and season with the salt and cayenne. Place the flour on another plate and thoroughly dredge both sides of the fish slices to coat.

4 To cook the zucchini, in a separate pan, heat the butter over medium-high heat and add the zucchini ribbons. Sauté until the ribbons are just tender. Season with salt and keep warm.

5 Heat the olive oil in a non-stick sauté pan over medium-high heat and sauté the fish for 1 to 2 minutes per side until golden. Pile the warm zucchini ribbons onto the center of two warm serving plates and arrange the fish slices overtop.

6 Add the garlic, white wine, reserved lemon zest, and lemon juice to the fish pan. Bring to a boil over high heat, scraping up any browned bits, and simmer for 3 minutes or until the liquid is reduced to ¼ cup (60 mL). Remove the pan from the heat and whisk in the 2 Tbsp (30 mL) of cold butter. Pour the hot sauce over the fish and zucchini, sprinkle with parsley, and serve immediately with steamed potatoes or rice. Serves 2.

Warm Poached Figs on Ice

When you need to impress someone, buy really good quality vanilla ice cream and top with this yummy, warm fig sauce. Serve with a pretty cookie on the side (look for crisp Belgium cookies, drizzled in white or dark chocolate, at any gourmet grocery). This is the perfect finale for a dinner date—you can make the fig sauce a few days in advance, and warm it just before serving. For a more virtuous dessert, just spoon the fig compote into a couple of stemmed dessert wine or small martini glasses and top with a dollop of lemon yogurt.

1 cup (250 mL) dried Mission figs, halved or
   quartered
1 cup (250 mL) granulated sugar
2 cups (500 mL) red wine

cinnamon stick
1 star anise
2 cloves
2 scoops vanilla bean ice cream

1 Clip the woody stems from the figs and put them in a small saucepan with the sugar and wine. Tie the cinnamon stick, anise seed, and cloves in a small cheesecloth bag (or use a tea ball to hold the spices) and submerge in the pan.

2 Bring to a boil over medium heat, then reduce the heat to low and simmer until the figs are soft. Continue to simmer until the sauce thickens slightly. Remove the spice package and discard, then cool the fig sauce slightly or chill. (If chilled, warm in the microwave before serving.)

3 To serve, scoop the ice cream into pretty dessert dishes and top with the warm poached figs and sauce. Serves 2 (with extra sauce).

WISE GUY: Make sure you start with good quality ice cream and remember, you get what you pay for. Inexpensive, commercial ice creams incorporate a lot of air into the mixture (this is called "overrun"). Next time you're at the supermarket, pay attention to how much that pint of ice cream weighs—the top-quality brands have only a 20 percent overrun, while others have a 50 percent overrun and more.

If you can, find a local artisan ice cream or gelato producer and serve something special.

Butter Pecan Banana Sundae

This is an adult sundae with a tropical island twist—a warm nutty sauce, shot with rum, and loaded with caramelized bananas. Simple and simply addictive, it's a dessert that's done in 5 minutes.

¼ cup (60 mL) unsalted butter
¼ cup (60 mL) packed dark brown sugar
¼ cup (60 mL) chopped pecans
1 medium banana, sliced

2 Tbsp (30 mL) dark rum
2 large scoops good-quality butter pecan or
   vanilla ice cream

1 Heat the butter in a small frying pan over medium-high heat. When the butter is melted, add the brown sugar and stir until the mixture is bubbly. Add the sliced bananas and pecans and cook for 1 to 2 minutes or until they're nicely caramelized. Stir in the rum. Simmer for a minute (or flambé with a long match if you're feeling dramatic—just stand back and be careful).

2 Scoop the ice cream into two attractive dessert dishes and top each with some of the banana mixture. Serves 2.

Happy Trails

As a kid, The Guy always loved to strap on the six-shooters and play cowboys and Indians. But these days, when he can't find the time to ride off into the sunset, some good southwestern cowboy grub can be almost as much fun.

A salad topped with grilled chicken and fresh corn on a summer evening, a chicken-fried steak sandwich on a weeknight or a fancy southwestern feast complete with apple turnovers keeps The Guy croonin' along happy trails. It's all part of that wild western thang!

Cowboy Steak

This is The Guy's way to stretch a single steak into a dinner for four. Serve it with Sweet Potato Mash with Chipotles (see page 215) and perhaps a few sautéed wild mushrooms when you're shooting for that artsy, New Mexican, urbane cowboy style.

The flank steak is a particularly lean cut so beware of overcooking—flank steak can't be cooked past medium rare or it will be tough as an old shoe. The trick is to cook it fast at a hot temperature to sear the juices inside—then let the meat rest for at least 10 minutes after grilling to let the juices settle. The steak actually continues cooking as it rests. Then slice it thinly across the grain—if you're seeing a lot of juice on the cutting board, you're slicing it too soon.

¼ cup (60 mL) rye whisky

2 Tbsp (30 mL) soy sauce

2 cloves garlic, minced

1 Tbsp (15 mL) Worcestershire sauce

1 Tbsp (15 mL) olive oil

2 tsp (10 mL) brown sugar

1 tsp (5 mL) chili powder

¼ tsp (1 mL) cayenne pepper or chipotle chili
   powder

1 tsp (5 mL) coarsely crushed black peppercorns

1½ lb (750 g) flank steak or hangar steak

1 In a small bowl, whisk together the whisky, soy sauce, garlic, and Worcestershire sauce. Place the steak in a zippered plastic bag with the whisky marinade and refrigerate overnight (or up to 2 days), turning occasionally.

2 Remove the steak from the refrigerator at least 30 minutes before grilling and pat dry. Rub the steak on both sides with the olive oil. Combine the brown sugar, chili powder, cayenne, and black peppercorns, and rub over both sides of the steak. Set aside.

3 Heat the barbecue to high and place the steak on the grill. Grill for 3 to 4 minutes per side for medium rare.

4 Transfer the steak to a cutting board and tent with foil. Allow to rest for 10 minutes to let the juices settle. When ready, thinly slice the steak across the grain on the diagonal, and then serve. Serves 4.

WISE GUY: You can serve even more people with a single flank steak if you serve it overmixed salad greens or fajita-style, wrapped in flour tortillas with grilled bell peppers, onions, and/or other vegetables. If you're planning a fajita party, slice some colorful peppers and onions into wedges, toss them with a little of the whisky marinade, and stir-fry them in a barbecue stir-fry basket designed for use on the grill until they start to char.

Grilled Quesadillas

The Guy's favorite way to start a dinner on the deck is with these gooey quesadillas, hot off the grill. Feel free to use a flavored flour tortilla, and fill your quesadillas with any kind of fillings. Just make sure you have the basics—salsa, cilantro, and grated cheese—and don't overfill the tortillas (or they'll be sloppy, not crisp). Also, remember to watch the tortillas on the grill as they burn quickly. Learn this simple technique, and you'll always have easy appetizers on a summer day.

Avocado-cream dipping sauce
1 ripe Haas avocado, peeled, pitted,
   and mashed
¼ cup (60 mL) mayonnaise
¼ cup (60 mL) sour cream

10 flour tortillas (plain, tomato, spinach, etc.)
1 cup (250 mL) spicy salsa
¼ cup (60 mL) olive oil
1 avocado, peeled, pitted, and slivered
½ cup (125 mL) cooked black beans (rinsed and
   drained well if canned)

2 tsp (10 mL) freshly squeezed lime juice
2 Tbsp (30 mL) chopped cilantro
1 green onion, chopped
¼ tsp (1 mL) Asian chili paste
salt and freshly ground black pepper to taste

6 thin slices smoked chicken or turkey, slivered
2 cups (500 mL) shredded Monterey Jack or
   mozzarella cheese
¼ cup (60 mL) chopped cilantro

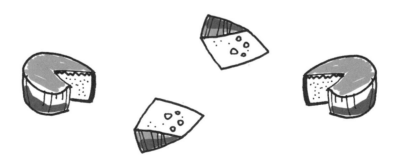

1   For the dipping sauce, combine all the ingredients in a blender or food processor and whirl until smooth. Chill. Pour the oil into a small bowl.

2   To make perfect quesadillas, learn this technique: using a pastry brush, very lightly coat one side of a tortilla with oil. Lay the tortilla, oiled-side down, on a plate. Spread a thin layer of salsa over the tortilla, spreading to the edges, top with a few slivers of avocado, a sprinkling of black beans, some bits of smoked turkey, and a smattering of chopped cilantro. Sprinkle with cheese. Top with a second tortilla, brush the tortilla lightly with oil, and press down with a spatula to seal the layers. Continue to make quesadillas in this manner (you can just stack them up on the plate as you go). Remember to fill the quesadillas sparingly—too much filling is counter productive, your quesadillas will be soggy and difficult to eat. They should be a little gooey, but crisp.

3   Heat the barbecue to medium-high heat and, using a wide spatula, carefully transfer each quesadilla to the grill. Cook on one side for 2 to 3 minutes, until it starts to brown and melt together, then quickly flip to cook the second side.

4   Repeat until all the quesadillas are crispy on the outside and cooked through. Watch carefully so they don't burn.

5   Set the grilled quesadillas aside on a cutting board for a few minutes to cool before cutting into wedges. Serve immediately with avocado dipping sauce. Makes about 24 wedges.

WISE GUY: Always start with salsa and shredded cheese, but vary your quesadillas with other fillings. The Guy likes some kind of protein (beans, crabmeat, slivered ham, or chicken), a vegetable or fruit (slivers of avocado, ripe peaches, pineapple, or roasted red peppers) and fresh herbs (cilantro, basil, green onions, or Italian parsley). Tex-Mex combinations can morph into Asian (barbecue pork or duck with hoisin sauce) or French (pears or fresh figs with blue cheese and chicken) or even Italian (ham and pineapple, or salami and peppers, with tomato sauce and basil). Use this same technique for making open-faced tortilla pizzas on the grill—the tortillas form a nice crispy crust for these speedy snacks.

Southwestern Chicken and Corn Salad

One of The Guy's favorite meals, this makes a yummy lunch or simple supper in late summer, when those first cobs of sweet peaches-and-cream corn are ready in the garden. Pick them, ferry them directly to your kitchen, and make this salad for your favorite buffalo gal.

Dressing

2 green onions, chopped

4 Tbsp (60 mL) freshly squeezed lemon or lime juice

1 tsp (5 mL) grated lemon or lime zest

1 tsp (5 mL) honey

1 tsp (5 mL) Dijon mustard

3 Tbsp (45 mL) chopped cilantro leaves or 1 Tbsp (15 mL) coriander chutney

¼ cup (60 mL) extra virgin olive oil

1 tsp (5 mL) light soy sauce

½ tsp (2 mL) chili paste or ¼ tsp (1 mL) cayenne

sea salt

Salad

4 ears fresh corn

1 small jicama or young turnip, peeled and diced (¼-inch/5-mm dice)

1 red bell pepper, seeded and diced

1 avocado, peeled and diced

2 large ripe tomatoes, seeded and chopped

1 lb (500 g) mixed salad greens

vegetable oil, for frying

6 corn tortillas

sea salt to taste

2 skinless, boneless chicken breasts

1 Preheat the oven to 350°F (180°C) or preset the grill to high.

2 In a blender or food processor, whirl the dressing ingredients together and taste. If you've used lemon instead of lime juice, it might need a touch more honey. Set aside.

3 Remove the leaves and cornsilk from the cobs. Holding the cobs upright on the cutting board, use a sharp knife to remove the kernels, cutting down from the top of the cob to the base. Place the corn kernels in a bowl, along with any of the sweet milky juice that's released.

4 Put the chicken breasts on a plate and drizzle with 1 Tbsp (15 mL) of the dressing. Rub all over to thoroughly coat the chicken. Bake the breasts in the oven for 30 minutes—or on the grill for about 15 minutes—until just cooked. Set aside to cool, then cut into chunks or shreds.

5 Add the chopped jicama (see page 505) or turnip, red pepper, avocado, and tomatoes to the corn in the bowl. Add half of the remaining dressing and toss to coat. Set aside.

6 In a non-stick pan, heat about ½ inch (1 cm) of canola oil over medium-high heat. Slice the corn tortillas into thin strips, and add to the hot oil, a few at a time. Deep-fry until the strips are curled and crisp. Drain them on paper towels and sprinkle with a little sea salt.

7 When you're ready to eat, toss the greens with the remaining dressing and divide among four plates. Top each salad with some shredded chicken and corn salad. Strew the crispy corn tortilla strips around and serve immediately. Serves 4.

WISE GUY:

Coriander chutney is an East Indian condiment that The Guy always keeps in the fridge. It's essentially like basil pesto but made with ground cilantro and chilies. Use it when you have no fresh cilantro in the house and when your recipe (whether it's Mexican, Southwestern, or Southeast Asian) is crying out for the flavor of this unique herb. You can find it at Indian groceries and large supermarkets—it's a lifesaver for the gourmet pantry.

Corn Sticks

Make this quick bread in a cast iron corn-stick pan or a muffin tin. Add a couple of chopped jalapeño peppers if you want to make it spicy.

1 cup (250 mL) stone-ground cornmeal
½ cup (125 mL) all-purpose flour
2 tsp (10 mL) baking powder
½ tsp (1 mL) baking soda
½ tsp (1 mL) salt
1 Tbsp (45 mL) granulated sugar

3 large eggs
¾ cup (175 mL) milk
¼ cup (60 mL) canola oil
1 cup (250 mL) corn kernels, fresh or frozen
½ cup (125 mL) grated aged cheddar cheese

1 In a mixing bowl, combine the cornmeal, flour, baking powder, baking soda, salt, and sugar. In a separate bowl, lightly beat the eggs and whisk in the milk and canola oil. Stir in the corn and grated cheese. Add the wet ingredients to the dry, and mix quickly with a fork just to combine. Don't overmix.

2 If you're using a cast iron corn-stick pan or muffin tin, brush with oil and preheat in a 400°F (200°C) oven for 10 minutes. Pour the cornbread batter into the hot pans, then bake for about 20 to 25 minutes or until firm and golden. Makes 1 dozen.

Chicken-Fried Chicken

Deep in the heart of Texas it's steak that's flattened, floured, and fried chicken-style but The Guy likes this idea for the ubiquitous boneless chicken thighs, so easy to find in almost any supermarket. Just season, flour, and fry—and serve with Corn Sticks (see page 213) and creamy coleslaw (see page 165) on the side. These flattened and fried chicken cutlets also make a great sandwich on a crusty bun or buttermilk biscuit (see page 64), with gravy, of course.

1 lb (500 g) boneless, skinless chicken thighs
½ tsp (2 mL) cayenne pepper or ancho
  chili powder
½ tsp (2 mL) granulated garlic
½ tsp (2 mL) onion powder
salt and freshly ground black pepper

1 tsp (5 mL) sweet paprika
½ cup (125 mL) all-purpose flour
1 egg beaten with ¼ cup (60 mL) cold water
canola oil for frying
2 cups (500 mL) of milk for the gravy

1 Open the boneless chicken thighs flat on a sheet of plastic wrap, cover with another sheet of plastic wrap, and pound lightly with a meat mallet to flatten into an even thickness.

2 In a small bowl, combine the cayenne, granulated garlic, onion powder, salt, pepper, and paprika. Sprinkle this seasoning evenly over both sides of the chicken.

3 Place the flour on a plate and dip the seasoned chicken in it, coating both sides, and shaking off any excess flour.

4 In a separate shallow bowl, whisk together the egg and water. Using tongs, dip each piece of floured chicken in the egg mixture, then dip again in the flour.

WISE GUY: This is one time when it's absolutely essential to have a couple of good pairs of metal chef's tongs (see page 487). Use them to pick up the chicken when dipping it into the flour, egg, and flour (to keep your hands clean) and for turning the chicken in the pan (always use a fresh pair of tongs to prevent cross contamination).

5 Heat ¼ inch (5 mm) of canola oil in a non-stick sauté pan over medium-high heat and fry the chicken until nicely browned on both sides. Drain the chicken pieces on a plate lined with paper towels and keep warm in a 200°F (95°C) oven while you finish cooking all the chicken.

6 Once the chicken is done, add about 4 Tbsp (60 mL) of the remaining seasoned flour to the drippings in the pan, stirring to form a paste (a.k.a. roux). Cook the roux over medium heat, stirring constantly, for a few minutes or until it turns a deep golden brown. Slowly stir in the milk and bring to a boil. Continue boiling until the gravy is nicely thickened. Spoon the gravy over the chicken and serve with biscuits or cornbread. Serves 4.

Sweet Potato Mash with Chipotles

When The Guy was in Texas, he had a nice grilled steak seasoned with a spicy rub and served with creamy and colorful sweet potatoes on the side. Adding a finely chopped chipotle pepper (the kind you can find in a can in adobo sauce) and a bit of sweet maple syrup gives this version of sweet potato mash a lovely depth that stands up well to steak.

1 lb (500 g) orange-fleshed sweet potatoes
    (about 1 large potato)
½ lb (250 g) Yukon Gold potatoes
¼ cup (60 mL) butter

1 Tbsp (15 mL) minced chipotle chilies, in
    adobo sauce
1 Tbsp (15 mL) maple syrup
salt and freshly ground black pepper

1 Place a steamer and about ½ cup (125 mL) of water in a large saucepan. Place the sweet potatoes and potatoes in the steamer. Bring the water to a boil over medium-high heat. Reduce the heat to medium-low and steam for 15 minutes or until the vegetables are easy to pierce with a fork. Drain the steaming water and remove the steamer from the pot. Return the potatoes to the pot and set over the heat to steam and dry slightly. Using a potato masher, mash with butter and stir in the syrup, chipotles, salt, and pepper. Serve hot alongside your steak. Serves 4.

Sloppy Roys

The Guy's childhood hero, Roy Rogers, was one of the tidiest cowboys on the range, so this wild western version of beef on a bun isn't quite as sloppy as the original. High-class ingredients, just like the gentleman cowboy himself.

Perfect to serve to a cowboy crowd on a summer afternoon, or to heat up for a tailgate party to support the home team.

3 lb (1.5 kg) beef brisket
salt and freshly ground black pepper
2 Tbsp (30 mL) olive oil
one 12-oz (375-mL) bottle dark beer
½ cup (125 mL) packed brown sugar
1 cup (250 mL) ketchup
1 large onion, minced
2 Tbsp (30 mL) Dijon mustard

1 Tbsp (15 mL) chili powder
1 Tbsp (15 mL) dried oregano
1 tsp (5 mL) ground cumin
3 cloves garlic, pressed
2 chipotle chili peppers in adobo (chopped) or
     1 tsp (5 mL) liquid smoke
dash or two of Worcestershire sauce
12 crusty whole wheat rolls

1 Preheat the oven to 300°F (150°C).

2 Rub the roast all over with salt and pepper. Heat the oil over medium-high heat in a Dutch oven on the stovetop. Brown the seasoned beef on all sides.

3 In a food processor, combine the beer, sugar, ketchup, onion, mustard, chili powder, oregano, cumin, garlic, chipotle chilies, and Worcestershire. Process until smooth. Pour the beer mixture over the meat, cover the pot tightly with foil and seal with the lid. Transfer to the oven and braise for 4 hours or until the meat is very tender.

4 Remove the beef from the Dutch oven and shred with a fork or coarsely chop.

5 Pour the cooking liquid from the Dutch oven into a glass measuring cup and spoon off any excess fat. Return the beef and sauce to the pot, cover, and simmer on low heat for 20 minutes. Keep warm and serve, or chill overnight and reheat to serve.

6 To serve, pile the beef on crusty buns. Serves 12.

WISE GUY: This is the kind of dish you can make in a slow cooker, too. After the roast is browned, place it in the slow cooker, cover with the sauce ingredients, and cook for 12 hours. Shred the meat and simmer the skimmed braising sauce on the stovetop until it's thick. Mix the sauce with the shredded beef. You can stretch this dish to feed an even bigger crowd by adding canned pinto beans. Coleslaw (see page 165) is good on the side.

Apple Turnovers

Out on the range, cowboy cooks made fried pies—pastries filled with apples, wild berries, or mincemeat that could be eaten in the saddle or around the campfire without a knife and fork. These flaky pies are baked and simple to make with frozen puff pastry.

4 Granny Smith apples, peeled and cored
1 tsp (5 mL) ground cinnamon
¼ cup (60 mL) packed brown sugar
1 Tbsp (15 mL) cornstarch

cranberries or raisins (optional)
frozen puff pastry, thawed
cream and granulated sugar

1 Preheat the oven to 350°F (180°C).

2 Thinly slice the apples and combine in a medium bowl with the cinnamon, sugar, and cornstarch. Toss well to coat the apple slices.

3 Place the puff pastry on a flat work surface and roll until it's about ¼ inch (4 mm) thick. Cut the pastry into 4-inch (5-mm) squares. Use a little cold water to moisten the edges of each square. Put some apple filling into the center of each square and fold the pastry over to form triangles. Press with your fingers or a fork to seal all the way around.

4 Line a baking sheet with parchment paper and place the turnovers on the baking sheet. Brush the turnovers lightly with cream (or milk) and dust with sugar.

5 Bake for 35 to 40 minutes or until the turnovers are puffed and golden. Serve warm. Makes 1 dozen apple turnovers.

The Greek God Guy

Think about it: The Greeks were the Adonis's of the ancient world. Every Guy should work on his inner Greek—that combination of fiery patriot and laid-back island Guy. You know, the one with the good tan, and the great stash of olive oil and red wine. Oh yeah, and The Guy who breaks into a slow, sexy dance at the drop of a plate!

Zorba's Mussels

A big bowl of these mussels, with garlicky pieces of toasted pita bread and a little ouzo on ice, takes The Guy right back to his favorite Greek taverna on the beach.

If you're in a hurry, just pick up some fresh tomato salsa or bruschetta topping at the supermarket to start this speedy dish. Farmed mussels don't require scrubbing or de-bearding, so will save you time, too.

3 Tbsp (45 mL) olive oil
2 ripe Roma tomatoes, chopped
¼ cup (60 mL) finely chopped red or
  white onion
2 cloves garlic, minced
1 green onion, chopped
1 Tbsp (30 mL) chopped Italian parsley
1 tsp (5 mL) chopped fresh mint

1 tsp (5 mL) basil
salt and freshly ground black pepper
¼ cup (60 mL) white wine
2 to 3 lb (1 to 1.5 kg) fresh, meaty blue mussels
  (scrubbed and de-bearded)
2 Tbsp (30 mL) freshly squeezed lemon juice
1 to 2 thick Greek pita breads, toasted and brushed
with garlic butter

1 In a deep saucepan or wok, heat the olive oil over high heat and sauté the tomato, red onion, and garlic for 5 minutes or until the onion is soft. Add the green onion, parsley, mint, basil, salt, pepper, wine, and the mussels. Cover the pan and steam the mussels, shaking the pan frequently, for 7 to 8 minutes or just until the shells open.

2 Pour the mussels and pan juices into two shallow soup plates, mounding the mussels high in the serving dishes, and discarding any that don't open. Sprinkle the mussels with lemon juice and serve with thick pita bread that's been toasted (on the grill or in a toaster oven) and brushed with garlic butter. Serves 2.

WISE GUY: De-bearding mussels is a little time consuming but necessary when you're using wild mussels (farmed mussels require less cleaning). De-bearding simply means pulling off the dark "beard" protruding from the side of the shell (it's the stuff that keeps the mussels attached to rocks in the sea). Grab it with your fingers and pull down (from the "fat" end of the mussel to the hinged end) to remove. Make sure you buy mussels from a reputable fish store, preferably stored on ice or living in circulating water (never packaged). Mussels must be alive before you cook them, so make sure the shells are tightly closed, or that they close when you tap the shell on the counter. Throw away any uncooked mussels that aren't closed or which don't open once cooked.

The Addictive Eggplant Antipasto

There's a Greek gal at The Guy's local farmers' market who turns out delicious traditional Greek take-out—including a rich eggplant and bell pepper condiment that's addictive. Serve it piled on crackers, pita, or sliced baguette for a simple appetizer (or consider using it to fill an omelet or serve atop a piece of grilled fish). This concoction also freezes beautifully—so make a double batch and you'll always have a sensational snack on hand.

2 medium purple eggplants, stems removed
1 Tbsp (15 mL) sea salt
1 red bell pepper, halved and seeded
1 green bell pepper, halved and seeded
1 large onion, peeled and quartered
½ cup (125 mL) olive oil

2 cloves garlic, minced
2 Tbsp (30 mL) freshly squeezed lemon juice
salt and freshly ground black pepper
1 Tbsp (15 mL) chopped fresh oregano
   (optional)

1 Use the large shredding disk on your food processor to shred the eggplant into long shreds (alternately, use the largest holes on your box grater, or slice the eggplant into thin strips by hand). Toss the shredded eggplant with sea salt, place in a colander and set in the kitchen sink to drain for 30 minutes. Rinse with cold water and squeeze dry with your hands.

2 Sliver the peppers and onions into similar, ¼- by 1-inch (5-mm by 2.5-cm) pieces.

3 Heat the olive oil in a wide sauté pan over medium heat. Add the garlic and onions, and cook until the onions begin to lightly brown. Add the eggplant and sauté for 10 minutes longer, until the eggplant softens. Add the slivered peppers, cover the pan, and continue to cook together over medium-low heat for 45 to 50 minutes, until everything is soft, jammy, and melting together.

4 Stir in the lemon juice and season to taste with salt and pepper. Stir in the oregano, cover, and refrigerate or freeze. Makes 2 cups.

Tomato and Lentil Soup

There could be nothing easier than this savory soup—flavored with olive oil and dill, it's like a trip to the Greek islands on a winter afternoon. It's a classic dish for Lent and other occasions that call for meatless meals. Use the food processor to chop the onions and purée the tomatoes and you'll be eating in 30 minutes flat. A slice of crusty bread, slathered with a piece of creamy, ripe cheese, and a bowl of black olives, will finish your meal. Or sprinkle some crumbled feta over each bowl for an added boost of authentic Greek flavor.

¼ cup (60 mL) extra virgin olive oil

1 large onion, finely chopped

2 cloves garlic, minced

one 16-oz (500-mL) can (about 2 cups) Roma tomatoes, with juice (or one 14-oz/398-mL can plain tomato sauce)

2 to 3 cups (500 to 750 mL) chicken broth

1 can brown or green lentils, rinsed and drained

1 Tbsp (15 mL) balsamic vinegar

2 Tbsp (30 mL) chopped fresh dill, divided

1 dried hot chili pepper, crumbled (optional)

salt and freshly ground black pepper

crumbled feta cheese (optional)

1 Heat the oil in a soup pot and sauté the onions over medium heat for 10 minutes or until soft.

2 While the onions are cooking, put the canned tomatoes (juice and all) into the food processor and purée until smooth. Add the purée to the cooked onions in the pot and stir in the broth.

3 Add the lentils to the soup. Stir in the balsamic vinegar and half the dill (if you're stuck with dried dill, use only 1 Tbsp/15mL). Crumble the dried chili into the soup.

4 Bring the soup to a boil, then reduce the heat to medium-low and simmer for 30 minutes.

5 Season the soup with salt and pepper to taste. Just before serving, stir in the remaining fresh dill. Ladle into shallow soup bowls and garnish each serving with crumbled feta and more fresh dill, if desired. Serves 4.

Braised Lamb with Lemony Roasted Potatoes

The Guy learned about this slow-cooked lamb dish at his favorite Greek restaurant. Seems the rebels were hiding in the hills and had to cook their meals without telltale smoke. Ergo, everything was done in a pit in the ground. You don't have to go to such lengths to get tender lamb, but for the best results, you'll need to start marinating it the night before. A lightly steamed green vegetable—like broccoli or green beans—dressed with a little lemon juice and fruity Greek olive oil, is the classic side dish.

3 to 4 lb (1.5 to 2 kg) lamb shoulder roast

zest and juice of 1 lemon (about 3 Tbsp/45 mL juice and 2 tsp/10 mL zest)

½ tsp (2 mL) freshly ground black pepper

1 tsp (5 mL) dried oregano

4 cloves garlic, minced

¼ cup (60 mL) Dijon mustard

2 cups (500 mL) finely chopped onion (1 large onion)

1 Tbsp (15 mL) dried Greek oregano

2 bay leaves

1 tsp (5 mL) mustard seed

2 cups (500 mL) water (or replace half the amount with white wine)

2 whole heads garlic, for roasting

olive oil

fresh rosemary sprigs

1 Break the lamb shoulder into large pieces, removing the excess fat and sinew as you go. Place the lamb in a glass bowl or zippered plastic bag.

2 Scrub the lemon well, then pat dry. Use a microplane grater to remove the yellow zest from the lemon (avoid the white pith) and squeeze the juice using a citrus reamer. If you don't have a microplane grater, remove the zest using the fine holes of your box grater or shave off with a vegetable peeler and mince.

3 Add the juice and zest to the lamb, then stir in the pepper, oregano, minced garlic, and mustard. Cover the bowl with plastic (or seal the bag) and refrigerate the lamb overnight.

4 The next day, place the chopped onion, rosemary, bay leaves, and mustard seed in a heavy Dutch oven. Pour the lamb, with its marinade, over top. Add the water and bring to a boil over medium-high heat. Cover the pot and transfer to a 300°F (150°C) oven. Roast for 2 hours, then remove the lid and continue to roast for 40 minutes or until the meat is very tender and the braising liquid has reduced. During the last hour of cooking, roast the whole heads of garlic and the Lemony Roasted Potatoes (recipe follows) alongside the lamb. To prepare the garlic, use a sharp knife to cut ½ inch (1 cm) off the top of each head, exposing the cloves. Set the heads on a square of foil, drizzle with a few drops of olive oil, and gather the foil up around the heads, loosely enclosing it but leaving the top slightly open. Set the foil packet directly on the oven rack next to the braising lamb—the garlic should be roasted by the time the lamb is done.

5 To serve, lift the lamb from the cooking juices and arrange on a warm platter. Squeeze the whole cloves from the heads of roasted garlic, and scatter them around and between the lamb pieces. Surround with the Lemony Roasted Potatoes and garnish with fresh rosemary. Drizzle a bit of the braising juices and serve family style. Serves 4.

Lemony Roasted Potatoes

2 lb (1 kg) large white potatoes, peeled
sea salt
zest and juice from 1 lemon (about 3 Tbsp/
   45 mL juice and 2 tsp/10 mL zest)
freshly ground black pepper

2 cloves garlic, pressed in a garlic press
   or minced
¼ cup (60 mL) extra virgin Greek olive oil
1 tsp (5 mL) minced fresh rosemary

1 Cut the potatoes in half lengthwise and then cut each half into three or four long, thick pieces. Place in a heavy, non-stick roasting pan and sprinkle the pieces with salt. Let stand for 5 minutes.

2 Add the lemon juice, pepper, and garlic to the potatoes and toss to coat. Drizzle the olive oil over top and then transfer the pan to the 300°F (150°C) oven, alongside the lamb. Roast for about 1 hour or until the potatoes are tender and golden. Sprinkle the finely minced rosemary over the potatoes and serve with the lamb. Serves 4.

Greek Salad

Yes, this is the simple salad you'll find in tavernas all over Greece. Make it in the summertime, or whenever you have good fresh tomatoes. The Guy likes to use small cherry or grape tomatoes—they usually have good flavor and the extra skin means more healthy stuff. This substantial salad also stands up well when hauled along to summer potluck parties—add some steamed new potatoes or chickpeas to make it even sturdier.

2 cups (500 mL) grape tomatoes, halved if large or 4 large Roma tomatoes, halved, seeds removed and diced

1 yellow bell pepper, seeded and diced

1 medium English cucumber, quartered lengthwise, seeded, and cut into chunks

½ cup (125 mL) good quality Greek olives (like kalamata)

½ red onion, slivered

½ cup (125 mL) cubed or crumbled feta cheese

Dressing

2 to 3 Tbsp (30 to 45 mL) freshly squeezed lemon juice

1 tsp (5 mL) Dijon mustard

1 clove garlic, minced or pressed in a garlic press

salt and freshly ground black pepper

⅓ cup (75 mL) extra virgin olive oil

2 to 3 Tbsp (25 to 45 mL) chopped fresh dill

1 Combine the tomatoes, bell pepper, cucumber, olives, onion, and feta in a large bowl and toss well.

2 Whirl the dressing ingredients together in a blender or food processor (or just whisk together by hand) and pour over the salad. Chill for up to 1 hour or serve immediately. Serves 4 as a side salad.

Honey and Walnut Baklava

While you're doing the Greek god thing, pull out one final classic: baklava, with layers of crisp phyllo pastry, walnuts and raisins, and a glossy honey glaze. Make this when you want to impress. It's easy—really just a construction project with store-bought pastry—but if it all seems too daunting, you can always buy baklava at a Greek or Middle Eastern bakery.

1 package frozen phyllo pastry (24 sheets)
½ cup (125 mL) unsalted butter, melted
1½ cups (375 mL) finely ground walnuts

½ cup (125 mL) raisins
¾ cup (175 mL) packed brown sugar
¼ cup (60 mL) melted honey

1 Thaw the phyllo in the refrigerator overnight. Cut sheets to fit your pan with kitchen shears.

2 Butter a 13- x 9-inch (3.5-L) baking pan and lay a sheet of phyllo in the bottom. Brush the phyllo lightly with melted butter and lay another sheet on top. Brush with butter, sprinkle with some ground walnuts, a few raisins, and 2 Tbsp (30 mL) of the brown sugar. Continue layering, with nuts, raisins, and sugar on every second layer, until the pan is full. If there's any pastry hanging over the edges of the pan, fold it under and press down around the pan.

3 Cut the baklava into 18 pieces, cutting completely through the layers of phyllo. Bake at 375°F (190°C) for 30 minutes. Reduce the heat to 325°F (160°C) and bake 30 minutes longer. Brush the baked baklava with honey to glaze while warm. Makes 18 pieces.

WISE GUY: You can buy pre-made phyllo pastry dough sheets in the freezer section of most supermarkets (it's in a long, narrow box). Make sure to cover the pastry with a clean, lightly dampened kitchen towel while you're working so it doesn't dry out.

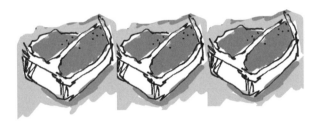

Steak House Suppers

Steak is the ultimate Guy thing—a nice, juicy piece of beef is essentially idiot-proof when you learn a few tricks from the steak house chefs. Herewith, The Guy's steak primer, whether it's a simple minute steak for supper on Tuesday or a strip loin on Saturday night. With a basic baked potato on the side (or a fancier stuffed version), a green salad, a pot of beans or a pile of sautéed mushrooms, all you need is a big, beefy Cabernet Sauvignon to make a steak supper a real feast.

Steak Basics

You can't pick a good steak without a program—some steaks are nicely marbled and perfect for grilling, others are so lean they need to be marinated, braised, or otherwise manipulated to get a tender result. Read the label for clues, some will say "grilling steak" or "simmering steak" so you'll know what to choose for the backyard grill and what to use for Swiss steak.

The highest grades of beef are the most marbled (that is, with the most intra-muscular fat flecked or streaked throughout the meat). The top grade is USDA Choice or AAA. But grass-fed beef—leaner because it's raised on grass and not on grain in the feedlot—has wonderful flavor as long as it's not overcooked. There's also organic beef, and branded beef from specific producers or specific types of cattle (think Angus, Galloway, or Kobe beef).

Aging also makes a difference when it comes to a tender steak. The steak that's bright cherry red (no age) won't likely be as tender as the steak that has that aged brownish-burgundy color. (If there's blood in the package, the meat may have been previously frozen and won't be as juicy.)

Pick the right cut for the recipe. Ask the butcher or use the following guidelines:

 Minute Steak

When a beef steak is "mechanically tenderized" it cooks quickly and is labeled "minute steak." This is the perfect cut for breaded or "chicken-fried" steak.

 Flank Steak

These long, flat steaks are best when marinated and grilled just until rare, then sliced diagonally, across the grain, for serving in sandwiches, rolled in fajitas, or over salad greens.

 Hanger Steak

The new darling of the bistro chef, this cut is a long, flat steak, similar to the flank steak.

 Round Steak

This steak, usually cut from the "bottom round," can be quite chewy—plan to braise it (this is the cut for beef stew) or slice thin and cook quickly for a stir-fry. If the steak is labeled "top round," you can get away with grilling it, but expect a chewier product.

 Sirloin Steak

This steak, from the rear portion of the loin, is the best value, in terms of price and flavor. It's not quite as tender as some grilling steaks, so make sure you don't cook beyond medium rare. Other steaks now available (cut from the bottom of the sirloin) include flap steaks (for braising), ball tip (for stir-fry or tenderizing), and tri tip (for stir-fries, fajitas, etc.).

 T-bone Steak

This classic steak (a.k.a. Porterhouse), includes both the meaty strip loin and tenderloin bits, and is still attached to the bone. Because cattle are getting larger all the time, it's hard to find a T-bone steak that's appropriate for one serving (and some supermarkets are simply cutting them too thin to cook properly). Ask for a thick T-bone, at least 1 inch (2.5 cm) thick, and share it if you want a tender steak on the bone.

Strip Loin

The top loin muscle becomes the strip loin steak, a nicely marbled, oval-shaped steak that's both tender and beefy. The best strip loins are the center-cut portions.

Rib Eye or Delmonico

The Guy's favorite butcher puts this steak above all others—it's tender enough when properly cooked, but has all the full, beefy flavor of a tougher cut. Find it on the bone, or boneless.

Tenderloin or Filet mignon

The tenderloin is the most tender bit of the beef, and when this long, lean muscle is cut into steaks, they're called filet mignon (the largest section, the center cut, is known as Chateaubriand). As it is the leanest steak, it's important not to overcook the filet mignon, or it will be dry and tasteless.

Basic Grilled Steak

Learn to grill a steak properly. It's a skill every Guy should know. And remember, the best chefs refuse to cook a steak beyond medium—it just ruins a great piece of beef. Add a bit of garlicky Blue Cheese Sauce (see page 232) to gild the lily.

1 tsp (5 mL) minced garlic
1 Tbsp (15 mL) olive oil
two 6-oz (175-g) beef steaks (rib eye, strip loin, or tenderloin), about 1 to 1½ inches (2.5 to 4 cm) thick

2 tsp (10 mL) Worchestershire sauce
freshly ground black pepper

1 In a small bowl, combine the minced garlic and the olive oil, and rub over the steaks. Drizzle and rub with Worcestershire, and then season with pepper.

2 Grill the steaks to rare or medium rare—about 5 minutes per side on medium-high heat. Transfer the steaks to individual plates and serve. Serves 2.

Touchy Feely

Wonder when your steak is done to your liking? Use the steak house chef touch test—something The Guy learned from a chef used to cranking out dozens of red-meat meals at a steak house. Call it the steak house "rule of thumb." If you know how a steak feels when it's done, you'll never be stuck with over- or under-cooked meat again.

 Relax your hand and press the triangle of flesh below your thumb. That's how a spongy rare steak feels.

 Holding your thumb and index finger together, press the spot again. It's firmer, like a steak cooked medium rare.

 When you touch your thumb and middle finger together, the spot gets even firmer, like a steak that's cooked to medium or medium well.

 Fourth finger—bouncy, tough, and well done. If you go any further, that steak is shoe leather!

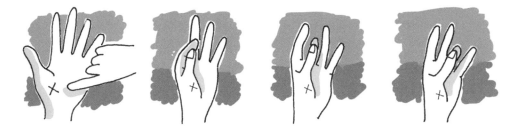

Seasoning Salt

Most steak houses have their own "secret" seasoning salt that they use on every steak. The mixture is usually a combination of salt, black pepper, paprika, garlic powder, and onion salt. You can make your own seasoning mixture to have at the ready, or use a commercial version of this universal steak spice.

Argentinian Steaks with Chimichurri Sauce

The light herb sauce in this recipe is perfect for spooning over steaks, like they do in South America. Chimichurri is best consumed soon after you make it, but The Guy has successfully kept it for a day or two in the refrigerator.

4 cloves garlic, minced
¼ cup (60 mL) freshly squeezed orange juice
1 Tbsp (15 mL) freshly squeezed lemon juice
1 Tbsp (15 mL) freshly squeezed lime juice

1 Tbsp (15 mL) dried oregano
3 Tbsp (45 mL) olive oil
six 8-oz (225-g) strip loin or tenderloin steaks,
    1-inch (2.5-cm) thick

1 In a small bowl, combine the garlic, orange juice, lemon juice, lime juice, oregano, and olive oil. Rub the marinade over the steaks and marinate for 2 hours.

2 Grill the steaks directly over medium-high heat, about 4 to 5 minutes per side for medium rare. Set the meat on a platter to rest, tent with foil, and set aside for 5 to 10 minutes. Serve the steaks drizzled with chimichurri sauce. Serves 4 to 6.

Chimichurri Sauce

½ cup (125 mL) fresh Italian parsley leaves
½ cup (125 mL) fresh cilantro leaves
4 large cloves garlic, peeled
½ cup (125 mL) extra virgin olive oil
2 tsp (10 mL) balsamic vinegar

1 Tbsp (15 mL) water
1 to 2 shallots, peeled and quartered
1 tsp (5 mL) salt
1 small dried red chili

1 Combine all of the sauce ingredients in a food processor and process until smooth. Let stand at room temperature for 20 minutes before serving with grilled steak. Makes 1 cup (250 mL).

Steak with Creamy Peppercorn Sauce

This is The Guy's version of Steak Diane, a dish that can only be described as pure retro cuisine. With a baked potato and a green vegetable such as beans or broccoli on the side, this makes a classic steak house–style dinner for two. Who knows who the mysterious Diane might be, but you can always change the name of this classic dish to woo whomever you want!

two 6-oz/175-g boneless beef steaks (tenderloin or strip loin), cut 1 inch (2.5 cm) thick
sea salt
2 Tbsp (30 mL) cracked mixed peppercorns (white, black, and pink)
1 Tbsp (15 mL) olive oil
2 Tbsp (30 mL) butter

¼ cup (60 mL) finely chopped shallots or green onions
⅓ cup (75 mL) beef broth (canned is okay)
¼ cup (60 mL) brandy or cognac
1 Tbsp (15 mL) Dijon mustard
1 tsp (5 mL) Worcestershire sauce
¼ cup (60 mL) heavy cream
1 Tbsp (15 mL) finely chopped chives

1 Season the steaks on both sides with salt. To crush the peppercorns, use a mortar and pestle or place them in a plastic bag and crush them with a rolling pin. Press the peppercorns over both sides of the steaks.

2 Heat a heavy sauté pan over medium-high heat and add the olive oil. Place the steaks in the hot pan and cook until nicely seared, about 4 minutes on each side for medium rare. Remove the steaks from the pan and set aside on a warm plate (tent with foil to keep warm).

3 Discard most of the fat from the pan and add the butter and shallots. Sauté for 2 minutes. Stir in the broth, brandy, mustard, and Worcestershire. Stir, scraping up any browned bits in the bottom of the pan, and bring to a boil. Continue boiling for a minute, to slightly reduce the liquid (flambé, by putting a match to the liquid, if you're feeling dramatic—but be careful), then stir in the cream. Bring the sauce back to a boil and continue to cook for 1 to 2 minutes longer or until it's nicely thickened.

4 Place the steaks on individual serving plates, drizzle the sauce over top, and sprinkle with chopped chives. Serves 2.

Classic Steak Sandwich

All steak sandwiches are not created equally. The Guy's favorite steak house uses a top-quality rib eye steak for sandwiches, which makes all the difference. Serve a pile of salad greens or a stuffed baked potato (see page 234) on the side. It's a "knife and fork" kind of sandwich.

two 6-oz (175-g) rib eye steaks
olive oil
seasoning salt (see page 229)

2 Tbsp (30 mL) softened butter
1 clove garlic, crushed
two 1-inch- (2.5-cm-) thick slices French bread

1 Preheat the grill to high.

2 Brush both sides of the steak with olive oil and sprinkle with seasoning salt. Place the seasoned steak on the grill, cooking for 3 to 4 minutes per side, shifting the steak a ¼-turn halfway through cooking each side (this method gives the steak its attractive cross-hatch, grill-mark pattern).

3 In a small bowl, combine the softened butter and garlic. Toast the bread and slather with the garlic butter.

4 Set the cooked steak on top of the garlic toast and serve. Serves 2.

Blue Cheese Sauce

On every steak sandwich—or steak for that matter—The Guy loves to gild the lily with this rich, creamy sauce. Try it as a dip, too, with skinny Italian bread sticks and spears of red, green, and yellow peppers.

2 cloves garlic, crushed
⅔ cup (150 mL) mayonnaise
⅔ cup (150 mL) mascarpone cheese
1 cup (250 mL) crumbled Stilton or other
   blue cheese

¼ cup (60 mL) fresh basil leaves
½ cup (125 mL) Italian parsley leaves
1 tsp (5 mL) Worcestershire sauce
freshly ground pepper to taste

1 In a food processor, combine the garlic, mayonnaise, mascarpone, Stilton, basil, parsley, Worcestershire, and pepper. Blend until smooth. Refrigerate.

2 Spoon a dollop of the sauce on your steak, or drizzle over your steak sandwich. Bring to room temperature before serving as a dip. Makes about 3 cups (700 mL).

Steak House Sides

That's the other thing about the classic steak house—you need to order almost everything on the side. Start with onion soup and don't forget the caesar salad and mushrooms.

French Onion Soup

This is the classic way to start a steak house meal—a bowl of intense beef stock (see page 40), flavored with sweet caramelized onions (see page 16), and topped with crisp croutons and gooey cheese.

¼ cup (60 mL) unsalted butter
4 large yellow onions, peeled and slivered
4 cups (1 L) homemade brown beef broth (or substitute low-sodium canned)

salt and freshly ground black pepper
4 slices French bread, or sourdough, toasted
½ cup (125 mL) shredded Gruyère cheese or a combination of Gruyère and Parmesan

1 In a large saucepan, heat the butter over medium low heat and slowly sauté the onions, stirring often, for 30 to 45 minutes or until they are browned and caramelized. Add the stock, salt, and pepper, and simmer together for 15 minutes longer.

2 Preheat the broiler. Place the toasted bread into 4 ovenproof bowls and set the bowls on a baking sheet.

3 Ladle the hot onion soup over the bread, dividing it evenly between the bowls. Top each bowl with 2 Tbsp (30 mL) of grated cheese. Place the soup directly under the broiler and broil for 3 minutes or until the cheese is melted and beginning to brown. Serve immediately. Serves 4.

Stuffed Baked Potatoes

The stuffed potato is a classic steak house side dish. These potatoes are delicious with or without the addition of cheese—your choice.

4 large baking potatoes, unpeeled,
    well-scrubbed, and rubbed with olive oil
4 Tbsp (60 mL) butter
½ cup (125 mL) sour cream

½ tsp (2 mL) seasoning salt (see page 229)
2 green onions, minced
1 cup (250 mL) finely grated Parmesan or cheddar
    cheese (optional)

1 Bake the potatoes at 400°F (200°C) for 30 minutes or until softened, then cut a slice off the top of each and scoop the flesh into a mixing bowl, leaving ¼-inch (6-mm) shells.

2 Set the shells on a baking sheet.

3 Mash the potato flesh with butter, sour cream and seasoning salt until smoothly puréed. Stir in the green onion and the grated cheese (if using), then spoon or pipe the filling back into the potato shells. Brush the tops of each stuffed potato with melted butter and reheat in a 450°F (230°C) oven for 10 minutes, until beginning to brown on top. Makes 4.

Sautéed Steak House Mushrooms

There's nothing quite like these garlicky mushrooms piled on top of your steak. Any kind of mushroom will do, but if you add a few wild mushrooms (chanterelles or morels) or even some interesting oyster mushrooms, it will take your steak into new territory.

2 lb (1 kg) sliced mushrooms (white, brown,
    oyster, portobello, or wild)
¼ cup (50 mL) butter
2 Tbsp (25 mL) extra virgin olive oil

2 Tbsp (25 mL) minced garlic
¼ cup (50 mL) white wine
salt and freshly ground black pepper

1 In a sauté pan, heat the butter and oil over medium-high heat. Add the mushrooms and garlic and sauté for 10 minutes or until the mushrooms give up their juices and begin to brown. Add the wine and season with salt and pepper. Continue to cook until most of the liquid is gone, and serve hot, on top of your steak. Serves 4 to 6.

WISE GUY:
Use any leftover sautéed mushrooms on pizza, pasta, or piled on toasts for appetizers.

Caesar Salad (from scratch)

Having your caesar salad made by a waiter, tableside, is a classic steak house specialty. You can add a bit of drama at home, too, if you make this salad for your guests from scratch.

2 cloves garlic, crushed
2 tsp (10 mL) finely chopped anchovies
1 tsp (5 mL) Dijon mustard
1 egg yolk
3 Tbsp (45 mL) freshly squeezed lemon juice (about half a lemon)
1 tsp (5 mL) Worcestershire sauce
3 drops Tabasco sauce
½ tsp (2 mL) freshly ground black pepper

pinch of salt
½ cup (125 mL) extra virgin olive oil
1 head romaine lettuce, chopped into small pieces
½ cup (125 mL) freshly grated Parmesan cheese
½ cup (125 mL) homemade croutons (see page 483)

1 In a large wooden bowl, whisk together the garlic, anchovies, mustard, and egg yolk. Stir in the lemon juice, Worcestershire, and Tabasco. Stir well to combine and season with pepper and salt. Slowly drizzle the olive oil into the dressing, whisking as you go, to form an emulsion. Add the lettuce to the bowl and toss to coat with dressing. Sprinkle the Parmesan cheese and croutons into the bowl and toss again. Serve immediately. Serves 3 to 4.

EGGS

WISE GUY: While traditional caesar salad dressing is made with a raw egg, there is a small danger of salmonella poisoning, so avoid serving dishes including raw eggs to the very young, the very old, and those with compromised immune systems. Never use cracked eggs. And to be safer when serving raw eggs, coddle them lightly first (immerse the eggs into barely simmering water for a minute or two, to make sure there are no contaminants on the shell).

Chrysanthemum Onion

Many steak houses serve onion rings alongside the beef, but others have come up with variations on that theme, including the whole onion, cut, breaded, and deep-fried like a flower. This crispy "chrysanthemum" onion is great for sharing at the start of a meal.

2 medium white or yellow onions, peeled
¼ cup (60 mL) all-purpose flour
½ cup (125 mL) very fine dry breadcrumbs
1 tsp (5 mL) paprika

1 tsp (5 mL) salt
1 tsp (5 mL) freshly ground white pepper
¼ tsp (1 mL) cayenne pepper
4 cups (1 L) vegetable oil, for frying

1 Peel and trim the onions. Cut the root end flat and slice ½ inch (1 cm) from the other end. Stand the onions upright, root-end down, and make several vertical cuts, ¼ inch (6 mm) apart and at right angles, down to, but not through, the root.

2 Put the onions into a big bowl of ice water and they will expand like flowers.

3 Combine the flour, breadcrumbs, paprika, salt, pepper, and cayenne in a bowl. Drain the onions well, then toss with the crumb mixture to coat all sides, making sure to spoon the mixture into the center of the onion. Shake off any excess crumbs.

4 Heat the oil in a wok or deep pot to 375°F (190°C). Fry the onions, one at a time, until golden brown, about 5 minutes. Drain them on paper towels and serve with Mojo Mayo (see page 259). Serves 4.

Chunky Chocolate Peanut Butter Ice Cream Pie

Not sure why this insanely filling dessert always seems to turn up on steak house menus (to order after you've already consumed a gigantic chunk of protein), but it does. This is the kind of dessert that little tykes (and guys who aren't watching their weight) will love—a layer of creamy peanut butter ice cream in a chocolate crust, with more chocolate stuff and whipped cream on top. Mmmmmm—peanut butter pie!

2 cups (500 mL) chocolate cookie crumbs
¼ cup (60 mL) unsalted butter, melted
6 cups (1.5 L) vanilla ice cream
1 cup (250 mL) chunky, natural peanut butter
   (no sugar or added fat)

8 oz (225 g) semi-sweet chocolate chips
2 cups (500 mL) whipping cream
2 Tbsp (30 mL) granulated sugar

1 Preheat the oven to 350°F (180°C).

2 In a medium bowl, combine the cookie crumbs and butter, and press into the bottom of a 10-inch (3-L) springform pan. Bake for 15 minutes, until firm, then cool and refrigerate to chill.

3 Allow the ice cream to soften in a large bowl and blend in the peanut butter. Spoon into the chilled crust and press down to smooth. Place the pan in the freezer for two hours until firm.

4 Meanwhile, melt the chocolate in a microwave-safe bowl, stirring every 30 seconds until smooth. Cool slightly, then drizzle artfully over the frozen pie. Return the pie to the freezer until serving time.

5 Using an electric mixer, whip the cream with the sugar until stiff. Release the pie from the spring form pan, cut into 12 wedges, and serve with a dollop of whipped cream on the side. Serves 12.

The Wine Geek Dinner

The Guy likes his wine—and likes to create dinners to showcase his favorite new finds. When there's serious wine to taste, a multi-course dinner is in order. Ask a few friends to help, then sup in style.

The Truth About Wine

There's nothing particularly complicated about the concept of making wine. It's a fermented beverage, created by squeezing the juice out of grapes and turning the sugars in that juice into alcohol, using yeast. The resulting beverage may be bottled when it's fresh and young or stored in a charred oak barrel that will add extra structure, in the form of wood tannins, and other layers of flavor to the wine. Here's what else you should know:

Grapes for making wine are grown in many parts of the world, from France to Napa Valley, India to England. But some parts of the world are better known for better wine, mostly because their terroir (climate, soil, and exposure to the sun) has long been recognized as perfect for growing a particular kind of grape. Burgundy, for example, is famous for its Pinot Noir while Germany's Rhine Valley is known for its Riesling.

Each varietal of grape makes wine that tastes a little different (Chardonnay to Pinot Noir, Cabernet Sauvignon, Gewürztraminer or Sangiovese) but how that grape tastes also depends on where it's grown. A Chardonnay grown in a hot climate will have tropical fruit flavors, owing to speed and degree of ripening, while one grown in a cool climate will express more mineral and tart citrus characters. Depends what you like.

You get what you pay for when it comes to wine, but not always. Sometimes you're paying a premium for a rare wine—like a specific Burgundy from a very small appellation—so it's supply and demand that raises the price. You can likely find a Pinot Noir from somewhere else in the world that's just as tasty and well made for half the price. Like anything, more hands-on, personalized care (versus large-scale, industrial production) adds to the price and usually, if not always, to the quality.

Red wine is made from red grapes and white wine is made from white grapes, but not always. It's the color of the skin that gives the wine its color (all grapes are white on the inside). So if you press red grapes and take the juice off the skins immediately, you'll get a white wine, or one with just a blush of pink. That's how rosé is made—from red grape juice with minimal skin contact. The deeper pink the rosé, the thicker and darker the skins and/or the longer they stuck around in the fermenting juice.

In some parts of the world, the vintage (the year the grapes for the wine were harvested) has a big influence on the quality of the wine in the bottle, because the weather can be very changeable. In other parts of the world, where the climate is more consistent, there will be less vintage variation in the wine so the year it was made doesn't matter that much. It does let you know, however, if a particular bottle is ready to open or might need more "bottle age" in your cellar to mature and smooth out the rough edges.

That said, most of the wine made in the world today has been designed for immediate consumption (and most of the wine purchased is consumed the same day). So don't feel you have to age your wine, unless you have cases of first growth Bordeaux in the basement.

When you're tasting wine, look at the color (a white that's darker will likely be older or has been aged in wood), smell the wine (aromas give you clues to how the wine will taste) and hold it in your mouth for a few seconds before swallowing to get the flavors all over your tongue. Drawing air over your tongue, with the wine in your mouth (that slurping thing wine geeks do) has a purpose—it makes the wine taste more intense, making it easier to describe more of the nuances and flavors.

Glassware is vital to the enjoyment of wine. Always use large glasses that taper at the top and don't overfill them. Then you can swirl the wine around, without spilling it, to release the aromas, which is half the joy of drinking wine. Some companies make specifically designed glasses for each grape varietal and style of wine, figuring that how the wine enters your mouth, and which area of your tongue it lands on (front, back, sides), will affect how it tastes. This does work but you'll need a lot of wine glass storage space.

There's nothing wrong with serving wine from a bottle that has a screw cap or a synthetic cork—in fact, it virtually guarantees that the wine will be fresh, clean, and free of the musty cork taint that is so common with wines closed with natural cork. The Guy looks for screw caps—especially for white wines.

The acidity or sweetness of the food you're eating will affect how your taste buds perceive the flavors in wine you drink with it. Imagine biting into something sweet, like a glazed doughnut, then drinking something sour, like homemade lemonade—it will seem all the more mouth-puckering because of the sugary taste left in your mouth from the food. But if you've just put a piece of fresh lemon in your mouth, that lemonade might taste rather sweet by comparison. It's the same with wine and food. So if the meat has a sweet sauce, you'll taste more dryness in the wine (ergo, a sweeter wine might taste more balanced while a very dry wine will just seem tart). Saltiness, bitterness, and umami (the protein flavor in food) also influence how the wine will taste. Think about how an acidic wine, or something spritzy, clears the palate of something salty and how a piece of cheese or steak can instantly smooth out the tannic and aggressive edges of a big red wine. So adjust your food to match the wine you want to drink. That's why you have things like salt, chili sauce, ketchup, and vinegar on the table or a slice of lemon and a drizzle of reduced balsamic on your plate. Slightly altering the flavour of your food—with a sweet, salty, or acidic condiment—will affect how your tongue perceives the next sip of wine. Try it. It works.

There's no right or wrong answer when it comes to wine and pairing it with food. Either you like it or you don't. Some people enjoy sweeter wines, while others only like big tannic reds. But you might prefer a sweeter white wine when you're eating something spicy, and a dry bubbly with something salty. Experiment. The choice is yours.

Gougères

These tiny cheese puffs are traditional snacks in Burgundy (where The Guy's favorite grape—Pinot Noir—is king). Gougères (goo-ZHAIRS) are particularly good when they're hot out of the oven, so you may want to plan to pop them in just after your guests arrive. You can, though, eat them at room temperature too. Learn the technique, and you'll soon be making sweet cream puffs and flavoring your gougères with blue cheese or your other favorites. Dead easy. Pop the cork on a good French champagne or pour a white Burgundy.

6 Tbsp (90 mL) unsalted butter, cubed
1 cup (250 mL) water
½ tsp (2 mL) sea salt
pinch cayenne pepper
pinch dry mustard

¾ cup (175 mL) all-purpose flour, sifted
3 eggs, lightly beaten
¾ cup (175 mL) grated imported Gruyère cheese, divided

1 Preheat the oven to 400°F (200°C).

2 Have all of your ingredients measured and ready to go into the pot. Combine the flour with the cayenne and mustard. Lightly whisk the eggs.

3 In a heavy saucepan, heat the butter, water, and salt together over high heat. When the mixture comes to a boil, remove the pan from the heat and add the flour all at once, beating with a wooden spoon until the batter looks smooth. Return the pan to the stove, reduce the heat to medium, and cook the batter for a minute or so, just to reduce some of the liquid in the mixture.

4 Remove from the heat and gradually add the beaten eggs, beating well with a spoon until the batter is shiny and is coming away from the sides of the pan. Stir in ½ cup (125 mL) of the grated cheese. The batter should be thick, like stiff mayonnaise.

5 Line a baking sheet with parchment paper. Transfer the dough to a piping bag or use a small spoon to scoop tiny 2-inch (5-cm) mounds onto the paper, about 1½ inches (4 cm) apart. Sprinkle lightly with remaining grated cheese.

6 Bake the puffs in the center of a preheated oven for 15 to 20 minutes, until they're golden brown. Test one puff to make sure they're done—they should be moist and steamy in the center, but not doughy.

7 Transfer the puffs to a rack to cool and pass them around in a basket. Don't forget your favorite white or red from Burgundy. Makes 24 to 30 gougères.

Shaved Fennel Salad with Prosciutto and Parmesan

This is a small salad course. It's not too acidic and the meat and cheese help to make it work with wine, whether you're serving a white Graves or a young Pinot Noir.

2 bulbs fennel, shaved or finely slivered

2 tsp (10 mL) freshly squeezed lemon juice

2 Tbsp (30 mL) extra virgin olive oil

¼ cup (60 mL) finely chopped green onion
   or chives

½ tsp (2 mL) salt

4 slices prosciutto, cut into fine slivers

2 oz (50 g) Parmesan cheese (or another aged,
   dry cheese)

freshly ground black pepper

herb oil (see page 20) or reduced balsamic
   (see page 17) to drizzle

1 To make the salad, trim the outer leaves from the fennel bulbs, and then trim the bases. Cut the bulbs in quarters, lengthwise, and remove the cores. Sliver the fennel into paper-thin pieces, slicing across the grain by hand or using a mandoline (see page 506). Toss the fennel with the lemon juice, olive oil, green onions, and salt. Set aside.

2 Toss the prosciutto with the fennel mixture just before serving. Arrange the salad on individual salad plates and, using a vegetable peeler, shave some of the Parmesan over each serving. Grind a little black pepper over each salad and drizzle a few drops of herb oil or reduced balsamic vinegar around the edge of each plate. Serves 4.

Creamy Beet and Potato Soup with Chard

Here's The Guy's take on traditional borscht—gussied up for a fancy dinner. The bright green chard adds texture and contrasting color to this wild fuchsia soup, which has the texture and richness to match with a creamy Chardonnay or a big South African Chenin Blanc.

1 lb (500 g) beets, whole
2 Tbsp (30 mL) butter
1 medium onion, chopped
3 cloves garlic, minced
1 lb (500 g) potatoes, peeled
   and cut into chunks
2 cups (500 g) water

2 to 3 cups (500 to 750 mL) vegetable
   or chicken broth
¾ cup (175 mL) half-and-half
salt and pepper
3 cups (750 mL) slivered rainbow chard
shaved mizithra (or other dry, salty cheese
   like aged ricotta, feta, or goat cheese)

1 Wrap the beets loosely in foil and roast in a 400°F (200°C) oven for 25 minutes. Cool, slip off the skins, and then chop.

2 In a large saucepan, melt the butter. Add the onion and sauté until it starts to brown. Add the garlic, potatoes, water, and 2 cups (500 mL) of the broth. Bring to a boil over high heat.

3 Reduce the heat to low and cook until tender for about 20 minutes. Add the roasted beets and simmer for 10 minutes.

4 Transfer the soup to a blender or food processor and purée until very smooth. Return the soup to the saucepan (you can strain the soup back into the saucepan if it seems too grainy). Stir in the half-and-half, salt, and pepper. Bring to a boil, then simmer for 10 minutes. Thin to taste with remaining broth if soup seems too thick.

5 Meanwhile, thinly slice the chard stems. Roll the leaves (like cigars) and slice into thin "chiffonade" strips. Heat a bit of butter in a sauté pan and cook the chard stems for a minute or two, until tender. Then add the leaves to the sauté pan and toss for a minute, just to wilt.

6 Divide the soup among shallow soup bowls. Pile some sautéed chard in the center of each bowl. Top each bowl with a little grated cheese. Serves 8.

Duck Breast with Fig Gratin

In the fall, when fresh figs are in season, buy boneless duck breasts from the butcher, and make this simple but seductive dish. A dish inspired by California wine country and chef Steve, it makes a nice small poultry course in a multi-course wine dinner or an elegant main course on its own. You'll need a ripe fruity California red—Zinfandel or Merlot—to stand up to this rich and intensely flavored dish.

4 duck breasts
salt and freshly ground black pepper
1 cup (250 mL) ruby port
¼ cup (60 mL) balsamic vinegar
black peppercorns
1 sprig thyme

3 cups (750 mL) whole fresh figs
1 slice wholegrain bread (use the crusty end)
1 large clove garlic, minced
2 Tbsp (30 mL) chopped Italian parsley
⅓ cup (75 mL) chopped pecans
1 Tbsp (15 mL) olive oil or melted butter

1 Score the fat side of duck breasts, being careful not to cut into the flesh. In a hot, non-stick pan, cook the duck breasts to render the fat. The pan should be very hot—so that a drop of water evaporates immediately when it hits the surface. Place the breasts in the hot pan, skin-side down, sear for 1 minute, then reduce the heat to medium-low and cook for 12 to 15 minutes, pouring off fat as you cook (reserve this fat for other recipes). The idea is to melt out all of the fat without cooking the meat. Remove the breasts from the pan and set on a plate.

2 Brush the uncooked side of the breasts with the rendered duck fat. Sprinkle with salt and pepper. Chill.

3 To the same sauté pan, add the port and balsamic vinegar to deglaze, scraping up any browned bits. Add the peppercorns and thyme and cook over medium-low heat until the sauce is reduced and thickened, about 10 to 15 minutes. Strain the sauce and keep warm.

4 Cut the figs in half lengthwise and arrange cut-side up in a shallow gratin dish. In a blender or food processor, combine and bread, garlic, parsley, and pecans and pulse until finely chopped. Season with salt and pepper and add the olive oil. Pulse to combine. Spread the crumb mixture evenly over the figs.

5 Heat the oven to 400°F (200°C). Place the seared duck breasts, seasoned-side down, in a roasting pan. When the oven is hot, place the figs and the duck in the oven. Bake for 10 to 15 minutes, until the duck is just medium rare and the figs are nicely browned.

6 To serve, arrange some of the figs on each of four individual warm plates. Slice each duck breast diagonally and fan the slices over the figs. Drizzle the duck with the port sauce. To serve as a main course, present with a purée of garlic mashed potatoes alongside. Serves 4 to 6.

Polenta with Goat Cheese

This is a simple flavorful dish to serve alongside any stew. Look for a coarse, stone-ground cornmeal or, if you're a southern boy, try this with good-quality grits.

5 cups (1.25 L) water
1 tsp (5 mL) salt
1 Tbsp (15 mL) butter

1 cup (250 mL) coarse, stone-ground polenta
1 cup (250 mL) soft goat cheese
1 Tbsp (15 mL) chopped fresh rosemary or sage

1 Bring the water to a rolling boil and add the salt and butter. Slowly add the polenta to the pot in a steady stream, whisking as you go to prevent lumps from forming. Stir for 5 minutes, then reduce the heat to low. Continue to cook for 15 minutes, stirring to make sure the polenta doesn't stick to the pot. Remove from the heat and stir in the goat cheese and herbs. Keep warm.

2 Serve the polenta in wide, shallow soup plates, topped with some Braised Lamb with Red Wine and Olives (see page 246). Garnish with a sprig of fresh rosemary. Serves 8.

The Cheese Course

The wine geek Guy likes nothing better than sitting around the table after a fine meal, sipping a fine vintage port (or the remains of the big reds) and nibbling on fine cheese. The recipe is simple—chose three fine artisan cheeses (one soft, creamy, and young like Camembert or bloomy brie; one aged and dry like Parmigiano Reggiano or aged Gouda; and one blue like Stilton or Gorgonzola). A few simple water biscuits or melba toasts, a handful of dried cherries or cranberries, and a few toasted walnuts or pecans will round out your cheese tray (and add some color). Then you can just pour the port and relax. Dinner's done!

Braised Lamb with Red Wine and Olives

Here's a beautiful braise for a wine dinner, inspired by the flavors of Provence and the slow food so popular with chefs these days. Don't forget to use good wine, fresh herbs, and the best tiny niçoise olives you can find for the sauce. Serve the lamb alongside creamy polenta flavored with goat cheese (see page 245) or garlic mashed potatoes and fresh, skinny green beans that have been barely steamed.

Like The Guy, this is a dish that gets better with age, so feel free to make it the day before your party. A meaty Châteauneuf-du-Pape is the wine of choice for this foray into the south of France. But with the rich flavorful lamb and bitter olives, it matches equally well with a dry Portuguese red from the Douro, an Australian Grange, or a good South African Pinotage.

4 lb (2 kg) boneless lamb shoulder, trimmed of
 visible fat and separated into fairly large
 pieces

Marinade

2 Tbsp (30 mL) extra virgin olive oil
1 onion, finely chopped
1 stalk celery, finely chopped
1 carrot, finely chopped

8 cloves garlic, halved
2 bay leaves
1 Tbsp (15 mL) chopped fresh rosemary
1 sprig fresh thyme
1 bottle dry red wine

Lamb

25 small boiling onions, blanched and peeled
⅓ cup (75 mL) flour
 salt and freshly ground black pepper
2 Tbsp (30 mL) extra virgin olive oil
2 thick slices double-smoked bacon, cut into
 matchstick pieces
1 stalk celery, chopped
6 cloves garlic, whole

2 medium carrots, cut into chunks
reserved marinade
1 cup (250 mL) niçoise olives or other good-quality,
 air-cured black olives
2 cups (500 mL) beef broth
2 cups (500 mL) red wine
fresh minced rosemary or Italian parsley to
 garnish

1 The day before you plan to serve the lamb, make the marinade. Heat the oil in a saucepan and sauté the onions, celery, carrot, and garlic until soft and starting to brown, about 10 minutes. Stir in the bay leaves and herbs, then add the bottle of wine and bring to a boil. Simmer 20 minutes. Remove from the heat and chill. When the marinade is cold, add the lamb pieces and marinate overnight in the refrigerator.

2 The next day, remove the lamb from the marinade. Strain the marinade, discarding the solid bits but reserving the liquid to add to the sauce later.

3 To peel the onions, bring a pot of water to a boil. Trim each onion at the base. Add the onions to the boiling water and blanch for 1 minute. Drain and cool in ice water, then slip off the papery skins. Set aside.

4 Combine the flour, salt, and pepper in a bag and toss in the lamb pieces, shaking to coat. In a large, non-stick sauté pan, heat the olive oil over medium-high heat and brown the floured meat in batches.

5 As it's browned, remove the lamb to a heavy covered Dutch oven. Add the bacon to the sauté pan and cook until the fat is rendered and the bacon is nearly crisp. Remove the bacon with a slotted spoon and add to the Dutch oven.

6 In the bacon fat, sauté the peeled onions over medium-low heat until they begin to caramelize. Remove the onions with a slotted spoon and add to the dish with the lamb. Lightly sauté the celery, garlic, and carrots in the same pan, until they begin to brown. Add to the Dutch oven. Add the reserved marinade to deglaze the pan, boiling until the liquid in the pan is reduced by half.

7 Pour this mixture over the meat and stir in the olives, beef broth, and red wine. Cover the Dutch oven and bake at 325°F (160°C) for 2 to 3 hours or until the meat is very tender and the sauce has thickened.

8 Before serving, skim any excess fat from the sauce and simmer, uncovered, on top of the stove to further thicken the gravy (a bit of flour mixed into some softened butter, or a solution of cornstarch and water can help thicken the sauce). Serve immediately, or chill overnight and reheat to serve with a sprinkling of herbs. Serves 8.

Sangria Ice

The Guy got this idea from Gary, a chef who devised this dessert when he had a bunch of sangria left over after an event. Into the freezer and voilà! A new recipe is born.

1 bottle red wine
½ cup (125 mL) Grand Marnier or brandy
½ cup (125 mL) orange juice

1½ cups (375 mL) lemon-lime soda (like Sprite or 7-Up)
fresh raspberries, blueberries, and strawberries to garnish

1 Combine the wine, brandy, orange juice, and soda. Pour into a shallow pan, cover with plastic wrap, and place in the freezer. Use a fork to scrape the mixture into icy granules as it freezes. Just before serving, shave the mixture with a fork again. Scoop it into chilled martini glasses and garnish with fresh berries. Serves 6.

Guy Meets Grill

What is it about men and fire? The Guy has always felt most comfortable when cooking over the flames of a barbecue (whether gas or charcoal), and apparently he's not alone. According to the marketing gurus who collect such information, North Americans are cooking over the coals 3 billion times a year. And yes, the majority of those who are grilling, smoking, and barbecuing supper are still guys (66 percent at last count).

So c'mon baby, light that fire!

COOKING WITH FIRE

Always heat the gas barbecue on high for 10 minutes, lid down, before cooking. Use a wire brush to clean the hot grill racks before putting new food on the grill.

Beware of sauces and marinades with sugary ingredients. It's best to brush the barbecue sauce over the chicken after it's cooked, or at least during the last five minutes, to avoid charred and blackened food.

When in doubt, use an instant-read thermometer to test the internal temperature of burgers, chicken, and other grilled meats. Remember, all ground meats must be cooked well done—155°F to 160°F (68°C to 71°C)—to avoid contamination.

Start bigger items over direct heat, then turn off one burner and move the food to the unlit side of the grill—it will continue to cook, but slower and without flare-ups.

WISE GUY: For really special beef burgers, go to a good butcher and ask for top-grade sirloin, ground to order. You want AAA or Prime grade beef (it has the highest fat content). While most chefs add nothing to their designer burgers but salt, pepper, and a little olive oil, you can also include minced onion and garlic, and your own favorite herbs and spices. This also works nicely with ground lamb.

The Big Ol' Burger

However you spice it, the big beefy burger is still one of the most popular items to slap on a barbecue grill. So here's The Guy's basic burger recipe, along with some ideas to take the big ol' burger into new territory.

Basic Burger

1 lb (500 g) freshly ground beef, coarse to medium grind (not too lean)

salt and freshly ground black pepper

2 cloves garlic, crushed

1 Tbsp (15 mL) olive oil

wholegrain buns

Typical (and not so typical) toppings

Sliced artisan cheese (aged cheddar, brie, blue cheese, Gruyère, etc.)

Heirloom tomatoes

Butter lettuce, shredded romaine, watercress

Mayonnaise (flavored with basil pesto, grainy mustard, or horseradish—see page 37)

Sliced cucumbers, avocado, caramelized onions, etc.

Crispy double-smoked bacon, grilled capicollo or prosciutto ham

Spicy cowboy ketchup, salsa, red pepper spread, mango chutney

1 Season the ground beef with salt and pepper, add the garlic, and form into four or five patties. Don't compress the meat too much, and try to create patties of an even thickness, not too fat in the middle—they'll shrink and get thicker in the center as they cook anyway. Brush each burger lightly with olive oil.

2 Heat the grill over medium-high heat and brush the racks lightly with oil. Grill the burgers on both sides until well done, about 5 to 7 minutes per side, until an instant-read thermometer inserted into the center of the patty reads 160°F (71°C). Ground meat should always be cooked to well done since any contamination on the outside of the meat (which is destroyed when you sear a steak or chop) gets mixed into the middle when you grind the meat.

3 Serve burgers immediately on toasted wholegrain buns with toppings of choice. Serves 4.

Grilled Flank Steak on Asian Greens

This is a main meal salad with exotic Eastern overtones, perfect for dining with friends on the deck on a warm evening. Marinate the steak in the morning and you'll be serving dinner in less than an hour. You can also serve the steak with slightly more traditional accompaniments with an Asian twist—think Sautéed Edamame Beans (see page 167) or Pickled Asian Slaw (see page 166).

Sauce

4 cloves garlic, chopped
1-inch (2.5-cm) piece of ginger, peeled and chopped
4 Tbsp (60 mL) granulated sugar
¼ cup (60 mL) soy sauce

2 tsp (10 mL) sesame oil
2 tsp (10 mL) Asian chili paste
1 tsp (5 mL) finely grated lime zest
4 Tbsp (60 mL) freshly squeezed lime juice

1 lb (500 g) flank steak

Salad

1 head butter lettuce, leaves separated
8 oz (225 g) fine rice vermicelli noodles
2 cups (500 mL) pea shoots
1 cup (250 mL) mustard greens or baby bok choy, shredded

½ an English cucumber, seeded and cut into fine, 2-inch- (5-cm-) long julienne strips
½ red bell pepper, seeded and slivered
3 green onions, chopped
1 bunch fresh mint or Thai basil, leaves only

1 In a food processor, combine the garlic, ginger, sugar, soy sauce, sesame oil, chili paste, lime zest, and lime juice. Process until smooth. Place the steak in a zippered plastic bag with half the sauce and refrigerate from 1 to 4 hours. Refrigerate the remaining sauce to dress the salad.

2 Wash the lettuce and spin dry in a salad spinner. Soak the rice noodles in hot water for 20 minutes to rehydrate. Drain well. (For bigger, flat rice noodles, soak first, then boil for a minute or two, drain, and refresh in cold water).

3 Place the well-drained noodles in a bowl and toss with half the reserved sauce.

4 Arrange the butter lettuce on a large serving platter. Top with the pea shoots and mustard greens. Arrange the rice noodles over the greens, down the center of the dish. Scatter the cucumber, bell pepper, and green onion overtop, and sprinkle the salad with the fresh mint leaves.

5 Remove the steak from the refrigerator 30 minutes before grilling and discard the marinade. Grill the steak over high heat for 4 to 5 minutes per side for medium rare—don't overcook, the meat should be nicely crusted on the outside but rare inside. Place the steak on a cutting board, tent with foil, and let it rest for 10 minutes. Thinly slice the steak across the grain and pile it on top of the salad. Drizzle the remaining sauce over the salad and serve immediately. Serves 4.

Grilled Vegetables

Whenever you're grilling a piece of protein, you should be grilling vegetables on the side. Just brush them with garlic-infused oil and grill until nicely charred. Dead easy and fantastic in sandwiches.

¼ cup (60 mL) extra virgin olive oil

1 clove garlic, crushed

1 large eggplant, sliced into ¼-inch (5-mm) rounds

1 medium zucchini, sliced lengthwise into ¼-inch (5-mm) strips

2 bell peppers, one red and one yellow, seeded and halved

2 large portobello mushrooms

salt and freshly ground black pepper

1 Tbsp (15 mL) balsamic vinegar

1 Combine the olive oil and crushed garlic and set aside to infuse for 10 minutes. Brush both sides of the eggplant, zucchini slices, pepper halves, and the mushrooms with the infused oil. Season with salt and pepper.

2 Grill the vegetables over medium heat for 5 minutes per side or until softened and slightly charred.

3 To serve, cut the warm, grilled bell peppers and mushrooms into strips. Add to a large bowl, along with the grilled eggplant and zucchini, and toss with balsamic vinegar before serving. Serves 4.

WISE GUY: To make 4 grilled vegetable sandwiches, start with 4 crusty wholegrain buns. Spread each bun with 1 Tbsp (15 mL) tapenade (see page 21) on one side and 2 Tbsp (30 mL) Boursin, brie, or other creamy cheese on the other side. Layer the grilled vegetables on each sandwich and top with some fresh basil leaves. Serve warm or cold (it's good picnic fare).

Grilled Halibut with Tapenade Drizzle and Tomato and Bocconcini Salad

Halibut is one of The Guy's favorite fish—and thick steaks cut from halibut fillets are easy to grill and very classy to serve with this simple sauce. A salad of tiny tomatoes and miniature bocconcini complements the dish perfectly.

Lemon Tapenade Drizzle

¼ cup (60 mL) extra virgin olive oil
1 clove garlic, crushed
2 Tbsp (30 mL) freshly squeezed lemon juice
¼ cup (60 mL) pitted niçoise olives

1 tsp (5 mL) grated lemon zest
1 tsp (5 mL) granulated sugar
¼ tsp (1 mL) chili paste
½ tsp (2 mL) fish sauce

Tomato and Bocconcini Salad

1 cup (250 mL) grape tomatoes, halved or quartered
¾ cup (175 mL) mini fresh bocconcini cheese balls
extra virgin olive oil

reduced balsamic vinegar (see page 17)
salt and freshly ground black pepper
chopped fresh basil and/or Italian parsley

Fish

2 Tbsp (30 mL) extra virgin olive oil
1 clove garlic, crushed
1 tsp (5 mL) finely grated lemon zest

1 tsp (5 mL) basil pesto
salt and freshly ground black pepper
four 5- to 6-oz (150- to 175-g) pieces of halibut, about 1 inch (2.5 cm) thick

1 To make the drizzle, combine the oil, garlic, lemon juice, pitted olives, zest, sugar, chili paste, and fish sauce in a blender. Whirl at a high speed until very smooth. Set aside.

2 For the salad, combine the tomatoes and cheese in a bowl. Drizzle with a bit of olive oil and a few drops of reduced balsamic vinegar, then season with salt and pepper, and scatter the herbs overtop. Set aside.

3 For the fish, combine the oil, garlic, zest, pesto, salt, and pepper in a small bowl. Rub over both sides of the halibut.

4 Heat the grill over high heat for 10 minutes. Clean the grill well, then brush with oil (the easiest way to do this is to soak a folded paper towel in canola oil, pick it up with tongs, and rub it over the grill racks). Grill the fish over direct heat until it's just opaque, about 4 minutes per side. Remove from the grill and serve immediately, drizzled with the lemon tapenade sauce and the tomato salad on the side. Serves 4.

Miso-Glazed Tuna with Grilled Bok Choy

There's nothing worse than cooking a fine piece of tuna until it's well done (and dried out). Tuna should be nicely seared on the outside, but rare and red on the inside. Buy a good piece of sushi-grade ahi (a.k.a. yellowfin) tuna and cook it quickly over very high heat for the best results. Don't put the lid down while grilling or you risk overcooking this delicate fish.

¼ cup (60 mL) mirin (Japanese rice wine)
1 tsp (5 mL) sesame oil
2 Tbsp (30 mL) liquid honey
½ cup (125 mL) white miso paste

four 6-oz (175-g) sushi-grade ahi tuna portions, each about 1½ inches (4 cm) thick
8 baby bok choy
1 Tbsp (15 mL) olive oil
salt and freshly ground black pepper

1 In a small saucepan, combine the mirin, sesame oil, honey, and miso paste. Bring to a boil and continue boiling for 5 minutes. Remove from the heat and let it cool to room temperature. With a basting brush, heavily coat both sides of the tuna with the cooled sauce. Transfer the fish to a plate, cover, and marinate in the refrigerator from 8 hours to overnight.

2 Trim the bok choy and cut each in half, lengthwise. Brush the cut sides with oil and season with salt and pepper.

3 Heat the grill over high for 10 minutes. Clean the grill well, then brush with oil (the easiest way to do this is to soak a folded paper towel in canola oil, pick it up with tongs, and rub it over the grill racks). Remove the excess marinade from the tuna, and place the fish on the hot grill. Cook quickly, about 1 to 2 minutes per side, just until the outside is seared but the inside is still red and rare. Cook the bok choy, cut-side down, on the grill at the same time, until it's just wilted and lightly charred.

4 Pile the grilled bok choy in the center of individual plates, and top each with a piece of seared tuna. Serves 4.

Spicy Jerk Chicken

When The Guy came back from Jamaica, he had a wicked sunburn and a new addiction—jerk chicken. Served from a barbecue pit at the side of the road, it was his first taste of this spicy island concoction.

Break out the beer and fire up the barbie, mon. Think about grilling some fat wedges of sweet potatoes or corn (brush them with oil) to serve alongside, or make some beans (see page 348) and rice cooked with coconut milk.

2 Tbsp (30 mL) freshly squeezed lime juice

2 Tbsp (30 mL) canola oil

2 green onions, roughly chopped

1 jalapeño, seeds removed, or 1 chipotle pepper in adobo sauce (canned)

1 Tbsp (15 mL) brown sugar

1 tsp (5 mL) salt

½ tsp (2 mL) crushed allspice berries

½ tsp (2 mL) thyme

½ tsp (2 mL) garlic powder

½ tsp (2 mL) freshly ground black pepper

3 ½ lb (1.75 kg) chicken pieces, on the bone, or 1 whole chicken

1 In a food processor, combine the lime juice, oil, green onions, and jalapeño. Whirl until chopped. Add the sugar, salt, allspice, thyme, garlic powder, and pepper. Whirl again, forming a paste. Rub the paste over all sides of the chicken pieces, then cover and refrigerate from 4 hours to overnight.

2 Heat the barbecue to medium-high heat and grill the chicken indirectly (turn off the burners on one side and cook the meat on the unlit side of the grill). Cover the barbecue and turn the chicken occasionally, for 30 to 45 minutes or until an instant thermometer inserted into the thickest part of the meat registers 175°F (79°C). To crisp the skin, transfer the chicken to the hot side of the barbecue and grill, skin-side down, during the last 5 minutes of cooking. Makes 4 servings.

WISE GUY: Try rubbing this marinade on a whole pork tenderloin. Marinate in the refrigerator overnight, then grill indirectly for about 30 minutes, to an internal temperature of 155°F (68°C). Set the grilled pork onto a cutting board and tent with foil for 10 minutes before slicing thinly or cutting into thick, fillet-like steaks. Crack open a cold beer and pass the red beans and rice.

Brined Chicken for the Grill

The Guy first learned about brining chicken from a chef who creates the crispest, juiciest chicken at his brasserie. You can use the brining method for a whole roast chicken, or just make a light brine—about one part sugar, one part salt, and 8 parts water—whenever you plan to grill or oven-roast chicken pieces.

The sugar in the brine helps caramelize the skin, resulting in a crisp, golden-brown chicken, while the salt and spices season the meat right down to the bone. But even a skinless, boneless chicken breast benefits from brining. Make the brine in advance and store it in the refrigerator to use whenever you want to serve chicken.

Since The Guy learned to brine, he now brines every piece of poultry that he serves. It takes a wee bit more time, but try it—the results are definitely worth the extra effort. No more dry or rubbery chicken breasts—when brined, they're always plump and juicy.

Brine
16 cups (4 L) water
½ cup (125 mL) kosher salt
¾ cup (175 mL) granulated sugar
2 cloves garlic, crushed

1 tsp (5 mL) whole juniper berries
1 tsp (5 mL) black peppercorns
1 tsp (5 mL) coriander seed
(or substitute your favorite spice combinations)

1 In a large pot, combine the brine ingredients and bring to a boil. Stir until the salt and sugar have dissolved, then remove the brine from the heat and cool. Store in a jar in the refrigerator.

2 Cut the chicken into serving pieces and put them into a large, heavy, zippered plastic bag. Add enough of the brine to submerge the chicken. Refrigerate for several hours or up to two days.

3 Before roasting or grilling, soak the chicken in cold water for 10 minutes to remove excess salt, then pat dry. The chicken needs no additional seasoning—simply grill it or roast it until it's cooked through. Sear the chicken, skin-side down, on the hottest part of the grill until brown, then move it to an unlit side of the gas grill and close the lid to finish cooking—about 20 minutes in total. Serves 4.

Pork Tenderloin with Southern BBQ Rub

The Guy loves pork tenderloin—a lean, boneless cut akin to a boneless chicken breast—quick to cook and always tender. You can rub a tenderloin with almost any spice mixture before tossing it on the grill or into the oven. Just remember to let the cooked meat rest to let the juices settle before slicing it.

Try tenderloin with this classic barbecue rub or riff on the spice mixture—try five-spice, lemon pepper, or garam masala. Start with the mustard, though, and make sure to use the sugar in the mix to create a nice crust.

2 tsp (10 mL) salt
3 Tbsp (45 mL) granulated sugar
1 Tbsp (15 mL) brown sugar
1 Tbsp (15 mL) ground ginger
1 Tbsp (15 mL) chili powder
1 Tbsp (15 mL) granulated garlic

1 tsp (5 mL) freshly ground black pepper
1 tsp (5 mL) ground cumin
3 Tbsp (45 mL) sweet Hungarian or Spanish paprika
2 pork tenderloins, about 1 lb (500 g) each
2 Tbsp (30 mL) ballpark mustard (not Dijon)

1 For the rub, combine the salt, sugars, ginger, chili powder, garlic, pepper, cumin, and paprika. Set aside in a spice jar. Any extra rub keeps for a long while.

2 Rub the tenderloins all over with the mustard. Sprinkle the spice rub heavily on all sides, massaging into the meat. Set the tenderloins aside for 10 minutes to allow the rub to get tacky—this will help to seal in the juices and form a tasty crust as the pork cooks on the barbecue.

3 Heat the barbecue to high and quickly sear the pork on all sides, about 2 to 3 minutes in total.

WISE GUY: Barbecue pork makes scrumptious pork sandwiches, piled on crusty buns with grainy mustard and coleslaw (see page 165). Or slice it thickly and pass around the potato salad (see page 410) and corn on the cob (see page 164). Too cold to cook outdoors? Just sear the tenderloins in a shallow roasting pan for a couple of minutes on each side, then fire them into a 425°F (220°C) oven for 20 to 25 minutes.

4 Turn off one burner and transfer the pork to the cool side. Close the lid and continue to cook the pork over indirect heat until just cooked through, about 20 to 30 minutes or until an instant-read thermometer inserted into the center of the meat registers 155°F (68°C). Pork tenderloin is lean and quickly dries out if overcooked. It shouldn't be rare but don't panic if it's a little pink—that's when it's juicy.

5 Remove the meat from the grill and set it on a cutting board, to rest for 5 minutes. Resting allows the juices to spread throughout the meat—if you slice it immediately all the juice will be left on the cutting board. Slice the pork thinly, on the diagonal, for sandwiches or to top a salad. Or cut it into thick medallions, like small tenderloin steaks, for plating. Serves 4.

Cuban Grilled Pork Loin with Mojo Mayo

This is a great way to cook a boneless loin of pork on the barbecue. Drizzle the sliced pork with Mojo Mayo and serve with sweet potato fries (see page 167). Or serve the pork on sandwiches with sliced tomatoes, avocado, and cilantro sprigs. This method also works well with pork tenderloin.

3 Tbsp (45 mL) olive oil
2 cloves garlic, crushed
1 boneless pork loin, about 2 to 3 lb (1 to 1.5 kg)
½ tsp (2 mL) ground cumin
½ tsp (2 mL) dried oregano

½ tsp (2 mL) paprika
½ tsp (2 mL) salt
½ tsp (2 mL) pepper
1 Tbsp (15 mL) brown sugar

Mojo Mayo
1 cup (250 mL) mayonnaise
8 cloves roasted garlic (see page 17)
½ tsp (2 mL) ground cumin

1 Tbsp (15 mL) freshly squeezed lime juice
2 Tbsp (30 mL) frozen orange juice concentrate
¼ tsp (1 mL) freshly ground black pepper

1 In a small bowl, combine the oil and garlic and let it stand 5 minutes to infuse the flavors.

2 To make the Mojo Mayo, in a blender or food processor, combine the mayonnaise, garlic, cumin, lime and orange juices, and black pepper. Blend until smooth. Refrigerate until ready to use.

3 Rub the pork on all sides with the garlic-infused oil. In a small bowl, combine the cumin, oregano, paprika, salt, pepper, and brown sugar. Rub this mixture over the pork, coating all sides.

4 Heat the grill to medium high and sear the pork until browned on all sides, about 10 minutes in total. Turn off one burner and move the pork to the unlit side of the grill. Cover the barbecue and cook the loin for 30 to 45 minutes longer, until the meat is cooked but still pink inside. Use an instant read thermometer—the internal temperature should be about 140°F (60°C).

5 Let the pork loin rest on the cutting board for 10 minutes before slicing. Drizzle with Mojo Mayo and serve alone or on sandwiches with sliced avocado, tomatoes, and cilantro. Serves 4.

Grilled Lamb Chops, Three Ways

Thick, juicy lamb chops are delightful straight off the grill. Get the butcher to cut the chops 1 inch (2.5 cm) thick, then rub your chops with one of the following easy combinations. Enjoy!

Basic Grilled Chops

1 Tbsp (15 mL) olive oil
1 clove garlic, crushed

8 thick lamb chops (loin or rib)
salt and freshly ground black pepper

1 In a small bowl, combine the olive oil and garlic. Set aside for 5 minutes to infuse. Rub the garlic-infused oil over both sides of the chops and season with salt and pepper.

2 Preheat the gas grill on high for 10 minutes. Keep one burner on high and reduce the heat to medium on the other side. Put the chops on the hot grill and sear, turning once, for about 2 minutes per side. Move the seared chops to the cooler side of the grill and cook for another 2 to 3 minutes per side (for medium rare). Remove from the grill to a warm plate and let rest for 5 minutes before serving.

Yogurt Rub

½ cup (125 mL) plain yogurt
1 Tbsp (15 mL) freshly squeezed lemon juice
½ tsp (2 mL) finely grated lemon zest
1 Tbsp (15 mL) olive oil
1 tsp (5 mL) minced fresh mint

1 tsp (5 mL) parsley
1 tsp (5 mL) minced garlic
½ tsp (2 mL) ground cumin
½ tsp (2 mL) Spanish paprika
salt and freshly ground black pepper

1 In a small bowl, combine the yogurt, lemon juice, zest, oil, mint, parsley, garlic, cumin, paprika, salt, and pepper. Rub over both sides of the chops. Refrigerate in a covered container for 2 hours. When fully chilled, brush off any excess rub, and then grill, following the instructions for Basic Grilled Chops.

Mixed Pepper Rub

3 Tbsp (45 mL) black peppercorns
2 Tbsp (30 mL) white peppercorns
1 Tbsp (15 mL) pink peppercorns

1 Tbsp (15 mL) allspice berries
1 Tbsp (15 mL) coriander seed

1 Grind the whole spices together in a blender or spice grinder (alternately, combine in a pepper mill and keep next to your stove to grind whenever you want to add an exotic note to a dish). Rub the chops with olive oil and season with Mixed Pepper Rub, then grill, following the instructions for Basic Grilled Chops.

Classic Rosemary Rub

2 Tbsp (30 mL) olive oil
2 cloves garlic, crushed
2 Tbsp (30 mL) finely minced fresh rosemary (or use 1 Tbsp/15 mL ground dried rosemary)

salt and freshly ground black pepper

1 Combine the olive oil and garlic. Set aside for 5 minutes. Rub the chops on both sides with the garlic-infused oil, sprinkle with minced rosemary, and season with salt and pepper. Grill, following the instructions for Basic Grilled Chops.

Stick Handling

The Guy likes to stick his food on skewers for grilling—it's easy to get sauces and marinades into every nook and cranny, and the small bite-sized pieces of meat and fish cook almost instantly.

Cut meat and poultry into uniform pieces for even cooking. You can cut meats into cubes or long strips (a.k.a. ribbons). The latter can be folded to thread onto skewers "accordion-style."

Marinate your protein in the refrigerator before threading on the skewers.

It's usually best not to combine meats with vegetables on one skewer, as they cook at different rates, although some food (like onions, peppers, and pineapple) can add flavor to the meats they're skewered next to. To grill dense vegetables (like potatoes, eggplant, or squash), make separate meat and vegetable skewers, then serve one or two of each to your guests.

When skewering large shrimp or prawns, use two bamboo skewers (one at the head and one at the tail end) to keep the fish flat. Easier to turn, too.

Veggies that take well to stick handling include grape tomatoes, chunks of bell peppers or onions, and cubes of summer squash and eggplant. Brush vegetables with garlic-infused olive oil and season with sea salt before grilling.

Soak bamboo skewers in warm water for 30 minutes before skewering the food and placing on the grill—otherwise, they can go up in smoke before your dinner's done!

Be careful when handling metal skewers. They get extremely hot while on the grill, so never pick them up without using an oven mitt.

Skewers look good presented over a bed of fluffy, mixed salad greens. Chunks of marinated, grilled meat, poultry, and vegetables are perfect to wrap in tortillas and pitas, or to pile onto toasted buns and then drizzle with flavored mayonnaise (see page 37). See index under kabobs for more stuff on sticks.

Pork Skewers with Thai Coconut Curry Sauce

You can substitute strips of chicken breast for the pork in this dish. The curry sauce permeates the pork with an exotic flavor—for an added shot of fiery Thai curry, drizzle the skewers with reserved sauce as it comes off the barbecue.

one 14-oz (398-mL) can light coconut milk

2 tsp (10 mL) hot Asian chili paste

¼ cup (60 mL) chopped cilantro (or 2 Tbsp/30 mL coriander chutney)

2 Tbsp (30 mL) oyster sauce

2 tsp (10 mL) curry powder

1 Tbsp (15 mL) brown sugar

2 cloves garlic, minced

1 pork tenderloin (about 1 lb/500 g), cut into long, thin strips

1 In a food processor or blender, combine the coconut milk, chili paste, cilantro, oyster sauce, curry powder, brown sugar, and garlic. Whirl until puréed.

2 Place the pork strips in a zippered plastic bag and add half of the marinade. Marinate the pork in the refrigerator for several hours. Cover the remaining marinade and refrigerate.

3 Thread the pork, accordion-style, onto flat, metal skewers. Grill the pork over medium-high heat for 8 minutes, turning several times, until it's just cooked.

4 Meanwhile, put the reserved marinade into a small pot and boil for 10 minutes to thicken. Brush some of the curry sauce over the pork as it comes off the grill. Serve the pork skewers over basmati rice, drizzled with the remaining curry sauce. Serves 4.

Souvlakia Skewers

This is The Guy's fallback for a simple supper—skewers of lemony chicken, pork, or lamb; Greek salad; and pita bread, toasted on the grill and brushed with olive oil for wrapping. Some plain yogurt, whisked with minced garlic, shredded cucumber, and dill (a.k.a. tzatziki) is nice on the side. Or make a pot of rice with spinach (see page 163) or hummus (see page 283) for a more traditional Greek meal.

2 lb (1 kg) skinless, boneless chicken breasts (or pork tenderloin or lamb), trimmed
¼ cup (60 mL) freshly squeezed lemon juice
¼ cup (60 mL) extra virgin olive oil

1 Tbsp (15 mL) dried oregano
¼ tsp (1 mL) freshly ground black pepper
1 tsp (5 mL) minced fresh rosemary
1 large clove garlic, minced

1 Cut the meat into long, skinny strips and thread, accordion-style, onto bamboo skewers that have been soaked for 30 minutes in water (this will prevent them burning up on the grill). In a small bowl, combine the lemon juice, oil, oregano, black pepper, rosemary, and garlic. Pour this over the meat and marinate in the refrigerator from 1 hour to 24 hours. Grill the chicken skewers over medium-high heat for about 7 to 8 minutes or just until the juices run clear. Serves 6.

Tandoori Lamb Skewers

Spicy skewers of grilled lamb and vegetables make a simple but elegant summer meal, with rice and spicy mango chutney on the side. This marinade works well on chicken, too, or can be rubbed over a piece of salmon before grilling.

1 lb (500 g) lamb leg, trimmed of visible fat

Tandoori Rub
⅓ cup (75 mL) plain yogurt
1 Tbsp (15 mL) curry powder or garam masala
½ tsp (2 mL) Asian chili paste
½ tsp (2 mL) salt
½ tsp (2 mL) granulated sugar

1-inch (2.5-cm) chunks of onion, zucchini, red and yellow bell peppers, and eggplant

2 green onions, minced
2 cloves garlic, crushed
½-inch (1-cm) piece fresh ginger, minced or puréed
2 Tbsp (30 mL) finely chopped fresh cilantro

1 Cut the lamb into 1 ½-inch (4-cm) cubes. In a medium bowl, whisk together the yogurt, curry, chili paste, salt, and sugar. Stir in the green onions, garlic, ginger, and cilantro. Reserve half the marinade for brushing the vegetables while grilling.

2 Add the lamb cubes to the remaining marinade in the bowl. Stir to coat well, then cover and refrigerate from 30 minutes to 12 hours.

3 Drain the lamb and discard the marinade. To cook the lamb, skewer the cubes of marinated meat on to pre-soaked bamboo or metal skewers. Make separate skewers of onion, zucchini, bell pepper, and/ or eggplant. Brush the vegetables with the reserved marinade.

4 Grill the skewers over medium-high heat until the lamb is medium rare and the vegetables are cooked, about 10 minutes in total. The lamb will be most tender if not cooked beyond medium rare.

5 Serve the lamb and vegetables with basmati rice and a little mango chutney on the side. Serves 4.

Mexican Fiesta

¡Hola! Crank up the mariachi music, shake up some margaritas, and pull out the pinatas—it's party time! Whether it's January or July, there's no better time for a Mexican fiesta. And this is the menu to match. Start with a traditional ceviche or chipotle chicken soup, then serve an elegant jalapeño-stuffed chicken breast or some garlicky fish, reminiscent of that Mexican beach holiday. Whatever you choose, this food is cause for celebration.

Chipotle Chicken Soup

This recipe makes a spicy bowl of chunky chicken and vegetable soup—a meal in itself. The chipotle chili adds an authentic smoky note. Look for canned chipotles in adobo sauce in any good grocery or supermarket, in the Mexican food section.

3 Roma tomatoes, roughly chopped
   (fresh or canned)
1 small onion, peeled and quartered
1 to 2 canned chipotle chilies, in adobo sauce
1 clove garlic, peeled
2 Tbsp (30 mL) olive oil
2 skinless, boneless chicken breasts, slivered
1 tsp (5 mL) sea salt

4 cups (1 L) chicken broth
1 small zucchini, cut into ¼-inch/5-mm) cubes
1 cup (250 mL) frozen corn, thawed
¼ cup(60 mL) chopped red bell pepper
1 Tbsp (30 mL) chopped fresh oregano
salt and freshly ground black pepper
½ cup (175 mL) tortilla chips
3 small key limes, halved

1 In a blender, purée the tomatoes, onion, chipotles, garlic, and ½ cup (125 mL) of water.

2 Heat the olive oil in a soup pot over medium-high and add the tomato/onion purée, frying until it begins to darken in color. Stir in the chicken and cook for 5 minutes, until the chicken turns white. Add the salt and broth to the pot and bring to a boil. Add the zucchini, corn, and red pepper and return the soup to a boil. Reduce the heat to low and simmer for 15 minutes.

3 Stir in the fresh oregano and season with salt and pepper to taste. Serve each bowl garnished with a few tortilla chips, and one piece of fresh lime for squeezing into the soup. Serves 6.

CHILI PEPPERS

WISE GUY: If you want to make this soup a little fancier, top each serving with some crispy tortilla strips made from scratch. Cut fresh corn tortillas into thin strips, and fry in hot oil until crisp.

Orange Scallop Ceviche

The acid in citrus juices will "cook" fish in a few hours—you never have to turn on the stove. This dish combines tender scallops, orange sections, and avocado in a ceviche inspired by The Guy's travels in Chile. You can try this with shrimp or a white fish such as halibut—or make a combination ceviche using a variety of seafood. Just make sure you start with extremely fresh fish.

1 lb (500 g) large sea scallops, sliced or cubed
2 medium navel oranges, juiced (about ¾ cup/175 mL)
2 large limes, juiced (about ½ cup/125 mL)
1 Tbsp (15 mL) ketchup
½ tsp (2 mL) Asian garlic chili paste
1 tsp (5 mL) honey
1 Tbsp (15 mL) extra virgin olive oil

1 medium navel orange, peeled and cut into sections
¼ cup (60 mL) finely chopped or slivered red onion
1 jalapeño or serrano chili, minced
½ ripe avocado, peeled and chopped
2 Tbsp (30 mL) chopped fresh cilantro
sea salt

1 Combine the scallops, orange juice, and lime juice in a non-reactive bowl (stainless steel or glass, but not aluminum). Cover and refrigerate for 4 to 5 hours (no longer). The scallops should be white and slightly firmed up.

2 Drain the scallops, discarding the citrus juice. In a large bowl, whisk together the ketchup, chili paste, honey, and oil. Stir in the scallops, orange segments, red onion, chili pepper, and avocado. Cover and refrigerate for 2 hours. Just before serving, stir in the cilantro and season with salt to taste.

3 Serve as an appetizer to scoop up with tortilla chips or as a starter course. Try presenting as a "ceviche cocktail" in a martini glass. Or serve the ceviche salad-style, piled atop sliced tomatoes with a few sprigs of baby greens. Serves 4.

WISE GUY: Choose only Haas avocados (the dark wrinkly kind) as the bigger, bright green ones are tasteless by comparison. A ripe avocado is neither hard as a rock nor soft and squishy—the tip should yield just slightly when pressed. To peel, hold the avocado with one hand and slice around the avocado lengthwise, just up to but not through the large pit. Twist the two halves apart, then lodge your chef's knife into the pit, and twist it out. Use a spoon to scoop the flesh into a bowl (discard any blackened avocado). Chop for salads or mash for guacamole. You can also "cube" the flesh while it's still in the skin—cut a grid pattern through the flesh, just to the skin, then turn the skin inside out to release your perfect pieces.

Guacamole

While you're passing the ceviche, guacamole is always in order. A few fresh taco chips are all you need for a perfect little appetizer. A little acidity (like a squeeze of fresh lemon juice) will help keep the guacamole from turning brown, but it's best to serve it soon after it's made.

3 large ripe avocados, peeled
1 Tbsp (15 mL) freshly squeezed lime or
    lemon juice

½ cup (125 mL) chunky tomato salsa (drain
    slightly if watery)
2 Tbsp (30 mL) minced cilantro

1 In a medium bowl, mash the avocado and citrus juice together with a fork. Fold in the salsa. Cover with plastic wrap and refrigerate up to 2 hours. Serve with chips or alongside other Mexican dishes. Serves 8.

Spicy Rice

This rice definitely has a southern thing going on. Serve it with any grilled fish, chicken, or seafood—even alongside a spicy piece of pork.

2 cloves garlic, minced
1 stalk celery, minced
½ cup (125 mL) minced onion (1 small)
1 Tbsp (15 mL) olive oil
2 cups (500 mL) long-grain rice
3 cups (750 mL) water

½ cup (125 mL) tomato sauce
½ to 1 tsp (2 to 5 mL) chili paste
½ tsp (2 mL) ground cumin
salt and freshly ground black pepper
2 Tbsp (30 mL) chopped fresh cilantro or parsley
    (optional)

1 Use the food processor, if you like, to finely mince the garlic, celery, and onion.

2 In a medium-sized saucepan, heat the olive oil over medium-high heat and sauté the garlic, celery, and onion mixture for 3 minutes or until the celery is wilted and the onion and garlic are tender and fragrant. Add the rice and stir for a minute or two, then add the water, tomato sauce, and chili paste. Season with the cumin, salt, and pepper and bring to a boil. Reduce the heat to low, cover, and simmer for 30 minutes.

3 Remove from the heat and let the rice steam for 5 minutes, then fluff with a fork, and stir in the cilantro, if using. Serves 4 to 6.

Chicken Rellenos

The Guy likes this nifty combination of cheese-stuffed chilies (rellenos) with tender chicken—it makes a nice party dish. But remember, jalapeño peppers can be tricky—some are super hot, others are pretty mild (depending on how and where they're grown). Taste them before you use them.

4 skinless, boneless chicken breasts
4 large jalapeño peppers (look for the biggest ones you can find or substitute 8 smaller peppers)
4 oz (100 g) Monterey Jack or Jalapeno Jack cheese
salt and freshly ground black pepper

½ cup (125 mL) all-purpose flour
½ cup (125 mL) milk
2 large eggs, lightly beaten
1 cup (250 mL) fine dry breadcrumbs or cracker crumbs
olive oil

1 Place the chicken breasts on the counter, between two sheets of plastic wrap, and use a meat mallet to gently pound the breasts into an even thickness. (Flattening the chicken will double its surface area.)

2 Cut the stem end off each jalapeño pepper and, using a small paring knife, cut a slit down the length of each. Work the knife inside the peppers to remove the ribs and seeds, then discard the ribs and seeds.

3 Cut the cheese into finger-sized chunks, just big enough to fill the cavity of each pepper. Fill each pepper with cheese.

4 Season the flattened chicken pieces lightly with salt and pepper. Place a stuffed pepper on one end of each piece of chicken and roll the chicken around the pepper to enclose it, tucking in the sides as you roll. Secure with toothpicks.

5 Place the flour on a plate. Beat the milk and egg together in a shallow bowl. Place the dry crumbs on another plate. Carefully roll the chicken bundles in flour to coat, shaking off any excess. Dip in the egg mixture, then roll in the plate of crumbs. The chicken bundles should be coated on all sides. Set the chicken bundles on a rack for 10 minutes while you heat the oil in a non-stick, ovenproof sauté pan. Cook the bundles over medium-high heat until browned on all sides (start with the seam side first and the meat will sear together so that you can remove the toothpicks and continue browning). Place the pan into a 350°F (180°C) oven for 10 minutes to finish cooking. Serve with Fresh Tomato Salsa (see page 77) and spicy rice. Serves 4.

WISE GUY:

Putting meat into the oven to finish cooking after an initial browning stage is a chef's trick that prevents overcooking. Keep this in mind when you're buying pans for the kitchen — plastic handles may stay cool on the stove top, but they can't go into the oven. Cook like a chef—buy ovenproof pans and use oven mitts!

Pescado Mojo de Ajo

The Guy recalls sitting at a little table under a shady *palapa* on a beach in Mexico whenever he makes this simple, garlicky dish. This recipe works well for cooking big tiger prawns, too. Serve some Spicy Rice (see page 269) on the side.

four 6-oz (175-g) fish fillets (whitefish, sole, pickerel, etc.)
3 Tbsp (45 mL) freshly squeezed lime juice
½ cup (125 mL) all-purpose flour
¼ tsp (1 mL) salt

¼ cup (60 mL) butter
2 Tbsp (30 mL) canola oil
12 cloves garlic, thinly sliced
freshly ground black pepper
chopped fresh parsley and lime wedges to garnish

1 Place the fish on a plate and pour the lime juice overtop. Set aside to marinate for 10 minutes.

2 On another plate, combine the flour and salt.

3 Heat the butter and oil in a non-stick skillet over medium-low heat. When the butter has melted, add the sliced garlic and cook, shaking the pan occasionally, until the garlic just begins to turn pale golden. Don't brown the garlic or it will become bitter. Remove the garlic from the oil with a slotted spoon and reserve.

4 Drain the fish fillets and dip, one at a time, in the flour to lightly coat both sides. Shake off any excess flour. Heat the garlic-flavored oil over medium-high heat and fry the fish until golden brown, about 2 to 3 minutes per side, depending on the thickness of the fish.

5 Arrange the fried fish on a platter. Sprinkle with the reserved garlic and drizzle with the garlic butter from the pan. Garnish with chopped parsley and lime wedges, then serve. Serves 4.

Margaritaville

Margs are the way to go to get your Cinco de Mayo party off on the right foot. Make a big container of these slushy margaritas in advance and pull it out of the freezer as your guests arrive. Otherwise, just shake up the classic margarita (see page 277), one at a time, like the cocktail king you know you are!

1 can frozen limeade concentrate
1 cup (250 mL) good quality tequila
½ cup (125 mL) Cointreau, Triple Sec, or other
    sweet orange liqueur
4 cups (1 L) crushed ice or about 30 ice cubes*

2 fresh limes, quartered
coarse sea salt
2 cups (500 mL) soda water or lemon-lime soda
    (like Sprite or 7-Up)

1 Combine the limeade, tequila, orange liqueur, and ice in your blender (you may have to do it in two batches). Whirl until the mixture is smooth and slushy. Store the slush in a covered container in the freezer until ready to serve.

2 To serve, fill a shallow bowl with coarse sea salt, ¼ inch (5 mm) deep. Rub the lime around the rim of each margarita glass (big martini-style glasses are classic) and press the rim into the salt to coat. Give the glass a tap to knock off any excess salt.

3 Using an ice cream scoop, fill the glass with a big scoop of the frozen margarita mix. Top with a bit of soda and serve with a straw. Makes 8 cocktails.

If you're using ice cubes, make sure your blender is powerful enough to take on the ice. Otherwise, start with crushed ice (or put your cubes in a plastic bag and bash them with a meat mallet).

Flan Kahlúa

Like your favorite crème caramel with a shot of coffee liqueur, this easy and impressive dessert is quite appropriate to end a Mexican meal in style. After inverting these individual flans on pretty dessert plates, drizzle each with a little extra Kahlúa. Mucho mocha!

1 cup (250 mL) granulated sugar
3 Tbsp (45 mL) water
two 13-oz (385-mL) cans evaporated milk
⅓ cup (75 mL) icing sugar
½ cup (125 mL) strong coffee
3 large eggs

2 egg yolks
pinch salt
¼ cup (60 mL) Kahlúa
chocolate-covered coffee beans and extra Kahlúa to
    garnish

1   Start by caramelizing the sugar. Put the sugar and water in a heavy saucepan over medium heat. The sugar will dissolve as the mixture heats, forming a clear syrup. Swirl the pan a few times at the beginning to help the sugar dissolve. When the syrup is clear, stop swirling the pan and turn the heat up to high. Let the sugar cook until it starts to turn a caramel color. Watch it carefully as it can burn quickly. When it's a nice rich amber color, pour it carefully into eight ovenproof, straight-sided ramekins, swirling each to coat both the bottoms and sides with caramel. Work quickly, as the caramel will set as it cools, but be careful—the sugar is very hot at this point. Set the ramekins aside.

2   Preheat the oven to 350°F (180°C).

3   In another pan, combine the evaporated milk, icing sugar, and coffee. Bring to a boil over medium-high heat. Reduce the heat and stir until the sugar dissolves completely. Remove from the heat and set aside.

4   In a large bowl, whisk the eggs and egg yolks with the salt. Slowly pour in the warm milk mixture, whisking constantly. Add the Kahlúa and mix well, then pour into the prepared ramekins. Place the ramekins in a large baking pan that has been filled with 1 inch (2.5 cm) of hot water. Place the pan in the oven and bake the flans for about 30 to 35 minutes or until they are nearly set. (They should still be a little jiggly in the center for the most tender result—overcooking makes a rubbery flan.)

5   Remove the ramekins from the hot water bath, cool for 30 minutes, then cover with plastic wrap and refrigerate overnight. To serve, run a knife around the edge of each ramekin to loosen the flan (or dip the base of the ramekin in hot water) then invert each onto an individual dessert plate. Garnish each flan with a chocolate-covered coffee bean and drizzle with a little Kahlúa. Serves 8.

The Cocktail Hour

The Guy likes to invite his friends by for some cool cocktails and nifty noshes. But you don't have to be a chef to organize a great schmooze. Just make a few instant noshes, like The Guy's spicy bar nuts and some simple crostini (a.k.a. toast) with a few spreads and slathers. Hit the local cheese shop for some imported cheese and pass by the bakery for some artisan walnut bread or sesame-crusted crackers (a.k.a. lavosh).

The Guy's Top Ten Cocktails

Shaken or stirred? The Guy loves to play bartender—there's nothing quite as sexy as working that shiny silver shaker. The cocktail world is vast but here's a taste of The Guy's current favorites, from classic martinis and pisco sours to mojitos. Cheers!

Dry Gin Martini

You can make this with vodka, but why would you when there's so much great gin?

1 oz (30 mL) dry vermouth
2 oz (60 mL) gin (Bombay Sapphire, Hendricks, or
   Tanqueray)

twist of lemon rind or green olive as garnish
   (optional)

1 Combine the vermouth and gin in a cocktail shaker with ice. Shake well to chill, then strain into a cocktail glass. Garnish, if you like, with a twist of lemon or a skewered green olive. Makes 1 cocktail.

Pisco Sour

The Guy learned to love this cocktail in Chile, where every meal begins with a pisco (the unique, locally made brandy). Whirled up in the blender with fresh lime juice, sugar, and egg white, it makes a smooth and surprisingly strong aperitif.

½ cup (125 mL) freshly squeezed lime juice (look for
   tiny, sweet Mexican or key limes)
1 cup (250 mL) pisco

2 Tbsp (30 mL) confectioner's sugar
1 egg white
dash angostura bitters

1 Combine the lime juice, pisco, sugar, egg white, and bitters in a blender, and blend until frothy. Add about ½ cup (125 mL) crushed ice and blend until smooth (or pour into a cocktail shaker and shake with ice). Strain into small glasses or champagne flutes. Makes 4 cocktails.

Cosmopolitan

The girls love this ruby red cocktail. Serve in a martini glass with a few frozen cranberries bobbing on top.

1 oz (30 mL) vodka
1 oz (30 mL) Cointreau
¼ cup (60 mL) cranberry juice

2 Tbsp (30 mL) freshly squeezed lime juice
frozen cranberries

1 Fill a cocktail shaker with ice and add the vodka, Cointreau and cranberry and lime juices. Shake until chilled. Strain into a martini glass and top with frozen cranberries. Makes 1 cocktail.

Mojito

Here's the drink to start a Latin or Caribbean meal—it's tall, cool, and refreshing on a hot day.

2 to 3 sprigs fresh mint
¼ lime
2 tsp (10 mL) sugar

¼ cup (60 mL) freshly squeezed lime juice
2 oz (60 mL) rum
crushed ice and soda water

1 Put the mint sprigs, quartered lime, and sugar in the bottom of a tall glass. Muddle (crush and mix) the ingredients around with a long spoon to dissolve the sugar, release the lime juice, and bruise the mint.

2 Add the lime juice and rum, and fill the glass with crushed ice. Top up with soda water, stir, and serve. Makes 1 cocktail.

Whisky Sour

One of The Guy's good friends always serves whisky sours, with smoked pheasant appetizers, before Christmas dinner. It's a good traditional cocktail to break the ice anytime.

2 oz (60 mL) rye whisky
2 oz (60 mL) Rose's lime cordial

crushed ice and soda water

1 Combine the whisky and lime cordial in a cocktail shaker filled with ice. Shake for 30 seconds until chilled, then strain into a cocktail glass. Top with a splash of soda water and serve. Makes 1 cocktail.

Margarita

The Guy loves a classic margarita—made with the best tequila you can buy—served shaken, never frozen. The best tequilas are labeled "100% blue agave." Use a "blanco" or white tequila when making margaritas—gold tequilas aged in oak like whisky are made for sipping.

1 lime, cut in half
coarse sea salt
1½ oz (45 mL) tequila

½ oz (15 mL) Cointreau or Triple Sec
2 Tbsp (30 mL) freshly squeezed lime juice
    (look for tiny, sweet key limes)

1 Rub ½ of the cut lime along the rim of a margarita or martini glass and then dip the rim in coarse sea salt to lightly coat. Shake off any excess salt.

2 Combine the tequila, Cointreau, and lime juice in a cocktail shaker filled with ice. Cover and shake hard for 30 seconds. Strain into the salt-rimmed glass and serve. Makes 1 cocktail.

Gin Tonic

The perfect antidote to the midday sun—to be imbibed on the deck.

2 oz (60 mL) gin
1 oz (30 mL) Rose's lime cordial

½ cup (125 mL) tonic water
1 slice of lime

1 Fill a tall glass with ice and add the gin, lime cordial, and tonic water. Stir to combine and garnish the glass with a slice of lime. Makes 1 cocktail.

Blueberry Tea

After a day out in the snow—skiing, walking, or whatever—a steaming blueberry tea by the fire is bliss.

1 oz (30 mL) amaretto
1 oz (30 mL) Grand Marnier

hot, brewed black tea
1 slice of fresh orange

1 Put the amaretto and Grand Marnier in a mug and fill with tea. Float a slice of orange on top and serve. Makes 1 serving.

Velvet Hammer

Could there be a better name for a creamy and seductive cocktail like this? The Guy thinks not.

1 oz (30 mL) vodka
½ oz (15 mL) white crème de cacao
½ oz (15 mL) Kahlúa

2 oz (60 mL) heavy cream
¼ cup (60 mL) crushed ice

1   In a blender, combine the vodka, crème de cacao, Kahlúa, cream, and ice. Blend until frothy and pour into a martini glass. Makes 1 cocktail.

Spicy Caesar

Created in Canada, eh? Yep, this is the classic morning eye-opener for your cowboy brunch crowd. And with its celery stick garnish, it makes a nice happy hour snack, too.

1 lime, cut in half
celery salt
1½ oz (45 mL) vodka
⅔ cup (150 mL) Clamato juice
   (tomato clam juice)

dash of hot sauce
double dash of Worcestershire sauce
leafy stalk of celery to garnish

1   Rub ½ of the cut lime along the rim of a tall glass and then dip the rim in a plate of celery salt to lightly coat.

2   Fill the glass with ice and add the vodka, Clamato, hot sauce, and Worcestershire. Sprinkle a bit of celery salt on top, stir with a stalk of celery, and serve. Makes 1 cocktail.

Champagne: The Ultimate Aperitif

Champagne is the king of sparkling wine—some aficionados would argue it's the pinnacle of the wine world, too. It's definitely a great drink to serve with cocktail noshes.

Champagne comes from the Champagne region of France. It's made from a very dry, still wine—made from Pinot Noir and/or Chardonnay grapes—that's re-fermented in the bottle to create the characteristic bubbles. International law states that only the French can label their bubbly "Champagne," although some other countries still do. Several, however, have developed their own unique names for their sparklers—"cava" in Spain, for example, or "prosecco" in Italy—while others label their bubbly "méthode traditionelle" to indicate it's made in the traditional bottle-fermented way.

Less expensive sparkling wines are re-fermented in a large tank (charmat method) or simply shot through with a fizzy blast of CO_2 before bottling—the former being quite acceptable, the latter being far inferior to the real thing.

While there are some good traditional-style bubblies from Italy, Spain, Australia, California, and Canada, you get what you pay for when it comes to sparkling wine. When it really matters, The Guy always goes for French champagne.

There's a lot of pressure built up in a champagne bottle so be careful where you're aiming that cork when you open it. Not that you want to eject the cork into the air—very déclassé. In fact, you don't want to "pop" the cork at all—as the sommeliers say, it should come away with a "sigh." So remove the foil and protective wire bale from the top of the bottle, drape the neck with a towel, and grasp the cork with one hand while twisting the base of the bottle with the other. The cork will gently ease out of the bottle and you won't waste any of the exquisite taste.

Make sure you have nice tall champagne flutes to keep the wine "lively" and give you a good look at all of those tiny bubbles.

Wine, Beer, and Other Stuff

Any good cocktail party should have a well-stocked bar. You can limit the offerings to wine and beer or go all out and mix whatever cocktails your guests request.

To make big parties easier, The Guy usually sticks to one red and white wine choice, a dark and a light beer, plus non-alcoholic juices and sparkling water. He also usually offers one signature cocktail to welcome each guest and set the mood. If it's a holiday party, that might be an eggnog or a martini. If it's a Mexican fiesta, a margarita or a mojito is in order. To start a cowboy barbecue (or brunch), a spicy Caesar.

Then just set up a bar area where guests can help themselves to drinks—or if it's a huge affair, hire a bartender to serve. A backyard barbecue calls for a big washtub filled with ice for chilling long-necked beers, coolers, and soft drinks.

Nifty Party Noshes and Finger Food

They call it finger food because you can eat it with your fingers and dunk it, dip it, slide it off a skewer, or pop it in your mouth the moment you take it from the tray. That's a rule for cocktail bites—they should be consumable in a bite (two at the most), and shouldn't require a plate or cutlery of any kind. Sit-down appetizers are for sitting down. Save them for your tapas party.

Chips and Dip

The Pita Chip

These are so much better than the commercial chips—and they're low in fat, too. Make sure the pita bread is fairly fresh to begin with—stale pita is harder to separate into rounds (but that's okay, too, just cut it up and make thicker chips).

½ cup (125 mL) extra virgin olive oil
3 cloves garlic, crushed
2 packages 6- to 8-inch (15- to 20-cm) pita breads (white and whole wheat make a nice contrast)

variety of dried herbs and spices, like basil, oregano, thyme, cayenne, paprika, and celery salt (or spice blends such as Cajun spice, herbes de Provence, five-spice powder, etc.).

1 Combine the olive oil and crushed garlic in a bowl and let steep for 15 minutes to infuse the oil. Using kitchen scissors, cut each pita into two rounds (cut around the edge to separate). Then cut the rounds into six wedges (or tear rounds into fat strips for a more rustic look).

2 Preheat the oven to 400°F (200°C). Using a pastry brush, very lightly brush the rough inner side of each piece with olive oil (several chips can be done with one brushful of oil) and lay them, rough-side up, on a cookie sheet.

3 Sprinkle with your choice of herbs and spices. (The Guy likes to change his spice mixes with every pan of chips he makes, so guests get a surprise, but try to stick to traditional combinations such as Italian with basil, oregano, and pepper or Mexican with cumin, coriander, and chili powder.) A light dusting of cayenne adds spark to any mixture.

4 When the sheet is full (a single but crowded layer), pop it into the oven for 3 to 4 minutes. Set the timer and watch carefully as the chips can burn quickly. While one batch is baking, start working on a second tray and you'll have them all done in less than half an hour. They keep well in a sealed bag, so you can make them several days in advance. Makes a huge basket of chips.

Hot Crab and Artichoke Dip

This decadent dip, inspired by one of The Guy's favorite chefs, combines two old favorites in one rich, creamy concoction. Serve it warm with pita chips, French bread, or vegetables for scooping.

one 4-oz (125-g) package fat-reduced cream cheese
2 Tbsp (30 mL) bottled chili sauce or tomato paste
1 tsp (5 mL) freshly squeezed lemon juice
1 tsp (5 mL) prepared horseradish
½ cup (125 mL) low-fat mayonnaise
½ cup (125 mL) low-fat plain yogurt or sour cream
1 cup (250 mL) finely grated fresh Parmesan or
    Romano cheese
freshly ground black pepper

½ tsp (2 mL) hot pepper sauce
one 14-oz (398-mL) can artichoke hearts, drained
    well and chopped
1 clove garlic, crushed
1 green onion, chopped
1 cup (250 mL) fresh or frozen crabmeat (or one
    7 ½-oz/213-g can, drained)
paprika, for garnish

1 Preheat the oven to 350°F (180°C).

2 In a food processor, add the cream cheese, chili sauce, lemon juice, horseradish, mayonnaise, yogurt, Parmesan, pepper, and the hot pepper sauce. Process until smooth. Using a rubber spatula, scrape down the sides of the bowl so that all of the ingredients are well combined. Add the artichoke hearts, garlic, chopped green onions, and crabmeat (make sure you pick through the crab to remove any bits of shell or cartilage). Pulse a few times, just to combine (not purée). Spoon the dip into a small baking dish, dust with paprika, and bake for 20 to 30 minutes or until it begins to bubble and starts to brown on top. Serve this dip hot, with pita chips or crostini. Serves 4 to 6.

WISE GUY:

You can make this dip in advance, cover, and chill overnight, then bake as needed.

Cilantro Hummus

This is a healthy dip to scoop up with pitas or sliced veggies, or even to slather on a sandwich. The cilantro gives it a lot of fresh flavor and a groovy green glow. If you want an orange hummus, whirl in a roasted red pepper (out of a jar) instead of all the green stuff.

one 19-oz (540 mL) can chickpeas, drained
 and rinsed
1 jalapeño pepper, seeded and finely chopped
1 tsp (15 mL) ground cumin
¼ cup (60 mL) extra virgin olive oil
¼ cup (60 mL) tahini paste
 (sesame seed paste)

2 tsp (10 mL) sesame oil
juice of one large lemon (about 5 to 6 Tbsp/
 75 to 90 mL)
2 cloves garlic, minced
1 tsp (5 mL) salt
¼ cup (60 mL) water
1 cup (250 mL) cilantro leaves

1 Drain the chickpeas in a sieve over the sink and rinse well under running water to remove excess salt. Place the chickpeas, jalapeño, cumin, olive oil, tahini, sesame oil, lemon juice, garlic, and salt in a food processor. Process until the hummus is smooth. Add a little water if the mixture seems too dry.

2 Toss in the cilantro and process to combine. Serve the hummus immediately with warm pita bread or Pita Chips (see page 281), or cover and refrigerate for up to 3 days. Makes 3 cups (750 mL).

BOWL OF DIP ☺

Roasted Onion and Garlic Dip

This is The Guy's tarted-up version of an old family favorite—a dip (or scoop as we knew it) created with sour cream and dehydrated onion soup. You can go that route in a pinch, or make this more sophisticated version. Pita chips make healthy dippers, but The Guy is also a sucker for a good rippled potato chip, for old times sake.

one 4-oz (125-g) package cream cheese
   (plain or herbed like Boursin)
¾ cup (175 mL) sour cream
2 tsp (10 mL) Worcestershire sauce

1 large onion, slivered and caramelized
   (see page 16)
1 head garlic, roasted (see page 17)
salt and freshly ground black pepper

1 In the food processor, whirl the cream cheese, sour cream, and Worcestershire until smooth. Add the caramelized onions and squeeze the roasted garlic out of its papery husk and into the processor. Season with salt and pepper to taste. Pulse everything together a couple of times until it's combined, but still nice and chunky. Serve warm or chilled. Makes 1½ cups (375 mL).

More Dip Shtick

Is there a cup of low-fat sour cream in the refrigerator? Can you add a spoonful or two of mayo? This is your dip baseline (or start with strained plain yogurt). Add some herbs and other flavorings—for dunking veggies, crackers, chips, bread sticks, etc.
Experiment with these easy additions:

 pesto

 curry paste (Indian or Thai)

 puréed salsa and chopped cilantro

 puréed sundried tomatoes, basil, oregano, and garlic

 canned sockeye salmon, chopped dill, and a drop of liquid smoke

 fresh basil, fresh rosemary, minced lemon zest, chives, thyme leaves, paprika

 crumbled bits of soft, but assertive cheese such as goat cheese or Stilton with herbs

 minced dill pickles and fresh dill

Toasty Stuff

Crispy Toast Cups

This is one good use for the kind of dense white bread you can find at any supermarket. Flattened and molded into mini-muffin tins, white bread makes perfect little toast cups for mini-mouthfuls of party food (from cheesy dips to more substantial stuff).

1 loaf dense white bread, sliced, crusts removed   sea salt
¼ cup (60 mL) extra virgin olive oil

1 Preheat the oven to 350°F (180°C).

2 Using a rolling pin, flatten the bread until thin. With a pastry brush, brush the bread lightly with olive oil and sprinkle with salt. Cut the flattened bread into rounds with a 2-inch (5-cm) glass or cookie cutter or cut into 2-inch (5-cm) squares. Lightly brush a mini-muffin pan with olive oil. Press the bread into the muffin pan (you will need to do this in three or four batches) and bake for 10 minutes or until golden and crisp. Remove the toasts from pan and cool. These crispy toast cups keep well at room temperature, in a plastic bag, for several weeks. Makes about 50 to 60 bread cups.

WISE GUY: Use toast cups to ferry anything drippy to your mouth, from the aforementioned crab and artichoke dip, to curried chicken, or beef in barbecue sauce. Be creative, a creamy herbed dip—created with cream cheese (or tangy goat cheese), softened with milk, yogurt or sour cream, and flavored with fresh minced chives, horseradish, citrus zest, curry paste, basil pesto, or blue cheese—can be dolloped into a toast cup and topped with anything from seafood or sausage to tiny tomatoes, eggplant purée, or grilled figs.

Crostini Toasts

The Guy figures that anyone can make toast—so why not make your own cool crostini for a party. Sure, you can buy commercial toasts but they're just not the same. Take a half hour and make your own—they'll last a week at room temperature in a plastic bag.

1 good-quality French baguette
⅓ cup (75 mL) extra virgin olive oil

1 large clove garlic, minced
½ tsp (2 mL) sea salt

1 Preheat the oven to 400°F (200°C).

2 Slice the baguette on the diagonal into ¼- to ½-inch (5-mm to 1-cm) slices.

3 In a small bowl, combine the olive oil with the garlic and let steep for 5 minutes to infuse the oil with flavor.

4 Using a pastry brush, lightly brush the garlic-infused oil over both sides of the bread. Lay the slices in a single layer on a baking sheet. Sprinkle with sea salt.

5 Toast in the oven for 4 to 5 minutes or until the bread just begins to turn golden brown. Watch carefully as the crostini can burn quickly. Cool and store in a plastic bag at room temperature for up to 1 week. Makes 40 toasts.

Slathers and Spreads

Chunky Smoked Salmon Spread

When The Guy last went salmon fishing on the left coast, he brought home some of his catch as Indian candy—a sweetly glazed and spiced, hot-smoked salmon product that's addictive on its own as a snack, or perfect to haul along on a cycling trip for a fast hit of protein. Mixed with some cream cheese and sour cream, it makes an awesome spread.

3 oz (75 g) cream cheese
¼ cup (60 mL) sour cream
1 cup (250 mL) flaked, hot-smoked salmon

1 Tbsp (15 mL) minced fresh dill
2 tsp (10 mL) chopped capers (optional)
freshly ground black pepper

1 Whirl the cream cheese and sour cream together in a food processor until smooth. In a bowl, flake the smoked salmon (making sure to remove and discard any skin and bones) and combine it with the cream cheese mixture. Stir in the fresh dill, capers, and black pepper. You've got a yummy spread for crostini or to pipe into crispy bread cups (see page xxx) with a caper or sprig of dill on top. Makes 1½ cups (375 mL).

Not Foie Gras Paté

While you'll see foie gras on almost every top restaurant menu these days, it's not the kind of thing The Guy has on hand at home. But this basic bistro alternative—creamy chicken liver paté—has almost as much cachet when slathered on crostini and topped with a dab of something to cut the richness (think spicy fruit chutney or sweet relish). Chic and cheap!

2 Tbsp (30 mL) butter
2 Tbsp (30 mL) olive oil
1 lb (500 g) chicken livers, trimmed
  and quartered
4 large shallots, minced
2 cloves garlic, minced
½ cup (125 mL) white wine or sherry
1 bay leaf
½ tsp (2 mL) freshly ground black pepper

½ tsp (2 mL) dried thyme
½ tsp (2 mL) dried sage
1 tsp (5 mL) minced fresh rosemary
½ tsp (2 mL) salt
⅓ cup (75 mL) whipping cream or sour cream
2 Tbsp (30 mL) brandy
3 Tbsp (45 mL) melted butter
bay leaves for garnish

1 In a non-stick sauté pan, heat the butter and olive oil over medium-high heat until sizzling. Add the chicken livers to the pan and sauté quickly, until firm but still pink inside. Remove the chicken livers and set aside.

2 Add the shallots and garlic to the pan and cook for 2 to 3 minutes, until fragrant. Stir in the wine, bay leaf, pepper, thyme, and sage. Simmer together for 10 minutes or until the liquid has cooked down to about ¼ cup (60 mL).

3 Transfer the contents of the pan to a food processor, discarding the bay leaf. Add the reserved chicken livers, minced rosemary, salt, cream, and brandy. Process until smooth. Add the melted butter and pulse to combine. Fill small molds or terrines with the paté mixture and decorate the tops of each with bay leaves. Cover with plastic wrap to seal, and refrigerate the terrines overnight or freeze. Serve with crostini or sliced French bread and savory rhubarb sauce (see page 474), prepared mango chutney, or tiny sweet pickles from the supermarket. Serves 8.

Savory White Bean Purée with Goat Cheese

Another hearty purée to slather on toast or dollop into a toast cup.

one 14-oz (398-mL) can white beans
  (canellini or navy beans)
1 Tbsp (15 mL) finely chopped fresh rosemary
1 Tbsp (15 mL) basil
1 Tbsp (15 mL) parsley
2 cloves garlic, minced

¼ cup (60 mL) extra virgin olive oil
½ tsp (2 mL) Asian chili paste
½ cup (125 mL) caramelized onions
  (see page 16)
½ cup (125 mL) goat cheese

1 Put the beans into a sieve and rinse well under running water. Shake off any excess water and set aside to drain.

2 In a food processor, combine the rosemary, basil, parsley, garlic, and olive oil. Whirl to purée. Add half the beans and process until smooth. Add the rest of the beans and the chili paste and pulse, leaving the purée a little chunky.

3 Heat the caramelized onions in a medium sauté pan and add the bean purée. Stir to heat through. Crumble the goat cheese into the pan and fold into the mixture. You want the cheese warm, but still intact in the mixture. Pile into a serving dish and serve immediately with crostini toasts or French bread. Makes 2 cups (500 mL).

Asian Eggplant

The Guy likes to serve this savory eggplant with pita or Chinese Chow Cow chips for scooping up. It also makes a nice side dish to an Asian-inspired meal (like the Crispy Fried Fish on page 314).

1 lb (500 g) Japanese eggplant
1 Tbsp (15 mL) olive oil
1 small onion or 4 shallots, finely chopped
2 Tbsp (30 mL) minced garlic

1 tsp (5 mL) minced fresh ginger
¼ tsp (1 mL) sesame oil
1 Tbsp (15 mL) minced fresh cilantro

Sauce
2 Tbsp (30 mL) water
2 Tbsp (30 mL) hoisin sauce
1 Tbsp (15 mL) soy sauce

1 Tbsp (15 mL) rice or white wine vinegar
1 Tbsp (15 mL) packed brown sugar
½ tsp (2 mL) Szechuan peppercorns, toasted and
  ground or ½ tsp (2 mL) Asian chili paste

1 Prick the eggplants all over with a fork. Place on a roasting pan and roast in a 400°F (200°C) oven for about 45 minutes or until very soft. Cool, peel, and mash the flesh. For a smokier version, cook the eggplants on the barbecue until blackened, then peel and chop the eggplant flesh.

2 In a small bowl, whisk together the sauce ingredients and set aside.

3 In a wok or sauté pan, heat the oil over medium high heat and stir fry the, garlic, and ginger for 5 minutes. Add the eggplant and quickly stir-fry to heat through and combine. Add the reserved sauce mixture and simmer until most of the liquid has boiled away. Serve the eggplant in a bowl, drizzled with sesame oil and sprinkled with cilantro. Serve warm or at room temperature. Serves 4 to 6.

Tuna Tapenade

The Guy loves this simple tapenade (olive paste) that's made with stuffed green olives and canned Italian tuna in olive oil. Nothing could be simpler served with a toasted baguette as an appetizer, but it's also awesome when tossed quickly with any short pasta such as rotini or orecchiette. Look for tiny tins of tuna packed in olive oil at Italian markets.

1 cup (250 mL) pitted green olives (if possible, use ones that are stuffed with anchovies)
1 Tbsp (15 mL) minced fresh garlic
2 Tbsp (30 mL) extra virgin olive oil
one 3 ½-oz (100-mL) tin tuna, packed in olive oil

1 tsp (5 mL) grainy mustard
½ tsp (2 mL) hot pepper sauce
juice and grated zest of ½ lemon
2 Tbsp (30 mL) chopped fresh parsley

1 In a food processor, combine the olives and garlic. Pulse until chopped but still chunky. Add the oil, tuna, mustard, hot sauce, and lemon juice. Pulse again to combine.

2 Process for a few more seconds—the tapenade should be partly pasty and partly coarse. Add the lemon zest and parsley, and pulse just to combine. Refrigerate and serve with crostini. Makes 1½ cups (375 mL).

> **WISE GUY:** For a speedy supper for four, cook ¾ lb (375 g) rotini or other chunky pasta in boiling water until al dente (tender but toothsome), drain well and toss with the tuna tapenade and 1 cup (250 mL) of grated Parmesan cheese. Season with freshly ground black pepper.

Bits and Bites

Crispy Dal Fritters with Onion Chutney

These fritters—like little pancakes—are easy to make and are very addictive. Make them in advance and reheat in a 300°F (150°C) oven when you're ready to serve. The sweet and sour flavors in the coconut onion chutney make a good foil for the rich, spicy fritters. This south Indian-style chutney, flavored with coconut, also makes a delicious appetizer on its own when scooped up with crisp pappadums.

Fritters

1 cup (250 mL) channa dal (split chickpeas)
1 clove garlic
1 tsp (5 mL) minced ginger
1 hot red serrrano chili pepper,
   stem and seeds removed

1 small onion, chopped
2 to 3 Tbsp (30 to 45 mL) water
2 Tbsp (30 mL) minced cilantro
salt and freshly ground black pepper
½ cup (125 mL) canola oil for frying

Onion Chutney

¼ cup (60 mL) canola oil
1 tsp (5 mL) whole black mustard seeds
½ tsp (2 mL) nigella seeds
   (a.k.a. kalonji seeds)
2 tsp (10 mL) cumin seeds
1 tsp (5 mL) salt
2 large onions, peeled and finely chopped
   (use the food processor)

4 fresh green or red chilies,
   seeded and finely chopped
2 Tbsp (30 mL) freshly squeezed lime juice
¼ cup (60 mL) water
1 Tbsp (15 mL) honey
2 tsp (10 mL) minced ginger
¼ cup (60 mL) dried, unsweetened coconut

1 To make the fritters, immerse the dal in enough water to cover. Soak for 2 to 3 hours.

2 Meanwhile, in a food processor, combine the garlic, ginger, chili pepper, and onion. Pulse to mince. Transfer to a mixing bowl and set aside.

WISE GUY: Dal (a.k.a. lentils and beans) is a staple in Indian cooking. You can find a variety of types, from masoor dal (red lentils), urad dal (black gram), and tiny moong dal (mung bean)—stewed with onion, ginger, and spices and scooped up with roti or naan bread. Channa dal is the split chickpea—slightly sweeter than regular split yellow peas, with a lovely nutty character. Channa flour may also be labeled "besan" or "gram flour"—it's used to make dosas and the light, crunchy batter for pakoras.

3 Drain the soaked dal and place it in the food processor. Add the water, 1 Tbsp (15 mL) at a time, and process until the dal forms a fairly smooth paste. Add the dal paste to the vegetables in the mixing bowl. Stir in the cilantro, salt, and pepper. Chill the batter for 1 hour.

4 For the chutney, heat the oil in medium skillet over low heat. Add the mustard, nigella, and cumin seeds and cook for 2 minutes or until fragrant. Add the salt, onions, and chilies. Sauté for 20 to 30 minutes or until the onion is softened and begins to brown. Add the lime juice, water, honey, ginger, and coconut. Simmer for 10 minutes or until the chutney is soft and jammy. Transfer the chutney to a covered container and store in the refrigerator until ready to use (makes about 1½ cups/375 mL).

5 To fry the fritters, heat the oil over medium high in a non-stick sauté pan. Drop the batter by rounded 1 Tbsp (15 mL) portions into the hot oil. Cook the fritters until browned on both sides. Drain on paper towels and then transfer to a 200°F (95°C) oven to keep warm while you make the rest. Serve the warm fritters with a dollop of onion chutney on top. Makes about 18 fritters.

Masala Prawns

People go mad for prawns at a party so this is one plate you'll want to pass around the room. The prawns are best straight out of the pan, so make the spicy butter in advance and sauté some up, mid-event...then watch them disappear. The butter in this recipe has a subcontinental flavor. For a southwestern twist, use cumin instead of the garam masala.

½ cup (125 mL) fresh cilantro leaves
4 green onions, chopped
½ lb (250 g) softened unsalted butter
1 tsp (5 mL) Asian garlic chili paste or minced chipotle pepper in adobo sauce

½ tsp (2 mL) garam masala or five-spice powder
¼ tsp (1 mL) salt
1 Tbsp (15 mL) freshly squeezed lime juice
2 lb (1 kg) large raw prawns, peeled and deveined, with tails

1 In a food processor, combine the cilantro and onions. Pulse until finely minced.

2 Add the butter, chili, garam masala, salt, and lime juice. Process until smooth. Place a piece of plastic wrap on the counter, spoon the cilantro butter in dollops along one edge of the plastic, then roll up to form a log. Refrigerate until firm. The cilantro butter will keep this way for up to two days.

3 To cook the prawns, heat about 6 Tbsp (90 mL) of the cilantro butter over medium-high heat in a shallow sauté pan until it sizzles. Quickly toss in a handful of prawns and sauté until just cooked through, about 2 to 3 minutes. Remove from the pan and keep warm. Add more butter to the pan and finish cooking the prawns in batches. Serve the prawns while hot. Serves 10.

Prosciutto Sticks

With a box of skinny Italian bread sticks and some paper-thin prosciutto from the deli, you have the makings of an instant appetizer. Not only are these prosciutto sticks fast to assemble, when arranged artfully in a tall container, they add drama and height to the appetizer table. Don't stint on the prosciutto—this is the time to shell out for authentic, air-dried ham from Italy and to enjoy all of its intense, nutty flavor.

very thin slices of lean Italian prosciutto

grainy mustard (try a roasted garlic or herbed
  mustard for extra interest)

thin Italian breadsticks

1 Trim any visible fat from the prosciutto and spread each slice with a little mustard. Place a breadstick across the thin end of the prosciutto, at a slight angle, and roll the meat around the breadstick, covering two-thirds of the breadstick. The mustard will help the thinly sliced meat adhere to the breadsticks.

2 To serve, set the prosciutto-wrapped breadsticks upright in a jar or other tall container that you've lined with a napkin, with the prosciutto ends sticking out.

Spicy Bar Nuts

It's the egg white that makes the sweet and spicy stuff stick to these nuts—makes 'em crispy, too.

1 egg white

1 tsp (5 mL) water

2 cups (500 mL) pecans

2 Tbsp (30 mL) granulated sugar

¾ tsp (4 mL) five-spice powder

¼ tsp (1 mL) cayenne pepper

1 tsp (5 mL) salt

1 Preheat oven to 300°F (150°C).

2 In a medium bowl, whisk the egg white and water until foamy. Stir in the nuts, sugar, five-spice powder, and salt.

3 Line a cookie sheet with parchment paper and spread the coated nuts in the pan. Bake for 30 to 40 minutes, turning once, until crisp. Makes 2 cups (500 mL).

WISE GUY:

Switch it up, with different spices—The Guy has also used sweet paprika instead of five-spice powder, or substituted minced fresh rosemary for the spice mix.

BBQ Duck Salad Rolls

Barbecue duck from the Chinese deli makes for a perfect summer appetizer when wrapped up in a rice paper roll with rice noodles and fresh vegetables.

3 Tbsp (45 mL) hoisin sauce
1 Tbsp (15 mL) granulated sugar
2 Tbsp (30 mL) freshly squeezed lime juice
½ tsp (2 mL) Asian chili paste
½ lb (250 g) Chinese barbecue duck, shredded
   or cut into slivers
2 cups (500 mL) rice noodles, soaked in hot
   water and cut into 2- to 3-inch (5- to 8-cm)
   lengths

2 cups (500 mL) shredded romaine lettuce
1 large carrot, cut into thin, 2-inch (5-cm) long
   matchstick strips
1 small English cucumber, unpeeled, cut into 2-inch-
   (5-cm-) long julienne strips
½ cup (125 mL) chopped fresh mint
   or cilantro leaves
twelve 6-inch (15-cm) rice papers

1 In a bowl, combine the hoisin, sugar, lime juice, and chili paste. Toss with the duck and noodles. Set aside.

2 Fill a shallow bowl with hot tap water. Slide the rice paper pieces through the water, one at a time, just to wet both sides. Set the wet rice papers on a clean dish towel to rehydrate. Place some of the duck and noodle mixture along the lower third of each rice paper. Top with some shredded lettuce, carrot, and cucumber strips. Sprinkle with chopped herbs. Fold the sides over the filling, then roll like a cigar. The rice paper will stick to itself. Set on a plate, seam-side down, and cover with a clean, damp towel and some plastic wrap. Continue making rolls with the remaining rice paper and filling.

3 Serve the rolls immediately or refrigerate, covered, up to 4 hours. Cut the rolls in half on a sharp diagonal to expose the filling and stand upright on a serving platter. Makes 24 rolls.

WISE GUY: Here's a tip for making your own breadsticks. Partially thaw a loaf of frozen bread dough and cut it lengthwise into 20 to 25 pieces. Roll and stretch each piece until it's about 15 inches (38 cm) long. Lay the breadsticks, side by side, on a large baking sheet lined with parchment paper. Lightly brush the breadsticks with extra virgin olive oil and sprinkle with coarse salt or other toppings (sesame seeds, poppy seeds, Parmesan cheese, granulated garlic, etc.).

Bake the breadsticks in a preheated 400°F (200°C) oven for 12 to 15 minutes or until golden brown and crisp.

Gorgonzola, Fig, and Prosciutto Bites

The Guy discovered these simple little appetizers being passed around the first-class cabin on an overseas flight. It's one of those simple combinations that transcends the sum of its parts (dead easy to make, too). But it's essential to use the best ingredients. Start with good quality dried figs, artisan blue cheese, and real air-dried Italian ham, and you'll marvel at the wonderful synergy of sweet, salty, and spicy flavors.

8 dried Mission or other California figs
8 thin slices Italian prosciutto ham
 (about 5oz/150 g)
2 cups baby arugula leaves or 1 bunch fresh
 watercress

2 oz (50 g) Stilton, gorgonzola, or other blue
cheese, crumbled

1 Cut the figs into quarters, discarding the woody stems. Carefully trim any visible fat from the prosciutto and cut slices into 1- x 4-inch (2.5- by 10-cm) strips.

2 Lay a strip of prosciutto on your work surface. Place a few sprigs of arugula or watercress across the base of the strip, with leaves overhanging and pointing in both directions (you want some of the greenery poking out of both sides of the finished roll). Press about ½ tsp (2 mL) of crumbled cheese over the greens and top with a piece of fig. Tightly roll the prosciutto over and around the filling, forming a small cigar-shaped package with greens protruding from each end. The prosciutto will adhere to itself, sealing the rolls. Serve immediately, or cover and chill in the refrigerator for several hours. Makes about 25 appetizers.

WISE GUY: The Guy hates to sound like a snob, but when you're talking prosciutto, it really pays to purchase the real thing, imported from Italy. Sure, there are domestic hams (also labeled "prosciutto") for half the price, but next time you're at the deli counter, ask to taste a sample of both before you buy. The nutty flavor and firm texture of a true prosciutto ham, salt-cured and air-dried in the hills of Parma, is unmistakable and vital for simple preparations like this.

Marinated Bocconcini Bites

The Guy loves bocconcini—the balls of freshly made mozzarella cheese from the local Italian market are so simple to use. A classic combination is the sliced fresh tomato and bocconcini salad, topped with a little extra virgin olive oil, balsamic vinegar, and fresh basil. You might consider using that kind of dressing on little mozza bites, or spice it up with fresh cilantro salsa (recipe below), a variation of a classic Latin chimichurri sauce, with roots in the tapas bars of Spain. Then pass the mojitos or the sangria. Olé!

Marinade
3 cloves garlic, minced
½ cup (125 mL) chopped cilantro leaves
¼ cup (60 mL) chopped Italian parsley
1 jalapeño pepper, seeded and chopped
½ cup (125 mL) extra virgin olive oil

2 Tbsp (30 mL) freshly squeezed lime juice or wine
  vinegar (red or white)
2 Tbsp (30 mL) cold water
¼ tsp (1 mL) salt
¼ tsp (1 mL) freshly ground black pepper

1 lb (500 g) fresh bocconcini cheese, preferably
  true buffalo milk mozzarella (look for mini
  balls the size of grape tomatoes)

24 small cherry or grape tomatoes
short skewers or toothpicks

1 In a blender, combine the garlic, cilantro, parsley, jalapeño, oil, juice, water, salt, and pepper. Blend until smooth. Toss the mini bocconcini balls (or larger cheese, chopped into ¾-inch/2-cm cubes), with the marinade in a bowl and refrigerate for several hours or overnight.

2 To serve, bring the marinated cheese to room temperature, then skewer each piece on a toothpick along with a grape or cherry tomato. Makes 24 appetizers.

Small Plates

(an International Tapas Party)

Tapas, izakaya, or small plates. Whatever you choose to call them, sharing a variety of little noshes is becoming the popular way to dine. No need to order—or offer—the usual courses starting with soup and salad and ending with dessert. Simply create a collection of interesting dishes, cold and hot, savory and sweet, to sample at the buffet or around the table.

It's the perfect way to organize a potluck party, too. Just ask your guests to bring something for the buffet—a small plate with a worldly pedigree for everyone to share. Then open the wine and let the conversation flow.

Garlic Clams

Another true tapas combination—you'll find this little nosh in Spanish bars, in cities like Barcelona in the north and Malaga in the south.

Make sure you clean your clams well to get rid of any grit before you cook them. Put them in a bowl, cover with cold water, add 1 Tbsp (15 mL) of cornmeal, and refrigerate overnight. The next day, lift the clams out of the water, leaving the sand behind.

¼ cup (60 mL) extra virgin olive oil
½ cup (125 mL) minced onion
4 cloves garlic, minced
½ cup (125 mL) dry white wine

1 dried chili pepper, whole
3 to 4 dozen small clams, cleaned
2 Tbsp (30 mL) minced Italian parsley
lemon wedges

1 In a large saucepan or wok, heat the oil over medium heat. Cook the onion and garlic for 5 minutes, until soft and fragrant. Add the wine and chili pepper and bring to a boil. Simmer until the wine is reduced by half.

2 Add the clams to the pan and increase the heat to high. Cover the pan and steam until the clams are open, about 5 minutes. Remove from the heat.

3 Transfer the steamed clams to a large serving dish and discard the chili pepper. Sprinkle with parsley and serve with lemon wedges to squeeze overtop. Serves 2 to 4.

Seared Beef Carpaccio

Carpaccio is a simple dish—paper-thin slices of lean beef tenderloin, lightly seasoned with olive oil and lemon juice. This version includes a light herb and black peppercorn crust, seared on the outside of the meat before slicing. While the beef tenderloin is served raw, searing the outside ensures there is no danger of contamination. It's traditional to serve thin slices of carpaccio, overlapped on a plate and drizzled with olive oil, as a first course, but consider rolling the thin slices of raw beef and skewering, along with a cube of Parmesan cheese, for more portable bites. Or pile on crostini toast with a sliver of Parmesan.

1 lb (500 g) beef tenderloin, in one piece
1 tsp (5 mL) minced fresh thyme
1 tsp (5 mL) minced fresh basil
1 tsp (5 mL) minced fresh oregano
1 tsp (5 mL) minced fresh rosemary
1 tsp (5 mL) black peppercorns
2 Tbsp (30 mL) canola oil

salt
extra virgin olive oil
freshly squeezed lemon juice
freshly ground black pepper
piece of fresh Parmigiano Reggiano cheese
   (for making shreds)

1 Trim any fat, sinew or silver skin from the beef. Cut it lengthwise, with the grain, into strips, each about 3 inches (8 cm) in diameter (you'll end up with 2 to 3 strips, depending on the size of the tenderloin).

2 Place the peppercorns inside a zippered plastic bag and pound them with a meat mallet, or press with a rolling pin, until all are thoroughly cracked. Combine the herbs and cracked peppercorns on a plate and roll the meat strips in the mixture to coat all sides. Wrap the seasoned meat tightly in plastic wrap and refrigerate for 6 to 8 hours.

3 To sear the beef, heat the canola oil in a non-stick pan over high heat until it is very hot and near smoking. Immediately add the tenderloin and sear it quickly on all sides, about 30 seconds to 1 minute per side—you want the meat to be browned on the outside, but still completely rare on the inside. Cool the meat to room temperature, wrap tightly in plastic wrap, and freeze for about 1 hour, until the meat is stiff but not solidly frozen.

4 Using a sharp slicing knife, cut the tenderloin across the grain into very thin slices. Arrange the carpaccio on individual plates or on a platter for sharing, overlapping the pieces in a pattern. Drizzle with extra virgin olive oil and season with pepper. Use a vegetable peeler to shave a few shards of Parmesan over the plates. Serves 6 to 8.

Cornmeal Crusted Calamari

This staple of the Greek taverna has become as ubiquitous as french fries and onion rings in casual restaurants and makes a great appetizer or meal with a simple Greek salad (see page 224) on the side. Start with pre-cleaned calamari tubes to make this classic dish super speedy.

2 cups (500 mL) cornmeal
2 cups (500 mL) all-purpose flour, divided
½ tsp (2 mL) dried thyme
1 tsp (5 mL) granulated garlic
1 tsp (5 mL) salt
1 tsp (5 mL) freshly ground black pepper

1 cup (250 mL) buttermilk
1 egg
2 lb (1 kg) squid (a.k.a. calamari) tubes, sliced into
   ¼-inch (5-mm) rings
canola oil for frying
1 lemon, cut into six wedges

1 In a large bowl, combine the cornmeal, 1½ cups (375 mL) of the flour, thyme, granulated garlic, salt, and pepper. In another bowl, whisk the buttermilk and egg together. Place the remaining ½ cup (125 mL) of flour in another bowl.

2 Dredge the squid rings (and tentacles) in the plain flour first. Shake off any excess, then dip them in buttermilk, and dredge in the spiced cornmeal coating. Place the cornmeal-crusted calamari on a parchment paper–lined baking sheet to allow the batter to set. When the batter is set, fry immediately, or cover with plastic wrap and refrigerate.

3 When ready to cook, heat the oil to 375°F (190°C) in a wok (check the temperature with a deep-fat or candy thermometer) or deep saucepan (the oil needs to be at least 1 inch/2.5 cm deep). Fry the calamari in batches in the hot oil until just golden. Drain on paper towels and then keep warm in a pan in a 200°F (95°C) oven until all the calamari is fried. When ready to serve, pile the calamari on a lettuce leaf–lined platter and surround with lemon wedges. Serve with Spicy Garlic Mayonnaise (see page 300) on the side for dipping. Serves 6.

Spicy Garlic Mayo

6 cloves garlic, peeled
1 Tbsp (15 mL) freshly squeezed lemon juice
1 tsp (5 mL) finely grated lemon zest

1 tsp (5 mL) Asian chili paste
1 cup (250 mL) good-quality commercial
 mayonnaise

1 Place the garlic in a small saucepan, cover with water, and bring to a boil and simmer until soft, about 10 minutes (alternatively, use 6 cloves of roasted garlic).

2 In a food processor, combine the cooked garlic with the lemon juice, zest, chili paste, and mayonnaise. Whirl until smooth. Makes 1¼ cups (310 mL).

Coconut Shrimp

Here's a popular appetizer from Cajun and Creole country, a dish with roots that's spread into the Caribbean. Make lots—your guests will inhale these addictive morsels.

½ cup (125 mL) all-purpose flour
1 Tbsp (15 mL) Cajun seasoning
1 large egg, beaten
½ cup (125 mL) milk

3 cups (750 mL) shredded unsweetened coconut
 (long shreds)
2 lb (1 kg) large raw shrimp, peeled, tail on
canola or corn oil, for frying

1 Combine the flour and Cajun seasoning on a plate. Whisk the egg and milk together in a small bowl. Place the coconut into another shallow bowl.

2 Holding the shrimp by the tail, roll in seasoned flour to coat, shaking off any excess. Dip the flour-coated shrimp in the egg mixture, then roll in the coconut to coat. Set the coconut-crusted shrimp aside on a rack, set over a baking sheet, until you're ready to cook.

3 Heat about ¼ inch (5 mm) of oil to 350°F to 375°F (180°C to 190°C) in a wide sauté pan. Fry the shrimp in the hot oil, in batches, until golden, about 1 minute per side. Transfer the fried shrimp to a paper towel–lined plate to drain, and place in a 200°F (95°C) oven to keep warm while you finish cooking them all. Makes about 2 to 3 dozen.

Supplis

This is the Italian word for a wonderful way to recycle leftover risotto into an appetizer extraordinaire. The Guy is addicted to the supplis—or fried rice balls—made with porcini-studded risotto and wrapped around gooey mozzarella cheese, at his favorite Italian deli. Here's a reasonable facsimile for your tapas party (or Tuesday lunch).

3 cups (750 mL) leftover mushroom risotto
    (see page 147), chilled overnight
eight ¾-inch (2-cm) cubes of mozzarella
    or Friulano cheese
1 cup (250 mL) all-purpose flour

1 large egg lightly beaten with
    2 Tbsp/30 mL milk
1 cup (250 mL) panko (Japanese breadcrumbs)
2 cups (500 mL) canola oil, for frying

1 Wet your hands and scoop up ¼ cup (60 mL) portions of cold, leftover risotto. Roll into 2-inch (5-cm) balls, around cubes of cheese (you can alternately make the ball first, poke a hole in the middle, insert the cheese, then enclose it again around the cheese). Set the suppli on a plate.

2 Put the flour, beaten egg, and panko crumbs into 3 separate bowls, then roll each rice ball in the flour (shake off any excess), dip it into the egg, and then toss in the crumbs to completely coat. Set the panko-crusted supplis back on the plate and chill for 30 minutes.

3 In a deep sauté pan or wok, heat the oil to 350°F (180°C)—it should be rippling on the surface, but you can test it with a deep-fat or candy thermometer to make sure. Add the supplis, 3 or 4 at a time, and cook until golden brown on all sides, about 5 minutes in total. Place the cooked rice balls on a paper towel–lined plate to keep warm in a 200°F (95°C) oven while you finish frying the remaining supplis. Makes 8 to 10 suppli.

WISE GUY: These days you can buy the fluffy white Japanese panko breadcrumbs at most grocery stores. Try them. You won't believe the amazingly crispy coating they make for any fried food.

Prawn and Sweet Bell Pepper Bites

This is one of those delicious appetizers that circulate on the dim sum carts, but it also makes a pretty starter for your next Asian dinner party or izakaya buffet. Prepare them in advance but cook just before serving for best results. You can also spread the shrimp filling over squares of bread or sandwich it inside wonton wrappers and deep-fry. This is a dish that requires a knife and fork so make sure your guests are sitting down.

1 lb (500 g) raw shrimp or prawns,
   shelled and deveined
1 egg white
2 Tbsp (30 mL) softened butter
½ tsp (2 mL) sesame oil
2 tsp (10 mL) light soy sauce
½ tsp (2 mL) granulated sugar

½ tsp (2 mL) minced ginger
   (use a garlic press to mince)
pinch of white pepper
2 tsp (10 mL) cornstarch, divided
1 green onion, minced
3 large bell peppers (one red, one yellow, and
   one orange)
canola or corn oil, for frying

Sauce
½ tsp (2 mL) granulated sugar
2 Tbsp (30 mL) oyster sauce

⅓ cup (75 mL) stock or water combined with ½ tsp
   (2 mL) cornstarch
¼ tsp (2 mL) Asian garlic chili paste

1 In a food processor, purée the shrimp, then add the egg white, butter, sesame oil, soy sauce, sugar, pepper and 1 tsp (5 mL) of the cornstarch. Process to combine. Transfer the shrimp mixture to a bowl, stir in the green onion, and set aside.

2 Cut the peppers into quarters lengthwise, and remove the stem, seeds, and ribs. Cut each quarter into three 2-inch (5-cm) squares. Dust the pepper pieces lightly with cornstarch on the inside surface, shaking off any excess.

3 Heat 2 Tbsp (30 mL) of oil in a large non-stick frying pan over medium heat. Spoon 1 to 2 tsp (5 to 10 mL) of the shrimp mixture into the inside curve of each square of pepper, mounding slightly, and smoothing into the corners to seal. Place the shrimp-stuffed peppers, filling-side down, into the oil, and cook for 2 to 3 minutes or until golden brown. You may have to brown the pieces in batches. Return the peppers to the pan, shrimp-side up. In a bowl, whisk together the sugar, oyster sauce, stock, and chili paste; add to the pan. Cover the pan and simmer for 5 minutes or until the sauce has thickened. Spoon the sauce over the stuffed peppers to glaze, and serve. Makes 24 to 30 pieces.

Grilled Paprika Shrimp with Garlic Sauce

San Sebastian is one of The Guy's favorite Spanish towns—loaded with great restaurants and tapas bars. This is where you'll find shrimp like this, piled on the bar, to enjoy with a glass of wine or a crisp, fino sherry. A real tapas bar specialty.

Garlic Sauce
½ cup (125 mL) mayonnaise
2 Tbsp (30 mL) extra virgin olive oil

1 lb (500 g) peeled and deveined large shrimp,
   tails on
2 cloves garlic, minced
¼ cup (60 mL) extra virgin olive oil

1 tsp (5 mL) Dijon mustard
2 cloves garlic, crushed
salt and freshly ground black pepper

1 tsp (5 mL) sherry vinegar or freshly squeezed
   lemon juice
1 tsp (5 mL) hot Spanish paprika
chopped fresh Italian parsley

1 To make the garlic sauce, whisk together the mayonnaise, 2 Tbsp (30 mL) olive oil, Dijon mustard, and minced garlic. Season with salt and pepper and refrigerate.

2 For the shrimp, combine the garlic and ¼ cup (60 mL) olive oil in a bowl and set aside for 30 minutes to infuse. Whisk in the vinegar and paprika, then add the shrimp, stirring to coat well.

3 Skewer each shrimp on parallel bamboo skewers, running the skewers through both the head and tail end of the shrimp (this helps the shrimp to lie flat on the grill). Grill the shrimp over medium-high heat for 1 minute per side or just until they turn pink and opaque.

4 Pull the shrimp from the skewers, toss with fresh parsley, and serve with the garlic sauce for dipping. Serves 4.

Southern Crab Cakes

Crab cakes are a little finicky to make, but everyone loves them. So if you're doing one hot appetizer for your party, make these spicy little morsels. You can cook them in advance and chill them overnight, then reheat in a 275°F (140°C) oven until warmed through.

A dollop of mustard mayonnaise and a tiny piece of Italian parsley makes these crab cakes look especially festive on the serving tray.

¼ cup (60 mL) finely minced red bell pepper
¼ cup (60 mL) finely minced green bell pepper
2 green onions, finely minced
1 clove garlic, minced
⅓ cup (75 mL) mayonnaise
1 Tbsp (15 mL) freshly squeezed lemon juice
½ tsp (2 mL) dried mustard
1 tsp (5 mL) Cajun spice mix

1 lb (500 g) fresh or thawed previously frozen
    crabmeat
1 cup (250 mL) breadcrumbs
salt
butter and vegetable oil for frying
mustard mayonnaise and Italian parsley,
    for garnish

1 Finely mince the peppers, onion, and garlic by hand or use a food processor to pulse until nicely chopped. In a bowl, combine the minced vegetables (and their juices) with the mayonnaise, lemon juice, dry mustard, and Cajun spice mix.

2 Pick through the crabmeat to remove any shell fragments. Fold the crab and breadcrumbs into the mayonnaise mixture. Season with salt to taste.

3 Line a baking sheet with parchment paper and scoop the crab-cake mixture onto the sheet in mounds, about 1 to 2 inches (2.5 to 5 cm) in diameter. You can use a small ice cream scoop to make even portions. Cover with plastic wrap and freeze for several hours.

4 To cook, heat equal parts of butter and oil, about 1 Tbsp (15 mL) of each, in a non-stick frying pan. Add the frozen crab cakes and sauté for 4 to 5 minutes per side or until golden. Return the cakes to the baking sheet and finish in a 350°F (180°C) oven for about 10 minutes. Serve hot with a dollop of mustard mayo and a parsley leaf for garnish. Makes 2 dozen crab cakes.

WISE GUY: The Guy loves homemade mayonnaise but the commercial Hellmann's brand (even the low-fat version) makes a good substitute. To make your own mustard mayo, just flavor some commercial mayonnaise with your favorite gourmet Dijon or honey mustard to taste.

Satay Sticks with Peanut Sauce

Use this Indonesian-inspired marinade for thin strips of chicken, pork, or lamb. The peanut sauce is tradi-

1 lb (500 g) boneless chicken, pork, or lamb
   cut into thin strips

Marinade

¼ cup (60 mL) kecap manis (sweet Indonesian soy
   sauce)

1 Tbsp (15 mL) freshly squeezed lime juice
1 clove garlic, crushed
1 tsp (5 mL) honey

Peanut Sauce

1 clove garlic, crushed
½ cup (125 mL) natural peanut butter
1 Tbsp (15 mL) kecap manis
   (sweet Indonesian soy sauce)

¼ cup (60 mL) chicken broth or water
1 Tbsp (15 mL) freshly squeezed lime juice
½ tsp (2 mL) Asian chili paste

1 In a large, zippered plastic bag, combine the meat with the marinade ingredients. Seal and marinate in the refrigerator overnight.

2 Drain the marinated meat and thread onto skewers. Grill over medium-high heat until browned on all sides, about 10 minutes in total.

3 To make the sauce, whisk the garlic, peanut butter, kecap manis, chicken broth, lime juice, and chili paste together in a small bowl.

4 Set the sauce in the center of a round platter, and arrange the skewers, like spokes, around the edges. Makes 16 skewers.

Pan-Fried Shrimp and Scallop Dumplings with Spicy Dipping Sauce

If you'd rather serve chicken dumplings, replace the scallops and shrimp in this recipe with ground chicken. Just remember to cook the chicken dumplings a little longer—when the water comes to a boil and the dumplings float, add 1 to 2 cups (250 to 500 mL) of cold water, cover the pot, and bring the water back to a boil a second time.

½ lb (250 g) bay or sea scallops
½ lb (250 g) peeled and deveined raw shrimp
1 egg white
4 green onions, minced
6 water chestnuts, minced
1 Tbsp (15 mL) dry sherry or sake
1 Tbsp (15 mL) light soy sauce

1 tsp (5 mL) sesame oil
½ tsp (2 mL) salt
2 tsp (10 mL) grated fresh ginger
1 clove garlic, crushed
2 tsp (10 mL) cornstarch
40 round or square wonton wrappers
   or dumpling skins

Dipping Sauce
2 Tbsp (25 mL) light soy sauce
1 Tbsp (15 mL) rice vinegar

1 tsp (5 mL) Asian chili paste
1 green onion, minced

1 In a food processor, combine the scallops and shrimp with the egg white. Pulse several times to coarsely chop (don't purée the seafood, just chop). Add the green onions, chestnuts, sherry, soy sauce, sesame oil, salt, ginger, garlic, and cornstarch. Pulse again, just to combine.

2 To fill the wontons, place a generous 1 tsp (5 mL) portion of filling on each wrapper. Use your finger to moisten the edges of the wrappers with water, then fold over, pressing the edges to seal. Dust a tray with cornstarch and set the dumplings on the tray. Cover and refrigerate until you're ready to cook them.

3 To make the dipping sauce, whisk together the soy sauce, rice vinegar, chili paste, and green onion in a small bowl. Set aside.

4 To cook the dumplings, bring 12 cups (3 L) of water to a boil. Add half the dumplings, stirring gently to prevent them from sticking together. The dumplings are cooked when they rise to the top and float there for about 20 seconds. Remove the cooked dumplings from the water with a slotted spoon and drain. Serve the dumplings immediately with the dipping sauce.

5 If you prefer pan-fried dumplings, heat 3 Tbsp (45 mL) of oil in a non-stick sauté pan over medium-high heat and arrange the dumplings, packed tightly together, sealed side up, in the oil. Fry them until golden brown on the bottom, then add 1 cup (250 mL) of water to the pan. Bring to a boil and cover. Reduce the heat to low, and cook for 10 minutes. Uncover, pour out the water, and return the pan to medium heat. Drizzle with 1½ tsp (7 mL) of oil and fry for 2 minutes longer to crisp. Invert the dumplings onto a platter, golden-side up, and serve with dipping sauce. Makes 40.

Sangria

This is the Spanish wine punch that will add an authentic edge to your tapas party. The perfect vessel for putting together a batch of sangria is a large glass jar with a spigot. Use a couple of large pitchers to make this if you haven't got a big enough punch bowl or jar. Serve your sangria in red wine glasses, with a few slices of marinated fruit bobbing around in each glass.

1 lemon, scrubbed and sliced

1 orange, scrubbed and sliced

2 peaches, slivered, or other sliced fruit
  (optional)

½ to ¾ cup (125 to 175 mL) Triple Sec
  or other orange liqueur

2 bottles fruity red or white wine

ice cubes

2 to 3 cups (500 to 750 mL) soda water or a
  lemon-lime soda (such as Sprite or 7-Up)

1 Scrub the lemon and orange, then thinly slice, rind and all, into rounds using a very sharp knife or mandoline (the slicing blade on a good food processor works, too). Place the citrus fruit into your vessel, along with other fruit, and the orange liqueur. Add the wine and let the sangria steep for several hours (refrigerate if you have space).

2 When your guests arrive, add the ice and soda water to chill and dilute to taste. Makes about 12 cups (3 L) of sangria.

Spicy Szechuan Dreams
You Say Szechuan, I Say Sichuan (or Peking)

When The Guy returned from his travels to China, it was the spicy food of Szechuan province that stuck in his mind and on his palate. There's something addictive about the tongue-numbing little Szechuan peppercorn, and the play of chilies, vinegar, and sugar in Szechuan sauces, that's unbeatable.

Plan a Szechuan potluck dinner with a variety of these spicy dishes. Don't forget to serve lots of fluffy basmati rice, and perhaps some sautéed bananas over ice cream for dessert (to help temper the fire in your mouth).

Marinated Lotus Root Salad

Serve this lightly pickled crisp vegetable as a side salad to counterbalance the spicy food on the table. Lotus root looks like a big buff-colored radish, sometimes in several bulbous sections. But once you peel and slice it, a lotus root is beautiful and delicate, like a flower-patterned paper doily.

¼ cup (60 mL) rice vinegar
¼ cup (60 mL) granulated sugar
1 tsp (5 mL) minced fresh ginger
1 small red chili, minced

1 lb (500 g) lotus root
sliced cucumber and chopped fresh cilantro, for
   garnish

1 To make the dressing, combine the vinegar, sugar, ginger, and chili in a blender or food processor. Purée and set the dressing aside.

2 Peel the lotus root and cut into very thin slices using a sharp knife. Bring a large pot of water to a boil, add the lotus root slices, and blanch for 30 seconds. Drain and immerse immediately in ice-cold water to stop the cooking process. Drain well and place the lotus root slices into a serving bowl.

3 In a small saucepan (or in the microwave), heat the dressing until boiling. Pour the dressing over the lotus root. Cover and refrigerate for several hours to chill. Serve the salad garnished with sliced cucumber and chopped cilantro. Serves 4.

Green Onion Pancakes with Shrimp

When The Guy was in the markets in Chengdu, China, there were vendors making all kinds of wonderful things to eat—from soy-glazed rotisserie rabbit to addictive little pancakes shot with slivers of green onions like these. You can make them with, or without, the tiny shrimp, but it makes them extra special. It's as easy as making pancakes.

1½ cups (375 mL) all-purpose flour
¼ cup (60 mL) cornmeal
1 cup (250 mL) water
3 large eggs
½ cup (125 mL) milk
½ tsp (2 mL) salt

¾ cup (175 mL) finely chopped green onions
   (or garlic chives)
½ lb (250 g) small shrimp, peeled and
   deveined (chopped if large) (optional)
oil, for frying
sesame oil, for brushing

1 Add the flour, cornmeal, water, eggs, milk, and salt to a food processor and whirl to combine. Pour into a bowl, or large measuring cup with a spout, and stir in the onions and shrimp (if using).

2 Heat a drop of oil over medium heat in an 8-inch (20-cm) non-stick pan. Pour or ladle about ¼ cup (60 mL) of the batter onto the pan, swirling to evenly cover the bottom of the pan.

3 Cook until the pancake is set and golden on one side, then flip and cook until the second side is speckled with brown dots.

4 Transfer the pancake to a platter and fold into quarters. Keep warm in a 200°F (95°C) oven while you make the rest of the pancakes. Eat the pancakes while still warm, brushed with sesame oil. Makes 8 to 10 pancakes.

WISE GUY: If you make these pancakes without the shrimp, they make great little wrappers for slivers of barbecue pork or duck from the Chinese deli.

Corn and Crabmeat Soup

In Chengdu, in Szechuan province, The Guy enjoyed a delicate corn soup flavored with creamy, bright-yellow crab roe. This version uses crabmeat and egg whites to mimic the texture and flavor.

6 cups (1.5 L) chicken stock

1 tsp (5 mL) minced ginger

2 Tbsp (30 mL) rice wine

1 cup (250 mL) creamed corn

1 Tbsp (15 mL) cornstarch mixed with 1 Tbsp
   (15 mL) cold water

1 small tin crabmeat (about ½ cup/125 mL)

2 egg whites lightly beaten with 1 Tbsp (15 mL) of
   water

1 tsp (5 mL) sesame oil

1 In a large pot over high heat, bring the chicken stock to a boil. Add the ginger, rice wine, and creamed corn. Heat through. Slowly add the cornstarch solution, stirring until the soup is thick and bubbly.

2 Drain the crabmeat well. Pick over the meat to remove any bits of shell, then shred with a fork.

3 Stir the crab into the soup and heat through for 1 minute. Remove from the heat and drizzle the beaten egg white into the hot soup, stirring gently with a fork to create delicate strands of egg throughout. Drizzle with sesame oil and serve immediately. Serves 6.

BOWL OF SOUP

Szechuan-Style Pork and Eggplant

This is a lovely, rich pork dish to serve over a bowl of brown rice on a Tuesday, or as part of a Chinese banquet on the weekend. The eggplant breaks down to make a rich, thick sauce for the tender pork. For an authentic Szechuan meal, serve it alongside thin strips of cucumber lightly marinated with rice wine, sugar, and crushed red chilies, or a Lotus Root Salad (see page 309).

⅓ cup (75 mL) canola or peanut oil, divided
1 large eggplant (about 1 5 lb/750 g), washed and
 cut into ½-inch (1-cm) cubes
1 lb (500 g) boneless pork (pork loin chops,
 etc.) trimmed of visible fat and sliced into
 ¼-inch (6-mm) strips
salt and freshly ground black pepper
1 large onion, finely chopped
8 cloves garlic, minced
1 tsp (5 mL) Asian chili paste, or to taste

3 Tbsp (45 mL) tomato paste
1 cup (250 mL) chicken broth
¼ cup (60 mL) wine vinegar
1 Tbsp (15 mL) tamari soy sauce
1 tsp (5 mL) Asian fish sauce (optional)
¼ cup (60 mL) packed brown sugar
½ tsp (2 mL) curry powder (optional)
1 red bell pepper, seeded and slivered
¼ cup (60 mL) chopped cilantro

1 In a wok, heat 1 to 2 Tbsp (15 to 30 mL) of oil over medium-high heat. Cook the cubed eggplant in batches until browned, adding more oil if necessary. Remove the eggplant from the pan as it's browned and reserve.

2 Season the pork strips with salt and pepper. Heat 2 Tbsp (30 mL) of the oil in the wok over medium-high heat until it starts to smoke. Add the pork in batches, cooking until nicely browned. Remove the pork from the pan with a slotted spoon and set aside.

3 Add a little more oil to the wok and add the onion. Stir and cook until the onion starts to brown. Add the garlic and cook together for 2 minutes. In a medium bowl, stir together the chili paste, tomato paste, chicken broth, wine vinegar, soy sauce, fish sauce, brown sugar, and curry powder. Add this sauce to the wok and bring to a boil over high heat. Simmer, uncovered, for 3 minutes, then return the cooked eggplant and pork to the pan. Stir in the bell pepper and return to a boil. Cover the pan, reduce the heat to medium-low, and simmer for 30 to 45 minutes or until the eggplant is very tender and the sauce has thickened. Taste and adjust the seasoning with more chili paste if desired. Stir in the cilantro and serve immediately over brown basmati rice. Serves 4 to 6.

Peking-Style Salt and Pepper Shredded Chicken

Peking is the name formerly given to the Chinese capital of Beijing, but at many Chinese restaurants in North America, you'll still find "Peking-style" dishes like this one. Serve it as part of a Chinese meal.

1 lb (500 g) boneless chicken breast,
   sliced in long, thin strips or shreds
1 egg, lightly beaten
1 Tbsp (15 mL) rice or white wine vinegar
1 Tbsp (15 mL) vegetable oil
2 cups (500 mL) cornstarch
1 cup (250 mL) all-purpose flour
2 cups (500 mL) water
2 cups (500 mL) canola oil for deep frying

1 tsp (5 mL) minced garlic
½ green or yellow bell pepper,
   seeded and julienned
½ red bell pepper, seeded and julienned
½ medium onion, slivered
1 tsp (5 mL) crushed red chili peppers
½ tsp (2 mL) salt
½ tsp (2 mL) granulated sugar
¼ tsp (1 mL) freshly ground white pepper

1 Place the chicken strips in a large bowl. Add the egg, vinegar, vegetable oil, cornstarch, flour, and water. Mix with your hands until well combined. Let the chicken mixture sit in the refrigerator for 30 minutes to tenderize.

2 In a large wok or deep sauté pan, heat the oil to 350°F (180°C). Use a deep-fry or candy thermometer to test the oil temperature—it should sizzle when you add the chicken.

3 Place the chicken into the hot oil, a handful at a time, and fry until golden brown and crispy. This will take about 5 minutes. Remove the chicken from oil using a slotted spoon and drain on a paper towel–lined plate. Keep warm in a 200°F (95°C) oven while you cook the rest of the chicken.

4 Discard the oil and wipe out the wok. Heat 1 Tbsp (15 mL) of canola oil and sauté the minced garlic, green pepper, red pepper, and onion for about 5 minutes. Stir in the crushed chili peppers and return the chicken to the pan. Add the salt, sugar, and white pepper. Toss to combine and heat through. Serve immediately. Serves 4 to 6 as part of a Chinese meal.

WISE GUY: For an excellent vegetarian option, try this recipe with eggplant instead of chicken. Slice slender Japanese eggplant into ¼-inch (6-mm) rounds and toss with cornstarch to coat lightly on both sides (no need to batter it). Fry the eggplant slices in batches until golden brown on both sides and drain well on paper towels. Finish it like the chicken, with the slivered peppers, onion, and spices. Addictive!

Crispy Fried Fish with Sweet and Sour Sauce

As a visitor in China, The Guy came face to face with many a fish (a whole fish is traditional at special banquets as it symbolizes prosperity and good luck). You can use a whole fish in this recipe if you like but The Guy prefers boneless fillets—they're easier to cook (and eat).

This is a typical Szechuan dish and a nice way to serve fish as part of a Chinese meal. Make some stir-fried Chinese broccoli with garlic and brown basmatic rice, and dinner's done.

Sauce

½ cup (125 mL) chicken broth
¼ cup (60 mL) chili sauce or ketchup
¼ cup (60 mL) rice vinegar (unseasoned or black)
¼ cup (60 mL) granulated sugar
1 Tbsp (15 mL) light soy sauce

1 tsp (5 mL) sesame oil
2 tsp (10 mL) cornstarch
½ tsp (2 mL) salt
1 tsp (5 mL) minced fresh ginger
1 clove garlic, minced

1.5 lb (750 g) sole, cod, sea bass, or catfish
   fillets, cut into 4-inch (10-cm) pieces
1 tsp (5 mL) salt
1 tsp (5 mL) grated fresh ginger

1 Tbsp (15 mL) rice wine
cornstarch
canola oil, for frying
3 green onions, slivered

1 In a medium bowl, whisk together the broth, chili sauce, vinegar, sugar, soy sauce, sesame oil, cornstarch, ½ tsp (2 mL) salt, minced ginger, and garlic. Set aside.

2 If the fish fillets are thick, use a sharp knife to cut, on the diagonal, ½-inch- (1-cm-) thick slices. Place the sliced fish on a plate. In a small bowl, combine the 1 tsp (5 mL) salt, grated ginger, and rice wine. Rub over the fish and set aside to marinate for 15 minutes.

WISE GUY: To sliver the green onions for this dish, wash the onions and trim away the root end and any wilted bits. Cut the onions into 1-inch (2.5-cm) lengths, then cut each piece lengthwise into skinny slivers. You can gather together several of the green bits to make this quicker.

3 Heat about 1 cup (250 mL) canola oil in a wok over medium-high heat until it is hot, about 375°F (190°C)—you'll need a deep-fry or candy thermometer to test the oil. Spread the cornstarch on a plate and roll the fish pieces in it, coating lightly on both sides and shaking off any excess. Slide the fish into the hot oil, a few pieces at time, and fry until golden brown, about 2 minutes per side. Remove with a slotted spoon and drain on paper towels. Keep warm in a 200°F (95°C) oven.

4 Discard the oil from the wok and add the reserved sauce mixture. Bring to a boil, stirring, and cook until nicely thickened, about 1 minute. Arrange the fried fish on a platter and drizzle with the hot sauce. Garnish with slivers of green onion and serve immediately. Serves 4.

Hot Chili Oil

If your food isn't hot enough, a drizzle of this fiery condiment always helps. Don't use it as a cooking oil—drizzle over your dish once it's done. Commercial chili oils are also available, but look for a good brand (Thai and Malaysian brands are hottest, Chinese versions more subtle, and Japanese brands are often superior in quality).

¼ cup (60 mL) sesame oil
¾ cup (175 mL) canola oil

½ cup (125 mL) dried hot chili peppers, crushed
2 Tbsp (30 mL) Szechuan peppercorns (optional)

1 In a small pot, heat the sesame and canola oils over medium heat. When the oil is very hot, add the chilies and peppercorns. Remove from the heat, cover, and let it steep from several hours to overnight. Strain the oil through a fine sieve or cheesecloth. Store in a small bottle in a dark place. It will keep indefinitely and is perfect for adding a little Szechuan kick to any soup or stir-fry dish.

WISE GUY: Szechuan peppercorns are distinctive little seeds from Szechuan province. A rusty brown in color, these wild peppercorns resemble little flower buds (and are sometimes called flower peppers in China) but the flavor is not like black pepper. In fact, the aromatic spice isn't even related to the traditional peppercorn—its culinary fame is in the tingly numb feeling it leaves on your tongue when you eat it.

Roast Szechuan peppercorns in a hot, dry pan for a minute before grinding to bring out all of their elusive fragrance.

Ma Po Tofu

When The Guy was in Szechuan province in China, he had to visit Mrs. Chen's famous restaurant in Chengdu, where this classic local dish was apparently created. The combination of chilies and aromatic ground Szechuan peppercorns will literally make your tongue numb, but the creamy tofu acts as an antidote to the spice. Remind your guests not to eat the chunks of chilies.

1 lb (500 g) package medium-firm tofu
½ lb (250 g) ground pork
2 Tbsp (30 mL) soy sauce, divided
2 Tbsp (30 mL) rice wine, divided
1 tsp (5 mL) sesame oil
1 Tbsp (15 mL) canola oil
2 green onions, minced, divided
2 cloves garlic, minced
½-inch (1-cm) piece ginger, peeled and minced

1 tsp (5 mL) chili paste or hot bean paste
1 cup (250 mL) chicken broth
½ tsp (2 mL) granulated sugar
1 large dried chili, seeded and cut into chunks
½ tsp (2 mL) cornstarch mixed with 2 tsp (10 mL) cold water
½ tsp (2 mL) Szechuan peppercorns, toasted and crushed to a powder

1 Wrap the tofu in a clean towel and drain on the counter under a weight (use a heavy saucepan or cutting board), for 15 minutes. Cut into small cubes and set aside.

2 In a bowl, combine the ground pork with 1 Tbsp (15 mL) of soy sauce, 1 Tbsp (15 mL) of rice wine, and the sesame oil. Set aside to marinate.

3 In a wok, heat the canola oil over medium-high heat. Add the ground pork and stir-fry for 5 minutes, breaking the meat up into small pieces. When cooked, remove the meat from the wok using a slotted spoon. Add half the green onions to the wok along with the garlic, ginger, and chili paste. Stir-fry for 10 seconds before adding the broth, sugar, remaining soy sauce, rice wine, reserved tofu cubes, and cooked pork. Bring to a boil, reduce the heat to medium, and simmer for 10 minutes or until the liquid is reduced by one quarter. Stir in the cornstarch solution and simmer until thickened.

4 Serve sprinkled with remaining green onions and Szechuan peppercorn powder. Serves 4.

WISE GUY: The easiest way to peel a gnarly piece of fresh ginger is with a spoon. Really. Just use the sharp edge of a teaspoon to scrape away most of the papery, brown skin. Before you mince, place the whole piece of ginger under the flat blade of your chef's knife and give it a whack—the ginger will nearly mince itself (the same trick works with whole cloves of garlic).

Spicy Szechuan Greens

The chilies in this dish add flavor but are not for eating. Just pick them out or eat around them—unless you're suicidal.

Some kind of sautéed greens accompanied every meal The Guy had in southwestern China—it's a good rule to follow for any meal. You can season any greens this way, whether you're sautéing spinach or collards. Makes a nice side dish to almost any grilled fish.

1 lb (500 g) baby bok choy or Chinese broccoli
2 Tbsp (30 mL) canola oil
1 hot red chili, cut into thick rings, seeds removed (fresh or dried)
2 cloves garlic, minced
1 tsp (5 mL) minced ginger

¼ cup (60 mL) water
1 Tbsp (15 mL) light soy sauce
1 tsp (5 mL) granulated sugar
1 tsp (5 mL) cornstarch dissolved in 1 Tbsp (15 mL) water

1 Slice the bok choy and immerse in a sink full of water to rinse off any grit (make sure you rinse the base bits well). Bring a large pot of water to a rolling boil, add the greens, and boil for 30 to 60 seconds or just until the bok choy turns bright green. Drain well.

2 In a wok, heat the oil over high heat. Add the chili, garlic, and ginger. Stir-fry for 30 seconds. Add the greens and cook for about 1 minute, stirring and tossing constantly. Add the water, soy sauce, sugar, and cornstarch solution and cook 1 minute or until the greens are nicely glazed with sauce. Serve immediately. Serves 4.

Tropical Fruit Brûlée

This is an easy and elegant way to serve fresh fruit—bathed in custard that's caramelized under the broiler. The bananas will help tame any of the chili fire left in your mouth from the main course.

1 cup (250 mL) pineapple chunks

2 bananas, peeled and sliced

4 large mangoes, peeled and chopped

Coconut Custard

1 cup (250 mL) coconut milk

1 cup (250 mL) milk

3 egg yolks, lightly beaten

1 Tbsp (15 mL) cornstarch

½ cup (125 mL) granulated sugar

pinch of salt

1 Combine the fruit and divide among eight ovenproof ramekins or shallow individual baking dishes. Set fruit-filled dishes on a baking sheet. Preheat the broiler.

2 Heat the coconut milk in a saucepan over medium heat until hot but not boiling. In a small bowl, whisk the egg yolks with the cornstarch, sugar, and salt. Slowly stir this egg mixture into the hot coconut milk, whisking constantly. Cook the custard over medium-low heat until thick, about 7 minutes. Remove from the heat and let it cool.

3 Just before serving, pour the custard over the fruit in the ramekins. Set desserts under the preheated broiler, about 4 inches from the heat source, and broil until just beginning to brown on top. Garnish with sprigs of fresh mint and serve immediately. Serves 8.

RAMEKIN

Doing Dessert

Dessert is the segue from savory to sweet that signals the end of the meal. Dessert does not always need to be slaved over—it can be as easy as a scoop of your favorite hazelnut gelato, with a store-bought biscotto on the side, or a plate of imported Belgian cookies from the local deli, to nibble with an espresso.

Never underestimate the power of a cheese course to cap a culinary occasion. Arrange small slices or chunks of three different cheeses (a dry aged, a creamy, and a blue) on plain white plates, with a few dried cherries, cranberries, or slivered apricots, and some toasted walnuts or pecans, then pass around some water biscuits and your best vintage or tawny port.

Match the dessert to the occasion and the season—slices of watermelon and chewy chocolate cookies (see page 468) are perfect for a picnic or barbecue. When cherries are ripe and juicy, present a glistening bowl for your guests to enjoy alfresco. Or bake a simple puff pastry tart shell and top it with a skiff of custard and a layer of perfect golden raspberries.

End an Asian meal with tropical fruit, such as fresh pineapple or crisp slices of Asian pears.

Fall means pies—apple, pumpkin, and squash—or pears poached in wine. During the dead of winter, concoct the perfect bread pudding, chocolate torte, or maple pecan pie.

So don't forget dessert. It makes life a little sweeter.

Chocolate Ginger Mousse

The Guy's favorite pieces in the artisan chocolate box are the chewy bits of ginger dipped in chocolate. He's also partial to the pickled ginger that comes with his sushi, and the candied ginger imported from Down Under. So what better way to get his ginger fix than with this elegant chocolate and ginger dessert. It's a sweet way to end a big meal, and works with both Asian and fusion menus.

10 oz (300 g) bittersweet chocolate

¼ cup (60 mL) brewed strong coffee or espresso

⅓ cup (75 mL) cold unsalted butter, cut into small pieces

¼ cup (60 mL) finely chopped, crystalized ginger, plus extra for garnish

4 large eggs, separated

½ cup (125 mL) granulated sugar

¼ cup (60 mL) brandy or rum

⅛ tsp (0.5 mL) cream of tartar

1 cup (250 mL) whipping cream plus ½ cup (125 mL), for garnish

fresh mint sprigs

1 Get out all of your mixing bowls—you'll need them.

2 Chop the chocolate into small pieces and, in a small saucepan, combine with the coffee and butter. Melt over low heat (or in the microwave on low), stirring every 10 seconds until smooth. Stir in the minced candied ginger and set aside.

3 In a stainless-steel bowl, whisk the egg yolks with the sugar until the mixture is pale and fluffy. Whisk in the brandy. Place the bowl over a saucepan of simmering water (a pan just large enough to balance the bowl on top is perfect—make sure the bowl isn't touching the water), and whisk until the mixture is thick and hot to the touch. Remove from the heat and whisk in the melted chocolate mixture. Cool to room temperature.

4 In a separate bowl, and using an electric mixer, beat the egg whites with the cream of tartar until stiff peaks form. In a separate bowl, beat the whipping cream until stiff.

5 Now it's time to mix and fold. Pile the stiffened egg whites on top of the chocolate mixture and, using a spatula, gently lift and fold together until incorporated. Fold the whipped cream into the mousse, using the same technique. Spoon the mousse into 8 wine glasses or small dessert dishes and refrigerate from 6 hours to overnight. Whip the remaining ½ cup (125 mL) of whipping cream. To serve, garnish the top of each mousse with a dollop of whipped cream, a sprinkling of chopped ginger, and a sprig of mint. Serves 8.

Simple Strawberry Trifle

A simple, no-bake dessert for a hot summer day. Only make this dessert in season, when fresh, juicy strawberries are available at the market—it's just not the same with those tasteless big imported berries you see in the supermarket in November. You can also make this dessert with canned peaches, drained and chopped, or mangoes. Be creative.

1 small pound cake
¼ cup (60 mL) sherry or Grand Marnier
3 cups (750 mL) hulled and sliced strawberries
2 Tbsp (30 mL) granulated sugar

1 tub of lemon or vanilla yogurt (look for a thick
   Balkan-style lemon yogurt)
fresh mint leaves, for garnish

1 Cut the cake into ½-inch (1-cm) cubes. Combine the sliced strawberries with sugar and stir to combine.

2 In individual cups or wine glasses, place a layer of cake cubes. Sprinkle 1 tsp (5 mL) of sherry or Grand Marnier over the cake. Top with a layer of sliced strawberries and just enough of the yogurt to cover. Continue layering the cake, berries, and yogurt until the glass is full, ending with yogurt. Decorate each serving with a few sliced berries and fresh mint. Cover with plastic wrap and refrigerate from 1 to 8 hours. Makes 4 to 6 individual desserts (or one medium trifle if you make the layers in a larger glass bowl).

TRIFLE BOWL

Orange Crème Brûlée

Whenever you're serving a fancy meal, crème brûlée makes a classy finale. And what guy doesn't love to get out his blowtorch to finish a meal? The new mini butane torches available at culinary and hardware stores create a bubbly caramelized sugar topping almost instantly. This impresses all guests and it really works. Believe me.

3-inch (8-cm) strip of orange rind
   (from a Seville or navel orange)
1 ⅓ cup (325 mL) whipping cream
⅔ cup (150 mL) milk
1 tsp (5 mL) pure vanilla extract
6 large egg yolks (use organic eggs if you can—
   the yolks are richer and deeper yellow in
   color)

½ cup (125 mL) plus 6 Tbsp (90 mL) granulated
   sugar
3 Tbsp (45 mL) orange liqueur
   (Cointreau or Grand Marnier)

1 Wash the orange well and pat dry. Use a vegetable peeler to remove a long strip of orange rind from the fruit (you want the orange bit only, not the bitter white pith).

2 Rinse a small saucepan with cold water. Pour the cream and milk into the wet pan, add the orange rind, and bring to a simmer over medium heat. When the mixture begins to steam and bubble around the edges, remove from the heat and stir in the vanilla.

3 Preheat the oven to 325°F (160°C).

4 In a large measuring cup, whisk together the egg yolks and ½ cup (125 mL) of the sugar. Whisk a few spoonfuls of the hot milk into the eggs to temper them (that is, heat up the egg yolks but not hot enough to cook them), then slowly add the egg yolk mixture to the hot milk, whisking constantly as you pour. Place a strainer over the measuring cup and strain the yolk-milk mixture back into the cup. Discard the orange rind and stir in the orange liqueur. Set six individual baking dishes (a.k.a. ramekins) in a baking pan. Make a "bain-marie" by pouring hot water around the dishes, filling the baking pan with about 1 inch (2.5 cm) of water. Divide the custard mixture evenly among the ramekins (each should be about ¾ full).

5 Set the pan in the oven and bake for 40 minutes or until the custards are just barely set. Don't overcook your crème brûlée or it will be rubbery. Remove custards from the baking pan, cool, and cover each with plastic wrap. Refrigerate until ready to serve.

6 Immediately before serving, top each custard with 1 Tbsp (15 mL) of sugar, sprinkling it evenly over the surface. Use a mini butane torch to melt the sugar until it caramelizes and turns golden brown and bubbly. If you don't have a torch, this can be done under a preheated broiler, but the results aren't always as even (and you can't impress your friends with your toys). Serves 6.

> **WISE GUY:** You can also dress these custards up with a nutty coconut crumble (which makes a nice dessert to follow an Asian or Caribbean feast). Just mix ¼ cup (60 mL) brown sugar with 1 Tbsp (15 mL) finely chopped pecans and ¼ cup (60 mL) flaked coconut. Sprinkle this mixture over the custards and brûlée with your torch until browned and bubbly.

Tiramisu

This is the Italian version of English trifle—booze-soaked cake (a.k.a. ladyfingers) layered with a creamy cheese custard and chocolate. That's amore!

one 1-lb (500-g) tub Italian mascarpone cheese
6 very fresh organic eggs, separated
6 Tbsp (90 mL) granulated sugar
½ cup (125 mL) espresso
   (or double-strength coffee)
1¼ cups (310 mL) liqueur (sambuca, Grand
   Marnier, Kahlúa, amaretto, etc.)

2 packages lady fingers
1 cup (250 mL) grated bittersweet Callebaut or other
   top-quality chocolate (with at least 55 to 65%
   cocoa mass)

1 Put the mascarpone into a mixing bowl and add the egg yolks and sugar. Beat with an electric mixer or whisk until smooth. In another bowl, use an electric mixer to beat the egg whites until stiff. Pour the beaten egg whites over the cheese mixture and, using a spatula, fold in the whites, just to combine and lighten the mixture.

2 In another bowl, combine the espresso and liqueur.

3 Lightly dip the ladyfingers into the liqueur mixture and fit them tightly together in a 9- x 12-inch (3.5 L) glass dish, completely covering the base of the pan. Top with half of the mascarpone mixture and half of the grated chocolate. Repeat with a second layer of soaked ladyfingers, mascarpone, and chocolate. Cover with plastic wrap and refrigerate overnight. Cut into squares to serve. Serves 8 to 10.

Deep Dish Chocolate Pecan Pie

Make this pie in a 9-inch (2.5-L) springform pan for a deep, down-home style pie, or use a larger tart pan with a removable bottom. The perfect sweet ending to a Mardis Gras feast or southern barbecue.

Crust
1¼ cups (310 mL) all-purpose flour
2 Tbsp (30 mL) brown sugar
pinch of salt
½ cup (125 mL) unsalted butter
1 egg yolk
1 Tbsp (15 mL) milk

Filling
4 oz (100 g) top quality bittersweet chocolate, chopped
3 large eggs
½ cup (125 mL) granulated sugar
1 cup (250 mL) corn syrup
¼ cup (60 mL) unsalted butter, melted
1 Tbsp (15 mL) all-purpose flour
2 Tbsp (30 mL) bourbon
pinch of salt
1½ cups (375 mL) chopped pecan halves

Bourbon Cream
½ cup (125 mL) whipping cream
1 Tbsp (15 mL) bourbon
2 Tbsp (30 mL) granulated sugar

1 To make the crust, combine the flour, sugar, salt, and butter in the food processor and process until crumbly. Add the egg yolk and milk and pulse until the dough forms a ball. Wrap in plastic and refrigerate for 1 hour to chill.

2 Preheat the oven to 350°F (180°C). Roll out the pastry on a lightly floured surface and press into the bottom, and at least 1 inch (2.5 cm) up the sides, of a 9-inch (2.5-L) springform pan. This pastry is totally forgiving, so don't panic—any rips or cracks can be repaired by pressing in extra bits of dough. Cover the pastry with foil and add some pie weights or dried beans (this helps the crust bake evenly). Bake for 20 minutes. Remove the foil and cool.

3 To make the filling, place the chopped chocolate in a microwave-safe dish and microwave for 30 seconds at a time, stirring every 30 seconds, until melted. Cool slightly and reserve.

4 Whisk the eggs, sugar, corn syrup, butter, flour, bourbon, and salt together in a bowl. Whisk in the cooled chocolate mixture. Pour the filling into the prepared crust and arrange the whole pecans artfully on top. Bake for 35 to 40 minutes in the preheated oven or until the filling is set. Cool to room temperature or chill before cutting.

5 To make the bourbon cream, in a small bowl, whip the cream, bourbon, and sugar just until soft peaks form. Chill until serving.

6 Slice the pie into thin wedges (this is wickedly rich stuff!) and serve with the bourbon cream. Serves 8 to 10.

Raspberry Crème Fraîche Tart

This sounds—and looks—so professional, but it's so simple to make, as long as you have a tart pan with a removable bottom. To make crème fraîche, just combine 2 cups (500 mL) of whipping cream with ½ cup (125 mL) of sour cream. Whisk them together in a bowl, cover with plastic wrap, and set aside at room temperature for 12 hours. The cream will thicken, and will keep, if refrigerated, for several days.

Crust

1½ cups (375 mL) flour (The Guy likes to use half whole wheat pastry flour and half cornmeal or barley flour)

2 Tbsp (30 mL) granulated sugar

pinch of salt

¼ cup (60 mL) cold unsalted butter, cubed

¼ cup (60 mL) cream cheese, cubed (or use all butter and no cheese)

1 large egg

Filling

3 large eggs

¾ cup (175 mL) crème fraîche

¼ cup (60 mL) all-purpose flour

⅔ cup (150 mL) granulated sugar

3 cups (750 mL) fresh raspberries (or half raspberries and blueberries)

icing sugar for dusting

1 Preheat the oven to 350°F (180°C).

2 To make the crust, combine the flour, sugar, salt, butter, and cream cheese in a food processor. Pulse until the mixture forms coarse crumbs. Add 1 egg and pulse just until the dough begins to come together. Dump it into a 10-inch (25-cm) shallow tart pan (the kind with a removable bottom) and press evenly over the bottom and up the sides, using your fingers or the back of a spoon. Bake the crust in the preheated oven for 15 minutes. Remove from the oven and set aside.

3 Meanwhile, to make the filling, in a medium bowl, whisk together 3 eggs and the crème fraîche. Slowly add the flour while you whisk, to prevent any lumps from forming, then whisk in the sugar.

4 Fill the pre-baked shell with the berries, then pour the custard mixture evenly overtop. Bake the tart in the preheated oven for 30 to 40 minutes or until the filling is set and the top is light brown. Cool before removing from the tart pan. Cut into wedges and dust each piece with icing sugar. Serves 6.

Easy Fruit Crisp

This is The Guy's fallback position whenever he needs a dessert—and fast! A fruit crisp is easy and adaptable to any fruit that's on hand. The classic combination is apple and cinnamon, but you can add other fruit as well (blueberries, cranberries, or rhubarb, depending on the season).

¾ cup (175 mL) granulated sugar
2 Tbsp (30 mL) honey
½ tsp (2 mL) ground cinnamon
¼ tsp (1 mL) ground nutmeg
3 Tbsp (45 mL) brandy, Calvados,
   or Grand Marnier

Topping
¼ cup (60 mL) whole wheat flour
3 Tbsp (45 mL) softened unsalted butter
½ cup (125 mL) packed brown sugar

2 cups (500 mL) blueberries, cranberries,
   or chopped rhubarb
5 large Granny Smith apples, peeled, cored,
   and sliced
2 Tbsp (30 mL) all-purpose flour

½ cup (125 mL) rolled oats or barley
pinch of salt
1 tsp (5 mL) cinnamon
gourmet vanilla ice cream or lemon yogurt

1 Preheat the oven to 350°F (180°C).

2 In a medium bowl, combine the sugar, honey, ½ tsp (2 mL) cinnamon, nutmeg, and brandy. Mix well. Toss with the blueberries and apples and marinate for 1 hour or until the fruit releases its juices. Sprinkle with all-purpose flour and stir to combine well. Pour into a greased, shallow baking dish.

3 For the topping, in a small bowl, combine the whole wheat flour with the butter and brown sugar, mixing to form coarse crumbs. Stir in the oatmeal, salt, and 1 tsp (5 mL) cinnamon. Scatter the crumble over the fruit.

4 Set the baking dish on a baking sheet to catch any juice that may run over. Bake for 45 to 55 minutes in the preheated oven or until bubbling and golden brown. Serve the crisp warm with vanilla ice cream or lemon yogurt. Serves 6 to 8.

WISE GUY: Change apple crisp to any kind of fruit crisp, just use about 6 cups (1.5 L) of fruit in all. In the summertime, try a nectarine/blueberry, peach/raspberry, or plum crisp (toss in an extra 1 Tbsp/15 mL of flour with juicier fruits) or combine 2 Tbsp (30 mL) of peeled and grated ginger and the grated zest of 1 lemon, with 6 cups (1.5 L) of pitted and quartered apricots for an exotic Apricot Ginger Crisp.

Virtuous Chocolate Espresso Cake

You'll never imagine that this dark chocolate cake has only 275 calories and 7 grams of fat per serving! Easy to whirl up in the food processor, too.

1 small jar prune baby food
¼ cup (60 mL) brandy
1 cup (250 mL) buttermilk
1 cup (250 mL) granulated sugar
6 Tbsp (90 mL) canola oil
1 Tbsp (15 mL) pure vanilla extract

1¼ cups (310 mL) all-purpose flour
⅔ cup (150 mL) Dutch cocoa powder
2 Tbsp (15 mL) instant espresso powder
1 Tbsp (15 mL) baking soda
powdered (icing) sugar and raspberries,
    for garnish

1 Preheat the oven to 350°F (180°C).

2 Add the prunes, brandy, buttermilk, sugar, oil, and vanilla to a food processor. Whirl to combine. In a medium bowl, combine the flour, cocoa, espresso powder, and baking soda. Add the dry ingredients to the batter in the food processor and pulse four or five times, just to combine.

3 Line the bottom of a 9-inch (2.5-L) springform pan with parchment paper and spray with cooking spray. Pour the batter into the pan and bake for 40 to 50 minutes in the preheated oven, or until the cake springs back when touched, and a toothpick inserted into the center of the cake comes out clean. Cool the cake on a rack, then release from the pan.

4 Cut into 12 wedges and serve dusted with icing sugar, and garnished with a few perfect raspberries.

WISE GUY: If it's not raspberry season, a nice raspberry sauce (a.k.a. coulis) goes well with this simple cake. Just thaw a package of frozen raspberries, press them through a sieve to remove the seeds, and add 1 Tbsp (15 mL) of icing sugar for sweetening (if necessary). Chill and drizzle alongside the cake.

Chocolate Lava Cakes with Crème Anglaise

These individual chocolate desserts are served at many fine restaurants. The gooey center can be achieved several ways, but The Guy prefers the method of enclosing a frozen ball of chocolate in the center of each cake, which gives you a blast of real dark chocolate with every bite.

8 oz (225 g) top quality bittersweet chocolate, chopped and divided
1 Tbsp (15 mL) unsalted butter, melted
2 Tbsp (30 mL) Dutch cocoa powder
⅔ cup (150 mL) whipping cream
3 large eggs, separated

2 Tbsp (30 mL) rum
pinch of cream of tartar
2 Tbsp (30 mL) granulated sugar
cocoa powder, for dusting
crème anglaise (see page 480)
    or vanilla bean ice cream

1 Melt 3 oz (75 g) of the chocolate in the microwave, stopping every 30 seconds to stir it until it's melted and smooth. Divide the melted chocolate into 8 portions in an ice cube tray and freeze.

2 Meanwhile, brush 8 individual soufflé dishes or ramekins with the melted butter and dust with a bit of cocoa. Chill the ramekins.

3 In a heavy saucepan, combine the remaining 5 oz (150 g) of chocolate, 2 Tbsp (30 mL) of cocoa, and whipping cream. Heat over medium-low, stirring occasionally, until the chocolate is melted. Remove from the heat and stir until cooled slightly.

4 In a mixing bowl, beat the egg yolks and rum together. Whisk in the melted chocolate mixture. In another bowl, beat the egg whites and cream of tartar together until starting to stiffen. Gradually add the sugar and continue to beat until the whites are very stiff and shiny. Pile the egg whites over the chocolate mixture and, using a spatula, carefully fold the whites into the chocolate.

5 Preheat the oven to 450°F (230°C).

6 Remove the prepared ramekins from the refrigerator and set them on a baking sheet. Pop the chocolate out of the ice cube trays. Divide half the chocolate batter among the dishes and place a piece of chocolate in the center of each dish. Fill with the remaining chocolate batter, until each ramekin is ¾ full. Don't overfill the dishes, and run a knife around the inside edges of the dishes just before cooking.

7 Bake the lava cakes for 8 to 10 minutes in the preheated oven or until they rise up above the rim of the ramekins and are firm. Remove from the oven and let the cakes cool for 10 minutes. Once cooled, run a knife around the edge of each cake to loosen, then turn out onto the center of individual dessert plates. Dust the plates lightly around the rims with cocoa powder. Serve the lava cakes while warm, with a drizzle of vanilla crème anglaise or a dollop of vanilla bean ice cream. Serves 8.

Baked Rice Pud'

Here's a simple dessert that can end an everyday dinner or an exotic Asian meal. It's a great way to use up leftover rice, too.

1 cup (250 mL) cooked, long-grain white or brown basmati rice (about ⅓ cup/75 mL raw rice)
3 large eggs, beaten
½ cup (125 mL) granulated sugar

2½ cups (625 mL) milk
2 tsp (10 mL) pure vanilla extract
grated fresh nutmeg

1 Preheat the oven to 300°F (150°C).

2 To cook the rice, bring ⅔ cup of water to a boil, add ⅓ cup of rice, and reduce the heat to low. Cover and simmer for 30 minutes or until tender.

3 In a medium bowl, whisk the eggs and sugar together, then whisk in the milk and vanilla. Stir in the cooked rice. Pour the rice pudding into 4 buttered baking dishes (or ramekins), or use one large 4-cup (1-L) buttered baking dish (for serving family-style).

4 Set the ramekins into a large baking pan and add enough hot water so that it comes halfway up the side of the ramekins (this is called a "water bath" or "bain-marie"). Bake the puddings for 45 minutes in the preheated oven. Serve warm or cold, with a grating of nutmeg on top. Serves 4.

WISE GUY: Tart up your pud' with boozy fruit—combine ½ cup (125 mL) raisins, cranberries, or dried papaya bits with ¼ cup (60 mL) rum or brandy, and microwave for a minute to soften. Stir the fruit into the puddings before baking.

Sticky Toffee Pudding with Rum Sauce

This homey and simple dessert is rooted in a British tradition and is gaining new cachet. It's easy to bake these steamy little date puddings in advance and reheat them later. Serve in a pool of warm rum sauce, with a big dollop of whipped cream. Brilliant!

Pudding
½ cup (125 mL) unsalted butter
1 cup (250 mL) packed brown sugar
1 large egg
1 tsp (5 mL) pure vanilla extract
1¼ cups (310 mL) boiling water

one 8-oz (227-g) package pitted dates
1¼ cups (310 mL) all-purpose flour
1 tsp (5 mL) baking powder
½ tsp (2 mL) baking soda
¼ cup (60 mL) blackstrap molasses
½ cup (125 mL) chopped pecans

Sauce
1 cup (250 mL) packed brown sugar
¼ cup (60 mL) corn syrup

¼ cup (60 mL) cold unsalted butter, cubed
¼ cup (60 mL) dark rum
1 cup (250 mL) whipping cream

Garnish sweetened whipped cream

RAMEKIN

1 Preheat the oven to 350°F (180°C).

2 To make the pudding, in a medium bowl, cream the ½ cup (125 mL) butter with an electric mixer until fluffy. Slowly add the brown sugar and continue to beat until well combined. Add the egg and vanilla and beat well. Set aside.

3 In another bowl, pour the boiling water over the dates and let them stand until cool, then chop.

4 In a third bowl, combine the flour, baking powder, and baking soda. Add the flour mixture to the batter and stir to combine. Stir in the cooled, chopped dates.

5 Butter 10 individual ovenproof ramekins or small soufflé dishes and divide the batter evenly among the ramekins. Place the ramekins on a baking sheet and bake for 20 minutes in the preheated oven. Reduce the heat to 300°F (150°C) and continue baking for an additional 30 minutes. (Alternatively, pour the batter into a buttered 9- x 12-inch/3.5-L baking pan and bake for 1 hour).

6 To make the sauce, combine the brown sugar and corn syrup in a saucepan. Bring to a boil over medium-high heat, stirring constantly. Boil for 2 minutes, then whisk in the butter. Add the rum and cream, return to a boil, and simmer until the sauce is reduced and thickened.

7 Remove the puddings from the oven and cool slightly on a rack. Run a knife around the edge of each ramekin to loosen the pudding, and then invert onto individual serving dishes. If you've made the pudding in a baking dish, cut into squares.

8 Serve the puddings warm, drizzled with some of the rum sauce, and topped with a dollop of sweetened whipped cream. You can make the pudding and sauce in advance, and then warm in the microwave for serving. Serves 10.

Creamy Ricotta Cheesecake

The Guy's friend, Carol, is the queen of cheesecakes. You'd never know you're eating a low-fat, low-sugar dessert when you dig into her ethereal ricotta cheesecake. Topped with a mixed berry compote, it's impressive and good for you, too.

Fruit Purée
3 ½ cups (875 mL) blueberries or strawberries
¼ cup (60 mL) Splenda Granular
    or granulated sugar

1 Tbsp (15 mL) cornstarch
¼ cup (60 mL) water
2 Tbsp (30 mL) freshly squeezed lemon juice

Crumb Crust
2 cups (500 mL) graham cracker crumbs
⅓ cup (75 mL) Splenda Granular
    or granulated sugar

½ cup (125 mL) unsalted butter or margarine

Filling
2 cups (500 mL) low-fat ricotta cheese
two 16-oz (475-g) packages light cream cheese
4 large eggs, separated
1½ cups (375 mL) low-fat or non-fat
    plain yogurt

1½ cups (375 mL) low-fat sour cream
1¼ cups (310 mL) granulated sugar
2 tsp (10 mL) pure vanilla extract
¼ tsp (1 mL) salt
⅓ cup (75 mL) all-purpose flour

1 To make the fruit purée, combine the berries, Splenda, cornstarch, and water in a saucepan and simmer over medium heat, stirring occasionally, until the mixture has thickened. Cool the mixture, transfer to a blender, add the lemon juice and purée (or leave it chunky). Chill.

2 Preheat the oven to 350°F (180°C). Combine the crust ingredients. Press into a 9-inch (2.5-L) springform pan and bake for 10 minutes. Cool.

3 In a food processor, blender, or electric mixer, whip the ricotta cheese until smooth. Add the cream cheese, egg yolks, yogurt, sour cream, vanilla, salt, and flour. Process until smooth.

4 In a separate bowl, use an electric mixer to whip the egg whites until stiff. Pour the beaten egg whites over the ricotta cheese mixture and, using a spatula, carefully lift and fold the two together—the result should be light and fluffy. Pour the filling over the crust.

5 Bake the cheesecake in preheated oven for 20 minutes, then reduce the heat to 300°F (150°C) and continue to bake for another 25 minutes. Turn the oven off, but leave the cake in the oven for 10 more minutes. Open the oven door a few inches, and let the cake sit for another 10 minutes—this will ensure that the cake cools slowly and doesn't crack. (Another trick to prevent cheesecakes from cracking is to put a pan of water in the oven while baking.)

6 Chill the cheesecake for several hours or overnight before cutting. Serve in wedges, with the berry purée on top. Serves 8.

Observance

The Big Holiday Dinner

The Big Bird (a.k.a. turkey) is usually at the center of every big holiday feast. But the real success of this harvest or holiday celebration is what you serve on the side. So make sure you know everything about preparing the main event, then turn your talents to a chic soup, something green to contrast all that golden brown meat and gravy, and an impressive seasonal dessert to cap it off in style.

Celery and Sage Bread Stuffing

This is The Guy's favorite thing to stuff into a big bird—classic, old-fashioned bread stuffing, flavored with celery, thyme, and sage. If you're into something more exotic, add some chopped apple or pear, cooked and crumbled pork sausage, or even toasted pecans or roasted chestnuts. You need about ¾ cups (175 mL) of bread per 1 lb (500 g) of turkey, so adjust the amount of bread cubes and other ingredients according to the size of your bird. This recipe provides enough stuffing for a 10- to 12-lb (4.5 to 5.5-kg) turkey.

1 loaf day-old French bread, cut into ½-inch
   (1-cm) cubes (about 8 cups/2 L)
¼ cup (60 mL) melted butter
1 cup (250 mL) finely chopped celery
   (including leaves)
1 large onion, chopped

2 tsp (10 mL) ground sage
2 tsp (10 mL) celery salt
2 tsp (10 mL) dried thyme leaves (or 2 Tbsp/30 mL
   chopped fresh thyme)
salt and freshly ground black pepper

1 Place the bread cubes in a large bowl and set aside.

2 Heat the butter in a sauté pan over medium heat and cook the chopped celery and onion for 7 to 10 minutes or until the onions are translucent and tender but not brown.

3 Pour the contents of the sauté pan over the bread cubes and toss to coat. Sprinkle evenly with sage, celery salt, thyme, salt, and pepper. Toss to evenly distribute the spices.

4 Stuff the turkey with the bread stuffing just before you're ready to put it in the oven. If you'd rather cook the stuffing on the side (but, really, who would ... you'll miss out on all the yummy turkey juices and flavors) you can bake it in a covered casserole dish for about 1 hour, alongside the bird. Just add 1 cup (250 mL) of the turkey broth you made with the giblets (or use canned broth), to moisten the stuffing while it cooks. Any leftover stuffing that won't fit into the bird can be cooked this way, too.

5 Remove all the stuffing from the turkey before carving and keep it warm in a covered casserole dish. Don't leave the stuffing inside the turkey after it's cooked—it will spoil. Makes enough stuffing for a 10- to 12-lb (4.5- to 5.4-kg) bird.

The Big Bird
(Ten Steps to a Perfect Turkey)

1 Buy a turkey. If it's frozen, you have to think waaayyy ahead. It takes about 4 hours per 1 lb (500 g), 10 hours per 1 kg (2 lb), to thaw a bird in the refrigerator (that's 2 to 3 days for a small bird). Never thaw it at room temperature or cook a partially frozen bird or you risk salmonella poisoning. To save time, place the turkey—still in its plastic—in a sink and completely cover it with cold water. Allow 1 hour per 1 lb (500 g), 2 hours per 1 kg (2 lb), to thaw. Make sure to keep the water cold.

2 Fresh turkey should be cooked within 2 to 3 days of purchase. Turkey labeled "previously frozen" must be cooked within 48 hours of purchase.

3 Don't blow calories and fat grams by buying a turkey that's "basted" (a.k.a. injected with saturated fat). It's not necessary for a tender turkey and just adds calories.

4 Wash your hands with soap and hot water before and after handling raw turkey. Remove the plastic, take the neck and giblets out of the cavity (they should be in a bag), rinse inside and out with cold water, and pat dry with paper towels. (Put the neck and giblets in a pot of water with some onion, whole black peppercorns, carrot, and parsley. Simmer to make a broth for your gravy.) After handling raw turkey, wash all the used equipment, utensils, and surfaces with hot soapy water to avoid bacteria transfer and contamination.

5 Place the turkey on a rack in a large roasting pan, breast-side up. Brush with oil or melted butter and season inside and out with a little salt and pepper.

6 If stuffing the bird, wait until just before roasting. Don't pack the stuffing, you should fill the bird loosely (or you can cook the stuffing separately in a covered baking dish alongside the bird, which is known as "dressing").

7 Roast the bird at 325°F (160°C) for about 15-20 minutes per pound, until the internal temperature reads 170°F (77°C). Use an instant-read meat thermometer, inserted in the thickest part of the thigh, to test the internal temperature (don't leave it in while the bird is roasting, just during testing). Make sure you take the temperature of the stuffing, too. It should be at least 165°F (73°C) in the center of the stuffing. It doesn't take as long as you think to roast a turkey to perfection—about 3 to 4 hours for a 12- to 16-lb (5.5- to 7-kg) stuffed bird. Start checking the temperature early as leaner, free-range birds will cook and dry out more quickly. Cover the bird loosely with foil if it is browning too fast.

8 When the turkey is cooked, remove the bird from the roasting pan and let it rest on the cutting board or platter, covered with a loose piece of foil, for 15 to 20 minutes. This allows the juices to set and gives you time to make the gravy. Don't leave the turkey (cooked or raw) at room temperature for longer than 2 hours. You can refrigerate cooked turkey for up to 4 days or freeze it for up to 4 months.

9 Pour the juices from the roasting pan into a heatproof glass measuring cup and set aside. Any excess fat will form a layer on top of the juices in the measuring cup—skim off as much as you like (but reserve 3 Tbsp/45 mL to start the gravy). To make the gravy, start with 3 Tbsp (45 mL) of fat in the roasting pan. Place the roasting pan on top of the stove over medium heat. Sprinkle 3 to 4 Tbsp (45 to 50 mL) of flour over the fat and browned bits in the roasting pan. Stir with a wooden spoon to moisten the flour and loosen the browned bits. Add the reserved (skimmed) juices and ¼ cup (60 mL) water (or the broth you've made from the neck and giblets). Stir well to create a thick paste. Add more water or broth (or leftover liquid from boiling potatoes or peas), a little at a time, stirring as you go to avoid lumps (a whisk works well at this point). Let the gravy come back to a boil each time, and add a little more liquid if it's still too thick. Season with salt and pepper to taste. Keep warm in a gravy boat or small pitcher.

10 Using a large spoon, remove all the stuffing from the cavity of the bird and place it in a covered dish in the oven to stay warm. Carve the turkey. Remove the leg and thigh pieces first and slice the meat from the bone, arranging the dark meat at one end of the platter. To slice the breast meat, start at the base of the breast (where you've removed the legs), and slice vertically, parallel to the breastbone, into thin, even slices. Arrange on a platter, pass the trimmings and the gravy, and you're done!

WISE GUY: Fresh chestnuts are only available in mid-winter and come from either Italy or Asia. The fattest, tastiest chestnuts are Italian. The Guy's favorite way to get them out of their shells is to roast them over hot coals in a fireplace, or on a barbecue. Like the classic song says, there's nothing quite like the toasty, smoky flavor of chestnuts roasted on an open fire. Who better to start this manly tradition of cooking over wood during the holidays?

Just cut an X in the bottom or side of each nut (to prevent exploding nuts), arrange them in a single layer in a grilling basket, and roast them for 20 to 30 minutes, turning occasionally until they steam and crackle and the shells split. You can also roast them in a 400°F (200°C) oven for 30 to 40 minutes, or boil them for 20 minutes, but it's not nearly as sexy. Whatever way you cook them, just score in an X first.

When they've cooled enough to handle, but are still warm, peel off the shells and bitter inner brown skin. Then eat them straight up, or refrigerate or freeze them for later. Chestnuts are good for you, too—lowest in calories of all the nuts. Chestnuts have less than 1/10 of an ounce (3 g) of fat in 1/4 lb (125 g) and are similar to brown rice in nutritional value (high in complex carbohydrates and fiber).

WISE GUY:

Okay, so this may not be the time to start talking about turkey soup, but once you get all of that tender turkey carved off the bones, don't chuck the carcass—save it for making soup stock. Really. Wonderful turkey stock is only a winter afternoon of simmering away. If you can't face cooking anything else for a month, just put the carcass into a heavy plastic bag and freeze it until that day in January when you feel a cold coming on. Then put the carcass into your stock pot (break it into pieces if it's too big) and pour in enough cold water to cover the whole carcass, plus 4 or 5 inches (10 or 12 cm) extra. Throw in a couple of washed and quartered carrots, a stalk of celery, a quartered onion, some whole black peppercorns, and bay leaves. Bring the whole thing to a boil, and let it simmer on medium-low heat for several hours (four, five, six, who's counting?). Add more cold water after a few hours, just enough to keep everything submerged, and continue to simmer. Skim off any gunk that rises to the top of the pot. Strain the stock through a fine mesh sieve into a clean pot and pitch the bones and veggies. Season with salt and pepper. Drink it as-is or add small egg noodles. Or put it into containers and freeze it to use later in soups and sauces. You'll be glad you did. And now you know how to make chicken soup (it's the same method if you start with a raw chicken; just take the chicken out when the broth is ready and serve the poached chicken separately).

Creamy Chestnut Soup

This is a rich and wonderful creamed soup—the perfect way to start an elegant holiday meal. If you're serving this soup when fresh chestnuts aren't in season, look for frozen or dried chestnuts in Asian groceries (which are also a great source for the shallots you'll need for this soup).

¼ lb (125 g) piece of lean prosciutto ham
2 Tbsp (30 mL) butter
1 medium onion, thinly sliced
1 cup (250 mL) sliced shallots
6 cups (1.5 L) whole chestnuts, peeled and brown
    inner skin removed
½ tsp (2 mL) of salt

½ cup (125 mL) chopped celery
1 tsp (5 mL) fennel seeds
1 bay leaf
6 to 8 cups (1.5 to 2 L) chicken broth
½ cup (125 mL) heavy cream
salt and freshly ground white pepper
finely chopped fresh parsley for garnish

1 Cut the prosciutto in half. Cut one half into small slivers for garnishing the soup later.

2 In a large pot, melt the butter over medium heat. Sauté the onions, shallots, and whole prosciutto piece together until the onions are tender, about 10 minutes. Add the chestnuts, salt, celery, and fennel seeds. Stir in 6 cups (1.5 L) of the stock. Raise the heat to medium-high and bring to a boil. Cover the pot, reduce the heat to medium-low, and simmer for 1 hour.

3 Cool slightly. Remove the prosciutto piece and discard. Purée the soup in a food processor or blender until smooth. Return the purée to the cooking pot, then add the cream. Bring to a simmer over medium heat and add as much of the remaining broth as you need to create a smooth, creamy soup. Season to taste with salt and white pepper.

4 In a small pan over medium heat, sauté the reserved slivered prosciutto with a little olive oil to crisp it slightly. Ladle the soup into individual shallow soup plates and garnish each serving with a little crispy prosciutto and chopped parsley. Serves 8.

Brussels Sprouts You'll Love

The Brussels sprout—that adorable miniature cabbage, and first of the mini-vegetables on the scene—often gets no respect. But whether you love or hate Brussels sprouts, give this recipe a try. It's a winner that everyone enjoys, and it will give your holiday plate the shot of color it needs.

1 lb (500 g) Brussels sprouts
   (the smaller, the better)
2 Tbsp (30 mL) butter
1 Tbsp (15 mL) extra virgin olive oil

salt and freshly ground black pepper
⅓ cup (75 mL) chopped pecans
   or roasted chestnuts
½ fresh lemon, seeds removed

1 Bring a large pot of salted water to a boil. Trim the sprouts by cutting the base cleanly and slicing a little X on the base of each. Pull off any loose or yellow leaves. Add the sprouts to the boiling water, cover the pot, and boil them for 10 minutes, no longer. (Alternately, you can steam them for 10 minutes.) The trick to tasty sprouts is cooking them until they're just tender, no more—overcooked Brussels sprouts have a strong flavor. Once cooked, drain and immediately immerse the sprouts in a bowl of ice water to stop the cooking process. Drain sprouts again, pressing lightly to remove excess water, then place in a covered bowl and refrigerate.

2 When you're ready to serve the sprouts, heat the butter and oil in a large sauté pan over medium heat. When the butter is bubbly and beginning to turn a bit brown, add the nuts and toast for a minute. Return the sprouts to the pan, and sauté for 3 to 4 minutes or until the sprouts are just heated though. Season with salt and pepper, and squeeze the lemon overtop. Serve immediately. Serves 4.

Honey-Roasted Parsnips

The parsnip is another vegetable some people like to disparage, but it's a seasonal, winter vegetable that's really at its best when dug out of the cold ground, after the first frost, when the holiday season is upon us. Parsnips also make an addictive creamy soup for a fancy dinner and, if cut into thin strips with a vegetable peeler, can be fried in hot oil for crisp, tasty chips.

1 lb (500 g) parsnips (about 4 to 5 medium-sized
   parsnips)
2 Tbsp (30 mL) butter
1 Tbsp (15 mL) wildflower honey

salt and pepper
1 tsp (5 mL) chopped fresh rosemary or thyme
   leaves

1 Preheat the oven to 400° F (200°C).

2 Heat the butter and honey together in a medium-sized bowl in the microwave for 1 minute, or until melted. Peel the parsnips and slice into ½-inch (1-cm) slices or chunks. Add to the bowl and toss to coat with butter and honey mixture. Season with the salt, pepper, and herbs and toss again.

3 Line a baking sheet with foil or parchment paper. Spread the parsnips in a single layer on the baking sheet and roast for about 30 minutes, turning once after 15 minutes, until the parsnips are golden. Serves 4.

Speedy Fresh Cranberry Sauce

The Guy has been caught carving the bird before remembering to make the cranberry sauce. This is an easy, last-minute version to whirl up in the food processor minutes before serving.

one 12-oz (375-mL) bag fresh cranberries
1 whole navel orange, with peel

½ cup (125 mL) granulated sugar

1 Pick through the cranberries and discard any soft berries or stems. Put the cranberries in the food processor.

2 Cut the orange into quarters and discard the seeds. Add the orange quarters to the processor, peel and all. Pulse to finely chop the berries and orange pieces. Add the sugar and whirl to combine.

3 Place in a serving bowl and serve immediately. Or cover and chill in the refrigerator for up to 8 hours. Makes 2 cups.

Pumpkin Pie with Crunchy Streusel Topping

While pumpkin pie is traditionally served at fall suppers, it's the kind of pie you can make any time of the year (if there's a can of pumpkin in the pantry). Everyone loves it, and with no top crust to make, it's easy. You can even use a frozen pie shell to speed things up. The crunchy streusel topping simply gilds the lily.

pastry for 1 single crust, 9-inch (23-cm) pie (the recipe on a box of lard makes a good crust or use a frozen pie shell)
1½ cups (375 mL) canned pumpkin (not pumpkin pie filling)
3 large eggs
½ cup (125 mL) packed brown sugar
2 Tbsp (30 mL) cognac or bourbon

1 tsp (5 mL) ground cinnamon
¼ tsp (1 mL) ground cloves
¼ tsp (1 mL) grated nutmeg
½ tsp (2 mL) ground ginger
½ cup (125 mL) whipping cream
½ cup (125 mL) whole milk
¼ tsp (1 mL) salt

Topping

¼ cup (60 mL) packed light brown sugar

2 Tbsp (25 mL) all-purpose flour

2 Tbsp (25 mL) unsalted butter, softened

¼ cup (60 mL) finely chopped pecans

1 Make the pastry according to the recipe on the box. Roll the pastry into a circle, larger than your pie plate, then fold it in half (this makes it easier to pick up) and flop it into the pie pan. Unfold, allowing the pastry to drape evenly over the edges of the pan. Use a sharp knife or kitchen shears to cut it into an even circle, about ½ inch (1 cm) larger than the pan. Roll the pastry under to form a double thick edge, then use your fingers to "flute" the pastry. (Press the index finger of your right hand up into the dough edge through a "V" formed by your left thumb and index finger on the top side—continue all around the pie to form a scalloped edge). Chill the crust in the refrigerator for 30 minutes.

2 To make the filling, whisk together the pumpkin, eggs, brown sugar, cognac, cinnamon, cloves, nutmeg, ginger, cream, milk, and salt in a large mixing bowl. If you want a really fluffy pie, separate the eggs. Add the yolks to the batter, then in a separate bowl beat the whites until they are stiff. Gently fold the egg whites into the pumpkin mixture.

3 In a small bowl, combine all the topping ingredients. Mix with your hands until the butter is incorporated with the sugar and flour, and the mixture is crumbly. Set aside.

4 Preheat the oven to 350°F (180°C). Pour the filling into the prepared pie shell. Bake for 40 minutes, then sprinkle with the topping and continue to bake for 15 minutes longer, until the center is set and the topping is browned. Remove from the oven and cool thoroughly before slicing.

5 Serve the pie wedges with a dollop of sweetened whipped cream or a small scoop of vanilla ice cream. A few slices of candied ginger make a nifty garnish, too. Serves 6 to 8.

Islands in the Sun

The Guy always likes to plan a wonderful meal to ring in the New Year—and when he can get away with donning his favorite Hawaiian shirt on a black-tie occasion—it's brilliant!

So to celebrate his love of sunny Caribbean climes he created this delicious island-inspired party menu. With some rum-based cocktails, a tropical seafood stew, and classic plantain appetizers, it's a meal to instantly take you away from winter. Herewith, The Guy's island feast to impress eight of your favorite friends. Decorate your table with seashells and sand pails, invite your guests to arrive in their beach best, then spin the reggae records and celebrate!

Three Kings' Punch

A traditional cocktail for the holidays in Puerto Rico, reminiscent of eggnog, but with added kick.

1 cup (250 mL) granulated sugar
1 cup (250 mL) water
1 cinnamon stick
one 14-oz (398-mL) can evaporated milk

4 egg yolks
1 cup (250 mL) white rum
1 cup (250 mL) anisette
ground cinnamon for garnish

1 In a small saucepan, combine the sugar, water, and cinnamon stick. Bring to a boil. Remove from the heat and let it cool for 10 minutes. Meanwhile, in a large bowl, whisk together the evaporated milk and egg yolks. Slowly whisk in the warm sugar and cinnamon syrup, being careful not to cook the egg. Stir in the rum and anisette. Pour into a bottle and refrigerate. It will keep a week or more. Just before serving, shake vigorously then pour into cocktail glasses, over ice, and sprinkle with ground cinnamon. Makes 6 cups, 12 servings.

Pineapple Rum Punch

Keep this frozen rum slush in the freezer for an exotic island cocktail at any time.

4 cups (1 L) unsweetened pineapple juice, divided
1½ cups (375 mL) granulated sugar
⅓ cup (75 mL) freshly squeezed lime juice

4 cups (1 L) white rum
angostura bitters
3 to 4 oz (75 to 100 g) soda water
lime slices for garnish

1 In a medium saucepan, combine half of the pineapple juice and all of the sugar. Stir over medium heat for 5 minutes or until sugar is dissolved. Remove from the heat and cool.

2 In a large plastic container, combine the cooled pineapple and sugar syrup with the remaining pineapple juice, lime juice, and rum. Cover and freeze.

3 When ready to serve, spoon 6 Tbsp (90 mL) of the slush into a short cocktail glass, add a dash or two of angostura bitters, and top with soda water. Garnish each cocktail with a slice of lime and serve. Makes 16 servings.

Tostones with Puerto Rican Red Beans

Serve tostones (plantain fritters) as appetizers, topped with this chunky and traditional red bean dish. Or purée the beans to form a smooth dip. Scoop it up with a variety of sturdy chips—corn, cassava, or plantain. For a vegetarian appetizer, eliminate the ham.

Beans

¾ lb (375 g) pumpkin or winter squash, peeled and cubed

1 lb (500 g) small dried red beans, presoaked
8 cups (2 L) water

Sofrito

2 Tbsp (30 mL) plus 1 tsp (5 mL) olive oil
1 small yellow onion, peeled
1 large green bell pepper, seeded

½ red bell pepper, seeded
3 cloves garlic
2 Tbsp (30 mL) chopped cilantro leaves
½ tsp (2 mL) dried oregano

To finish

3 cups cooked beans
1 cup (250 mL) minced ham
3 to 4 Tbsp (45 to 60 mL) sofrito (above)
½ cup (125 mL) minced bell pepper
½ cup (125 mL) onion
⅓ cup (75 mL) olive oil
1 tsp (5 mL) curry powder

1 tsp (5 mL) paprika
1 cup (250 mL) chicken stock
½ cup (125 mL) tomato sauce
1 bay leaf
¼ cup (60 mL) white wine
1 cup (250 mL) chopped cilantro leaves, divided
salt and freshly ground black pepper to taste

1 In a saucepan, combine the pumpkin, red beans, and water. Bring to a boil over high heat.

2 Reduce the heat to medium-low, cover, and simmer for 1 hour or until the beans are almost tender. Drain and mash the pumpkin and the beans. Set aside.

3 To make the sofrito, in a blender, combine 2 Tbsp (30 mL) of the olive oil, the onion, peppers, garlic, cilantro, and oregano. Purée until smooth. In a frying pan, heat the 1 tsp (5 mL) of oil over medium heat and fry the purée for 20 minutes, stirring occasionally. Cool the sofrito and set aside 3 to 4 Tbsp (45 to 60 mL) for the beans. Freeze any leftover sofrito in ice cube trays for future use.

4 To finish the beans, sauté the ham and the reserved sofrito in a large saucepan. Add the pepper, onion, ⅓ cup (75 mL) of olive oil, curry powder, and paprika. Cook for 2 minutes. Stir in the stock, tomato sauce, bay leaf, wine, and reserved mashed beans and pumpkin. Add half the cilantro and bring to a boil. Reduce the heat to low and simmer, uncovered, for 30 to 45 minutes. Stir in remaining cilantro; season with salt and pepper to taste. Serve warm with tostones. Serves 8.

Tostones

Make these crispy plantain fritters to serve with drinks.

3 green plantains	2 Tbsp (30 mL) salt
4 cups (2 L) water	canola oil for frying
2 cloves garlic, peeled and crushed	

1 Peel plantains and cut on the diagonal into 1-inch (2.5-cm) slices. In a large bowl, combine the water, garlic, and salt. Add the plantain slices and soak for 15 minutes. Remove the soaked slices and pat the slices dry. Reserve the liquid.

2 In a sauté pan, heat 1 to 2 inches (2.5 to 5 cm) of oil to 350°F (180°C). Fry the plantain slices for 7 to 8 minutes. Drain the fried plantains on paper towels.

3 Set the slices on a flat surface. Use the bottom of a small pot to gently mash and flatten the slices. Quickly dip the slices in the reserved salt water, then fry a second time in 375°F (190°C) oil until crisp and golden on both sides.

4 Drain the tostones on paper towels, season with salt, and serve with the red beans (above) or a mojito sauce (a mixture of 2 Tbsp/30 mL sofrito, ½ cup/125 mL ketchup, 1 Tbsp/15 mL lime juice, a pinch of oregano, and a dash of Tabasco). Makes 12 to 18 tostones.

Island Bouillabaisse

This bouillabaisse has tropical overtones—a meal in itself when you're feeling exotic. It's very rich and creamy, so serve it in shallow bowls over mounds of fragrant basmati rice. For a traditional New Year's treat, instead of cooking the rice in water, cook it with coconut milk, a touch of minced jalapeño pepper, some cooked red beans, and a sprinkle of chopped fresh thyme.

The Base

2 medium tart apples, peeled and chopped

2 medium bananas, peeled

¾ cup (175 mL) raisins

¼ cup (60 mL) Madras-style curry powder

3 cloves garlic, minced

½ tsp (2 mL) ground cumin

2 tsp (10 mL) Worcestershire sauce

4 cups (1 L) coconut milk

4 cups (1 L) chicken stock

¼ tsp (1 mL) crushed saffron threads or turmeric

4 Tbsp (60 mL) freshly squeezed lemon or lime juice

4 Tbsp (60 mL) brown sugar

1½ cups (375 mL) whipping cream

To finish

1 cup (250 mL) finely diced red bell peppers

1½ lb (750 g) cubed snapper, halibut, or other firm white fish

32 large prawns, peeled and deveined

32 sea scallops

24 large mussels, scrubbed and debearded

½ cup (125 mL) chopped fresh cilantro, divided

4 to 5 cups hot, cooked basmati rice (about ½ cup/125 mL cooked rice per person)

1 In a large saucepan, combine the apple, banana, raisins, curry powder, garlic, cumin, Worcestershire, coconut milk, stock, saffron, lemon juice, and brown sugar. Bring to a boil over medium-high heat. Reduce the heat to medium-low, cover, and simmer for 30 minutes. Cool the mixture slightly and purée with a food processor or a hand blender until smooth. Add the cream and whirl to combine. (You can make this portion of the soup a day in advance. Simply refrigerate until you are ready to finish before serving.)

2 Reheat the soup base over medium heat in a deep Dutch oven or wok. When it boils, add the red peppers and cubed fish. Simmer for 5 minutes. Add the prawns, scallops, and mussels. Cover the pot and raise the heat to medium-high. Simmer for 3 to 5 minutes or until the shrimp are pink and the mussels are open.

3 Discard any mussels that don't open and stir in half the cilantro.

4 To serve, mound ½ cup (125 mL) of rice in the center of eight shallow soup plates (you can press the rice into a small ramekin or custard cup and unmold in the middle of the bowl to make it look more professional).

5 Surround the rice with the seafood and ladle the soup overtop. Sprinkle with reserved cilantro and serve. Serves 8 to 10.

Mango and Jicama Salad on Mixed Greens with Mango Vinaigrette

A simple salad with island overtones. Make sure the mangoes are ripe—they should be a red-orange color and have an alluring aroma.

1 lb (500 g) mango, peeled, pitted, and cubed
   (½-inch/1-cm cubes)
3 Tbsp (45 mL) brown sugar
¼ cup (60 mL) rum
¼ cup (60 mL) freshly squeezed lime juice
2 stalks celery, finely chopped
1 medium jicama, peeled and cubed
   (¼-inch/5-mm cubes)

½ red bell pepper, seeded and finely chopped
¼ cup (60 mL) minced red onion
⅓ cup (75 mL) olive oil, divided
8 cups (2 L) mixed greens (including some
   spicy mustard greens or arugula)
¼ cup (60 mL) chopped cilantro
sea salt

1 In a glass bowl, combine the mango, brown sugar, rum, and lime juice. Cover and refrigerate for 1 to 2 hours. Drain the mangos and reserve the marinade.

2 Add the chopped celery, jicama, red pepper, onion, and 1 Tbsp (15 mL) of the olive oil to the marinated mango. Toss and set aside.

3 Whisk the reserved marinade with the remaining olive oil to form a vinaigrette. Toss the greens with just enough vinaigrette to lightly coat the leaves.

4 Divide the dressed greens among 8 salad plates. Toss the chopped cilantro with the mango mixture and spoon equally over each salad. Sprinkle with sea salt and serve. Serves 8.

Key Lime Pie

This kind of "open-faced" pie is The Guy's specialty—just buy a frozen pie shell and you're on your way—no need to make a finicky pastry. Make this pie when the tiny, aromatic key limes are available at your supermarket.

4 eggs
one 14-oz (398-mL) can sweetened
  condensed milk
2 tsp (10 mL) lime zest

½ cup (125 mL) key lime juice
½ cup (125 mL) granulated sugar
½ tsp (2 mL) cream of tartar
frozen single-crust pie shell

1 Bake the frozen pie shell according to the directions on the package. Set aside to cool.

2 Wash the limes well (preferably start with unsprayed, organic fruit). Use your microplane grater (see page 487) to remove the zest (just the top green layer of the skin). Set aside. Then cut the limes in half, crosswise, and use a reamer or citrus press to squeeze the juice. Set aside.

3 Preheat the oven to 250°F (120°C). Separate the egg yolks and whites into two bowls. Be very careful not to get any of the yolks into the whites as this will impede the whites from reaching the proper volume and stiffness.

4 Using an electric mixer, beat the egg yolks until they look pale yellow. Add the condensed milk and lime juice and continue beating until thick. Stir in the lime zest. Pour the filling into the pre-baked pie shell.

5 Clean the beaters and dry them well. Beat the egg whites, adding cream of tartar and sugar, a little at a time, until the whites are very stiff and shiny. Pile this meringue on top of the pie filling. Use the back of a spoon to swirl it into an artful, spiky creation.

6 Place the pie on the middle rack of the oven and bake until the tips of the meringue spikes are golden brown, about 45 to 55 minutes. Serves 6 to 8.

High Holidays

It's always important to accommodate your guests' food preferences, but this meal satisfies whether you're keeping kosher or not. A nice roast chicken or a tender pot roast is a possibility for most high holidays. Start with latkes and gefilte fish from the local deli, then finish with an old-fashioned Orange Cranberry Bundt Cake (see page 454) or traditional rolled cookies called ruga-lah. Here are some traditional favorites that will delight your Jewish friends.

Grandma's Chicken Soup

Also known as "Jewish penicillin," chicken soup, made from scratch by grandmothers the world over, has a reputation for curing whatever ails you. A guy who can make chicken or turkey soup from scratch will have friends for life. It's dead easy—especially after you've roasted a bird. Never pitch a chicken or turkey carcass. Add some veggies and water, simmer for a few hours, and you'll have stupendous soup.

one 4-lb (2-kg) stewing hen, cut up (or a chicken or turkey carcass)
2 to 3 parsnips, peeled and cut into chunks
2 to 3 carrots, peeled and cut into chunks
2 stalks celery, with leaves, cut into chunks
1 onion, quartered

16 cups (4 L) cold water
2 tsp (10 mL) salt
4 to 5 black peppercorns
3 sprigs fresh parsley or dill
1/2 cup (125 mL) dried egg noodles (tiny diamond or thin egg noodles are best)

1 Place everything, except the noodles, into the tallest stock pot you can find. Bring to a boil over medium-high heat, making sure the chicken is well submerged. As the water comes to a boil, a foamy scum will rise to the surface—use a slotted spoon to skim this off.

2 Reduce the heat to low and simmer for 2 to 3 hours, adding extra water if necessary to keep the chicken submerged. Keep the heat very low—the soup should barely bubble (this makes the clearest broth).

3 After 2 or 3 hours, taste the broth—when it's concentrated to your liking, remove it from the heat and strain the liquid through a fine sieve into a heat-proof glass bowl or measuring cup. Discard the vegetables and bones. If you've used a whole stewing hen, you can reserve the meat for another dish, although most of the flavor will be in the broth.

4 As the strained broth cools you will see a layer of fat rise to the top. Skim this off with a spoon if you plan to use the broth right away. Alternately, refrigerate the broth overnight, then discard the solidified fat.

5 To serve, reheat the broth to boiling. Season with salt and pepper to taste and add the egg noodles. Boil for 5 to 10 minutes, or until the noodles are tender. Serves 6.

WISE GUY: For a truly traditional dish, skip the noodles and add matzo balls. Combine 1 cup (250 mL) of matzo meal with 3 Tbsp (45 mL) chicken stock and enough olive oil to moisten. Season with salt, chopped parsley, and a pinch of nutmeg. Bind with 2 beaten eggs. Refrigerate the batter overnight, then form into golf-ball sized dumplings. Poach in boiling water for 30 minutes or until the matzo balls float to the surface. Serve 1 to 2 balls in each bowl of soup.

Perfect Roast Chicken

Make sure you find a good free-range chicken producer or a butcher who regularly carries fresh roasting chickens from a local farmer. If you have time, brine it (this adds flavor and moisture to even any chicken and turkey—see page 257) or simply follow these five simple steps to a fabulous roast chicken in just over an hour.

Step One Buy a fresh free-range chicken—about 5 to 6 lb (2.2 to 2.7 kg). It will cost more than the usual commercial fryer, but the taste will be far, far better (trust me). Remove everything from the inside of the chicken (you might find the neck and/or gizzards in a bag). Wash the chicken, inside and out, under cold tap water and pat dry with paper towels (the skin will crisp better if dry).

Step Two Combine ¼ cup (60 mL) butter, softened with 2 Tbsp (30 mL) finely minced fresh herbs (The Guy likes to use rosemary or thyme). Reserve a few sprigs of fresh herbs for the chicken cavity.

Step Three Starting around the neck, at the top of the breast, carefully reach your fingers under the skin, forming a pocket on each side of the breastbone. Push the herbed butter under the skin and lightly press it along to evenly distribute the butter over the breast.

Step Four Place several whole sprigs of fresh herbs (the same herbs used in the butter) inside the cavity of the chicken. Wash a lemon, cut it into quarters, and place three of the quarters inside the chicken with the herbs. Tie the legs together with string. Place the chicken on a rack in a roasting pan, breast-side up. Rub the chicken with 1 tsp (5 mL) olive oil and squeeze the remaining lemon quarter over top.

Step Five Roast the chicken at 450°F (230°C) for 20 minutes. Reduce the heat to 350°F (180°C) and roast for 1 hour longer. The chicken is ready when the juices run clear and the internal temperature reaches 180°F (85°C). Test with an instant-read thermometer if you're unsure. When fully cooked, remove the chicken from the oven and let it rest for 15 to 20 minutes. Discard the lemon and herbs from the cavity and carve. Serves 6.

WISE GUY: While you're roasting that chicken, roast some garlic to squeeze into your mashed potatoes. Just cut the ¼ inch (5mm) from the pointed end of a whole head of garlic. Place the garlic on a piece of heavy foil, drizzle with a few drops of olive oil, and close the foil around the garlic. Roast alongside the chicken for 45 minutes. The softened, roasted garlic can be squeezed right out of the husks and straight into your potatoes. Mash the garlic and potatoes with butter and cream (or milk). Perfection!

WISE GUY: While The Guy roasts his perfect chicken, there's nothing easier than doing some roasted vegetables. Chop up 1lb (500 g) each of some chunked sweet potatoes, carrots and parsnips with a large red onion and a red or yellow bell peper. Toss with 2 Tbsp (30 mL) of extra virgin olive oil, salt and black pepper. Line a large baking sheet (or two) with parchment paper. Spread the vegetables in a single layer on the baking sheet and roast in a 400°F (200°C) oven for 45 to 60 minutes, stirring once, until browned. Toss the roasted vegetables with 1 Tsbp (15 mL) each of vinegar and parsley. Delicious!

Double Potato Latkes

You can shred the potatoes for these colorful latkes, like a real Jewish grandmother, with a box grater or save time and use the shredding disk on your food processor. You can even use the grater to shred the onion.

1 lb (500 g) sweet potatoes, peeled
    and shredded
1 lb (500 g) red potatoes, peeled and shredded
salt
1 medium onion, minced
2 eggs

freshly ground black pepper
1 Tbsp (15 mL) minced fresh dill
½ cup (125 mL) melba toast crumbs (or other fine,
    dry breadcrumbs)
olive oil for frying
sour cream or applesauce for garnish

1 Place the shredded potatoes in a colander, season with salt, then let them sit for 15 minutes to drain. Squeeze the potatoes with your hands to remove excess water and pat dry with paper towels.

2 In a large bowl, combine the potatoes, onion, eggs, pepper, dill, and melba toast crumbs.

3 Heat a large, non-stick sauté pan over medium heat with ¼ inch (5 mm) of oil in the bottom. When the oil is hot (a drop of water will sputter on top), drop in 1 to 2 Tbsp (15 to 30 mL) of the shredded potato batter and flatten to form small pancakes. Don't make them too big—aim for bite-sized noshes.

4 Cook the latkes for 3 to 4 minutes per side until nicely browned and crispy. Drain the fried latkes on a plate lined with paper towels, and place them into a 200°F (95°C) oven to keep warm while you cook the rest of the pancakes. Serve the latkes hot with sour cream and/or apple sauce. Serves 6.

Rugalah

The Guy likes to fill his rugalah with ground walnuts but he's seen recipes that include everything from pecans with cinnamon and cocoa, to raspberry jam.

Pastry
½ cup (125 mL) cold butter
1½ cups (375 mL) all-purpose flour

1 egg yolk
½ cup (125 mL) sour cream

Filling
1 egg white
drop of pure vanilla extract

1 cup (250 mL) ground walnuts or pecans
⅓ cup (75 mL) granulated sugar

1 egg white

granulated sugar to sprinkle

1 In a food processor, combine the butter and flour. Pulse until the mixture resembles coarse crumbs.

2 In a small bowl, whisk together the egg yolk and sour cream. Add this mixture to the processor and pulse until the dough comes together. Dump the contents of the food processor out onto your work surface and gather into a ball. Wrap in plastic and refrigerate for 30 minutes.

3 Preheat the oven to 350°F (180°C).

4 For the filling, lightly beat the egg white and vanilla, then stir in the walnuts and sugar.

5 Divide the chilled dough into three pieces and roll each into a 10-inch (25-cm) circle, about ¼ inch (5 mm) thick. Spread each round with filling, right out to the edges. Cut into 12 pie-shaped wedges.

6 Starting at the wide end, roll the wedges tightly. Bend the rolls into crescent shapes and place all of them on a parchment paper–lined baking sheet, setting the cookies about 2 inches (5 cm) apart. Lightly beat the egg white and brush over the rugalah, then sprinkle lightly with granulated sugar. Bake cookies in the preheated oven for 15 minutes or until golden brown. Makes 3 dozen.

 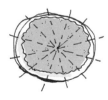 

BEER

St. Pat, Burns, and Other Celtic Guys of Note

The Guy's predilection for a good creamy stout must be a sign of the Highland Gael in his distant past—and he's always keen for a party. So what better way to celebrate (and raise a pint and a dram or two) than a mid-winter dinner devoted to one of those classic Celts of note, from patron saints like Patrick (Ireland: March 17) and Andrew (Scotland: November 30), to the bard Robbie Burns (another great Scot fêted every January 25).

Oat Cakes with Smoked Salmon

Oat cakes are a kind of savory cookie made with oatmeal. Make these for the bread basket, to pass with the soup, or serve them as an appetizer topped with a little dilled sour cream and thin slices of cold-smoked salmon.

Oat Cakes
3 cups (750 mL) quick-cooking oatmeal
½ tsp (2 mL) salt

¼ tsp (1 mL) baking soda
3 Tbsp (45 mL) melted butter
½ cup (125 mL) hot water

½ cup (125 mL) sour cream
1 green onion, minced
2 Tbsp (30 mL) minced fresh dill

salt and freshly ground black pepper
½ lb (250 g) cold-smoked salmon,
   cut in thin slices

1 To make the oat cakes, combine the oatmeal, salt, and baking soda in a medium bowl.

2 Pour in the melted butter and stir in just enough water to make a stiff dough. (Start with half of the hot water—you may have to wait a few minutes for the oats to absorb the water to accurately check the consistency before adding more.) The mixture should hold together but be stiff, not sticky.

3 Turn the dough onto a floured surface and knead quickly for 30 seconds. Roll out to ¼-inch (5-mm) thickness on a sheet of plastic wrap or parchment paper, then cut into rounds with a 3-inch (8-cm) cookie cutter or water glass.

4 Lightly grease a baking sheet and line it with parchment paper. Use a spatula to transfer the rounds to the baking sheet. Bake at 350°F (180°C) for 30 minutes or until the oat cakes begin to brown. Transfer to a rack to cool, then store in an airtight tin.

5 Meanwhile, combine the sour cream, green onion, dill, salt and pepper. Serve the crackers topped with the salmon and a dollop of the sour cream sauce. Serves 4.

Creamy Sweet Potato, Parsnip, and Caramelized Onion Soup

In the dark days of winter, there's nothing much in the cellar but onions, potatoes, and root vegetables. But never fear. The Scots have a knack for making something tasty out of the most humble ingredients (think about that famed oatmeal and offal concoction called haggis). How else do you think they can afford those pricey single malts!

¼ cup (60 mL) olive oil or butter
4 large onions, thinly sliced
2 Tbsp (30 mL) brown sugar
2 lb (1 kg) sweet potatoes, peeled and cubed
1 lb (500 g) parsnips, peeled
  and cut into chunks

8 cups (2 L) chicken stock
2 Tbsp (30 mL) whisky
1 tsp (5 mL) thyme leaves
salt and white pepper

1 Heat the oil in a large saucepan over medium-low heat. Add the onions, cover the pot, and sweat them for 10 minutes or until soft. Remove the lid, stir in the brown sugar, and sauté, stirring frequently, for 30 to 40 minutes until the onions are brown and jammy.

2 Remove ¼ cup (60 mL) of the caramelized onions and reserve for garnish.

3 Add the sweet potatoes and parsnips and cook for 5 minutes. Stir in the stock, whisky, and thyme. Bring to a boil over medium-high heat. Reduce the heat to medium-low and simmer for 20 minutes or until the vegetables are tender.

4 Remove the pot from the heat and, using a hand blender, blend until smooth (you can also pour everything into a blender or food processor to purée).

5 If you used an upright blender, return the puréed soup to the pot. Heat the soup through, over medium heat. Add more broth to thin the soup to your liking. Season with salt and white pepper to taste.

6 Serve in wide soup plates. Garnish the center of each bowl with a spoonful of the reserved caramelized onions. Serves 6 to 8.

Colcannon

This is a classic peasant dish from the Celts—a mash of potatoes, onions, parsnips, and cabbage that exceeds the sum of its parts. With the addition of a little butter and cream, it's a winter feast on its own, or perfect as a side dish with these tender braised lamb shanks.

6 medium potatoes, peeled and quartered
1 large onion, finely chopped
1 cup (250 mL) peeled and chopped parsnips, (about 2)
3 cups (750 mL) finely shredded or chopped green cabbage (about ½ of a small cabbage)

2 cups (500 mL) water
1 tsp (5 mL) salt
freshly ground black pepper
2 Tbsp (30 mL) butter
¼ cup (60 mL) whipping cream

1 In a large, heavy saucepan, layer the vegetables—half of the potatoes, onions, parsnips, and cabbage—then repeat. Add the salt to the water, and pour it overtop.

2 Cover the pan and bring to a boil over medium-high heat. Reduce the heat to low, and simmer, covered, for 1 hour.

3 Drain and use a potato masher to mash everything together to form a chunky purée. Season with pepper, and stir in the butter and cream. Serves 6.

Braised Lamb Shanks in Dark Beer

The Guy loves the meaty lamb shank—and the Scot in him loves the way you can eat like a king on a pauper's cut, if you're willing to put in the time. Just pop it in the oven on a winter afternoon and wait for the slow simmer to work its magic. The traditional colcannon (a mash of potatoes and cabbage) is another simple dish that transcends its parts and is perfect to soak up the lamb's princely sauce.

4 lb (2 kg) lamb shanks
6 cloves garlic, thinly sliced, divided
2 Tbsp (30 mL) olive oil
2 large carrots, chopped
2 stalks celery, chopped
2 large onions, halved and
  cut into half-moon slivers
1½ cups (375 mL) dark beer

1 cup (250 mL) tomato purée (use canned,
  crushed tomatoes or purée canned tomatoes
  in a blender)
1½ cups (375 mL) beef stock or water
¼ cup (60 mL) packed brown sugar
4 sprigs fresh thyme, or 1 tsp/5 mL dried
½ tsp (2 mL) coarsely ground black pepper
¼ tsp (1 mL) salt

1 Preheat oven to 275°F (140°C).

2 Trim the visible fat from the lamb. Cut slits in the lamb shanks and insert half the sliced garlic into the meat. Heat the olive oil in a Dutch oven or large heavy-bottomed pot over medium-high heat and brown the shanks on all sides. Remove the lamb from the pot and set aside.

3 Pour off any excess fat and add the chopped carrots, celery, onion, and remaining garlic to the pot. Cook until the vegetables begin to brown. Stir in the beer, scraping up any browned bits from the bottom of the pan. Add the tomato purée, stock, brown sugar, and thyme. Season with salt and pepper.

4 Return the shanks to the pot and bring to a boil.

5 Cover the pot and transfer to the oven. Braise the lamb shanks for 3 to 4 hours. Check occasionally, adding more beer or water, if necessary, to keep them submerged in the braising liquid. Remove the lid during the last 30 minutes to thicken the pan juices. When the lamb is tender and falling off the bone, it's done.

6 Using a slotted spoon, transfer some of the vegetables to a deep platter or shallow casserole dish. Place the shanks on top, cover loosely with foil and keep warm in a low oven.

7 Pour the braising liquid into a glass measuring cup and let the mixture settle for 5 minutes. Skim off the visible fat and return the liquid to the pan. Use a hand blender to purée any of the remaining vegetables into the gravy and season to taste with salt and pepper. Drizzle the meat and vegetables with the gravy and serve with colcannon or mashed potatoes on the side.
Serves 4.

Serving Single Malts

The Guy can't say enough about the joys of discovering the many nuances of real malted whisky. Go to the source in Scotland, along the River Spey, if you get the chance and taste Scotch whisky as it should be tasted.

Real Scotch whisky is only made in Scotland, so when you're buying Scotch, just make sure you're getting the real thing. Real Scotch is an artisan product, still made according to specific rules in Scotland. Single malts are made with nothing but malted barley (barley that has been sprouted then dried), yeast, and water. There are cheaper, blended Scotch whiskies on the market but they can be made almost anywhere, with any kind of bulk grain alcohol. It's still whisky, but it's nothing like a pure single malt Scotch.

Try Scotch from several parts of Scotland to discover the vast array of regional and stylistic characters. There are sweet versions, peaty ones, and aromatic Scotches aged in recycled sherry and port casks. The distinct, smoky flavor you can taste in some Scotch comes from the peat fires used to dry the malt in certain parts of Scotland. The briny character in others comes from being aged in the salty seaside air. The water, the wood, the age of the whisky, and the shape of the pot it was distilled in, all affect the style and flavor of a single malt.

Lowland malts are generally "softer" while there are all types of styles among the generally firmer Highland malts. Within the Highlands, Speyside malts are considered the most refined. Campbeltown, in the south and surrounded by the sea, is known for its briny malts, while Islay, an island nearby, makes peaty and complex malts with hints of seaweed and iodine.

The Guy always likes to keep a selection of malts on hand for guests, whether he's serving whisky to begin or end a meal.

Drink it as they do in Scotland, straight up—perhaps with a wee splash of water. A Scot would never have a dram on ice, but you might like it.

Boozy Bread Pudding with Whisky Sauce

More whisky? Why not—it's the Celtic way. The Guy likes to include booze in his cooking whenever possible, and nothing lifts an old-fashioned bread pudding into gourmet territory like this creamy caramel-colored whisky sauce. It's a good trick to haul out anytime you need to take a dessert up a notch.

6 cups (1.5 L) day-old white bread cubes
   (challah or egg bread makes a richer pudding
   but French or Italian bread works well, too)
1 cup (250 mL) raisins
½ cup (125 mL) rye or Scotch whisky
2 cups (500 mL) whole milk

1 cup (250 mL) whipping cream
4 eggs, lightly beaten
½ cup (125 mL) packed brown sugar
½ cup (125 mL) melted unsalted butter
2 tsp (10 mL) pure vanilla extract
½ tsp (2 mL) salt

Caramel Whisky Sauce
one 14-oz (398-mL) can sweetened
   condensed milk

½ cup (125 mL) whipping cream
¼ cup (60 mL) rye or scotch whisky

1 Preheat the oven to 350°F (180°C).

2 Cut the bread into ¾-inch (2-cm) cubes and place in a large bowl.

3 Combine the raisins and whisky in a bowl and microwave for 1 minute. Set aside to cool and macerate for 30 minutes.

4 In another bowl, use a whisk to combine the milk, cream, egg, sugar, butter, vanilla, and salt. Pour over the bread and stir to combine. Let the mixture rest for 10 minutes, so that the bread soaks up the custard, then stir in the raisins and whisky.

5 Pour into a buttered, 10-cup (2.5-L) baking dish. Cover and chill overnight, or bake immediately. Bake the pudding at 350°F (180°C) for 1 hour or until puffed and golden.

6 While the pudding is baking, make the sauce. In a small saucepan, boil the sweetened condensed milk with the cream over medium heat until it turns a nice caramel color. This will take about 15 minutes. Stir the mixture frequently to make sure it doesn't burn on the bottom. Remove from the heat and slowly stir in the whisky. Keep warm until ready to use.

7 Cool the pudding slightly before cutting into squares. You can also chill the pudding, cut into squares and reheat in the microwave before serving. Serve the pudding warm, drizzled with whisky sauce. Serves 8 to 10.

WISE GUY: You can switch up this pudding by adding different dried fruits (dried cranberries, blueberries, or chunks of dried apple), by using different booze (Grand Marnier with some grated orange zest; Amaretto and chopped almonds), or by tossing some chopped bittersweet or white chocolate into the mix. You can also try starting with raisin bread, grainy apricot- and nut-studded muesli bread, or a seasonal fruit bread like Italian panettone. With any variation, the soaking and baking instructions stay the same.

 # Whisky Cream Liqueur

Just a little tot to sip alongside pudding or to add to your coffee.

1 cup (250 mL) Irish whisky (or substitute rye or
   Scotch whisky)
one 14-oz (398 mL) can sweetened condensed milk
3 Tbsp (45 mL) chocolate syrup

¼ cup (60 mL) espresso (or instant espresso,
   dissolved in hot water)
3 large eggs

1 In a blender, combine all of the ingredients and blend until smooth. Pour into clean bottles and refrigerate. This will keep for up to one month in the refrigerator. Shake well before serving. Makes 3½ cups (875 mL).

He's Got Game(s)

There comes a time—perhaps for the annual finales to football/hockey/baseball seasons (or every week for the sport-obsessed)—when The Guy and the other guys get together to watch the big game. While they chew the fat over batting averages, leading rushers, or who's ahead in the hockey pool, they also like to nosh.

So the next time the guys gather for the game, earn extra points with a decent selection of snacks, and something more substantial for half time.

Yes, it's all bad for you—but who's keeping score?

Suicide Chipotle Wings

The Guy prefers to use meaty "drumettes" for his wings—the fat half of the wing—but you can also use whole wings.

5 chipotle chili peppers in adobo sauce or dried chipotle chili peppers, rehydrated in warm water

3 cloves garlic, crushed

2 Tbsp (30 mL) freshly-squeezed lime juice

½ cup (125 mL) tomato ketchup

2 Tbsp (30 mL) liquid honey or corn syrup

2 lb (1 kg) chicken wing drumettes (about 24)

1 Combine chipotles, garlic, lime juice, ketchup, and honey in a food processor and process until smooth. In a bowl or a zippered plastic bag, combine the chicken wings with the sauce. Marinate in the refrigerator from 30 minutes to 3 hours.

2 Line a baking sheet with foil (the non-stick kind is best but any will do—it makes cleaning up a lot easier). Place wings in a single layer on the sheet and bake at 375°F (190°C) for 45 minutes, turning occasionally, until both sides are nicely browned. Serves 4.

ASIAN CHILI PASTE = SAMBAL OELEK

WISE GUY: If you want your wings even hotter, spice up the marinade with hot pepper sauce (Asian garlic chili paste is The Guy's favorite pantry staple for adding heat to almost anything). To temper the heat, consider serving a dipping sauce alongside—mash a ripe avocado with some mayonnaise and season with a little salt and minced cilantro for a classic, southwestern flavor. Yum!

Crispy Wings

Marinated in hot sauce and lime juice, then breaded in cornmeal, these wings are tender and crispy at the same time—a nice contrast to the spicy, sticky wings on your party platter.

½ cup (125 mL) freshly squeezed lime juice
¼ cup (60 mL) hot pepper sauce
3 Tbsp (45 mL) olive oil, divided
2 lb (1 kg) chicken wing drumettes (about 24)
½ cup (125 mL) cornmeal

¼ cup (60 mL) all-purpose flour
1 tsp (1 mL) paprika
½ tsp (2 mL) garlic powder
½ tsp (2 mL) cumin
salt and freshly ground black pepper

1 Combine the lime juice, hot sauce, 2 Tbsp (30 mL) of the olive oil, and wings in a zippered plastic bag. Seal the bag and shake well to mix. Refrigerate from 3 to 12 hours.

2 When you're ready to bake the wings, remove them from the refrigerator and bring to room temperature. Drain the marinade and discard. Preheat the oven to 400°F (200°C) and grease a non-stick baking sheet with olive oil.

3 In another bag, combine the cornmeal, flour, paprika, garlic powder, cumin, salt, and pepper. Toss the wings in the flour mixture to coat all sides.

4 Set the wings on the greased baking sheet and bake for 10 minutes. Turn the wings over, and bake for 15 to 20 minutes longer or until they are crisp and golden. Serves 4.

Boozy BBQ Sausage Bites

Add booze to anything and it becomes a Guy thing. In this case it's a lean and smoky sausage—the kind The Guy buys from his local butcher—glazed in a whisky-laced barbecue sauce.

1 lb (500 g) lean garlic ham, elk, or bison
    sausage, available at good butchers (about
    1 sausage ring)
½ cup (125 mL) rye whisky

½ cup (125 mL) barbecue sauce
¼ cup (60 mL) maple syrup
1 tsp (5 mL) hot Asian chili paste with garlic

1 Cut the sausage into ½-inch (1-cm) slices on a slight diagonal.

2 Combine the whisky, barbecue sauce, maple syrup, and chili paste in a saucepan. Bring to a boil over medium heat. Simmer for 10 minutes to reduce and slightly thicken. Add the sausage and simmer for 5 minutes more. Adjust the flavor—adding a little more chili paste if you like it hotter—and cook until the sausage is nicely glazed. Pour everything into a deep serving dish and pass the toothpicks. Serves 8.

Buttery Popcorn

The Guy can't think of any snack food (except perhaps thick, kettle-cooked ripple chips) that can hold a candle to freshly popped corn. And I don't mean the kind that comes out of the microwave reeking of "butter flavored" topping. Real popcorn should be popped on the stove, in a little oil, and doused in real butter. That's good enough for The Guy — but you can add some grated cheese and spices for a fancier version, too.

2 to 3 Tbsp (30 to 45 mL) canola oil
½ cup (125 mL) popping corn

3 to 4 Tbsp (45 to 60 mL) butter
salt

1 In a heavy-bottomed saucepan (The Guy has his own designated popcorn pot), heat the oil and corn over medium-high heat. When the corn starts to pop, start shaking the pan.

2 At first, the popping will be slow—but soon it will be furious and fast. Lower the heat to medium-low and keep shaking the pan over the burner—this ensures the pot stays hot but the kernels don't burn. When the popping stops, immediately dump the contents of the pot into the biggest bowl you have.

3 Add some butter to the hot pan and swirl it around to melt. Drizzle the melted butter over the popped corn, flipping the bowl to toss the popcorn and distribute the butter. Do the same with the salt. Stop when it's salty and buttery enough. Eat it while it's hot. Serves 2 to 4.

WISE GUY: Add some finely grated hard cheese (like Parmesan) to the hot popcorn, or sprinkle barbecue spice or Cajun spice mix over the popped corn with the salt.

Chili Con Queso

This is one of those times when only processed cheese will do—it simply melts to the perfect consistency for dunking your favorite taco chips or drizzling over tostadas.

½ cup (125 mL) whole milk
6 oz (175 g) cream cheese
14 oz (400 g) processed cheese
   (like Velveeta), cubed
one 14-oz (398-mL) can diced tomatoes, drained
one 3 ½-oz (110-mL) can diced green chilies
3 green onions, finely chopped

½ tsp (2 mL) chili paste
½ tsp (2 mL) cumin
1 Tbsp (15 mL) chili powder
1 Tbsp (15 mL) chopped cilantro
corn tortilla chips
broccoli and cauliflower florets

1 Combine the milk and cream cheese in a double boiler and stir over simmering water until hot and melted, about 10 minutes. Add the cubes of processed cheese, stirring until melted and smooth.

2 Stir in the diced tomatoes, green chilies, green onions, chili paste, cumin, and chili powder. Simmer and stir frequently for 20 to 30 minutes.

3 Just before serving, stir in the cilantro. Keep the dip warm in a fondue pot (an electric pot or one with a solid fuel heat source). Serve with tortilla chips and vegetables for dipping, or drizzle over your Hungry Man Chili Con Carne Tostadas (see facing page). Serves 6 to 8.

WISE GUY: A tostada is like a loaded Mexican pizza—a crispy corn tortilla topped with chili, cheese sauce, shredded lettuce, tomatoes, and olives. Just fry a dozen corn tortillas in oil until crispy, set out the chili, cheese sauce, and garnishes—then let your guests create their own spicy combinations.

Hungry Man Chili Con Carne Tostadas

Make this chili the night before, then on game day put it in the slow cooker to simmer. You can serve it during the half-time show without ever leaving the couch during critical plays. Just set up the tostada buffet in the kitchen and let the guys loose to build their own meals.

1 Tbsp (15 mL) canola or olive oil

1½ lb (750 g) medium ground beef

1 large onion, chopped

2 cloves garlic, minced

½ red bell pepper, seeded and diced

1 jalapeño pepper, seeded and minced

2 Tbsp (30 mL) chili powder

1 tsp (5 mL) each cumin and paprika

½ tsp (2 mL) salt

one 14-oz (398-mL) can tomatoes, puréed in the blender

one 14-oz (398-mL) can pinto beans, rinsed and drained

½ tsp (2 mL) Asian chili paste (or more to taste)

¾ cup (175 mL) water or broth

¼ cup (60 mL) tomato paste

salt and freshly ground black pepper

For garnish chopped green onions, sliced black olives, sour cream, shredded cheddar cheese, crispy corn tortillas, or whole wheat tortillas (optional)

1 In a large sauté pan, heat the oil over medium-high heat. Fry the ground beef, breaking it up with a fork, until it begins to brown.

2 When the beef is nicely browned, drain any excess fat from the pan and add the onion, garlic, red pepper, and jalapeño pepper. Sauté for 5 minutes, then stir in the chili powder, cumin, paprika, and salt. Cook for one minute more, until the spices are fragrant, then stir in the puréed tomatoes, beans, chili paste, water, and tomato paste.

3 Bring the chili to a boil, then reduce the heat to low. Cover and simmer for 20 minutes. Remove the lid and continue to simmer until the chili is thick, about 30 minutes longer. Season with salt and pepper to taste. Add a little more chili paste if you like it hotter.

4 Transfer the chili to a slow cooker to keep it warm. When ready to serve, pass around a platter of crispy corn or whole wheat tortillas, with the garnishes, and let your guest create their own tostadas (see Wise Guy tip) or wraps. Or you can simply serve the chili on its own, without the garnishes. Serves 4 to 6.

Roughin' It
(The Backpacking, Canoe, or Ski Trip, with the Guys)

The Guy loves to head out into the great outdoors—backpacking into the mountains, canoeing a northern lake, kayaking a wild river, or cycling up a rutted trail to an isolated cabin.

Sometimes The Guy falls back on dried foods to sustain him through these excursions, the kind of dried soups and dehydrated meals you can buy at any good outdoor equipment or health-food store. It's easy to pack along bread and cheese for simple sandwiches, dried fruit and nuts, chocolate, and grainy cookies to keep the muscles pumping for a journey into the wild.

But when he's planning a major outdoor adventure with his friends, there's usually a simple division of labour (i.e. each participant is required to supply and prepare at least one major meal for the group). And depending on the destination and the conveyance (you can pack a cooler into a canoe and a fair bit of food into a bike pannier), those meals can be very simple or quite elaborate.

It's all about planning and preparation. Many soups and stews can be pre-made and frozen, then reheated at your destination. Meats can be marinated and frozen for grilling upon arrival. Dry ingredients for pancakes or spice mixtures can be pre-mixed. Wine can be transferred from heavy glass bottles into plastic ones. You can even pre-cook your sauces, double-bag them in zippered plastic freezer bags and freeze flat, creating "cooler packs" for other perishable ingredients.

Make a comprehensive list of what you need and keep it all together in one place (in the refrigerator or on the counter) the night before you leave. There's nothing worse than arriving in the middle of nowhere with a can of food and no can opener, or a meal that's missing a vital ingredient. The Guy knows—it's been done.

So, take the plunge and plan to get away on your own steam. Just remember, there's no need to suffer culinary deprivation just because you're miles away from civilization. Rough it well.

The Camp Cook

Whether you have a base camp, a rustic mountain hut, or a portable backpacker's stove, you can cook on the trail and eat well when you're out in the woods. Just make sure to pack out any garbage and keep the food stash away from marauding bears, raccoons, and other wildlife.

Make-and-Take Pancake Mix

There's a locally made wholegrain pancake mix that The Guy usually brings on camping trips, but it's easy to make your own specialty mix. Pack along a frozen box of pasteurized beaten eggs and you'll be ready to make a lot of pancakes for the guys. Just don't forget to bring a little plastic bottle of syrup.

3 cups (750 mL) all-purpose flour
3 cups (750 mL) dark flour and grains (equal parts
    whole wheat flour, oat bran, buckwheat flour,
    rye flour, rolled oats, flax, or any combination)
1 Tbsp (15 mL) salt

6 Tbsp (90 mL) baking powder
6 Tbsp (90 mL) granulated sugar
2 cups (500 mL) powdered buttermilk
    or skim milk

1 Combine all the ingredients and store the mix in portioned airtight containers (or zippered plastic bags).

2 One portion (1½ cups/375 mL) makes 8 to 10 pancakes. Make sure to write cooking instructions on the package and bring along the eggs and oil you'll need to finish the pancakes.

3 At the campsite, combine the 1½ cups (375 mL) of pancake mix with 1 cup (250 mL) of water, 1 beaten egg, and 1 Tbsp (15 mL) of oil or melted butter. Spoon the batter into a lightly oiled non-stick pan and cook the pancakes on your propane or gas stove until golden on both sides (flip the cakes when you see bubbles bursting on the top). Makes 8 to 10 pancakes.

WISE GUY: If you comes across wild blueberries or raspberries on the trail, add them to your breakfast pancakes. Just set the berries into the pancakes after you ladle the batter into the pan—this way, the berries will stay whole and won't bleed into the batter.

BLUE-BERRIES

WISE GUY: Substitute any chopped nuts for the pecans in the Great Granola recipe. If you can't find dried cranberries or blueberries, substitute currants, dried cherries, or dried mango bits.

Great Granola

So you're a crunchy granola guy—what of it? This great granola makes an instant gourmet breakfast when you're out backpacking, and is an impressive alternative to the usual boxes of commercial cereal. Bake up a bunch—it will keep in the cupboard for several weeks and for several months in the freezer. On the trail, enjoy your granola for breakfast with skim milk or yogurt, or munch it as a snack straight up.

8 cups (2 L) rolled oats
2 cups (500 mL) wheat germ
2 cups (500 mL) unsweetened
  shredded coconut
1 cup (250 mL) chopped pecans
1 cup (250 mL) slivered almonds
2 cups (500 mL) shelled, raw sunflower seeds
½ cup (125 mL) sesame seeds
½ cup (125 mL) flaxseeds or milled flax
1 cup (250 mL) canola oil

1 cup (250 mL) honey
1 tsp (5 mL) salt
2 tsp (10 mL) ground cinnamon
1 tsp (5 mL) freshly grated nutmeg
1 Tbsp (15 mL) pure vanilla extract
2 cups (500 mL) raisins, dried cranberries,
  or blueberries
2 cups (500 mL) chopped dried apricots
3 oranges (preferably organic)

1 Preheat the oven to 300°F (150°C).

2 In a large bowl, combine the oats, wheat germ, coconut, pecans, almonds, sunflower seeds, sesame seeds, and flaxseeds.

3 In a small saucepan over medium-high heat, bring the oil, honey, salt, cinnamon, nutmeg, and vanilla almost to the boiling point. Remove from the heat and drizzle over the dry ingredients. Mix well.

4 Spread the granola in a single layer over one or two large baking sheets. Bake in the preheated oven for 30 to 45 minutes, stirring often to prevent it from burning, until the granola is nicely browned. Remove from oven and let cool.

5 Scrub the oranges and remove the zest using a zesting tool or a microplane grater (the finer the better, but make sure not to grate any of the bitter white pith).

6 Stir the dried fruits and orange zest into the cooled granola mixture. Store in a large covered jar in a cool place. Serve with milk or yogurt. Makes a bunch (a huge 17-cup/4-L container full of healthy breakfast cereal).

Campfire Seafood Bake

Here's a classy meal to make the first night out on the trail (or to celebrate when you've arrived at an isolated cabin). If the seafood is frozen when you leave, it will be nicely thawed and ready to steam on the open fire. Now's the time to pour that Sauvignon Blanc you hauled in.

four 18-inch (45-cm) squares of heavy
   aluminum foil
16 small new red potatoes, halved or quartered
1 large onion, thinly sliced
2 to 3 ears of fresh corn, cut into 2-inch
   (5-cm) pieces
16 whole live mussels, scrubbed and debearded

16 large shrimp, peeled and deveined
2 Tbsp (30 mL) chopped fresh parsley
salt and freshly ground black pepper
½ cup (125 mL) white wine
¼ cup (60mL) butter
baguette and extra butter for spreading

1 Place the squares of foil on your work surface. Divide the potatoes, onion slices, corn, mussels, and shrimp evenly among the packages.

2 Season with chopped parsley, salt, and pepper. Pull up the sides to partially enclose the ingredients. Add 2 Tbsp (30 mL) of wine and 1 Tbsp (15 mL) of butter to each package. Tightly fold the seams to seal the packages well.

3 Build a fire and when the flames have died down and the coals are glowing, set a grill over the coals and place the packages on the grill. Cook for 20 minutes or until the vegetables are lightly steamed and the seafood is cooked (the mussels will open and the shrimp will be pink).

4 Place the packages into bowls to serve. Open carefully to release steam and serve with a crusty baguette and butter on the side. Serves 4.

STRawBerries

WISE GUY:

Fresh strawberries, blueberries, and peaches, marinated with a bit of brandy and sugar (do this at home), and served with a dollop of sweetened sour cream and store-bought pound cake or cookies, make an elegant Day One dessert on the trail.

Bannock

On the trail, bannock is the best bread. If you don't want to haul in a frying pan, leave the oil at home and roll this bread into ropes, wind it around a green branch, and cook it over the campfire until golden brown.

2 cups (500 mL) all-purpose flour
1 tsp (5 mL) salt
½ tsp (2 mL) baking powder

⅔ cup (150 mL) warm water
¼ cup (60 mL) olive oil

1 Combine the flour, salt, and baking powder in a zippered plastic bag. Label with recipe.

2 At camp, add the water to the plastic bag and knead in the bag to combine the ingredients and form a stiff dough. Let it sit for an hour to relax the gluten, and then knead again for a minute or two.

3 Heat a pan until hot, then add the oil. Form the dough into 4 rounds and pat until as thin as possible. Fry the rounds, one at a time, in the oiled pan about 2 minutes per side, or until lightly browned. Serve the warm bannock with savory dishes or sprinkle it with sugar and cinnamon. Serves 2 to 4.

Rules of the Back Roads

When you're exerting yourself you need a snack every 60 to 90 minutes—whether you're skiing, biking, or backpacking. But don't rely on junk food to keep you going. You want high quality snacks, whole foods such as nuts and dried fruit, wholegrains, and vegetables. The oldest, densest cheeses have the most protein, so pack along aged cheddar, Parmesan, Romano, or Asiago cheese. Take something salty along, whether it's pretzels, sesame sticks, or corn nuts.

GORP (Good Old Raisins and Peanuts) is the classic snack mix, but you can beef it up with whatever fruit and nuts you like, plus some chocolate chips or yogurt-covered raisins. Make your own savory snack mixes and bring high-energy spreads like nut butters, bean dip, and hummus or a portable protein like jerky or dried salami.

Plan for sturdy carbs—heavy breads, bagels, pita breads, and rye crispbreads—which can survive in your pack. Pack more fragile crackers or cookies in plastic containers or clean milk cartons to prevent breakage. Flour tortillas make excellent wraps for lunches or roll them with spreads into pinwheels for easy appetizers.

How many calories you'll need each day depends on several factors—your body weight, the weight of your pack, and the terrain you're hiking or skiing—but a 155-lb (70.5-kg) male will need at least 4,000 calories a day. Sports nutritionists agree that the kind of calories you consume are important, too. Sixty to 70 percent of those calories should come from complex carbohydrates, 10 to 15 percent from proteins, and 20 to 25 percent from fats. Remember, your body uses carbs to produce glycogen, the fuel that muscles draw upon to keep going hour after hour, so this is no time to skimp.

Fireside Fondue

Fondue may well be the best thing to enjoy around a roaring fire—whether it's in the woods or the living room. Buy a sealed pouch of pre-mixed fondue, and freeze it before you head out, or make the fondue from scratch and seal it in a zippered plastic bag to heat over your single-burner camp stove. Fondue is definitely the best reason to haul a baguette and a box of wine up the trail—and makes perfect sense when there's only one burner to cook dinner.

2 cups (500 mL) grated Gruyère cheese
2 cups (500 mL) grated Emmenthal cheese
1 Tbsp (15 mL) cornstarch
pinch of grated nutmeg
pinch of granulated garlic
½ cup (125 mL) white wine

splash of brandy or Kirsch
  (if anyone's carrying it)
crusty loaf of French or Italian bread,
  cut into cubes
lightly steamed broccoli, asparagus,
  or cauliflower

1 At home, combine the grated cheeses, cornstarch, nutmeg, and garlic. Toss to combine. Seal in a zippered plastic bag. Chill or freeze.

2 At camp, heat the wine in a pot over medium high heat until it just begins to boil. Gradually add the cheese mixture, a handful at a time, stirring until melted and smooth. Add the brandy and gently heat, but don't boil. Keep the fondue warm over very low heat on the stove or on the edge of the campfire while you dip the bread cubes and vegetables. Pickles or olives are good on the side. Serves 4.

WISE GUY: You can make this more substantial by stirring in a can of crabmeat. Or create a more casual dip by substituting cheddar and mozzarella cheeses, then adding canned green chilies, and serving tortilla chips or cubes of cornbread for dunking.

Fasta Pasta

This is a pasta dish created almost completely from jars and cans—pack the ingredients and a single-burner stove in your backpack and you've got a glorious gourmet meal in the wilderness. Or toss this together for a speedy supper when you're back at the ranch. Even when it seems like the cupboard is bare, you can still feast on this speedy pantry pasta.

For an easy vegetarian version, replace the meat with canned white beans or chickpeas.

¼ cup (60 mL) extra virgin olive oil

6 oz (175 g) slivered, cooked ham
　　or smoked turkey

3 cloves garlic, minced

¾ cup (175 mL) chopped sun-dried tomatoes in oil

¾ cup (175 mL) pitted and chopped black olives (a tasty kind like niçoise or kalamata)

one 14-oz (398-mL) can artichoke hearts, drained and chopped

1 to 2 crushed dried red chilies

1 lb (500 g) short pasta (gemelli, rotini, penne, etc.)

2 Tbsp (30 mL) basil pesto
　　or chopped fresh basil

½ lb (250 g) crumbled goat cheese
　　or feta cheese

salt and freshly ground black pepper

1 In a large sauté pan, heat the oil over medium-high heat. Add the ham and garlic to the pan and cook for 2 minutes, or just until the garlic sizzles. Add the sun-dried tomatoes, olives, artichokes, and chilies. Heat through. Reduce the heat to low and keep warm. Meanwhile, bring a very large pot of salted water to a boil. Add the pasta and cook until al dente, about 8 to 10 minutes for most short pasta.

2 When the pasta is cooked, drain, then return to the pot. Add the contents of the sauté pan and toss with the pasta. Stir in the pesto. Crumble the cheese overtop and toss until the cheese just begins to melt. Serve immediately. Serves 4.

Instant Noodle Salad

This is an instant salad that doesn't require cooking—one of those hiker recipes that sounds weird but actually tastes pretty good. Make it the night before you plan to eat it or mix it up in a zippered plastic bag in the morning and carry it in your backpack until you stop for supper. If you have any leftover cooked chicken or pork, just pile it on top.

Dressing

2 Tbsp (30 mL) rice wine vinegar
2 Tbsp (30 mL) liquid honey
1 Tbsp (15 mL) soy sauce
½ tsp (2 mL) Asian chili sauce

2 Tbsp (30 mL) canola oil (or half canola and
   half sesame oil)
1 Tbsp (15 mL) chopped cilantro, or 1 tsp (5 mL)
   coriander chutney (optional)

Salad

1 package ramen noodles, broken apart
2 cups (500 mL) finely shredded cabbage or
   supermarket coleslaw mix

2 green onions, thinly sliced
1 carrot, coarsely shredded
2 Tbsp (30 mL) chopped dry-roasted peanuts

1 Combine all of the dressing ingredients in a jar and shake to emulsify.

2 In a medium salad bowl, combine the noodles, cabbage, green onions, carrot, and dressing. Toss, cover with plastic wrap or a lid, and keep in the cooler overnight (or mix it up in a zippered plastic bag and carry it in a cool part of your pack until suppertime).

3 Serve the noodles with chopped peanuts sprinkled on top. Serves 2 to 4.

Banana's Forester

When in the wild, improvise dessert with what's on hand. This works when you have a banana or two, some chocolate chips in your GORP (good old raisins and peanuts) or a chocolate bar, and a piece of tin foil.

2 bananas, in the skin
butter
rum or whisky (whatever you've put in the flask)

brown sugar
chocolate chips or dark chocolate bar chunks
heavy tin foil

1 Using a sharp knife, cut a slit lengthwise into the inside curve of the bananas, through the skin and flesh, being careful not to pierce through the other side. Press the ends of the bananas inwards lightly to spread the cut open, forming a space for filling.

2 Set the bananas on pieces of heavy foil. Fill the openings with a bit of butter, brown sugar, and a splash of rum or whisky. Top with as many chocolate chips as you can find in the GORP (or use some broken up chunks of dark chocolate bar).

3 Wrap the bananas in foil and heat on the fire (directly over coals or on the grill) until hot and gooey. Eat directly from the foil package. Serves 2.

Portable Lunches and Trail Snacks

Oatmeal Poppy Seed Squares

These squares are the perfect breakfast bar, whether you're bushwhacking through the woods or jostling among the throngs of morning rush-hour commuters. Usually parchment paper is used to line baking sheets, but in this case it goes right into the bottom and up the sides of a baking pan to make removing these bars easy. To make these squares even healthier, substitute canola oil for the melted butter.

½ cup (125 mL) butter, melted
2 large eggs
¼ cup (60 mL) liquid honey
1 tsp (5 mL) pure vanilla extract
¼ cup (60 mL) milk
1 cup (250 mL) all-purpose flour
¾ cup (175 mL) rolled oats
1 tsp (5 mL) baking powder

¼ tsp (1 mL) baking soda
1 cup (250 mL) packed brown sugar
½ tsp (2 mL) salt
½ cup (125 mL) unsweetened shredded
  coconut
½ cup (125 mL) poppy seeds
½ cup (125 mL) sliced almonds

1 Preheat the oven to 350°F (180°C).

2 In a bowl, combine the butter, eggs, honey, vanilla, and milk. Beat lightly with an electric mixer.

3 In another bowl, combine the flour, oats, baking powder, baking soda, sugar, and salt.

4 Add the dry ingredients to the batter and beat for 3 to 4 minutes. Fold in the coconut, poppy seeds, and sliced almonds. Stir well.

5 Line the base and sides of a 9- x 13-inch (3.5-L) baking pan with parchment paper. Pour the batter into the pan and use a spatula to spread the batter evenly and smoothly. Bake in the preheated oven for 25 to 30 minutes or until the top is a deep brown color and springs back when lightly pressed.

6 Set the pan on a rack to cool for 10 minutes before scoring into 24 squares. Cool completely and cut into squares. Makes 24.

The Guy's Turkey Jerky

The Guy recently discovered turkey jerky at the local butcher. Turkey provides a lean protein for your trip—you can make this with lean beef, too.

2 lb (1 kg) skinless turkey breast, slightly frozen

Marinade
1 tsp (5 mL) salt
1 tsp (5 mL) pepper
2 Tbsp (30 mL) brown sugar
2 Tbsp (30 mL) Worcestershire sauce

¼ cup (60 mL) soy sauce
1 tsp (5 mL) liquid smoke
1 tsp (5 mL) lemon pepper
½ tsp (2 mL) dried granulated garlic

1 Using a very sharp knife, cut the turkey across the grain into very thin slices.

2 Combine the marinade ingredients in a zippered plastic bag and shake to combine. Add the sliced turkey, seal, and marinate in the refrigerator for 2 hours.

3 Set racks over a baking sheet and lay the marinated turkey slices across the racks in a single layer. Bake at 150°F (65°C) for 10 hours (or use a dehydrator) until the meat is dry and chewy, but not brittle. Seal in a bag to take on the trail. Makes 8 servings.

The Best Peanut Butter Cookies

The Guy has a bit of an addiction to peanut butter. A peanut butter sandwich may well be his favorite snack and, when it comes to cookies, these crunchy oatmeal-and-peanut butter gems are a close second. Always buy crunchy natural peanut butter with no added sugars or fats.

1½ cups (375 mL) rolled oats
1 cup (250 mL) whole wheat flour
½ tsp (2 mL) baking powder
½ tsp (2 mL) baking soda
½ tsp (2 mL) salt
½ cup (125 mL) softened butter

6 Tbsp (90 mL) crunchy peanut butter
1 cup (250 mL) packed brown sugar
½ cup (125 mL) granulated sugar
1 large egg
2 Tbsp (30 mL) water
½ tsp (2 mL) pure vanilla extract

1 Preheat the oven to 350°F (180°C). Combine the oats, flour, baking powder, baking soda, and salt. Set aside.

2 In a large bowl, cream together the butter, peanut butter, and both sugars, by hand or using an electric mixer. Beat in the egg, water, and vanilla.

3 Gradually add the dry ingredients to the creamed mixture, stirring until well mixed.

4 Drop batter by heaping 1-Tbsp (15-mL) balls onto greased or parchment-lined cookie sheets, about 2 inches (5 cm) apart. Bake for 12 minutes. Makes 3 dozen.

COOKIES & BARS

Mountain Man Cookies

This is The Guy's version of that monster coffee shop cookie that, with a steamy latte, has sustained him on many a morning. Chock-full of good things like rolled oats, nuts, and seeds, and as big as a bear claw, these are truly cookies for the mountain man.

2 cups (500 mL) butter, softened
2 cups (500 mL) packed brown sugar
4 large eggs
¾ cup (175 mL) plain yogurt (or use buttermilk)
2 cups (500 mL) all-purpose flour
2 cups (500 mL) whole-wheat flour
½ cup (125 mL) wheat bran

1 Tbsp (15 mL) baking powder
2 tsp (10 mL) baking soda
4 cups (1 L) rolled oats
¾ cup (175 mL) chocolate chips
¾ cup (175 mL) sunflower seeds
¾ cup (175 mL) sliced almonds

1 Preheat the oven to 350°F (180°C).

2 In a large bowl, use an electric mixer to beat the butter and sugar for 5 minutes or until fluffy. Add the eggs, one at a time, then add the yogurt and continue beating until combined.

3 In another bowl, combine both of the flours with the wheat bran, baking powder, baking soda, and rolled oats.

4 Use a wooden spoon to stir the flour mixture into the batter. Mix until well incorporated. Stir in the chocolate chips, sunflower seeds, and almonds. The batter will be quite stiff.

5 Rub a heavy baking sheet with butter or oil and line with parchment paper. Spoon mounds of batter (3 to 4 Tbsp/45 to 60 mL per cookie) onto the sheet. Leave 3 inches (8 cm) between cookie batter (it will spread as it bakes). Flatten the mounds slightly with the back of a spoon and bake for 15 to 18 minutes or until the tops are golden brown. Makes 3 dozen large cookies.

Calzones

Calzones are The Guy's secret weapon for all outings. These pockets of Italian flavor make great lunches. Bake a bunch, freeze, then grab and go—they'll be thawed by noon. Vary the filling according to what you like—carnivores can augment this vegetarian filling with chopped cooked chicken, Italian sausage, prosciutto slices, or salami.

Calzones make great portable lunches for hiking or cycling because they don't get squished in your pack.

1 large onion, halved lengthwise
    and thinly sliced
1 Tbsp (15 mL) olive oil
1 large red pepper, seeded and slivered
1 small chili pepper, minced
3 cloves garlic, minced
2 Tbsp (30 mL) chopped fresh basil
1 tsp (5 mL) dried oregano
salt and freshly ground black pepper
6 sun-dried tomatoes, soaked in warm water
    to rehydrate, then drained and chopped

2 oz (50 g) crumbled feta or shredded
    Parmesan cheese
1 cup (250 mL) 1% cottage cheese or ricotta
½ cup (125 mL) shredded mozzarella
    or three-cheese Italian mix
one 14-oz (398-mL) can artichoke hearts,
    drained and chopped
⅓ cup (75 mL) pitted, chopped black olives
2 loaves frozen whole wheat bread dough,
    thawed

1 Heat the olive oil in a non-stick pan over medium-low heat. Slowly cook the onions until caramelized and golden brown, about 30 minutes.

2 Add the red pepper and chili pepper. Cook for 5 minutes or until tender. Stir in the garlic and cook 3 minutes longer. Remove the pan from the heat and stir in the basil, oregano, salt, pepper, and sun-dried tomatoes. Set aside to cool slightly, then stir in the feta, cottage cheese, mozzarella, artichokes, and olives.

3 Preheat the oven to 400°F (200°C). Cut each bread dough loaf into 6 equal pieces. On a floured board, roll each piece into a 5-inch (12-cm) circle. Wet the edges of each and fill with 3 Tbsp (45 mL) of filling. Fold in half, forming a pocket, and press the edges together well to seal. Brush the calzones with milk and poke each with a fork to allow steam to escape during baking.

4 Brush a baking sheet lightly with oil, then sprinkle with cornmeal. Arrange the calzones on the sheet and bake for 20 minutes or until browned. Cool on a rack. Serve warm or at room temperature. Alternately, you can freeze calzones—just thaw and reheat briefly in the oven or microwave to serve warm. Makes 1 dozen calzones.

WISE GUY: Here are some other ideas for creative calzone fillings:

● cooked Italian sausage, asiago cheese, and chopped broccoli rabe (rapini) sautéed with olive oil and red pepper flakes

● lightly sautéed and drained spinach, chopped fresh dill, caramelized onion, feta cheese, and toasted pine nuts

● grilled eggplant and zucchini (brushed with olive oil and pesto), chopped sun-dried tomatoes in oil, roasted peppers, pesto, and creamy goat cheese

● eggs scrambled with sausage meat or chopped bacon, shredded cheese, and hash browns fried with onions and red peppers

● ground beef or chopped eggplant sautéed with chopped mushrooms, garlic, and onions, then mixed with grated cheddar and seasoned with fresh dill

Crispy Chocolate Cranberry Granola Bars

These easy no-bake bars are reminiscent of store-bought cereal bars, but with the goodness of ground flax-seed and oats. Wrap individually in plastic wrap for carrying on the trail.

4 cups (1 L) crisp rice cereal
½ cup (125 mL) rolled oats or barley
¼ cup (60 mL) ground flaxseed
½ cup (125 mL) chocolate chips
½ cup (125 mL) dried cranberries

½ cup (125 mL) corn syrup
½ cup (125 mL) packed brown sugar
1 tsp (5 mL) pure vanilla extract
2 Tbsp (25 mL) cocoa powder
¼ cup (60 mL) canola oil

1 In a large bowl, combine the cereal, oats, flaxseed, chocolate chips, and cranberries.

2 In a saucepan, heat the corn syrup and brown sugar over medium heat for 5 to 10 minutes, stirring until the sugar dissolves. Stir in the vanilla, cocoa, and oil. Pour this mixture over the dry ingredients and mix gently to combine.

3 Use your hands or a big spoon to press the mixture firmly into a lightly oiled 9- x 13-inch (3.5-L) pan, then chill. Cut into bars and serve from the pan, or wrap individually in plastic for the backpack. Makes 16 bars.

Peanut Butter Granola Bars

These classic granola bars actually get better after a couple of days—wrap them individually in plastic and keep them at the ready for carrying into the great outdoors.

1½ cups (375 mL) old-fashioned rolled oats
1½ (375 mL) cups all-purpose flour
2 tsp (10 mL) baking powder
1 tsp (5 mL) cinnamon
1 tsp (5 mL) ground ginger
½ tsp (2 mL) salt
½ cup (125 mL) chopped dried apricots
½ cup (125 mL) raisins
½ cup (125 mL) chopped pecans

½ cup (125 mL) shredded coconut
¼ cup (60 mL) toasted sunflower seeds
½ cup (125 mL) butter, softened
½ cup (125 mL) crunchy peanut butter
½ cup (125 mL) packed brown sugar
2 eggs
½ cup (125 mL) light molasses
2 tsp (10 mL) vanilla extract

1 In a large bowl, combine the oats, flour, baking powder, cinnamon, ginger, and salt. Add the apricots, raisins, pecans, coconut, and sunflower seeds. Stir to blend.

2 In another large bowl, cream the butter, peanut butter, and brown sugar with an electric mixer until light and fluffy. Add the eggs, one at a time, beating well after each addition. Beat in the molasses and vanilla until blended.

3 Gradually add dry ingredients, stirring with a wooden spoon, until thoroughly blended.

4 Evenly press the mixture into a lightly buttered 13- x 9-inch (3.5-L) baking pan. Preheat the oven to 350°F (180°C). Bake for 35 to 40 minutes, or until the edges just begin to pull away from side of pan. Cool on wire rack before cutting into bars. Makes 24 bars.

Après Outdoors

These are the one-dish wonders The Guy likes to feed the gang
after any outdoor pursuit—just pop into the oven, toss a salad,
slice a loaf of bread, and set up the buffet. All of these dishes
taste even better when made a day in advance and reheated.

Canadian Cassoulet

The Guy loves to come home on a chilly day to something bubbling in the oven—you can make this dish up to two days ahead, or use the slow cooker and simmer everything all day long, then finish it in the oven. With a green salad and a slice of crusty sourdough on the side, this Canadian-ized version of a classic French cassoulet—complete with back bacon, whisky, and maple syrup—makes for the ultimate après-ski feast when you've been playing in Rocky Mountain powder.

Beans

2 cups (500 mL) dried Flageolet or other small
    white beans
¼ lb (125 g) Canadian back bacon, chopped

6 whole cloves garlic, peeled
2 bay leaves
2 sprigs thyme

Sauce

one 2-lb (1-kg) boneless shoulder of pork (or
    shoulder chops)
2 Tbsp (30 mL) olive oil
1 lb (500 g) fresh Italian pork sausage with fennel
3 carrots, chopped
2 cups (500 mL) chopped onion
2 stalks celery, diced
2 cloves garlic, minced

½ cup (125 mL) rye whisky
1 cup (250 mL) chicken stock
one 14-oz (398-mL) can tomatoes, whirled in a
    blender to purée
¼ cup (60 mL) maple syrup
2 Tbsp (30 mL) chopped fresh rosemary, or
    2 tsp (10 mL) dried
salt and freshly ground black pepper

Topping

1 cup (250 mL) dry breadcrumbs
3 Tbsp (45 mL) olive oil

2 Tbsp (30 mL) chopped fresh parsley
2 cloves garlic, minced or pressed
salt and freshly ground black pepper

1 Place the beans in a large pot and generously cover with cold water. Soak overnight. To speed up this step, bring the beans and water to a full boil, cover, remove from the heat and let them sit for 1 hour before cooking.

2 Drain the soaked beans and return to the pot. Cover with 8 cups (2 L) of water. Add the bacon, garlic, bay leaves, and thyme. Bring to a boil. Cover, reduce the heat to low, and simmer until tender, about 1 to 2 hours, depending on the age of your beans.

3 Meanwhile, cut the pork into large 2- to 3-inch (5- to 8-cm) pieces, removing any visible fat. In a Dutch oven or large heavy-bottomed pot, heat the olive oil over medium-high heat and brown the pork pieces. Remove the pieces and set aside. In the same pot, brown the sausages. Remove the sausages, slice, and set aside with the pork. Add the carrots, onions, celery, and minced garlic to the pot and sauté until soft, about 5 minutes. Pour in the whisky, stirring up any browned bits stuck to the bottom of the pot, and bring to a boil. Continue boiling for 5 minutes or until liquid has reduced to half. Add the stock, puréed tomatoes, maple syrup, and rosemary. Bring to a boil. Return the browned pork and sausage to the pot, then season with salt and pepper. Cover, reduce the heat to low, and simmer for 1 hour or until the meat is tender.

4 Drain the beans, retaining their cooking liquid in a separate bowl, and discard the herbs and bay leaves. To assemble the cassoulet, layer the cooked beans and meat sauce in a deep earthenware casserole dish or heavy enameled roasting pan. Start with ⅓ of the beans and ½ of the sauce, then repeat, ending with a layer of beans. Add enough of the reserved bean liquid to the dish so you can just begin to see it through the top layer of beans (if making ahead, the dish can be prepared to this point, covered, and refrigerated for up to 2 days).

5 To finish, combine the topping ingredients and sprinkle evenly over the cassoulet. Bake in a 350°F (180°C) oven for 1 hour or until bubbly and nicely browned. Serves 8 to 10.

Braised Lamb with Chickpeas and Couscous

Like many braised dishes, this one is even better the second day, once the flavors are well married. So make it the night before you go skiing or cycling, and reheat it for your friends when you return from your exploits. The couscous is ready in 10 minutes. Toss a salad to serve alongside, and you're done!

¼ cup (60 mL) all-purpose flour
salt and freshly ground black pepper
4 lb (2 kg) lamb shoulder, fat trimmed,
    cut into large cubes
¼ cup (60 mL) olive oil
2 large onions, thinly sliced
2 cloves garlic, minced
¼ cup (60 mL) tomato paste

2 cups (500 mL) chicken stock or water
½ cup (125 mL) white wine
1 tsp (5 mL) ground coriander
1 tsp (5 mL) cumin
1 tsp (5 mL) cinnamon
1 tsp (5 mL) Asian chili paste
1 small whole orange, quartered
1 Tbsp (15 mL) brown sugar

recipe continued on next page

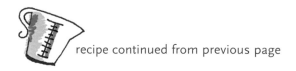recipe continued from previous page

one 19-oz (540-mL) can chickpeas,
   rinsed and drained
½ cup (125 mL) dried currants

¼ cup (60 mL) chopped parsley or cilantro
handful of grape tomatoes, halved

Couscous
2 cups (500 mL) couscous
3 cups (750 mL) chicken stock

1 Preheat the oven to 325°F (160°C).

2 Combine the flour, salt, and pepper. Dust this flour mixture over the lamb cubes to coat.

3 Heat the olive oil over medium heat in a Dutch oven (or other heavy ovenproof pot). When the oil is hot, add the lamb, a few pieces at a time, and brown quickly on all sides. Set the browned meat aside as you finish browning the remaining lamb, adding more oil to the pot if necessary.

4 Add the sliced onions to the pan and sauté for 5 minutes, until soft and starting to brown. Add the garlic, tomato paste, stock, wine, coriander, cumin, cinnamon, chili paste, orange quarters, and brown sugar. Stir to combine. Return the meat to the pan and bring to a boil. Cover, transfer to the oven, and braise for 2 hours or until the meat is tender. Remove the orange pieces from the pot and discard. Stir in the chickpeas, cover, and return to the oven for another hour.

5 To make the couscous, bring the stock to a boil over high heat. Stir in the couscous, remove the pot from the heat, and let stand, covered, for 10 minutes. Fluff the cooked couscous with a fork, then spoon onto a platter. Pour the lamb stew over the couscous and garnish with chopped parsley or cilantro and grape tomatoes. Serves 6.

Pork Goulash

The Guy loves using pork in stews like this—it's inexpensive and incredibly tender. Always keep dried porcini mushrooms in the pantry to add to your soups and stews. Goulash is a great dish to make ahead, but if you do, remember to stop before adding the sour cream and noodles. Instead, freeze the meat mixture and finish the goulash at the cabin or ski chalet.

½ cup (125 mL) crumbled dried porcini
   mushrooms
1½ lb (750 g) pork shoulder
   (or shoulder steaks)
1 Tbsp (15 mL) olive oil
2 medium onions, thinly sliced
2 large cloves garlic, minced
2 medium bell peppers, seeded and slivered
¾ cup (175 mL) white wine

one 7 ½-oz (213-mL) can tomato sauce
1½ tsp (7 mL) sweet Spanish paprika
salt and freshly ground black pepper
2 Tbsp (30 mL) flour
⅓ cup (75 mL) light (low-fat) sour cream
½ lb (250 g) cooked wide egg noodles or
   polenta or mashed potatoes
2 to 3 Tbsp (30 to 45 mL) chopped parsley

1 Put the dried mushrooms in a bowl, cover with boiling water, and soak for 10 minutes to soften. Drain.

2 Remove as much fat as possible from the pork shoulder, then cut the meat into bite-sized strips or cubes. Heat the olive oil in a Dutch oven or large heavy-bottomed pot over medium-high heat until almost smoking. Add the pork and sauté for 10 minutes until browned on all sides. Add the onions to the pot and continue to cook, stirring, until the onions begin to brown. Add the garlic and peppers and sauté for 5 minutes longer. Add the wine, stirring up any browned bits, then add the tomato sauce, paprika, and soaked mushrooms. Bring the mixture to a boil, then reduce the heat to low. Cover and simmer for 45 minutes, or until the pork is very tender. (At this point you can cool the goulash and chill it overnight or even freeze it for finishing another day.)

3 In a small bowl, combine the flour and sour cream. Heat the stew to a low boil, and whisk the sour cream mixture into the simmering sauce. Continue to simmer for another 10 minutes, over medium-low heat, until the sauce is thick enough to coat the back of a spoon.

4 Meanwhile, cook the egg noodles in boiling water until al dente (cooked but still a little firm to the bite), about 8 to 10 minutes. Drain well and combine the cooked noodles with the stew. Stir in the fresh parsley and season to taste. Serves 4.

Lamb Moussaka

The classic Greek casserole of layered eggplant, potatoes, and meat sauce is the perfect one-dish meal—whether you're serving a gang of hungry skiers or heading off to a potluck party. Topped with a layer of creamy béchamel sauce and shot through with salty sheep feta cheese—it's highly addictive.

2 large eggplants (the fat, dark purple kind),
   sliced into ¼-inch (5-mm) rounds
2 large red potatoes, peeled and thinly sliced
½ cup (125 mL) olive oil, divided
¾ lb (375 g) lean ground lamb
   (or substitute lean ground beef)
1 large onion, minced
3 to 4 cloves garlic, minced
1 medium red bell pepper, seeded and minced
1 carrot, peeled and shredded

one 28-oz (796-mL) can chopped tomatoes
   with juice
2 Tbsp (30 mL) tomato paste
⅓ cup (75 mL) dry white wine
1 bay leaf
1 tsp (5 mL) dried oregano
¼ tsp (1 mL) ground cinnamon
¼ tsp (1 mL) brown sugar
salt and freshly ground black pepper

The Béchamel
3 Tbsp (45 mL) butter
3 Tbsp (45 mL) all-purpose flour
1¼ cups (310 mL) milk

pinch of nutmeg
2 eggs, beaten
2 cups (500 mL) crumbled sheep-milk feta, divided

1 Place the eggplant rounds in a colander and salt each piece. Set in the sink to drain and leach the bitter juices for 30 minutes. When fully drained, rinse with water and pat the slices dry with paper towels.

2 Preheat the oven to 450°F (230°C). Lightly brush two non-stick baking sheets with olive oil. Arrange the sliced eggplant in a single layer (overlapping slightly if necessary) on one sheet, and the sliced potatoes on the other sheet. Lightly drizzle the potato and eggplant slices with 2 to 3 Tbsp (30 to 45 mL) of olive oil, then season with salt and pepper to taste. Bake the eggplant and potatoes for 10 to 15 minutes or until they begin to brown. Remove from the oven and cool.

3 Reduce the oven temperature to 350°F (180°C).

4 To make the meat sauce, heat 2 Tbsp (30 mL) of olive oil in a large sauté pan over medium-high heat and crumble in the ground lamb. Cook, stirring, for 10 minutes, until the meat is nicely browned. This is an important step—the brown, caramelized bits add extra flavor to the finished dish. Add the onion, garlic, bell pepper, and carrot to the pan, with a little more olive oil, and sauté for 5 minutes or until the vegetables are tender and fragrant.

5 Stir in the chopped tomatoes, tomato paste, wine, bay leaf, oregano, cinnamon, and brown sugar. Bring to a boil, then reduce the heat to low and simmer for 20 minutes, until the sauce has reduced substantially and is very thick. Set aside to cool.

6 To make the béchamel, in a saucepan, melt the butter over medium heat, and whisk in the flour. Cook for 1 minute before slowly whisking in the milk. Keep whisking until the mixture begins to bubble. Season with the nutmeg and continue to cook, stirring, for 2 minutes or until the sauce is nicely thickened. Remove the pan from the heat and whisk for 2 to 3 minutes to cool the sauce slightly. Add the eggs, one at a time, and whisk to incorporate. Stir in 1 cup (250 mL) of the feta cheese.

7 To assemble the moussaka, lightly coat a 9- x 13-inch (3.5-L) baking dish with olive oil.

8 Arrange the potatoes in the bottom of the dish. Top with ¼ cup (60 mL) of the remaining feta cheese. Layer with ⅓ of the eggplant—overlapping the slices to fill the pan. Add ⅓ of the meat sauce and sprinkle with ¼ cup (60 mL) of feta. Repeat layers—eggplant, sauce, and feta—twice more to use up the ingredients. Pour the béchamel sauce over the casserole, smoothing with a spatula to evenly cover. Bake in the preheated oven for 50 to 60 minutes or until it's bubbly and golden. Let the moussaka rest for 20 minutes before cutting. Serves 6 to 8.

EGGPLANT

Chicken and Sausage Jambalaya

You can get everything ready, right up until you add the rice, and finish this dish when you get back to your kitchen after a day in the great outdoors. The Guy has even been known to freeze the cooked sauce, pack along the rice, and cook his jambalaya at a rustic hostel in the woods. This makes a nice, spicy, one-pot meal to warm you to your toes.

1 medium onion, chopped

1 large red bell pepper, seeded and chopped

¼ cup (60 mL) canola oil

2 lb (1 kg) skinless, boneless chicken thighs

1 lb (500 g) spicy pork or chicken sausage (look for a good quality fresh chorizo or spicy Italian sausage for this dish)

1 lb (500 g) brown mushrooms, sliced

one 28-oz (796-mL) can Roma tomatoes, puréed in a blender or food processor

3 cloves garlic, minced

2 Tbsp (30 mL) chopped fresh rosemary

1 Tbsp (15 mL) chopped fresh sage

2 tsp (10 mL) salt

1 tsp (5 mL) freshly ground black pepper

½ tsp (2 mL) ground saffron threads

¼ tsp (1 mL) cayenne pepper or crushed chilies

2 cups (500 mL) short-grain rice like arborio or sushi rice

6 cups (1.5 L) chicken stock

1 cup (250 mL) peas (frozen is okay)

one 14-oz (398-mL) can chickpeas, rinsed and drained

chopped Italian parsley and lemon wedges to garnish

1 In a large, heavy sauté pan, heat the oil over medium-high heat and sauté the onion and red pepper until soft, about 10 minutes. Remove the vegetables from the pan and set aside.

2 Cut the chicken into large, 2-inch (5-cm) chunks and add to the pan. Sauté for 10 minutes, until nicely browned on all sides. Remove and set aside. Slice the sausage and sauté in the same pan for 5 minutes or until nicely browned. Set the sausage aside.

3 Add the mushrooms to the pan and sauté for 5 minutes, until soft and most of the liquid is gone. Purée the tomatoes in the blender or food processor, then stir into the pan with the garlic and reserved onion and pepper mixture. Bring to a boil and simmer for 20 minutes. Add the rosemary, sage, salt, black pepper, saffron, cayenne, and rice. Stir in the stock, chicken, and sausage and bring to a boil.

4 Reduce the heat to medium-low and simmer uncovered for 30 to 40 minutes longer, until rice is almost cooked. Stir in the green beans and chickpeas and continue to cook for 10 minutes. Serve from the pan, garnished with parsley and lemon wedges. Serves 8.

Mamma's Boy

While Easter holidays are an excuse to eat chocolate and feast on the first lamb of the season, spring also means Mother's Day. Fill the house with tulips and celebrate new life—let the mother in your life know she's special with this spring buffet menu.

Spring Crudités

A simple dressing for dipping takes fresh spring vegetables to new heights. Arrange the asparagus, green beans, carrots, bell peppers, and radishes individually in drinking glasses, for an artful presentation on the buffet.

5 medium carrots, peeled and cut lengthwise
    into sticks
1 lb (500 g) thin asparagus spears
½ lb (250 g) green beans
1 each red and yellow bell pepper, seeded and
    cut into strips

16 small radishes, washed and trimmed
mayonnaise sauce for dipping
    (see variations on page 37)

1 Break off the tough bottom end from each asparagus spear. Remove the stem end from each green bean.

2 Bring a big pot of salted water to a boil. Drop the carrot sticks into the water and blanch for 1 minute. Remove the blanched carrots from the water with a slotted spoon and plunge into a bowl of ice water to cool. Once cooled, drain well. Repeat with the asparagus and beans.

3 To serve, place five medium-sized drinking glasses on a tray around a bowl of dipping sauce. Fill one glass with whole radishes. Fill each of the remaining glasses with a different vegetable, standing them upright. Serves 4 to 6.

 ASPARAGUS

Gravlax

This is a traditional way to cure and serve salmon. Start with a piece that's scrupulously fresh or has been frozen at sea, hopefully something wild. Ask the fishmonger to scale and fillet the salmon, and remove any pin bones with tweezers. It takes a few days to "cook" the fish in this marinade but it's dead easy and makes an impressive nosh for a spring party buffet.

one 4- to 5-lb (2- to 2.2-kg) whole spring salmon, cut into 2 boneless fillets, skin intact
2 cups (500 mL) chopped fresh baby dill
½ cup (125 mL) coarse sea salt
½ cup (125 mL) packed brown sugar
1 tsp (5 mL) freshly ground white pepper
¼ cup (60 mL) aquavit, gin, or brandy

1 Find a glass or ceramic dish just large enough to hold the salmon fillets. Sprinkle ½ cup (125 mL) of the chopped dill over the bottom of the dish. Pat the salmon fillets dry and set them on a plate.

2 In a small bowl, combine the salt, sugar, and pepper. Rub the flesh side of both fillets with the salt mixture.

3 Sprinkle the flesh side of each fillet with aquavit. Lay one fillet, flesh-side up, in the dish. Evenly sprinkle the fillet with ¾ cup (175 mL) of chopped dill, then lay the second fillet on top, flesh-side down. (To create an even thickness for curing, lay fillets in opposite directions—tail end to head end). Sprinkle any remaining dill, aquavit, and seasoning mixture overtop of the fillets. Cover with plastic wrap.

4 Find a board or square plate that will fit into the dish and set it directly on top of the plastic wrap covering the salmon. Place something heavy over the board—bricks, cans of food, etc.—and transfer the dish to the refrigerator. Refrigerate for 2 to 3 days, basting twice a day with the salty juices that will accumulate in the dish. When the fish is properly cured, the flesh will become opaque and slightly lighter in color. To serve, drain the excess liquid and brush off the excess dill and salt mixture. Set the cured fish on a platter, skin-side down, and slice the gravlax on the diagonal into paper-thin strips, freeing each slice from the skin as you cut. Serve gravlax with mustard-flavored mayonnaise (see page 37) atop small squares of thinly sliced dark rye bread or crostini. Makes 4 lbs (2 kg).

WISE GUY: Aquavit is a Scandanavian spirit made from potatoes, similar to vodka, but with the addition of aromatic herbs and spices such as coriander, lemon, dill, and caraway seed. Like vodka, it's usually consumed ice cold and straight up in northern European countries—and that's the way to serve it with gravlax. If you buy a bottle, also try it in a Bloody Mary, instead of vodka, or, as the Swedes do, to lace the warm, spiced red wine mixture they call *glogg*.

Devilled Eggs on Baby Arugula

Any Guy can boil water. If you've got some eggs in there when it boils, you're halfway to devilled eggs. Everyone loves them and they're classic finger food. They make a perfectly spring-y first course, perched upon a plate of spicy arugula and drizzled with buttermilk dressing. And what else were you planning to do with all those hard-boiled oeufs you colored for Easter?

Buttermilk Dill Dressing
¼ cup (60 mL) mayonnaise
½ cup (125 mL) buttermilk
1 tsp (5 mL) Dijon mustard

½ (2 mL) tsp granulated sugar
1 tsp (5 mL) freshly squeezed lemon juice
1 tsp (5 mL) chopped fresh dill
¼ tsp (1 mL) salt

Devilled Eggs
6 large eggs (a few days old are better than super fresh)
3 Tbsp (45 mL) fat-reduced mayonnaise
1 Tbsp (15 mL) fat-free sour cream
½ tsp (2 mL) salt

¼ tsp (1 mL) freshly ground black pepper
½ tsp (2 mL) dry mustard
1 Tbsp (15 mL) minced fresh parsley, preferably Italian
1 Tbsp (15 mL) minced fresh chives

6 cups (1.5 L) fresh arugula (or watercress leaves)

1 To make the salad dressing, whisk together the mayonnaise, buttermilk, Dijon, sugar, and lemon juice. Add the chopped dill and salt. Chill.

2 Place the eggs in a pot large enough so they all fit in a single layer. Cover with cold water, 1 inch (2.5 cm) above the eggs. Bring to a boil over medium-high heat. Just as the water hits a full, rolling boil, remove the pot from the heat, cover, and let it stand for 15 minutes. Drain off the hot water and add cold tap water to cover the eggs. Throw in a few ice cubes to make sure the water gets really cold. Tap each egg on the wide end to crack the shell and put it back into the water to cool. (Don't forgo this step—the water will seep in under the shell and make the eggs infinitely easier to peel.)

3 Roll each egg between the palms of your hands to loosen the shell. Peel and discard the shells. Slice each egg in half lengthwise and remove the yolks. In a small bowl, mash the yolks with the remaining ingredients, reserving a little parsley or chives for garnish.

4 Heap or pipe the filling back into the egg whites. Serve devilled eggs as appetizers, or perch two devilled eggs alongside a small pile of baby arugula and drizzle with a little buttermilk dill dressing. Makes 12 devilled eggs, enough for six salads.

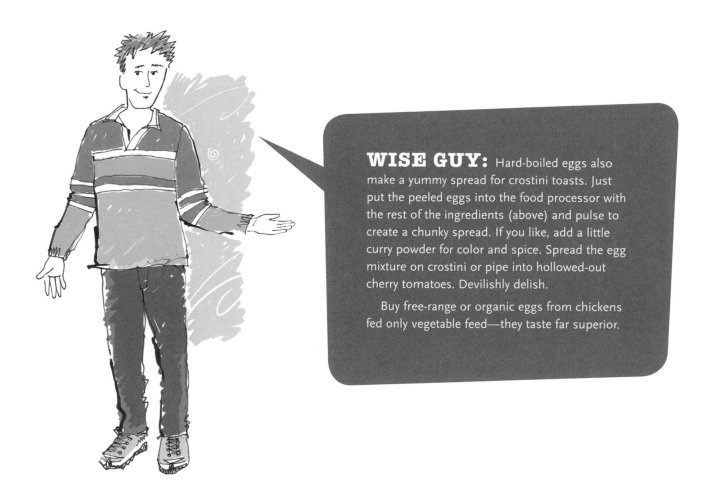

WISE GUY: Hard-boiled eggs also make a yummy spread for crostini toasts. Just put the peeled eggs into the food processor with the rest of the ingredients (above) and pulse to create a chunky spread. If you like, add a little curry powder for color and spice. Spread the egg mixture on crostini or pipe into hollowed-out cherry tomatoes. Devilishly delish.

Buy free-range or organic eggs from chickens fed only vegetable feed—they taste far superior.

Spinach and Leek Tart

The Guy has a soft spot for this rich, creamy tart with its fresh spring colors. A flatbread crust or pre-baked pizza shell from the supermarket makes it all come together almost instantly. This is one of those dishes you can make in advance, then assemble and finish just before serving.

2 Tbsp (30 mL) olive oil
2 large leeks, white and pale green parts only
3 cloves garlic, minced
¼ cup (60 mL) white wine
one 12-inch (30-cm) flatbread or precooked
   thin-crust pizza shell
¼ cup (60 mL) mayonnaise

¾ cup (175 mL) ricotta or quark
1 egg
1 cup (250 mL) freshly grated Parmesan cheese
2 cups (500 mL) finely chopped fresh spinach
salt and freshly ground pepper
cayenne pepper or paprika

1 Clean the leeks well. Cut each in half, lengthwise, and thoroughly rinse under running water to remove any sand caught between the layers. Slice the leeks crosswise, discarding the tough green tops or freezing them to use later in vegetable stocks. Heat the olive oil over medium heat in a large sauté pan. Add the sliced leeks, garlic, and white wine; cover and sweat (steam) for 10 minutes. Remove the lid, reduce the heat to medium-low and simmer until the liquid has evaporated and the leeks are soft. Set aside to cool.

2 Preheat the oven to 350°F (180°C).

3 In a food processor, combine the mayonnaise, ricotta, and egg. Process to combine. Add the Parmesan and whirl a second or two. Stir in the chopped spinach and pulse just to combine. Season with salt and pepper. (This filling may be made a day in advance and refrigerated.)

4 Set the flatbread or pizza crust on a baking sheet. Spread the filling evenly over the crust and scatter the leeks overtop. Dust lightly with cayenne or paprika and bake in the preheated oven for 45 minutes or until the tart is golden. Set aside to cool slightly before cutting into 12 wedges.
Serves 6 (2 pieces per person).

Poached Chicken and Olives

This is a room-temperature dish that you can make several days in advance—it gets better the longer it marinates. Serve as part of a spring buffet, or at a summer party.

2 to 3 lb (1 to 1.5 kg) skinless, boneless chicken breasts
¼ medium onion
1 small stalk celery, cut into chunks
1 tsp (5 mL) salt
6 cloves garlic, minced
¾ cup (175 mL) extra virgin olive oil
juice and finely grated zest of 1 lemon
    (about 3 Tbsp/45 mL juice and 1 Tbsp/15 mL zest)

1 tsp (5 mL) dried basil or Italian herb mixture
1 tsp (5 mL) Asian chili paste
1 cup (250 mL) air-cured black or small niçoise olives, pitted
1 Tbsp (15 mL) chopped parsley
1 bunch fresh watercress, large stems removed

1 Place the chicken breasts in a single layer in a shallow sauté pan. Add enough water to just cover the chicken. Add the onion, celery, and salt to the pan. Bring to a low simmer over medium heat. Gently poach for 10 minutes or until the chicken is just barely cooked (the internal temperature should be 165°F/70°C). Remove the chicken breasts from the poaching liquid. Cut the breasts across the grain into 1-inch (2.5-cm) slices, returning any underdone chicken slices to the still simmering poaching liquid for a minute or two until their centers are no longer pink (strain the broth and freeze to use in soups).

2 In a food processor, combine the garlic, olive oil, lemon juice and zest, basil, and chili paste. Whirl to combine.

3 Place the warm chicken into a deep dish and pour the olive oil mixture overtop. Toss to coat the chicken. Add the olives and toss again. Cover and refrigerate for up to 3 days. When ready to serve, return the chicken to room temperature and toss with parsley. Serve the chicken on an attractive platter, over a bed of fresh watercress, couscous, or chunky cooked pasta. Serves 8.

Strawberry Rhubarb Shortcakes

This is one of those seasonal desserts that must wait for the first field berries of spring—and for the young rhubarb stalks, sending up their first shiny leaves. Get out to the garden and pick the juiciest berries yourself, then mix them with sweet stewed rhubarb to top home-baked biscuits and cream. She'll swoon.

3 cups (750 mL) rhubarb, cut into ½-inch (1-cm) chunks
¾ cup (175 mL) granulated sugar
juice and zest of 1 orange (about ½ cup/ 125 mL juice and 1 Tbsp/15 mL finely grated zest)

3 cups (750 mL) fresh strawberries, halved
2 cups (500 mL) whipping cream or thick vanilla yogurt
2 Tbsp (30 mL) granulated sugar
fresh mint leaves for garnish

Cream Biscuits
2 cups (500 mL) all-purpose flour
¼ tsp (1 mL) salt
1 Tbsp (15 mL) baking powder

½ cup (125 mL) granulated sugar
½ cup (125 mL) cold butter, cut into cubes
½ cup (125 mL) whipping cream
melted butter for brushing

1 Preheat oven to 425°F (220°C).

2 In a medium saucepan, combine the rhubarb, sugar, orange juice, and zest. Bring to a boil over medium heat. Reduce the heat to low and simmer for 10 minutes or until the sauce thickens. Stir in the strawberries, then remove from heat and set aside to cool.

3 To make the biscuits, combine the flour, salt, baking powder, ¼ cup (60 mL) of the sugar, and the butter in a food processor. Pulse until the butter is chopped into small bits and the mixture resembles oatmeal. Drizzle the whipping cream into the batter and pulse quickly—just once or twice—to mix.

4 Dump the mixture out of the food processor, onto a lightly floured surface, and quickly gather the dough together, kneading gently. The trick to fluffy biscuits is a light hand—your biscuits will retain that ethereal quality. Pat the dough into a large circle, about ¾ inch (2 cm) thick.

5 Use a floured water glass or biscuit cutter to cut the dough into 3-inch (8-cm) rounds—press straight down without twisting. You can also cut the dough into 6 to 8 pie-shaped wedges. Reshape any leftover pieces of dough and cut additional biscuits (you should end up with 6 or 8 biscuits).

6 Line a baking sheet with parchment paper. Set the biscuits onto the parchment paper and lightly brush them with melted butter and sprinkle with the remaining sugar. Bake the biscuits until golden, about 12 to 15 minutes. Cool for 10 minutes (shortcake is best when the biscuits are warm).

7 Meanwhile, using an electric mixer, whip the cream and sugar until stiff.

8 To assemble the shortcakes, cut the biscuits in half horizontally and arrange the bottom halves on individual dessert plates. Top each with a little strawberry rhubarb sauce and a dollop of whipped cream. Set the second half of each biscuit on top, then drizzle the whole shortcake with more fruit sauce. Top each with more whipped cream and garnish with a fresh mint leaf. You can make the shortcakes to order, or set out the ingredients and let your guests construct their own desserts. Makes 6 to 8 servings.

Strawberries

Potlucky

(Or How to Score Big on the Salad Circuit)

The Guy is often invited to potluck parties—the office, the neighbors, the squash club—you never know when someone will utter those fateful words "Just bring a salad...."

While you can occasionally show up with a good loaf of bread, a watermelon, or the fixings for a decadent dessert drink, it's best to have at least a few good portable salads and one-pot wonders up your sleeve. Your reputation depends on it.

Who knows, your culinary skills may impress that other attractive single on the guest list. So whip up something simple but fabulous. It might be your night to get potlucky!

Lemony Lentil and Tabbouleh Salad

This is The Guy's torqued-up version of tabbouleh salad. Bulgar wheat is traditional, but you can also substitute couscous, or chewy pot barley (if you want to up the health quotient). This is a totally portable potluck dish that you can (and should) make in advance so the flavors have time to marry.

2 cups (500 mL) chicken broth
1 cup (250 mL) coarse bulgar wheat or whole
   wheat couscous or cooked pot barley
1 tsp (5 mL) ground cumin
one 19-oz (540-mL) can lentils, rinsed and drained
⅓ cup (75 mL) freshly squeezed lemon juice
¼ cup (60 mL) fruity extra virgin olive oil
3 green onions, finely chopped

2 cloves garlic, minced
2 Roma tomatoes, seeded and finely chopped
¼ cup (60 mL) chopped niçoise olives
½ cup finely chopped yellow bell pepper
½ cup finely chopped parsley
2 Tbsp (30 mL) chopped fresh mint (optional)
salt and freshly ground black pepper

1 In a large pot, bring the broth to a boil over high heat. Add the bulgar and cumin, cover, and remove from the heat. Let it sit for 15 to 20 minutes or until the bulgar is softened, then fluff with a fork.

2 Transfer the cooked bulgur to a bowl and stir in the lentils, lemon juice, and olive oil. Add the chopped onion, garlic, tomatoes, olives, bell pepper, parsley, and mint. Stir to combine. Cover and refrigerate for 2 hours. About a half an hour before serving, remove the tabbouleh from the refrigerator and bring it to room temperature. Season with salt and pepper to taste and garnish with a sprig of parsley. Serves 6 to 8.

WISE GUY: Bulgar—an ancient Middle Eastern ingredient—is whole wheat that's been steamed, dried, and cracked to make it quick and easy to cook. There are various grinds available but The Guy likes to use coarse bulgar for pilafs and salads. Look for it at health food stores or Middle Eastern groceries, and don't buy "cracked wheat"—it's not the same thing.

Chinese Chopped Salad

This is The Guy's perfect side dish when there's something glazed with soy sauce and honey (like salmon, chicken, or pork) on the grill. This salad is easy to make, colorful, yummy, and totally portable. And if you add some chopped leftover grilled chicken or pork (marinated in a little of the dressing before grilling), it's a meal in itself.

Dressing

1 Tbsp (15 mL) sesame oil

2 Tbsp (30 mL) canola oil

2 thin slices peeled fresh ginger

2 cloves garlic

2 Tbsp (30 mL) light soy sauce

2 Tbsp (30 mL) honey

1 Tbsp (15 mL) freshly squeezed lime juice

½ tsp (2 mL) Asian chili paste

3 cups (750 mL) chopped Chinese or Napa cabbage

3 cups corn (750 mL), cut from 3 cobs of corn, or substitute frozen kernel corn, thawed

1 cup (250 mL) shelled green soy beans (edamame), steamed

1 cup (250 mL) finely diced red bell pepper

2 cups (500 mL) chopped fresh snow peas (or edible pod peas)

½ cup (125 mL) celery, diced or sliced on the diagonal into thin slivers

1 large carrot, cut into fine matchstick slivers

3 green onions, minced

¼ cup (60 mL) minced cilantro

1 In a blender or food processor, combine the dressing ingredients and purée.

2 In a bowl, combine the cabbage, corn, soy beans, bell pepper, pea pods, celery, carrots, green onions, and cilantro. Toss in just enough dressing to coat. Chill before serving. Serves 8.

WISE GUY: You can buy green soy beans (a.k.a. edamame) in the freezer section of your local Asian grocery. They're sold in the pod or shelled. The latter are what you want for this salad, but the former make wonderful snacks with beer (the Japanese equivalent to a bowl of peanuts). Just nuke the whole pods for a couple of minutes, sprinkle with coarse sea salt and serve hot. To eat, pull the pods through your teeth to release the sweet, neon-green beans, and toss away the shells. A simple snack loaded with protein and other good stuff.

Cobb Salad

The cobb salad is the original composed salad and it's easy to make with basic supermarket ingredients. Haul the components along to the party individually, then arrange the salad on your best platter just before dinner is served. Who (or what) was Cobb? Who knows? But they say this is a salad with roots in Hollywood back when every big movie had a cast of thousands. So it's a salad with a story that might help you get a conversation started. Which is always a plus at a party.

Dressing

¾ cup (175 mL) extra virgin olive oil

¼ cup (60 mL) red wine vinegar

2 Tbsp (30 mL) freshly squeezed lemon juice (about half a lemon)

1 tsp (5 mL) granulated sugar

1 clove garlic, crushed

1 Tbsp (15 mL) Dijon mustard or other good-quality mustard

1 tsp (5 mL) Worcestershire sauce

salt and freshly ground black pepper

Salad

10 cups (2.5 L) salad greens (including chopped romaine, butter lettuce, and something peppery such as arugula or watercress)

1 cup (250 mL) grape tomatoes, halved

1 lb (500 g) cooked and shredded chicken (from a supermarket rotisserie chicken)

2 ripe avocados, peeled, pitted, and cubed

4 hard-boiled eggs, peeled and cut into quarters

6 slices of thick, double-smoked bacon, slivered and fried crisp

½ cup (125 mL) crumbled blue cheese

2 green onions, chopped

1 In a blender or food processor, combine all of the dressing ingredients and whirl until smooth. Pour the dressing into a jar and chill (shake it up again before using).

2 In a large bowl, toss the greens and tomatoes with just enough of the dressing to coat—about 4 to 6 Tbsp (60 to 90 mL). In another bowl, toss the cubed avocados with 1 to 2 Tbsp (15 to 30 mL) of the dressing.

3 Arrange the greens on a large platter or in a wide, shallow bowl. (The Guy has a big, white, round platter to add instant style to salads like this.)

4 Arrange the shredded chicken over the greens, in a row down the center. Artfully place the cubed avocados and quartered eggs around the edge of the platter. Sprinkle the bacon over the chicken, then scatter the blue cheese and green onions overtop.

5 Just before serving, drizzle some of the remaining dressing over the salad. Serves 6 to 8.

Perfect Potato Salad

This salad works all year round—but it's best when the first summer veggies appear at the market. With baby new potatoes, fresh peas, radishes, and dill, this potato salad is sublime and simple … a real keeper.

2 lb (1 kg) small new potatoes, scrubbed
¼ cup (60 mL) reduced-fat mayonnaise
¼ cup (60 mL) low-fat sour cream
   or plain yogurt
2 tsp (10 mL) Dijon mustard
1 Tbsp (15 mL) chopped fresh dill
   (or 1 tsp/15 mL dried dill)

1 Tbsp (15 mL) freshly squeezed lemon juice
salt and freshly ground black pepper
½ cup (125 mL) finely chopped celery
2 to 3 green onions, chopped
6 radishes, sliced
½ cup (125 mL) freshly shelled green peas,
   in season

1 Put a steamer basket in a large saucepan and add about 2 inches (5 cm) of water. Place the potatoes into the steamer basket and steam until tender, about 15 to 20 minutes. Cool for 20 minutes and cut into large cubes.

2 In a large bowl, whisk together the mayonnaise, sour cream, mustard, dill, lemon juice, salt, and pepper. Add the chunks of potato to the bowl and toss with the dressing to coat. Add the celery, green onions, radishes, and peas. Gently mix to combine, being careful not to break up the potatoes (The Guy hates mushy potato salads).

3 Serve immediately as a warm salad or chill for several hours and serve cold. For a more substantial salad, add a few chopped hard-boiled eggs along with the celery and other ingredients. Instead of the shelled peas, you can use chopped edible pod peas or lightly steamed green beans, cut into small pieces. Serves 6.

Tossed Salade Niçoise

This is a potato salad with gourmet cachet—a version of that classic composed salad of potatoes, beans, tuna, and garlicky mayonnaise. Serve it in a big shallow salad bowl lined with butter lettuce leaves to make it look extra appetizing on the potluck table. If clothes make the man, this well-dressed potato salad will make your picnic seriously stylish.

¼ cup (60 mL) reduced-fat mayonnaise
¼ cup (60 mL) low-fat sour cream
   or plain yogurt
2 tsp (10 mL) Dijon mustard
2 Tbsp (30 mL) extra virgin olive oil
4 cloves roasted garlic
   (or 1 clove crushed fresh garlic)
1 tsp (5 mL) finely chopped fresh rosemary
2 Tbsp (30 mL) freshly squeezed lemon juice
   (plus some grated lemon zest)
salt and freshly ground black pepper
2 lb (1 kg) small new red or yellow fingerling
   potatoes, scrubbed

1 cup (250 mL) fresh green beans, steamed
   lightly and chopped
2 to 3 green onions, chopped
1 can solid white tuna (packed in water),
   drained and broken into chunks
1 small head butter lettuce, leaves separated,
   washed and spun dry
½ cup (125 mL) tiny grape tomatoes, halved
½ cup (125 mL) niçoise olives
1 egg, hard-boiled, peeled, and chopped
1 Tbsp (15 mL) chopped fresh parsley

1 In a large bowl, whisk together the mayonnaise, sour cream, mustard, olive oil, roasted garlic, rosemary, lemon juice, zest, salt, and pepper.

2 Put a steamer basket in a large saucepan and add about 2 inches (5 cm) of water. Put the potatoes in the steamer basket and steam until tender, about 15 to 20 minutes. Cut into chunks. Add the warm potatoes to the dressing and toss.

3 Add the green beans to the steamer and steam until just tender, about 2 to 3 minutes. Rinse them under cold tap water to stop the cooking process, then chop into bite-size pieces. Mix the beans, green onions, and tuna into the salad, being careful not to break up the potatoes. Cool to room temperature, or chill and bring it back to room temperature before serving.

4 To present, line a wide bowl or deep platter with lettuce leaves and arrange the salad on top. Scatter the grape tomatoes and olives around the edge of the salad, pile the chopped egg on top, and sprinkle with parsley. Serves 6.

Roasted Eggplant, Onion, and Chickpea Salad

Reminiscent of days spent lolling in the south of France, this salad is perfect in the summer alongside grilled chicken or fish. The Guy has won raves for this dish at potluck parties in the past (and leftovers taste great stuffed into pita bread with some crumbled feta cheese). Who knows, it may be your day to get potlucky!

3 Tbsp (45 mL) freshly squeezed lemon juice

1 tsp (5 mL) sea salt

2 cloves garlic, minced

¼ tsp (1 mL) cayenne pepper

2 medium Roma tomatoes, seeded and chopped (or 1 cup/250 mL of grape tomatoes, quartered)

1 roasted red bell pepper, chopped (from a jar is fine)

one 14-oz (398-mL) can chickpeas, rinsed and drained

¼ cup (60 mL) olive oil, divided

2 slender Japanese eggplants, diced (unpeeled)

1 medium onion, peeled but whole

1 tsp (5 mL) each minced fresh basil and thyme leaves

2 Tbsp (30 mL) chopped parsley

1 Combine the lemon juice, salt, and garlic in a bowl. Add the pepper, cayenne, tomatoes, chopped roasted pepper, chickpeas, and 3 Tbsp (45 mL) of the olive oil. Toss and set aside.

2 Preheat the oven to 400°F (200°C).

3 Spread the diced eggplant on a baking sheet and drizzle with 1 Tbsp (15 mL) of the olive oil. Wrap the onion in foil, drizzling a little olive oil over it before loosely closing the package. Roast the eggplant and onion for 45 minutes, stirring the eggplant occasionally.

4 When the eggplant is brown and the onion is tender, remove from the oven. Add the eggplant to the salad bowl and stir.

5 Unwrap the onion, cut it in half lengthwise and cut it into thin crescent slices. Add the roasted onion to the salad. Toss gently with the basil, thyme, and parsley. Serve the salad warm or at room temperature. Serves 6.

Cold Noodles in Sesame Peanut Sauce

The Guy loves peanut sauce—this dressing is great over noodles and equally good for glazing satay chicken kabobs on the grill. Make sure you use real peanut butter (check the label; the only ingredient should be peanuts), as many brands are loaded with sugar and hydrogenated vegetable oils.

Dressing

1 Tbsp (15 mL) sesame oil

2 cloves garlic, minced (optional)

⅓ cup (75 mL) chunky or smooth natural peanut butter

¼ cup (60 mL) soy sauce

2 tsp (10 mL) brown sugar

1 Tbsp (15 mL) sushi vinegar (or wine vinegar)

1 tsp (5 mL) Asian chili paste

¼ cup (60 mL) chicken stock or water

½ lb (250 g) fresh Chinese egg noodles (the lightly steamed kind found in the supermarket produce department)

1 Tbsp (15 mL) canola oil

1 red bell pepper, seeded and thinly sliced

1 large carrot, peeled and grated

2 cups (500 mL) fresh bean sprouts

2 green onions, sliced diagonally into ½-inch (1-cm) slivers

¼ cup (60 mL) finely chopped cilantro

2 Tbsp (30 mL) toasted sesame seeds or finely chopped roasted peanuts

1 To make the dressing, combine the sesame oil, garlic, peanut butter, soy sauce, sugar, and sushi vinegar in a blender or food processor and purée until smooth. Add the chili paste and the chicken stock and pulse to combine. Set aside in the refrigerator.

2 Bring a large pot of salted water to a boil. Add the noodles and cook for 2 to 3 minutes or until the noodles are al dente (tender but still a bit firm).

3 Drain well, rinse in cold water, and place in a large bowl. Toss with the canola oil, then add the dressing and toss again to coat well.

4 Add the bell pepper, carrots, bean sprouts, green onion, and cilantro. Toss.

5 Arrange the salad in a serving bowl and top with the sesame seeds. Serves 4 to 6.

WISE GUY:
For individual, main-meal salads, serve these nutty noodles over chopped romaine lettuce, and top with grilled or roasted chicken.

Cold Comforts or Cool Stuff for Hot Times

Revenge may be one dish best savored cold, but there are many other things that offer simple satisfaction from the ice box. When the mercury soars in mid-summer, and you can barely face food (never mind a hot stove), having something ready-to-eat from the refrigerator is truly a blessing. Cold foods are also perfect for busy days or when you've promised someone a picnic supper.

Cool Tomato and Cucumber Soup

A chilled vegetable soup is just the thing to cool you off on a searing summer evening. Drink your veggies.

3 cups (750 mL) V-8 vegetable juice
2 ripe Roma tomatoes, seeded and finely chopped
   (or 2 from a can)
one 6-inch (15-cm) piece of English cucumber,
   seeds scooped out and grated
¼ cup (60 mL) minced white onion

1 clove garlic, minced
½ tsp (2 mL) salt
1 Tbsp (15 mL) balsamic vinegar
½ tsp (2 mL) chili paste
extra virgin olive oil

1 Combine all the ingredients, except the olive oil, in the blender or food processor and pulse a few times, just to break things up a bit. Transfer to a covered container and refrigerate from 2 hours to overnight. When you're ready to serve, thin the soup with ice water, to taste, and adjust the seasoning. You can add a couple of ice cubes to the thermos bottle when you tote it along for a picnic to keep it nice and cold.

2 When you serve, top with a splash of your tastiest olive oil. Serves 4.

Potato and Spicy Sausage Frittata

A Spanish-style frittata is an all-purpose egg dish, and this is one of those "mother" recipes that you can modify to suit what's in the fridge. Always bake or boil an extra potato or two on the weekend, and you'll have the basis for a fast frittata during the week (or substitute 1 to 2 cups/250 to 500 mL of frozen hash browns). Use any kind of cheese you like, and add vegetables like sautéed mushrooms or steamed asparagus, or different meats or fish such as ham, prosciutto, bacon, or smoked salmon.

Enjoy frittata for a fast supper or breakfast, straight out of the refrigerator. Or cut it into appetizer-sized bites for a party.

4 Tbsp (60 mL) olive oil, divided
1 large potato, cooked, chilled,
    and thinly sliced or chopped
½ cup (125 mL) chopped onion
2 bell peppers (1 red and 1 yellow),
    seeded and slivered
2 cloves garlic, minced
½ lb (250 g) fresh spicy Italian or chorizo sausage,

removed from the casings
    and crumbled
8 large eggs
½ cup (125 mL) grated old fontina
    or aged cheddar cheese
3 Tbsp (45 mL) grated Parmesan cheese
Spicy Salsa (see page xx)

1 In a large, non-stick, ovenproof frying pan, heat 2 Tbsp (30 mL) of the oil over medium-high heat. Add the potatoes and sauté for 5 minutes, until they begin to brown. Add the onion to the pan and cook for 3 to 4 minutes. Add the peppers, garlic, and crumbled sausage. Cook until the meat is no longer pink.

2 Beat the eggs in a bowl and pour over the ingredients in the pan. Reduce the heat to medium and stir the mixture until the eggs begin to set. Reduce the heat to low and let the eggs cook on the bottom, shaking the pan to keep the frittata from sticking.

3 Meanwhile, preheat the broiler. When the frittata is nicely browned on the bottom, remove the pan from the heat, top with the grated cheeses, and place the pan under the broiler. Broil for a minute or two, just until the top of the frittata sets and the cheese melts and begins to brown.

4 Let the frittata cool for a few minutes, then cut into four wedges. Serve warm or cold, with salsa on the side. Serves 4.

Niçoise Salad Sandwich

No mayo—no problem. Use crusty baguette-style loaves (long or individual) and keep the sandwiches wrapped and chilled for a few hours before serving. You may wish to hollow out the rolls a little to enclose the filling entirely. If you're using a long baguette, double the filling and make one big sandwich, then cut it on the diagonal into four sandwich-size chunks to serve. Can you say "romantic picnic"?

one 4-oz (184-g) tin white albacore tuna in water, drained well

¼ cup (60 mL) sliced black olives or Tapenade (see page 21)

1 Tbsp (15 mL) freshly squeezed lemon juice

¼ cup (60 mL) finely chopped roasted red bell pepper (from a jar is fine)

1 Tbsp (15 mL) chopped fresh basil

2 green onions, finely chopped

1 tsp (5 mL) tiny capers

2 Tbsp (30 mL) extra virgin olive oil

freshly ground black pepper

2 crusty rolls or a mini-baguette

extra virgin olive oil

sliced Roma tomatoes

arugula or mixed baby greens

1 In a bowl, combine the tuna, olives, lemon juice, roasted pepper, basil, green onions, capers, olive oil, and black pepper. Mix well, cover, and chill several hours (the filling should be cold before making sandwiches).

2 Cut the rolls in half lengthwise and scoop out some of the bread in the center, leaving a thick shell. Lightly brush the interior with olive oil. Line both sides of the bun with greens to prevent soggy sandwiches. Add the tuna salad and tomatoes. Wrap well and chill 2 to 3 hours before serving. Serves 2.

Southern Fried Chicken

This may not be the healthiest way to cook chicken, but hey, it's delicious, so get over it. The Guy loves crispy home-fried chicken, with some homemade Classic Coleslaw (see page 165) or Perfect Potato Salad (see page 410) on the side. It's an ideal food for a picnic (no cutlery required—but napkins sure are).

1 cup (250 mL) buttermilk or plain yogurt

1 tsp (5 mL) salt

¼ tsp (1 mL) cayenne

3 lb (1.5 kg) chicken pieces, bone-in and skin on
   (The Guy likes thighs and breasts)

1 cup (250 mL) all-purpose flour

1 cup (250 mL) cornmeal

1 tsp (5 mL) baking powder

2 tsp (10 mL) dried thyme

½ tsp (2 mL) freshly ground black pepper

½ tsp (2 mL) Hungarian paprika

½ tsp (2 mL) onion powder

½ to 1 cup (125 to 250 mL) canola or peanut oil

1 In a large, non-reactive bowl, combine the buttermilk, salt, cayenne, and chicken. Stir so the chicken is coated on all sides. Cover and refrigerate for 30 to 60 minutes.

2 Combine the flour, cornmeal, baking powder, thyme, black pepper, paprika, and onion powder in a shallow dish or paper bag. Remove the chicken from the marinade and shake off any excess buttermilk. Roll the chicken pieces in the flour mixture or shake them in the paper bag to coat well. Set a rack over a baking sheet, and place the chicken pieces on the rack for 10 minutes to allow the coating to set.

3 Preheat the oven to 200°F (95°C).

4 In a deep, heavy-bottomed skillet (cast iron is ideal), heat the oil over medium heat (the oil should be 375°F/190°C). Add half the chicken pieces to the pan, skin-side down, and cook until golden brown, about 10 minutes. Turn pieces over and cook for 8 to 10 minutes longer until browned on all sides. Keep checking the temperature of the oil—if it's not hot enough, the coating will absorb the oil and the chicken will be greasy, not crisp. That's why it's best not to crowd the pan while frying—if you put too much food into the oil at once, the temperature drops—so cook the chicken in batches.

5 Line a plate with paper towels and place the cooked chicken on the plate to drain excess fat. Then transfer the chicken to a baking sheet in the preheated oven to keep warm. Finish cooking the chicken, draining on paper towels as it's cooked, then keep warm in the oven until ready to serve.

6 You can also make the chicken ahead of time as it can be refrigerated for up to 2 days. Either serve it cold or reheat it in a 375°F (190°C) oven for about 15 minutes, until crisp. Serves 4.

Marinated Seafood Salad

This Mediterranean seafood salad can be served as a cold course to start a summer dinner party or as the main dish for your picnic.

1 small red onion, cut into thin rings
¾ lb (375 g) calamari tubes, cut into ¼-inch
   (5-mm) rings
¾ lb (375 g) medium shrimp, peeled and
   deveined
1 lb (500 g) mussels, scrubbed and debearded
¼ cup (60 mL) extra virgin olive oil
2 cloves garlic, crushed
4 Tbsp (60 mL) freshly squeezed lemon juice

½ tsp (2 mL) Asian chili paste
½ tsp (2 mL) salt
¼ tsp (1 mL) freshly ground black pepper
2 tsp (10 mL) finely grated lemon rind
   (use a microplane grater)
⅓ cup (75 mL) pitted black olives, sliced
¼ cup (60 mL) slivered fresh basil leaves
fresh salad greens for garnish

1 In a small bowl of ice water, soak the sliced onion for 1 hour.

2 Meanwhile, bring a large pot of salted water to a boil. Add the sliced calamari and simmer for 1 minute. Drain the calamari and immediately plunge into ice water to stop the cooking process. Drain and set aside. Cook the shrimp in the same manner, simmering in the pot of boiling salted water for about 1 minute, then plunging in a bath of ice water. Drain. Place the mussels in a large pot with a splash of water (or wine, if you like). Cover and steam over high heat for a few minutes until all the shells have opened (discard any mussels whose shells did not open). Remove the meat from the shells.

3 To make the dressing, combine the olive oil and garlic in a medium bowl. Set aside for 10 minutes. Whisk in the lemon juice and chili paste.

4 Drain the onion rings well and combine with the calamari, shrimp, and mussels in a glass bowl. Toss with the dressing, salt, pepper, lemon rind, and olives. Marinate in the refrigerator for several hours or overnight. Just before serving, stir in the fresh basil. To serve, line a platter with greens and pile the seafood salad in the center. Serves 6 to 8.

Caponata

Here's an addictive chunky condiment with spicy Sicilian roots. Serve it antipasto style with a sliced baguette, or toss with your favorite pasta and a little Parmesan for a fast supper. It's equally delicious hot and at room temperature. It takes a plain piece of grilled chicken or halibut into gourmet territory. The Guy likes to make caponata when just-picked local eggplants, peppers, and squash are easy to scoop up for a song at the farmers market. It keeps well in the fridge, and you can even freeze it!

2 lb (1 kg) eggplant, skin on, cut into cubes
1 lb (500 g) zucchini or other summer squash, cubed
2 tsp (10 mL) salt
½ cup (125 mL) extra virgin olive oil
2 cups (500 mL) chopped onion
4 large cloves garlic, minced
1 red bell pepper, chopped
1 yellow bell pepper, chopped
one 14-oz (398-mL) can Roma tomatoes, chopped or puréed

1 Tbsp (15 mL) brown sugar
¼ cup (60 mL) tomato paste
3 Tbsp (45 mL) balsamic vinegar
½ cup (125 mL) black olives, pitted and chopped
2 to 3 Tbsp (30 to 45 mL) chopped fresh basil or rosemary
salt and freshly ground black pepper
hot pepper sauce (optional)

1 Put the eggplant and zucchini cubes in a colander. Toss with salt and set in the sink to drain for half an hour. Rinse quickly under running water and pat dry with paper towels.

2 Heat the oil in a large sauté pan or Dutch oven over medium heat. Add the onion, garlic, and peppers. Sauté for 5 minutes. Add the eggplant and zucchini cubes and sauté for 5 to 10 minutes longer or until the vegetables begin to soften. Stir in the tomatoes, and cover the pan. Cook for 20 minutes. Remove the lid and continue to simmer for another 10 to 15 minutes or until the vegetables are very soft and the liquid in the pan has been reduced.

3 Whisk together the brown sugar, tomato paste, and vinegar. Add to the pan and mix well. Stir in the olives and remove from the heat. Add the fresh herbs and season with salt and pepper to taste (and a little hot sauce if you like it spicy).

4 Cool to room temperature and serve. (If refrigerated, in a covered container, caponata will keep for a week, or it can be frozen for several months.) Makes about 6 cups.

Chicken and Avocado Muffaletta

This is the perfect sandwich to take almost anywhere, and The Guy's favorite picnic nosh. Start with a crusty French baguette for this non-traditional muffaletta. For the filling, you can buy roasted, sliced chicken or turkey breast at the deli counter, or just shred a supermarket rotisserie chicken.

¾ lb (375 g) roasted chicken or turkey breast, sliced

1 Tbsp (15 mL) olive oil

1 Tbsp (15 mL) freshly squeezed lime juice

½ tsp (2 mL) ground cumin

½ tsp (2 mL) chili powder

½ tsp (2 mL) hot sauce

1 firm but ripe avocado, halved, peeled, and chopped

1 large Roma tomato, seeded and chopped

½ cup (125 mL) pitted and chopped black olives

⅓ cup (75 mL) mayonnaise, divided

1 crusty French baguette

½ cup (125 mL) fresh cilantro sprigs, stems removed

1 cup (250 mL) mixed salad greens or baby spinach

1 In a medium bowl, combine the olive oil, lime juice, cumin, chili powder, and hot sauce. Set aside.

2 Chop the avocado and rinse the slices under cold water to prevent browning. Coarsely chop the tomato and combine it with the avocado in a bowl. Stir in the black olives, half of the olive oil/lime juice dressing, and 1 to 2 Tbsp (15 to 30 mL) of the mayonnaise.

3 To make the muffalettas, cut the baguette into 4 equal pieces, then cut each section in half lengthwise. Press the cut side of the bread to compact and form a hollow (or pull some of the bread out). Spread both halves of each sandwich with the remaining mayonnaise.

4 On one side of the bread, layer the sliced chicken, cilantro, and salad greens. Drizzle with the remaining dressing. Top with the tomato and avocado salad and the remaining bread. Press the sandwiches to seal. Wrap in plastic wrap or foil and chill for 2 hours. Cut into 3-inch (8-cm) chunks to serve. Serves 4.

WISE GUY: For a more traditional look, you can make this sandwich on one large round loaf. Slice one large round loaf of Italian bread in half, horizontally. Pull out some of the bread from the insides, and fill as described. After the sandwich is chilled, cut it into wedges to serve.

Japanese Cold Noodles

While it may sound like a strange combination, the cold noodle, pork, and seaweed salad at the local sushi joint has long been The Guy's favorite supper on a hot summer day. Sadly, Ken and Tom closed the place, so now it's cold noodles at home—or nothing.

Serve this delicious cold dish with sushi on the deck and your friends will understand why you take the time to hunt down all of the oddball ingredients at the local Asian grocery store.

Make it when you have leftover roast pork or pork tenderloin (or grill a tenderloin from scratch, see page 258, to serve on top). Make sure to slice everything as finely as possible (let the slim Japanese soba noodles be your guide).

Sauce
½ tsp (2 mL) instant dashi broth powder
2 cups (500 mL) boiling water

¼ cup (60 mL) dark Japanese soy sauce
1 Tbsp (15 mL) sugar
¼ cup (60 mL) mirin (Japanese rice wine)

Salad
1 lb (500 g) soba or buckwheat noodles
2 tsp (10 mL) granulated sugar
2 tsp (10 mL) soy sauce
6 dried shiitake mushrooms
2 eggs, beaten with 2 Tbsp (30 mL) water

3 green onions, slivered
½ English cucumber, seeded and finely slivered
1 carrot, peeled and slivered
½ sheet nori (seaweed for making sushi) slivered
½ cup (125 mL) finely slivered cooked pork or
   chicken

1 To make the sauce, combine the dashi powder with the boiling water in a small saucepan and simmer for 1 minute. Stir in the soy sauce, sugar, and mirin. Remove from the heat, cool, and chill.

2 To make the salad, cook the noodles in boiling salted water until tender, about 5 minutes, then immerse in cold water to stop the cooking process. Drain and set them aside in a bowl.

3 In a small saucepan, heat 1 cup (250 mL) of water with the sugar and soy sauce. Add the mushrooms and bring to a boil over medium heat. Simmer, uncovered, for 15 minutes, until most of the liquid is gone. Remove the mushrooms, cool, and slice into very thin slivers, discarding the stems.

4 Beat the egg with the water. Heat a small, non-stick frying pan over medium-high heat. Pour the egg into the hot pan and cook for 2 to 3 minutes, then cook the second side. Place the omelet on a cutting board to cool and then cut into very small julienne strips, about 1 inch (2.5 cm) long and 1/16 inch (1.5 mm) wide.

5 Cut the cucumber, green onion, carrot, and nori in similarly fine julienne strips. Toss the cold noodles with the slivered mushrooms, omelet, green onion, carrot, nori, and cucumber, saving some of each for garnish. Divide the noodles among four individual serving bowls. Top with pork (or chicken). Serve with individual bowls of the cold sauce for dipping or pouring over the noodles. Serves 4.

Slow-Roasted Salmon

The Guy likes to serve a cold side of salmon for summer buffets, garnished with chopped tomatoes and black olives, niçoise-style, or slathered in a mayonnaise sauce and decorated with sliced radish "scales."

It can be tricky to poach a side of salmon—most people don't have the special vessel for such a task. But anyone can slow-roast a side of salmon in the oven, which provides similar results—a clean, simple, unembellished piece of fish that goes well with whatever sauce or accompaniment you choose. It's idiot-proof. Just preheat the oven, rub the fish with oil and salt, and it's done in 30 minutes flat. Try this technique with other fish like snapper, cod, and even tuna.

1 side of salmon, skin on, about 1 to 1½ inches thick (1½ to 2 lb/750 g to 2 kg)

2 tsp (10 mL) olive oil
salt

1 Preheat the oven to 275°F (140°C).

2 Rub the salmon all over with olive oil and season with salt. Place it on baking sheet, or in a baking pan, lined with parchment paper. Bake for 25 to 30 minutes, or until the salmon flakes easily and has an internal temperature of 120°F (60°C). Transfer to a serving platter and serve warm, garnished with a simple sauce or glaze (see Catch of the Day recipes, page xx). Or cool the fish to room temperature, cover, and refrigerate for several hours to serve cold. Any of the aiolis (see page 37) or herb oils (see page 20) are perfect to drizzle on top. Serves 4 to 6.

WISE GUY: You can also "poach" a side of salmon in the oven. Wrap the entire fillet in a sheet of heavy foil (season the salmon with salt and pepper and throw in a splash of white wine, then seal it up). Slide the package onto a baking sheet and bake at 250°F (120°C) for 45 to 60 minutes. Let it cool in the foil, pour off the juices, and refrigerate until you're ready to serve.

Strawberry Rhubarb Meringue Fool

Layers of crisp sweet meringues with creamy rhubarb mousse and tangy rhubarb sauce make a spectacular spring dessert. Make this trifle-style, in a glass bowl for the buffet, or layer the crumbled cookies, mousse, and sauce in tall champagne flutes for individual desserts. It's super summery and very chic for a wedding or anniversary party.

Meringue

6 egg whites, at room temperature

½ tsp (2 mL) cream of tartar (or 1 tsp/5 mL white vinegar)

pinch of salt

1½ cups (375 mL) granulated sugar

1 tsp (5 mL) pure vanilla extract

2 tsp (10 mL) finely grated orange zest (use a microplane grater)

Strawberry-Rhubarb Sauce

1 cup (250 mL) granulated sugar

⅔ cup (150 mL) freshly squeezed orange juice

5 cups (1.25 L) chopped red rhubarb

3 cups (750 mL) hulled and chopped strawberries

1 Tbsp (15 mL) finely grated orange zest

dash of pure vanilla extract

Mousse

2 cups (500 mL) whipping cream

2 Tbsp (30 mL) granulated sugar

¼ cup (60 mL) orange liqueur

1 Preheat the oven to 250°F (120°C).

2 To make the meringues, in a clean bowl, beat the egg whites with the cream of tartar and salt until they begin to stiffen. Gradually beat in the sugar and continue beating until the mixture is stiff and glossy. Stir in the vanilla and zest.

3 Line a baking sheet with parchment paper and spoon the meringues onto the sheet in mounds that are about 4 inches (10 cm) in diameter (later, you can layer the meringues whole, or break them into pieces). Bake in the preheated oven for 1½ hours until dry but not brown. Turn off the oven, with the meringues still inside, and let them continue drying for another hour.

4 For the sauce, combine the sugar, orange juice, rhubarb, and strawberries in a large saucepan. Simmer slowly, over medium-low heat, for about 15 minutes or until the rhubarb is tender. (The rhubarb will break down and thicken the sauce.) Stir in the orange rind and vanilla. Remove from the heat and cool. Purée 1 cup (250 mL) of the sauce in a blender and set aside. Cover and refrigerate the remaining sauce until ready to use.

5 To make the fool (a.k.a. mousse), beat the cream with the sugar, using an electric mixer, until thick. Add the liqueur and continue to beat until the mixture is stiff. Fold in the 1 cup (250 mL) of puréed sauce.

6 To assemble, spoon a layer of reserved fruit sauce in a large glass bowl or in individual stemmed glasses. Top with a layer of whole or broken meringues, then add a layer of mousse. Repeat these layers twice more and then top with crumbled meringues.

7 This dessert can be made a day ahead, or several days ahead and frozen. If frozen, let it soften for 30 minutes before serving. Serves 6 to 8.

TRIFLE BOWL

Frozen Chocolate Soufflés

This is a cross between chocolate mousse and wickedly decadent, homemade ice cream. Make it with the finest dark chocolate you can find, something with at least 60 to 70% cocoa. A little store-bought Belgian cookie on the side is all you need for an exquisite ending. When you have a batch of these babies in the freezer, it's like money in the bank.

6 oz (175 g) bittersweet dark chocolate
   (top quality), in small chunks
⅓ cup (75 mL) strong brewed black coffee
   or espresso
4 eggs, separated

1 Tbsp (15 mL) butter
2 Tbsp (30 mL) rum or coffee liqueur
¼ cup (60 mL) granulated sugar
½ cup (125 mL) whipping cream

1 In a medium saucepan, heat the chocolate and coffee together over medium-low heat until the chocolate is melted. Stir until nicely incorporated, then remove from the heat and stir to cool slightly.

2 Whisk the egg yolks in a bowl. Add a little of the chocolate sauce to the egg yolks, and continue whisking to combine. Slowly pour in the rest of the sauce, whisking until the chocolate is fully incorporated. Whisk in the butter and rum before setting aside to cool.

3 In another bowl, beat the egg whites with an electric mixer until foamy and thick. Slowly add the sugar and continue beating until the whites form stiff peaks.

4 With a large spatula, pile the stiffened egg whites over the chocolate mixture. Using the spatula, lift the chocolate over and through the egg whites until it's combined but still fluffy (the idea is not to deflate the egg whites as you fold in the chocolate, but to get rid of all of the white streaks).

5 Beat the whipping cream in a separate bowl until stiff, then fold into the mixture the same way. Pour the mixture into individual ramekins or custard cups, cover with plastic, and freeze overnight. Dust the tops with a bit of powdered sugar before serving. Serves 4 to 6.

WISE GUY: For the real WOW factor, use this chef's trick to make these cool desserts look more like classic soufflés. Make them in small, straight-sided ramekins or mini soufflé dishes. Make stiff collars out of pieces of parchment paper that have been folded into 3-inch (8-cm) strips and then wrapped around the dishes, then tied with string. This lets you pile the mousse high above the rim of the dishes before you freeze. Remove the collars just before serving, and dust with cocoa or icing sugar.

Catch of the Day

When The Guy hits the West Coast fishing lodges he always comes home with lots of salmon and halibut for the freezer. A big king or Chinook salmon can top out at 50 pounds so you'll need to know what to do with your salmon fillets when you get home. Have the lodge turn some of it into hot-smoked Indian candy, or have some canned and take the rest boneless, with the skin on, for grilling on the barbecue or baking in the oven.

If you're a freshwater fisher, use those delicate trout, pickerel, and arctic char fillets for fast pan frying. Wild fish is one of nature's perfect foods—eat it as often as you can.

Poached Salmon with Red Wine Sauce

When you want to serve salmon with your favorite northwest Pinot Noir, this is the perfect recipe. It may sound odd to cook fish with red wine, but it works.

Sauce

½ cup (125 mL) freshly squeezed orange juice

1 Tbsp (15 mL) brown sugar

½ cup (125 mL) ripe, fruity red wine (like the Pinot Noir you plan to serve)

1 Tbsp (15 mL) balsamic vinegar

1 Tbsp (15 mL) tomato paste

1 Tbsp (15 mL) cold butter

2 lb (1 kg) skinless salmon fillet, cut into 4 to 6 pieces, or four salmon steaks, wrapped into medallions (see technique below)

1 cup (250 mL) fish stock or bottled clam broth

1 cup (250 mL) water

1 tsp (5 mL) whole peppercorns

1 sprig fresh thyme

2 sprigs parsley

1 In a small saucepan, bring the orange juice, brown sugar, wine, vinegar, and tomato paste to a boil over medium heat. Continue simmering until the liquid has reduced to about ⅓ cup (75 mL). Remove from the heat and whisk the butter into the reduction until fully incorporated and the liquid has thickened slightly. Keep the sauce warm over minimum heat.

2 Meanwhile, in a large skillet, bring the stock, water, peppercorns, thyme, and parsley to a boil over high heat. Reduce the heat to medium-low so the liquid barely bubbles. Slide the salmon pieces into the broth. Cover the pan and keep the heat low to maintain an even simmer. Poach for 7 to 9 minutes, or until the salmon is firm but barely cooked through. Use a slotted spoon to lift the salmon from the poaching liquid.

3 Serve the salmon drizzled with the warm red wine sauce. Serves 4 to 6.

WISE GUY: To make your poached salmon look a little more interesting on the plate, cut the fillet into four or six lengthwise strips, each about ½ to ¾ inch (1 to 2 cm) thick. Wrap the strips into coils or rosettes, with the thickest part at the center, then secure the pieces with a toothpick before poaching. For salmon steaks, remove the skin and bones from each steak, creating two comma-shaped pieces. Lay the two halves, side by side, in opposite directions, then wrap the "tails" around the outside, wrapping in the same direction, to create a salmon medallion. Secure with toothpicks. Rosettes will cook a little faster than whole pieces of fish.

Salmon with Honey Mustard Glaze

When The Guy wants a fast, elegant presentation, he serves this simple glazed salmon atop a pile of wilted greens (slivered spinach, chard, and beet greens that have been quickly sautéed in butter and olive oil with shallots, garlic, and a splash of balsamic vinegar) or over Lemony Lentil and Tabouli Salad (see page 407).

Glaze
2 Tbsp (30 mL) Dijon mustard
2 Tbsp (30 mL) honey

1 Tbsp (15 mL) freshly squeezed lime juice
1 clove garlic, pressed through a garlic press
2 Tbsp (30 mL) butter

1½ to 2 lb (750 g to 1 kg) salmon fillet, about 1 inch (2.5 cm) thick, skin on

olive oil
salt and freshly ground black pepper

1 Combine the Dijon, honey, lime juice, garlic, and butter in a small saucepan. Heat and stir over medium heat for a few minutes, until smooth. Set aside.

2 Preheat the oven to 500°F (260°C).

3 Cut the salmon into 4 individual servings. Pat the salmon dry with a paper towel, and season the flesh side with a little salt and pepper. Rub a baking sheet with olive oil and place the fish in the pan, skin-side down.

4 Place the salmon in the preheated oven and bake for 5 minutes. Remove it from the oven and liberally brush with the glaze. Return the salmon to the oven and bake for 5 to 7 minutes more, until the fish is just barely cooked through, still translucent and a bright coral color in the middle. (You're shooting for an internal temperature of 150°F/65°C.)

5 Remove the pan from the oven and let it stand for 3 to 4 minutes to finish cooking.

6 Serve the fish with rice and wilted greens or steamed broccolini. Serves 4.

WISE GUY: Remember, frozen salmon will retain more of its just-caught qualities if defrosted slowly. Defrost fish in its packaging, on a plate, overnight in the refrigerator.

Pan-Fried Pickerel in Cornmeal Crust

The Guy loves to eat pickerel—and it's fun to catch in Canada's northern lakes. It's also one of the few freshwater fish that's still fished commercially, which means you're likely find fresh pickerel fillets at the local supermarket or fishmonger. Pickerel cooks quickly and has a mild and delicious flavor.

1 lb (500 g) pickerel fillets, bones and skin
    removed
salt and freshly ground black pepper
¼ cup (60 mL) all-purpose flour

½ cup (125 mL) stone-ground cornmeal
½ tsp (2 mL) paprika
2 to 3 Tbsp (25 to 45 mL) canola oil for frying
fresh lemon wedges

1 Season the fillets with salt and pepper on both sides. On a plate, combine the flour, cornmeal, and paprika. Roll the fillets in the cornmeal mixture to coat well on both sides. Heat the oil in a large, non-stick frying pan over medium-high heat and pan-fry the fish until brown and crisp on both sides, 4 to 5 minutes in total. Serve immediately, with a little fresh lemon squeezed overtop. Serves 3 to 4.

WISE GUY: This simple technique works with almost any fish fillet, from halibut to whitefish. Fried fish goes with most typical side dishes, whether brown rice and broccoli, or baked potatoes and a caesar salad. Or do as they do in the fast-food world and take your fried fish to go—stacked on a toasted whole wheat hamburger bun and topped with lettuce, tomato, and tartar sauce (mayo and sweet pickle relish), or wrapped with spicy salsa into a fish taco.

Seared Halibut with Tomato and Olive Relish

You can make this simple relish in advance and sear the halibut just before you plan to serve it. Lemony Potatoes (see page 223) and Sautéed Spinach (see page 162) will balance the plate nicely.

2 lb (1 kg) boneless halibut fillet,
   cut into 4 portions

Relish
½ cup (125 mL) sun-dried tomatoes in oil, drained
   and finely chopped
½ cup (125 mL) pitted kalamata or green olives,
   finely chopped
1 clove garlic, minced

salt and freshly ground black pepper, to taste
2 Tbsp (30 mL) extra virgin olive oil

1 Tbsp (15 mL) extra virgin olive oil
½ tsp (2 mL) chili paste
2 Tbsp (25 mL) chopped fresh parsley
1 Tbsp (15 mL) basil pesto
freshly ground black pepper to taste

1 In a small bowl, combine the relish ingredients and set aside for 20 minutes at room temperature to meld the flavors. Cover and refrigerate if making in advance—but return to room temperature for serving.

2 Season the fish on both sides with salt and pepper. Heat the oil in a nonstick sauté pan over medium-high heat. When the pan is hot, sear the fish, flesh-side down, for 5 minutes.

3 Turn the fish over, skin-side down, reduce heat to medium, and continue to cook for 5 minutes longer, just until the fish is cooked through. A 1-inch- (2.5-cm-) thick piece of fish will take 10 minutes in total to cook.

4 Set each piece of fish on a warmed individual serving plate and top each portion with a spoonful of the tomato and olive relish. Serves 4.

Simple Salmon Cakes

When there's leftover grilled salmon and mashed potatoes (or even a can of sockeye in the pantry) you're already well on your way to making these comforting cakes for a fast supper. Just serve with a salad and you're done.

1 small onion, minced (or 2 green onions)
2 Tbsp (30 mL) butter, divided
2 cups (500 mL) leftover mashed potatoes
1 cup (250 mL) cooked salmon (leftover or canned), bones removed and flaked

1 egg
salt and freshly ground black pepper
1 tsp (5 mL) chopped parsley
¼ cup (60 mL) cornmeal

1 Sauté the onion in 1 Tbsp (15 mL) of butter until tender. In a medium bowl, combine the mashed potatoes, salmon, egg, salt, pepper, and parsley. Stir in the cooked onion. If there's time, chill before forming into small cakes with your hands. Evenly sprinkle the cornmeal onto a plate. Roll the salmon cakes in the cornmeal to coat all sides and then set them aside on a rack until ready to cook.

2 Heat the remaining 1 Tbsp (15 mL) of butter in a non-stick sauté pan over medium heat. Fry the cakes until golden brown on both sides, about 3 to 5 minutes per side; add more butter to the pan if necessary. Serve with tartar sauce. Serves 4.

Beer Batter for Fish

This is the best way to make fish and chips at home. Serve the fish with a splash of malt vinegar or freshly squeezed lemon juice, Oven Fries (see page 116), Classic Coleslaw (see page 165), and a simple mayonnaise-based tartar sauce (see below).

Batter

1 cup (250 mL) all-purpose flour

1 tsp (5 mL) salt

1½ lb (750 g) boneless white fish fillets
(cod, halibut, sole, pickerel, etc.)

one 12-oz/375-mL bottle beer (any lager will do)

½ tsp (2 mL) hot pepper sauce (optional)

1 egg

½ cup (125 mL) all-purpose flour

canola or corn oil for frying

1 To make the batter, in a bowl, combine the 1 cup (250 mL) of flour with the salt. In another bowl, whisk the beer, hot sauce, and egg until smooth. Stir this into the flour and salt mixture. Cover the bowl with plastic wrap and let it rest for 1 to 2 hours.

2 Preheat the oven to 200°F (95°C).

3 To fry the fish, heat about 2 inches (5 cm) of canola or corn oil in a deep sauté pan. The oil should be about 375°F (190°C)—use a deep-fat or candy thermometer to test it. Put the ½ cup (125 mL) of flour on a plate. Roll the fillets in this flour and shake off any excess. Using tongs, pick up a piece of floured fish, dip in the batter to coat both sides, then set it gently into the hot oil. Fry the fish, a few pieces at a time, until brown and crisp on both sides. Drain on a paper towel–lined plate, then place in the preheated oven to stay hot. Serve with fries, coleslaw, and tartar sauce. Serves 4.

WISE GUY: To make tartar sauce from scratch, combine ½ cup (125 mL) mayonnaise, 1 Tbsp (15 mL) lemon juice, 2 Tbsp (30 mL) sweet pickle relish, and pepper to taste.

Salmon Burgers

This is the place to use the rich "belly fat" from those big sides of king salmon. Trim the fat from the bottom of the fillets and save it for these juicy burgers.

1 lb (500 g) salmon pieces, skin and bones
   removed
2 tsp (10 mL) light soy sauce
1 green onion, finely chopped

1 egg white
½ cup (125 mL) dry breadcrumbs
   or cracker crumbs
salt and freshly ground black pepper

1 Chop the salmon by hand or use a food processor (don't purée the fish, just pulse to chop it into a chunky mass).

2 In a medium bowl, combine the chopped salmon, soy sauce, green onion, egg white, and enough breadcrumbs to make a mixture that holds together. Season with salt and pepper.

3 Form into patties and pan-fry in a non-stick pan for 3 to 4 minutes per side. You can also freeze the burgers and cook them, still frozen, on a hot, well-oiled grill for about 5 minutes per side. Makes 4 to 6 burgers.

Halibut Chowder

Make a fish stock to start this elegant fish chowder, using the bones reserved from filleting your fish. Any extra stock can be frozen to use in future soups and sauces.

Fish stock

1 medium carrot, peeled and cut into chunks
1 large onion, cut into chunks
1 tsp (5 mL) salt
6 whole black peppercorns

3 stalks celery, with leaves
1 sprig of thyme or parsley (or both)
1 bay leaf
2 lb (1 kg) fish trimmings (bones, heads, etc.)
16 cups (4 L) cold water

Chowder

¼ cup (60 mL) butter
3 Tbsp (45 mL) all-purpose flour
6 cups (1.5 L) fish stock
1 cup (250 mL) finely diced carrots
½ cup (125 mL) finely diced parsnips
1 lb (500 g) skinless halibut (or other white fish)
    fillet, cubed

½ cup (125 mL) cleaned and finely sliced leeks,
    white part only
2 egg yolks
salt and freshly ground black pepper
3 Tbsp (45 mL) minced parsley
½ cup (125 mL) sour cream

1 To make the stock, combine the carrot, onion, salt, peppercorns, herbs, bay leaf, celery, fish trimmings, and water in a large stock pot. Bring to a boil over high heat. Reduce the heat to low, cover, and simmer for 30 minutes. Strain, discarding the solids, then return the stock to the pot. Simmer, uncovered for 15 minutes to reduce slightly. You will have about 12 cups (2½ L) of stock—it keeps for a long time in the freezer, or for a week in the refrigerator.

2 To make the chowder, in a large saucepan over medium-low heat, melt the butter and whisk in the flour. Cook for 1 minute, then slowly whisk in the stock. Stir until the mixture comes to a boil and thickens slightly. Add the carrots, parsnips, and leeks. Simmer for 10 more minutes, then add the cubed fish. Cook for 5 minutes or until the halibut turns translucent.

3 In a small bowl, beat the egg yolks. Whisk in ½ cup (125 mL) of the hot soup broth, 3 Tbsp (45 mL) at a time, just to heat the eggs. Remove the soup from the heat and stir in the egg mixture. Season with salt and pepper to taste. Serve immediately in wide, shallow bowls. Garnish with a dollop of sour cream and a sprig of parsley. Serves 6.

Candied Salmon on Asian Greens

This is The Guy's favorite "buffet" dish—it uses a whole side of fresh salmon. The fish is lightly cured with a spiced salt and sugar rub before being baked in a sweet glaze. Start preparation of this dish the day before you plan to serve it.

3 Tbsp (45 mL) sea salt
3 Tbsp (45 mL) brown sugar
3 Tbsp (45 mL) granulated sugar
1 or 2 chipotle chilies in adobo sauce, minced
2 tsp (5 mL) minced garlic
2 to 3 lb (1 to 1.5 kg) fresh wild Pacific salmon
  fillet, skin on

2 Tbsp (30 mL) sweet Indonesian soy sauce
  (known as kecap manis) or oyster sauce
3 Tbsp (45 mL) brown sugar
1 Tbsp (15 mL) crushed black peppercorns
baby spinach, pea shoots and/or shredded
  bok choy

1 In a small bowl, combine the sea salt, brown sugar, granulated sugar, chilies, and garlic. Rub this over the flesh side of the fillet. Place the fish, flesh-side down, into a non-reactive baking pan. Cover and refrigerate for 24 hours. Remove the salmon from the refrigerator and brush off the excess rub. Place the fillet on a parchment paper–lined baking sheet, skin-side down. Allow the salmon to dry at room temperature for 30 minutes.

2 Preheat the oven to 400°F (200°C).

3 Brush the salmon flesh with kecap manis or oyster sauce, then sprinkle the brown sugar and cracked black peppercorns evenly overtop.

4 Bake the fillet in the preheated oven for 10 to 15 minutes.

5 Serve the fish warm on a platter of greens. Serves 6.

> **WISE GUY:** Kecap manis is a thick, sweet soy sauce from Indonesia. You can substitute oyster sauce or use half dark soy sauce and half corn syrup or maple syrup.

Home-Smoked Salmon or Trout

The Guy uses this method to prepare his catch of rainbow trout, lake trout, or small pink salmon fillets for smoking on the barbecue or home smoker. Add fresh herbs or citrus zest to your rub for a gourmet touch, and try using a little green willow or alder in your fire for an authentic Native-style smoke.

If you're still out at your fishing camp, you can smoke whole, butterflied fish over an open fire. Just impale the fish on a green willow branch and weave a few smaller sticks through the fish, crosswise, to keep it flat and open. Position the fish over the fire and wait for the smoke to work its magic.

½ cup (125 mL) coarse kosher salt
¼ cup (60 mL) packed brown sugar
   or maple sugar
1 Tbsp (15 mL) crushed black peppercorns
¼ tsp (1 mL) paprika

1 tsp (5 mL) crushed juniper berries
4 rainbow or lake trout fillets, skin on (scaling is
   not necessary for trout but should be done
   for larger-scaled fish like salmon)
4 Tbsp (60 mL) olive oil

1 In a small bowl, combine the salt, sugar, peppercorns, paprika, and juniper berries.

2 Lay two fillets, skin-side down, in a shallow ceramic dish and spread the flesh side with the salt cure mixture. Top with the remaining two fillets, skin-side up.

3 Cover the fish with plastic wrap. Place a plate or small board overtop, add some weight to the top (a brick or cans of food will do), and refrigerate the fish from 10 to 24 hours. Rinse the fish and pat dry. Let the fish air dry, uncovered, for 1 hour in the refrigerator. Brush the flesh side lightly with olive oil and smoke in the top rack of a smoker for 2 to 3 hours, over the wood of your choice. To smoke on your gas barbecue, heat only one burner. Soak some wood chips and wrap them in a foil packet. Punch holes in the packet to release the smoke and place it over the lowest flame. Cook the fish indirectly, on the unlit side of the grill, skin-side down. Smoke over low heat until just cooked through, about 30 to 40 minutes.

4 Serve the smoked fish on small pieces of heavy rye bread or thin flatbread crackers. Top with a dollop of sour cream and a garnish of chive sprigs or minced red onion. Makes about 2 lb (1 kg) of smoked fish. (Smoked fish freezes well and will keep frozen for several months.) Serves 4 to 6.

Grilled Salmon with Tomato Mango Salsa

Here's another stylish way to serve that catch of wild king salmon. The sweet sauce glazes the salmon as it cooks, and the fruited salsa adds another layer of sweet, exotic flavor. Think about serving a dry German Riesling to balance the flavors of this chic supper.

Salsa
3 Roma tomatoes, seeded and chopped
1 mango, peeled and finely diced
1 clove garlic, minced or pressed
2 green onions, chopped

2 Tbsp (30 mL) chopped fresh mint or cilantro
1 Tbsp (15 mL) freshly squeezed lime juice
½ tsp (2 mL) fish sauce or soy sauce
1 Tbsp (15 mL) light brown sugar
½ to 1 tsp (2 to 5 mL) Asian chili sauce

four 5-oz (150-g) salmon fillets, skin on
olive oil
salt and freshly ground white pepper
2 Tbsp (30 mL) butter

2 Tbsp (30 mL) honey
2 Tbsp (30 mL) dark soy sauce
¼ tsp (1 mL) Asian chili paste
2 tsp (10 mL) oyster sauce

basmati rice for four (3 cups/750 mL cooked rice)

1 In a medium serving bowl, combine the tomatoes, mango, garlic, green onions, mint or cilantro, lime juice, fish sauce, brown sugar, and chili sauce. Set aside.

2 Meanwhile, cut each 5-oz (150-g) portion of fish into two pieces. Rub the skin side of the fish with a little olive oil to prevent it from sticking to the grill. Season the flesh side with salt and white pepper. Set aside.

3 Heat the butter, honey, and soy sauce together in a small saucepan over medium heat until the butter melts and the mixture is smooth and thick. Stir in the chili paste and oyster sauce, remove from heat and let cool.

4 Brush the flesh side of the salmon liberally with the cooled sauce and set aside to marinate for 10 minutes. Preheat the barbecue to medium-high heat and brush the grill with oil. Place the fish, skin-side down, on the grill. Close the lid on the barbecue and grill until the fish is barely cooked through, about 10 to 12 minutes. (Brush the fish with sauce once or twice more during grilling time.)

5 Pile equal amounts of basmati rice in the center of four plates and arrange the pieces of grilled salmon on top. Top with a spoonful of the tomato-mango salsa and a sprig of cilantro. Serves 4.

The Big Smoke

The Guy loves to take a Saturday afternoon off to bask in the sun with a cool one in hand. But it can be hard to justify that kind of lazy downtime these days—unless, of course, he's stoking the smoker.

Yes, during these lazy, hazy days of summer, The Guy's best friend is Little Joe, his boxy backyard smoker. Little Joe must be fed, slowly stoked with hot coals and wet wood chips, all day long if The Guy wants to enjoy the flavor of slow-smoked brisket, chicken, ribs, or pulled pork. This is the true barbecue of the South.

You can't rush The Guy or smoky Joe—plan on a good eight to 12 hours in the hammock for this kind of cooking. It's the ultimate slow food for summertime.

The Secrets of Competition Barbecue

The Guy loves to hang out with his smoker. But when you want to win at competition barbecue, there's more to cooking than smoke (and mirrors). Flavor is one thing, but presentation is important, too. The Guy picked up some great barbecue basics (and some inside information that can help you win) at barbecue boot camp, taught by big barbecue guys like Bob Lyons and Paul Kirk, a couple of legends on the competition barbecue circuit. Herewith, a little of their collective barbecue wisdom:

Barbecue is a noun, not a verb—referring to the slow-cooked, smoked beef brisket, pork butt, chicken, and ribs that come off a hot smoker after hours of indirect heat and smoke.

Buy a smoker that fits your smoking future—an inexpensive domed R2-D2 model if you're just planning to compete among friends, or a fancy custom-made smoker on a trailer to haul behind your pick-up if barbecue is your life. But remember, many a serious competition has been won by a careful cook on a simple Weber kettle barbecue, with the right coal and well-soaked wood, and a quality cut of meat.

When your barbecue is falling off the bone and ready to be presented to those picky judges, carefully slice the meat (or separate the ribs into neat sections) and arrange in the competition container (usually a styrofoam box or plate). Keep things neat and tidy, perfectly fanned over a bit of fresh lettuce. But don't get too fancy—barbecue judges are big on consistency and rules—too much flair will cost you points, so stick to the basics.

Beer-Can Chicken

The Guy isn't quite sure who first plunked a whole chicken upright over an open can of beer to roast, but the technique—spawned no doubt somewhere among the wild and crazy slow barbecue crowd in the southern states—has become such a popular way to cook a whole bird that there are now a variety of porcelain and metal stands available to prop your chicken up while it cooks.

The beauty of a beer can—half-filled with beer, cola, or even wine—is twofold. It's inexpensive and always available at a backyard barbecue. And it serves as both a stand and a receptacle for the liquid that keeps your chicken moist while it bakes on the barbie (or in the oven).

You can use any rub, and any liquid in the can, from alcohol to pop or fruit juice. Just make sure the can is open and partially drained (always use a bottle opener to punch a couple of extra holes in the top and you'll never have an exploding beer-can chicken on your hands). The results will be tastiest if you cook your chicken over charcoal and throw some chunks of soaked mesquite or applewood on the fire to create some smoke, but you can easily do this on a gas barbecue or even in your oven on a baking sheet.

1 whole chicken, about 4 lb (2 kg)
2 Tbsp (30 mL) ballpark-style yellow prepared
   mustard

Rub
1 Tbsp (15 mL) brown sugar
1 tsp (5 mL) salt
½ tsp (2 mL) paprika

1 beer or pop can, half-filled with beer, wine, pop,
   or fruit juice

½ tsp (2 mL) granulated garlic
½ tsp (2 mL) onion powder
½ tsp (2 mL) cumin
½ tsp (2 mL) freshly ground black pepper

1 Remove the neck and giblets from the chicken cavity, then rinse the chicken with water, inside and out. Dry the bird—inside and out—with paper towels. Pull the excess skin over the neck cavity and flip the wings around to the back of the chicken, using the wings to hold the skin in place.

2 Rub the outside of the chicken with the mustard. Combine the rub ingredients in a bowl and sprinkle over the entire surface of the bird. Rub a little on the inside, too.

3 If using beer, open the beer can, pour out half of the beer, and use a bottle opener to punch two or three additional holes around the top of the can. Stand the can on the counter and slide cavity of the chicken over the can.

4 Preheat the barbecue to medium heat. If you're using a gas barbecue, turn one burner off and cook the bird indirectly by placing it on the unlit side of the grill. If you're using charcoal, bank the coals beneath one side of the grill and set the bird on the opposite side. Place a disposable foil pie pan under the grill to catch any fat that drips from the roasting chicken. Throw some soaked wood chips directly onto the charcoal or place a metal smoker box filled with soaked wood chips over the fire bricks inside your gas grill.

5 Carefully transfer the chicken to the grill and balance it upright, using the can and the two chicken legs to form a tripod. Close the grill lid and cook the chicken for about 75 to 90 minutes or until a thermometer, inserted into the thickest part of the thigh, reaches 180°F (85°C).

6 If you're cooking the chicken in the oven, preheat to 350°F (180°C). Set the chicken upright on the can, then place on a baking sheet to catch the drips. Roast for 75 minutes or until a thermometer, inserted into the thickest part of the thigh, reaches 180°F (85°C).

7 Using oven mitts, remove the chicken and the can from the grill, taking care to support the can (it's filled with boiling liquid that can burn you if you spill it). Let the chicken rest, still balanced on the can, for 10 minutes. Remove the can, discard the beer, and carve the bird as usual. Serves 3 to 4.

A CAN OF HIS FAVOURITE BEER

PUNCH EXTRA HOLES!

Secret BBQ Sauce

Coca Cola may be the real thing, but any cola will do to add that je ne sais quoi to your next barbecue sauce. Keep this a secret and use it to win the next neighborhood cooking contest, whether you're basting chicken, ribs, or steak.

1 Tbsp (15 mL) canola oil
1 medium onion, minced
2 cloves garlic, minced
1 Tbsp (15 mL) minced fresh ginger
one 14-oz (398-mL) can tomato sauce
½ cup (125 mL) ketchup or chili sauce

1 cup (250 mL) cola
1 Tbsp (15 mL) Worcestershire sauce
1 whole chipotle chili in adobo sauce, minced
¼ tsp (1 mL) ground cinnamon
salt and freshly ground black pepper

1 In a saucepan, heat the oil over medium heat. Add the onion, garlic, and ginger. Sauté for 10 minutes or until it's fragrant and beginning to brown. Add the remaining ingredients and stir to mix well. Bring to a boil. Reduce the heat to medium-low and simmer, uncovered, for 15 minutes. Cool the sauce, then purée it in a blender or food processor. Season with salt and pepper to taste. Pour into a clean jar and refrigerate for up to 2 weeks. Makes about 2 cups.

WISE GUY: Use this sauce to marinate chicken or ribs for 30 minutes before grilling. Make sure you cook your meats away from direct flames, or over medium-low heat (no more than 300°F/150°C) as this sauce is sweet and burns quickly. Baste the meat lightly with this sauce as it cooks or wait until the last 15 minutes of cooking and top your meat with extra sauce.

Smoky BBQ Ribs

This is the time to lay out the big coin for baby back ribs. Never trust anyone who suggests you boil these meaty racks before putting them on the grill—this doesn't make ribs tender, it just removes the fat your ribs require to stay juicy during low, slow smoking.

The real competition barbecue trick lies in preparing the ribs for the barbecue or smoker. Always peel off the translucent skin on the back of the racks—this helps guarantee that the flavor goes right into the meat. Look for the best deals on pork ribs at Asian markets and opt for the meatiest (heaviest) specimens.

2 to 3 sides baby back ribs (close to 2 lb/1 kg apiece)

Barbecue Sauce (see facing page)

1 Trim the ribs. Cut off the flap of meat on the inside of the ribs (save it for the soup pot). Cut off the rib tips and the pointed end to form a nice rectangular rack (freeze the trimmings to use later in soup stock).

2 Remove the membrane from the back of the rack of ribs. This membrane, or "fell", is tough and your ribs will be tough if you leave it on. Using a knife, free a corner of the membrane, then grasp it tightly with a paper towel or clean cloth and pull it away in one piece.

3 Coat the ribs on both sides in barbecue sauce and marinate in the refrigerator from 1 to 8 hours.

4 Heat the barbecue to medium-low (300°F/150°C). Turn off one burner so you can grill the ribs over indirect heat. Brush the unlit side of the grill with oil and place the ribs on the grill, meaty-side down. Cover and grill the ribs indirectly for about 1 hour, turning and basting with extra sauce often. Watch to make sure the temperature stays at an even 250° to 300°F (120° to 150°C). You can also do this on a charcoal smoker—just make sure to keep the heat constant and low.

5 Stop basting about 15 minutes before the ribs are done. The ribs are done when the meat pulls away from the ends of the bones. To serve, cut each rack into 3 or 4 sections. Serves 4.

WISE GUY: Add some real southern smoky flavor while you grill your ribs by placing some soaked wood chips (wrapped in a punctured foil pouch or in a special smoker box) on the hot side of the grill. Make sure to keep the lid down while they burn and smoke.

Barbecue Beef Brisket

A beef brisket can be slow-cooked in the oven, a covered gas barbecue, or a wood-fired smoker. If you have the time, the smoker yields the best smoky flavor. You can sear the roast on the grill to give it some charcoal character, and finish it in a slow oven.

On a hot summer day, start up the smoker early in the morning and cook it low and slow—you'll be serving brisket 12 to 18 hours later. Or try the speedier method.

Spice rub
2 Tbsp (30 mL) chili powder
2 Tbsp (30 mL) brown sugar
2 Tbsp (30 mL) kosher salt

1 tsp (5 mL) each: cumin, oregano, garlic powder, onion powder, black pepper, paprika, and mustard powder

one 6-lb (2.7-kg) beef brisket or chuck roast
3 Tbsp (45 mL) olive oil

1 In a small bowl, combine the chili powder, brown sugar, kosher salt, cumin, oregano, garlic, onion powder, black pepper, paprika, and mustard powder. Rub the meat on all sides with olive oil, then coat evenly with the spice mixture. Place the roast in a zippered plastic bag and refrigerate from 2 hours to overnight.

2 Bring the roast to room temperature before grilling or smoking. Serves 8 to 10.

WISE GUY: Buy a good quality barbecue sauce or make your own (see page 444). To torque up a basic store-bought sauce, add your favorite spices (try garlic, cayenne, chili powder, cinnamon, and chipotle pepper powder), something sweet like honey or molasses, and something secret like strong black coffee, beer, or hoisin sauce.

Slow Style:

1 Heat the smoker. Light a pile of charcoal briquettes in the firebox. Soak 1 lb (500 g) of wood chunks, hickory or mesquite, in a pail of warm water. When the charcoal briquettes are uniformly white, add more charcoal and a chunk of wood.

2 Fill the smoker's water pan with water or beer and set over the coals. Place one of the racks above the water pan and set the roast on the rack. Cover the smoker and smoke until the internal temperature reaches 160° to 170°F (71° to 77°C). This will require at least 12 hours of cooking, depending on the ambient air temperature.

3 While the beef is cooking, feed the fire every hour with additional coal and a few wood chips. The idea is to keep the temperature between 200° and 250°F (93° and 120°C). Low-and-slow cooking makes tough cuts like brisket extremely tender. If you wish, when feeding the fire, spritz the meat with your favorite "mop"—apple juice, beer, or wine are often used to keep the outside of the meat moist.

4 The brisket is done when the meat is easily shredded with a knife and fork.

Faster Style:

1 Heat the grill (charcoal or gas) over medium heat. Place the roast on the grill. Cook the brisket, turning, for about 30 minutes, until nicely browned on all sides. If you're using coals, toss on some pre-soaked apple or mesquite wood chips to generate smoke (if you're using gas, put the wet wood chips into a metal smoking box or a pouch of heavy foil, punched with holes, and set it right on top of the fire bricks).

2 Cover the barbecue to smoke the brisket while grilling. When the roast is nicely charred, place it into a roasting pan, cover the pan tightly with foil, and roast in a 200°F (95°C) oven for 5 hours (1 hour per 1 lb/500 g).

3 Slice or shred the meat and serve with Secret Barbecue Sauce (see page 444). You can also heat the shredded meat in the barbecue sauce and pile it onto buns to serve. Serves 8 to 10.

Pulled Pork Butt with Mustard Sauce

Of all the great things The Guy has served off his simple home smoker, the lowly pork shoulder (a.k.a. pork butt) is an all-time favorite. This is the idiot-proof cut to smoke, naturally larded with just enough fat to keep it moist and juicy for hours on the grill, even if you accidentally let the heat rise above the magic 225°F (105°C) mark.

1 pork butt or shoulder, bone in, about 3 lb/
    1.5 kg (leg is too lean for this process)

¼ cup (60 mL) regular ballpark mustard
    (don't use fancy Dijon, it doesn't contain
    enough sugar)

Dry Rub

1 Tbsp (15 mL) salt
¼ cup (60 mL) white sugar
2 Tbsp (30 mL) each: brown sugar, cumin, ground
    ginger, chili powder, black pepper, and garlic
    powder

¼ cup (60 mL) Hungarian paprika (or other good-
    quality, sweet paprika)
1 Tbsp (15 mL) dry mustard

Mustard Sauce

1 Tbsp (15 mL) mayonnaise
¼ cup (60 mL) mustard
1 Tbsp (15 mL) ketchup

2 Tbsp (30 mL) honey
1 Tbsp (15 mL) cider vinegar
1 tsp (5 mL) Tabasco sauce
1 clove garlic, pressed

6 to 8 crusty rolls

1 Rub the pork with mustard to coat all sides. Combine the dry rub ingredients and massage generously into the pork to coat well (any unused extra rub can go back into your spice cupboard). Leave the pork at room temperature for 10 minutes, for the rub to get tacky. The salt will draw some of the moisture out of the meat, which will form a crust as it cooks to seal in the juices.

2 Preheat the smoker and place the pork above the coals on a rack. If you're using a gas grill, turn one burner off and place the roast on the unlit side of the grill. If you're using coals, toss on some pre-soaked apple or mesquite wood chips to generate some smoke (if you're using gas, put the wet wood chips into a metal smoking box or a pouch of heavy foil, punched with holes, and set it right on top of the fire bricks).

3 Keep the heat constant and low (about 200° to 225°F/95° to 105°C) and cook the pork until the internal temperature reaches 180°F (85°C). The pork should be tender and falling apart, easy to "pull" into shreds with a fork. This will take 6 to 8 hours.

4 Combine the mustard sauce ingredients in a saucepan over medium heat. Whisk until warm and well combined.

5 Pile the pulled pork on crusty rolls, then drizzle with the mustard sauce. Serve the sandwiches with coleslaw, either on the side or piled on the sandwich. Serves 6.

WISE GUY: Pork is safe to eat at an internal temperature of 165° F (73°C). At this point the pork will be cooked and sliceable. But for pulled pork you must cook the meat to the "falling apart" stage.

The Fabulous Baker Boy

There are times when The Guy needs to bring home the baking. Birthdays, holidays, other significant milestones—they all must be marked with a cake. A bit of homemade baking comes in handy at other times, too, whether the school is holding a bake sale or there's a potluck party on the horizon.

Without the brilliant artisan baker guy down the street kneading sourdoughs at all hours of the morning, The Guy would starve. But there are times when only a bit of homemade baking will do.

Herewith, his favorite simple cakes, and other baked goodies.

Lemony Yellow Pound Cake

Make this lemony pound cake in a springform pan. In the summer, top it with fresh fruit and whipped cream or lemon sauce. For your honey's birthday, dust it with icing sugar and decorate with fresh flowers and candles. A pound cake with panache!

¾ cup (175 mL) cubed unsalted butter
1 cup (250 mL) granulated sugar
4 large eggs
2 cups (500 mL) pastry flour

1½ (7 mL) tsp baking powder
¼ tsp (1 mL) salt
¼ cup (60 mL) freshly squeezed lemon juice
1 Tbsp (15 mL) finely grated lemon zest

1 Preheat the oven to 325°F (160°C).

2 In a mixing bowl, use an electric mixer to cream the butter and sugar together until light and fluffy. Add the eggs, one at a time, and beat until the mixture is silky smooth.

3 In another bowl, combine the flour, baking powder, and salt. Add the dry mixture to the batter in small amounts, alternating with a bit of the lemon juice and zest, stirring with a whisk until smooth.

4 Spoon the batter into a buttered, 8-inch (2-L) springform pan. Bake for 40 to 50 minutes in the preheated oven or until the top is golden and a skewer inserted into the center of the cake comes out clean. Cool in the pan before transferring to a plate. Serve dusted with icing sugar or topped with lemon curd sauce (see below). Serves 8.

WISE GUY: To make an ethereal lemon sauce to dollop over this cake (or over a bowl of fresh summer fruit) combine ½ cup (125 mL) of lemon curd (homemade or from a jar) with ½ cup (125 mL) of whipped cream (or ½ cup/125 mL of mascarpone cheese or ½ cup/125 mL of plain yogurt). Use a microplane grater to add a little fresh lemon zest. You can even split the cake horizontally and fill with fresh berries and this lemon sauce for a summer lemon shortcake.

The Guy's Chocolate Birthday Cake

Nothing says Happy Birthday better than this old-fashioned chocolate layer cake, fancied up with a bit of raspberry jam in the middle. Take it anywhere someone is marking another anniversary, and you'll earn brownie points.

¾ cup (175 mL) Dutch cocoa powder
1 cup (250 mL) boiling water
2 eggs
2 cups (500 mL) all-purpose flour
1½ cups (375 mL) sugar
1 tsp (5 mL) baking powder
1 tsp (5 mL) baking soda

½ tsp (2 mL) salt
1 cup (250 mL) buttermilk
½ cup (125 mL) melted unsalted butter
   or canola oil
2 tsp (10 mL) pure vanilla extract
⅓ cup (75 mL) raspberry jam (or substitute
   cherry or blueberry jam)

1 Preheat the oven to 350°F (180°C) .

2 Butter and flour two 9-inch (1.5-L) round cake pans and set aside.

3 Measure the cocoa into a mixing bowl and stir in the boiling water. Cool for 5 to 10 minutes, then use an electric mixer to beat in the eggs one at a time.

4 In another bowl, combine the flour, sugar, baking powder, baking soda, and salt.

5 Gradually add the dry ingredients to the chocolate mixture, beating on a low speed. Then add the buttermilk, melted butter, and vanilla. Continue beating for 2 to 3 minutes.

6 Divide the batter among the prepared pans and bake in the preheated oven for 25 to 30 minutes or until a toothpick inserted in the center of each cake comes out clean.

7 Cool the cakes on a wire rack for 15 minutes before removing from the pans. Return the cakes to the rack and let them cool completely.

8 With a long, serrated bread knife, slice the rounded top from one cake to make it totally flat. In a medium bowl, chop or crumble the removed cake layer. Bind these pieces with the raspberry jam, then spread evenly over the layer from which it was removed (this becomes the bottom layer). Place the bottom layer of the cake on a plate or a thick piece of cardboard covered with foil. Position the second layer over the filling and frost the top and sides of the cake with chocolate icing. Decorate with chocolate sprinkles, if desired, add the candles, and sing "Happy Birthday."

Creamy Chocolate Icing

½ cup (125 mL) unsalted butter, softened
½ cup (125 mL) Dutch cocoa powder
2 tsp (10 mL) pure vanilla extract (or other flavoring like brandy or Kahlúa)

2 cups (500 mL) icing sugar
¼ cup (60 mL) whipping cream or milk
chocolate sprinkles (optional)

1 In a small bowl, use an electric mixer or whisk to beat the butter until fluffy. Stir in the cocoa and vanilla, then gradually add the icing sugar until the icing is thick. Beat in enough cream to create a spreadable icing.

Carrot Spice Cake

This is a popular cake recipe—the kind of big cake you can take anywhere (from a church supper to a neighborhood potluck to a birthday at the office). For more formal cake occasions, you can use this recipe for a layer cake (three 9-inch/23-cm layers). It also makes an impressive birthday cake, especially if you make it in layers, or into frosted carrot cupcakes for kids' birthday parties (line your muffin pans with colorful paper cups, get some sparklers, then dim the lights). You'll need either a 10-inch (4-L) Bundt pan, a 9- x 13-inch (3.5-L) baking pan, or three 9-inch/1.5-L cake pans.

½ cup (125 mL) raisins
2 Tbsp (30 mL) Grand Marnier
4 cups (1 L) peeled and grated carrots (about 1 lb/500 g)
2½ cups (625 mL) all-purpose flour
1 tsp (5 mL) baking soda
2½ tsp (12 mL) baking powder
1 Tbsp (15 mL) ground cinnamon
½ tsp (2 mL) ground cloves

½ tsp (2 mL) ground nutmeg
1¼ cups (310 mL) canola oil
2½ cups (625 mL) packed dark brown sugar
¼ cup (60 mL) molasses
1 Tbsp (15 mL) pure vanilla extract
4 eggs
1 Tbsp (15 mL) freshly squeezed lemon juice
3 Tbsp (45 mL) orange marmalade
1 cup (250 mL) walnuts, coarsely chopped

Frosting
one 4-oz (114-g) package cream cheese
1½ cups (375 mL) icing sugar
¼ cup (60 mL) unsalted butter, softened

3 Tbsp (45 mL) Grand Marnier
1 Tbsp (15 mL) heavy cream or milk
finely chopped toasted walnuts (optional)

recipe continued on next page

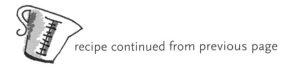 recipe continued from previous page

1 Preheat the oven to 375°F (190°C).

2 Put the raisins into a small bowl with the Grand Marnier and microwave on high for 30 seconds. Remove and set aside to allow the raisins to plump and soak up the liqueur.

3 Scrub the carrots well and grate them, using a hand grater (small holes) or the grater attachment on your food processor. Set aside.

4 In a bowl, combine the flour, baking soda, baking powder, cinnamon, cloves, and nutmeg. Set aside.

5 In another larger bowl, use an electric mixer or stand mixer to beat the oil, brown sugar, molasses, vanilla, and eggs until well combined. Stir in the lemon juice and marmalade. Slowly add the dry ingredients, beating to create a silky batter. Stir in the plumped raisins, grated carrots, and walnuts.

6 Rub your baking pan(s) with butter—you can use one deep 10-inch (4-L) Bundt pan or three 9-inch (1.5-L) cake pans—and dust with flour (put some flour in the greased pan, shake around to coat, then tip out the excess).

7 Pour the batter into the pan(s), making sure the pans aren't filled more than 2/3 full to allow for rising during baking. Bake for 35 to 40 minutes or until a skewer inserted in the center of the cake comes out clean. A Bundt cake will take up to 30 minutes longer to cook than the layer cakes (65 to 70 minutes in total).

8 Remove the cake from the oven and place on a wire rack to cool.

9 To make the frosting, use an electric mixer to cream together the cream cheese and butter until smooth. Beat in the Grand Marnier and enough cream to make a spreadable frosting. Make a stiffer frosting (a little more icing sugar) if you're making a layer cake. If you're making a Bundt cake, add a little more cream so you can drizzle the frosting over the top and sides of the cake (or over each piece as you serve it).

10 If you're making a layered cake, frost the layers and the top and sides of the cake. Press ground toasted walnuts around the outside of the layer cake to finish (or sprinkle over a Bundt).
Makes 1 cake (serves 12).

Orange Cranberry Bundt Cake

With its festive color and seasonal ingredients, this is The Guy's favorite cake to take to a holiday potluck but it's also nice for brunch. Look for one of the new soft, silicon Bundt pans: cakes pop out as easy as ice cubes from this miracle baking material and, amazingly, they brown beautifully.

You can substitute chopped apples or blueberries for the cranberries in this moist cake.

1 cup (250 mL) unsalted butter, softened
2 cups (500 mL) granulated sugar
4 eggs
3 Tbsp (45 mL) orange marmalade
2 cups (500 mL) all-purpose flour
1 tsp (5 mL) baking powder
½ tsp (2 mL) baking soda
½ tsp (2 mL) salt

2 tsp (10 mL) ground ginger
1 tsp (5 mL) ground cinnamon
½ tsp (2 mL) ground nutmeg
½ cup (125 mL) buttermilk
2 cups (500 mL) cranberries, fresh or frozen
2 tsp finely grated orange rind
   (use a microplane grater)

Glaze
½ cup (125 mL) icing sugar
3 to 4 Tbsp (45 to 60 mL) freshly squeezed orange
   juice

1 Tbsp (15 mL) orange marmalade (or finely grated
   orange rind)

1 Preheat the oven to 350°F (180°C). Using an electric mixer, cream the butter and gradually add the sugar, beating until fluffy and light. Add the eggs, one at a time, beating after each addition. Stir in the marmalade.

2 In another bowl, combine the flour, baking powder, baking soda, salt, ginger, cinnamon, and nutmeg.

3 Gradually add the flour mixture to the batter, in portions, alternating with the buttermilk, and beating after each addition.

4 Fold the cranberries and grated orange rind into the batter.

5 If using a silicon Bundt pan, place it on a baking sheet to stabilize, and pour in the batter, smoothing the top. Bake for 1 hour and 10 minutes in the preheated oven or until a skewer inserted into the center of the cake comes out clean. Let the cake cool in the pan on the wire rack for 15 minutes before turning it out onto the rack to cool completely.

6 To make the glaze, combine the sugar, orange juice, and marmalade. Drizzle over the cake. Serves 12.

Ginger Cake with Warm Apple Compote

Warm gingerbread with a chunky applesauce—what could be more comforting? Add a dollop of honey-sweetened whipped cream or mascarpone, just because.

1½ cups (325 mL) cake flour
1 tsp (5 mL) baking soda
¼ tsp (1 mL) salt
1 large egg
¼ cup (60 mL) blackstrap molasses
¼ cup (60 mL) maple syrup

½ cup (125 mL) buttermilk
½ cup (125 mL) unsalted butter
½ cup (125 mL) packed brown sugar
1 Tbsp (15 mL) grated lemon zest
1 Tbsp (15 mL) grated fresh ginger

Compote
6 apples, peeled, cored, and cut into wedges
2 Tbsp (30 mL) unsalted butter
½ cup (125 mL) packed brown sugar

¼ cup (600 mL) water
½ tsp (2 mL) ground cinnamon
¼ tsp (1 mL) ground ginger
2 Tbsp (30 mL) Calvados or brandy

1 Preheat the oven to 350°F (180°C).

2 Butter and flour a 9-inch (1.5-L) round cake pan.

3 In a medium bowl, combine the flour, baking soda, and salt. Set aside. In another bowl, whisk together the molasses, maple syrup, and buttermilk.

4 With an electric mixer, cream the butter until soft. Add the brown sugar and continue to beat until fluffy. Continue mixing while you slowly add the egg.

5 Alternately add the molasses mixture and flour mixture to the batter, beating after each addition until smooth.

6 Stir in the lemon zest and ginger by hand, using a wooden spoon. Pour the batter into the prepared pan and bake in the preheated oven for about 45 minutes or until a skewer inserted into the center of the cake comes out clean. Let the cake cool in the pan on the wire rack for 15 minutes before turning it out onto the rack to cool completely.

7 To make the apple compote, melt the butter in a large, non-stick sauté pan over medium-high heat. Add the apples and cook until just tender, about 5 minutes. Add the brown sugar, water, cinnamon, and ground ginger. Continue cooking until the apples begin to caramelize, about 10 minutes longer. Remove from the heat and stir in the Calvados.

8 Cut the cake into wedges, top with the warm apple compote, and dust lightly with icing sugar. Serve with a dollop of whipped cream or mascarpone if desired. Serves 6 to 8.

Pumpkin Muffins

This recipe makes two 9- x 5-inch (2-L) loaves or 18 big muffins—enough for the gang on the trail or for the bake sale. You can even use this recipe to make cupcakes with cream cheese icing (see page xx) for birthdays or Halloween parties—just bake in colorful paper cups in smaller muffin tins.

3 cups (750 mL) all-purpose flour
1 cup (250 mL) quick-cooking rolled oats
2 tsp (10 mL) baking soda
1 tsp (5 mL) ground cinnamon
1 tsp (5 mL) ground ginger
½ tsp (2 mL) baking powder
½ tsp (2 mL) salt
3 large eggs

2 cups (500 mL) canned pumpkin (about one 19-oz/540-mL can) (not pumpkin pie filling)
1½ cups (375 mL) granulated sugar
1½ cups (375 mL) packed brown sugar
½ cup (125 mL) cold water
½ cup (125 mL) canola oil
½ cup (125 mL) evaporated milk
¾ cup (175 mL) chopped walnuts or pecans
¾ cup (175 mL) raisins

1 Preheat the oven to 350°F (180°C).

2 In a large mixing bowl, combine the flour, oats, baking soda, cinnamon, ginger, and baking powder. Set aside. In another bowl, use an electric mixer or whisk to beat the eggs, pumpkin, sugars, water, oil, and evaporated milk until well combined.

3 Fold the flour mixture into the pumpkin mixture, whisking or beating on low speed, until blended. Stir in the nuts and raisins.

4 Line the muffin tins with paper cups or spray pans with non-stick cooking spray. For muffins, spoon the batter into the muffin cups and bake in the preheated oven for 35 to 45 minutes. For loaves, spoon the batter into the greased pans and bake in the preheated oven for 50 to 60 minutes. The batter is cooked when a toothpick inserted into the center comes out clean. Makes 18 muffins or 2 loaves.

Black and White Cupcakes

Old-fashioned cupcakes have become all the rage for birthdays and other occasions that call for cake. You can make any cake into a cupcake—just use your deepest muffin tins, lined with pretty paper cups, and swirl on your favorite icing. Here's a plain white cake recipe and a chocolate cake recipe (both morph well into cupcakes), and a recipe for basic white icing. Vary the white cake with whatever flavorings you like (add lemon juice, grated lemon rind, and poppy seeds or orange rind, Grand Marnier and winter spices, etc.) and add your favorite flavorings and food colorings to the icing. Sprinkles always add drama.

Black (Chocolate) Cupcakes

1¼ cups (310 mL) all-purpose flour
6 Tbsp (90 mL) Dutch cocoa
1 tsp (5 mL) baking powder
1 cup (250 mL) granulated sugar
pinch of salt

1 cup (250 mL) water
1 large egg
⅓ cup (75 mL) melted unsalted butter
2 tsp (10 mL) pure vanilla extract or Kahlúa liqueur
icing and chocolate sprinkles

1 Preheat the oven to 350°F (180°C).

2 In a medium bowl, combine the flour, cocoa, baking powder, sugar, and salt.

3 In another bowl, whisk together the water, egg, butter, and vanilla. Add the dry ingredients to the liquid mixture, mixing to combine.

4 Line a muffin pan with paper cups and fill the cups ¾ full with the batter. Bake for 20 to 25 minutes or until the tops of the cupcakes spring back when touched. Cool, then decorate with icing and chocolate sprinkles. Use the white icing recipe that follows, or Creamy Chocolate Icing (see page 453). Makes 1 dozen.

White Cupcakes

1½ cups (375 mL) all-purpose flour, sifted
2 tsp (10 mL) baking powder
¼ tsp (1 mL) salt
½ cup (125 mL) unsalted butter, cubed
1 cup (250 mL) sugar
2 eggs, separated

1 tsp (5 mL) vanilla (or cognac or rum, orange
    liqueur, etc.)
½ cup (125 mL) buttermilk, milk, cream, or sour
    cream
multi-colored candy sprinkles

1 Preheat the oven to 350°F (180°C).

2 In a medium bowl, combine the flour, baking powder, and salt. Set aside.

3 In another bowl, use an electric mixer to cream the butter and sugar together until fluffy and light. Add the egg yolks and beat for several minutes to dissolve the sugar. Add the vanilla and mix well.

4 Stir half of the flour mixture into the batter, then half of the buttermilk. Repeat.

5 Beat the egg whites in another bowl until stiff. Use a spatula to gently fold the egg whites into the batter. Line a muffin pan with paper cups and fill the cups ¾ full with the batter. Bake for 25 to 30 minutes in the preheated oven or until the tops of the cupcakes spring back when touched. Cool, then decorate with icing and sprinkles. Makes 1 dozen.

Icing

3 large egg whites
1 cup (250 mL) powdered sugar or icing sugar
pinch of salt

¼ cup (60 mL) corn syrup
1 tsp (10 mL) pure vanilla extract (or peppermint
    extract, lemon extract, etc.)

1 In a medium stainless-steel bowl combine the egg whites, icing sugar, salt, and corn syrup. Set over a saucepan of simmering water. Use a whisk or electric mixer to beat the mixture as it heats. Continue beating until stiff peaks form. Beat in the vanilla, and add a few drops of food coloring, if you like. Makes about 1½ cups (375 mL).

Speedy Cinnamon Rolls

The Guy loves the cinnamon rolls freshly baked from the funky coffee house in the mountain town where he skis. The good news is that they're based on a simple quick bread—leavened like a basic biscuit with baking powder—instead of the usual time-consuming yeast-raised buns. Invest in a good quality, non-stick extra-large muffin pan for these addictive rolls.

Dough

3 ¼ (800 mL) cups unbleached, all-purpose flour
3 Tbsp (45 mL) granulated sugar
2½ tsp (12 mL) baking powder
½ tsp (2 mL) salt

1 cup (250 mL) buttermilk
½ cup (125 mL) whipping cream
⅓ cup (75 mL) unsalted butter, melted and cooled
  plus extra for brushing

Filling

¼ cup (60 mL) unsalted butter, softened
¼ cup (60 mL) packed brown sugar

¼ cup (60 mL) granulated sugar
2 tsp (10 mL) ground cinnamon

1 Preheat the oven to 400°F (200°C).

2 In a large mixing bowl, combine the flour, sugar, baking powder, and salt. In another bowl, whisk together the buttermilk, cream, and melted butter. Add the liquid to the dry ingredients and stir until the liquid is just absorbed—don't worry if it looks a little dry. Turn the dough out onto the counter and knead it lightly, just until it holds together. Knead in a little more flour if the dough seems sticky.

3 On a piece of parchment or waxed paper, lightly form the dough into a rectangle. Use your hands or a rolling pin to gently roll until it's about 18 by 10 inches (45 by 25 cm).

4 Spread the dough with the softened butter. Combine the brown sugar, white sugar, and cinnamon. Dust the mixture evenly over the dough.

5 Starting with the long end, roll the dough as tightly as you can, using the parchment paper to aid you (like rolling a jelly or sushi roll, the paper is just used to facilitate rolling). Pinch the seam to seal and place the roll, seam-side down, on the counter. Cut the dough roll into 12 even slices using a sharp knife or a piece of dental floss (to slice with floss, simply slide the floss under the log, cross the ends of the floss over the log and pull to slice through the dough).

6 Pick up each slice carefully, pinching the base slightly to fit each roll into a cup in an extra large, non-stick muffin pan. Brush the rolls lightly with melted butter.

7 Bake in the preheated oven for 25 minutes or until golden brown. Turn the rolls out onto a cooling rack and serve while still warm. Makes 12 cinnamon rolls.

SPEEDY CINNAMON

WISE GUY: No buttermilk in the fridge? Plain yogurt stands in perfectly well. Or make your own buttermilk by mixing 1 Tbsp (15 mL) of lemon juice or white vinegar into 1 cup (250 mL) of milk and letting it stand for 10 minutes.

COOKIES & BARS

SQUARES

Don't Sweat the Sweet Stuff

There are times when something really sweet is all that works. Don't indulge every day, but enjoy something sweet once in a while and don't sweat it. Hey, every guy has his vices.

Apple Walnut Squares

Another super simple sweet to make and take almost anywhere, from a picnic to a potluck. Makes a decent bake sale contribution when the kid's hockey team comes calling, too.

2 cups (500 mL) all-purpose flour
1 cup (250 mL) packed brown sugar
2 tsp (10 mL) ground cinnamon
1 cup (250 mL) chopped walnuts
½ cup (125 mL) unsalted butter, cubed

one 8-oz (250-mL) package light cream cheese
1 egg, beaten
¼ cup (60 mL) granulated sugar
1 tsp (5 mL) pure vanilla extract
4 cups (1 L) peeled and chopped apples

1 Preheat the oven to 350°F (180°C).

2 In the food processor, combine the flour, brown sugar, cinnamon, and walnuts. Pulse until the nuts are finely chopped. Add the butter and pulse until the mixture resembles coarse crumbs.

3 Remove 2 cups (500 mL) of the crumbs and set aside. Press the remaining mixture into a lightly greased 9- x 12-inch (3.5-L) baking pan.

4 In a mixing bowl, use an electric mixer to beat the cream cheese, eggs, sugar, and vanilla until smooth. Pour the cheese mixture over the crust and scatter the chopped apples evenly overtop. Sprinkle with the reserved crumbs.

5 Bake in the preheated oven for 30 to 40 minutes or until golden. Cool before cutting into squares. Makes 1 dozen large squares.

Date and Nut Balls

This is one of those easy, old-fashioned, no-bake Christmas treats that The Guy remembers making as a kid. Make some with your kid, or for the kid in you.

½ cup (125 mL) unsalted butter
1 cup (250 mL) packed brown sugar
1½ cups (375 mL) chopped dates
1 egg, beaten
2½ cups (625 mL) crispy rice cereal

¾ cup (175 mL) chopped walnuts or pecans
½ tsp (2 mL) pure vanilla extract
pinch of salt
shredded coconut or icing sugar

1 In a saucepan, combine the butter, sugar, dates, and egg. Cook over medium heat, stirring constantly until the mixture boils and thickens, about 6 minutes.

2 Cool to lukewarm and stir in the rice cereal, nuts, vanilla, and salt. Mix well and roll into small balls about the size of a walnut. (If your hands are wet the mixture won't stick.) Roll the balls in coconut or icing sugar to coat. Chill. Makes 24 balls.

WISE GUY: You can also press the mixture into a buttered 9-inch (2.5-L) square baking pan and sprinkle with coconut. Chill and cut into bars. Wrap individually and take on a hike or in your backpack for breakfasts on the run.

The Chocolate Addict's Bar

One of The Guy's friends—who claims she can't cook—creates this insanely addictive sweet for the holidays. It's so easy to make, you'll become addicted, too. Use the best chocolate you can find—and don't say I didn't warn you!

1 box graham wafer cookies
1½ cups (375 mL) unsalted butter
1 cup (250 mL) brown sugar

3 cups (750 mL) chopped bittersweet Belgian
   chocolate (or chocolate chips)

1 Preheat the oven to 350°F (180°C).

2 Line a baking sheet with parchment paper. Cover the entire pan with a layer of graham crackers.

3 In a saucepan, combine the butter and sugar. Bring to a boil over medium heat. Boil for 5 minutes.

4 Carefully pour the hot sugar syrup evenly over the graham crackers (go slow, this is hot stuff!). Put the pan in the preheated oven and bake for 5 minutes.

5 Pour a layer of chocolate chunks, or chips, over the pan. As they melt, use a butter knife to spread the chocolate evenly over the entire sheet. Refrigerate. That's it. Break up into pieces, like peanut brittle. Makes 6 cups.

LIQUIDS! DRY!
GLASS / PLASTIC OR METAL
MEASURING CUPS

Easy-Bake Oatmeal and Date Cookies

These cookies are easy to make ahead and bake when the mood strikes. You can even freeze the cookie dough.

1 cup (250 mL) finely chopped pitted dates
¾ cup (175 mL) cubed, cold unsalted butter
1 cup (250 mL) granulated sugar
1 cup (250 mL) packed brown sugar

2 large eggs
2 cups (500 mL) all-purpose flour
1 tsp (5 mL) baking soda
3 cups (750 mL) quick-cooking oats

1 Preheat the oven to 350°F (180°C).

2 To make chopping the dates easier, especially if they're really dry, heat them briefly in the microwave with a little water. Then use the food processor to chop them, pulsing several times until the pieces are quite small.

3 In a mixing bowl, use an electric mixer to cream the butter with the white and brown sugar until fluffy. Add the eggs, one at a time, and beat to combine. Mix in the chopped dates, using a wooden spoon.

4 In another bowl, combine the flour, baking soda, and oats.

5 Stir the flour mixture into the batter by hand to form a stiff dough. Divide the dough into three portions, and form into three logs, each about 1½ inches (4 cm) in diameter. Wrap the dough tightly in waxed paper, then plastic wrap, and refrigerate overnight (or freeze).

6 To bake the cookies, slice the logs into rounds, about ¼ inch (6 mm) thick. Arrange on a parchment paper–lined baking sheet and bake at for 12 to 15 minutes or until the cookies are crisp and brown. Cool on wire racks. Makes 3 dozen.

Nutty Chocolate Chip Biscotti

The Guy loves biscotti—they're a not too sweet treat and they work well with coffee. They're also an elegant way to end a meal. If you don't like nuts, substitute dried cranberries. This recipe makes a big batch.

¾ cup (175 mL) softened unsalted butter
2 cups (250 mL) granulated sugar
3 eggs
3 ½ cups (825 mL) sifted pastry flour
2 tsp (10 mL) baking powder

1 cup (250 mL) lightly toasted slivered almonds
   or pistachios
1 cup (250 mL) dark chocolate chips
extra bittersweet chocolate for dipping or
   drizzling (optional)

1 Preheat the oven to 350°F (180°C).

2 In a large mixing bowl, use an electric mixer to cream the butter and sugar together until fluffy. Add the eggs, one at a time, beating after each addition.

3 In a separate bowl, combine the pastry flour and baking powder. Gradually add half the flour mixture to the batter, beating to incorporate. With a wooden spoon, mix in the nuts and chocolate. Stir in the remainder of the flour mixture and incorporate. Turn the dough onto a lightly floured surface and separate into 3 equal portions. Roll each portion into a rope about 12 to 14 inches (30 to 35 cm) long.

4 Line a baking sheet with parchment paper and place the ropes side by side, leaving at least 3 inches (8 cm) of space for the cookies to expand into slightly flattened logs as they bake.

5 Bake for 20 to 30 minutes in the preheated oven, or until the logs are firm to the touch. Remove from oven and let them cool for 20 minutes. With a serrated knife, cut each log on an angle into ½-inch- (1-cm-) thick biscotti. Lay the biscotti on the baking sheet and return to the oven for 10 minutes to crisp. If desired, drizzle melted chocolate over the biscotti once they've cooled, or dip one end of each biscotto in melted chocolate and chill until chocolate sets. Makes 4 to 5 dozen.

Chocolate Chunk Cookies
(for Ice Cream Sandwiches)

A chocolate bar can melt in your pack but these soft, chewy cookies won't. Make sure you use good-quality chocolate—a trip to the chocolatier for Callebaut or Valrhona chocolate makes all the difference. These cookies are not only great on their own, they form the chewy chocolate base for The Guy's special ice cream sandwiches.

1 cup (250 mL) unsalted butter
1½ cups (375 mL) granulated sugar
2 large eggs
2 tsp (10 mL) pure vanilla extract
1¼ cups (310 mL) all-purpose flour

1 cup (250 mL) Dutch cocoa powder
1 tsp (5 mL) baking powder
4 oz (100 g) white chocolate
4 oz (100 g) milk or bittersweet chocolate

1 Preheat the oven to 350°F (180°C).

2 In a mixing bowl, use an electric mixer to cream together the butter and sugar. Beat for 5 minutes or until fluffy and light.

3 Add the eggs, one at a time, beating well after each addition on medium speed. Mix in the vanilla.

4 In another bowl, combine the flour, cocoa, and baking powder. Mix well.

5 Stir the dry ingredients into the batter to combine. Chop the white and milk chocolate into small chunks, then fold them into the dough. Refrigerate the cookie dough for 1 hour.

6 Line a baking sheet with parchment paper and mound the cookie dough on the sheet, using about 2 Tbsp (30 mL) of batter per cookie. Leave at least 2 inches (5 cm) between cookies (they will spread). Bake in the preheated oven for 13 to 15 minutes or until the cookies are set but still soft. (Be careful not to over-bake—the cookies should remain chewy when cooled.)

7 Let the cookies cool slightly on the baking sheet, then use a wide spatula to transfer them to a rack to continue cooling. Makes 2 dozen.

WISE GUY: This is the perfect cookie to use for making decadent ice cream sandwiches. Sandwich a thick layer of gourmet coffee or vanilla bean ice cream between two cookies and freeze on a tray for several hours before wrapping in plastic. Serve whenever you feel the need for a frozen dessert to take the heat off!

Decadent Dream Bars

Sweetened condensed milk is an essential ingredient in Iced Vietnamese Coffee, The Guy's Quickie Caramel Sauce (see page 482), and these decadent little sweets. This recipe is infinitely adaptable—use any kind of chocolate chips, butterscotch chips, or even chopped apricots or dried cranberries. Coconut, chopped nuts, and condensed milk are the sweet things that glue it all together. Dreamy!

1½ cups (375 mL) graham wafer crumbs
   or crumbled chocolate cookies
½ cup (125 mL) unsalted butter, melted
1 cup (250 mL) chopped pecans or walnuts
1½ cups (375 mL) semi-sweet chocolate chips

½ cup (125 mL) white chocolate
   or butterscotch chips
1 cup (250 mL) sweetened shredded coconut
one 14-oz (398-mL) can sweetened
   condensed milk

1 Preheat the oven to 350°F (180°C). If you're using a glass baking pan, adjust the temperature to 325°F (160°C).

2 In a bowl, combine the cookie crumbs and melted butter. Stir well. Press the crumb mixture into a 9- x 13-inch (3.5-L) baking pan. Top with the chopped nuts, chocolate chips, white chocolate chips, and coconut, in that order. Pour the sweetened condensed milk evenly over the top and bake in the preheated oven for 25 to 30 minutes. Cool, and cut into bars. Makes 24 to 36 bars.

Sauces, Dressings, and Extra Info

Get Saucy

The Guy has observed that everyday stuff—whether it's a steak or a cake—is exponentially better when it's jazzed up with a little saucy stuff on the side.

First and foremost are the secret salad dressings, sauces, slathers, and chutneys seen on every restaurant menu. Steak comes with Chimichurri Sauce (see page 230), topped with a piece of herb-enhanced compound butter (see page 195) or dolloped with Horseradish Aioli (a.k.a. mayo) (see page 37). Fish has a Mango Salsa (see page 438) or lemony Tartar Sauce (see page 433) .

Then there are the sweet caramel sauces and fruity compotes that take simple cakes and puddings into gourmet territory. Something saucy is the way to make a basic meat/starch/veg meal into something special.

Pesto Sauce

Good pesto is available in jars at any Italian grocery store, but you can easily make your own (in season) and save a bundle. The Guy likes to freeze pesto in plastic ice cube trays. Then he can pop out the cubes, store them in a zippered freezer bag, and pop them into soups or stews whenever a shot of fresh basil is in order and there's none at hand.

Pesto is made simply—fresh basil leaves, olive oil, toasted pine nuts or walnuts, Parmesan cheese, and a touch of garlic. Use the best olive oil you can afford and real Parmigiano Reggiano cheese. If you plan to freeze your pesto, leave the cheese out and add it when you're ready to serve it.

2 cups (500 mL) fresh basil leaves
1 large clove garlic
3 Tbsp (45 mL) pine nuts, toasted

½ cup (125 mL) extra virgin olive oil
½ cup (125 mL) grated Parmigiano Reggiano cheese

1 Wash the basil well and dry it thoroughly before you start.

2 Whirl all ingredients in a food processor until smooth. Add more oil if you want a thinner pesto. Pour the pesto into clean jars or ice cube trays and freeze or refrigerate (if the surface is covered with oil, the pesto will keep in the refrigerator for several weeks). Makes 1½ cups (375 mL).

WISE GUY: While classic Italian pesto sauce is made with basil, you can also make "pesto" (herb pastes) with cilantro, mint, or parsley. Just leave out the cheese and season with a little freshly squeezed lemon juice. Thai-style cilantro pesto can be made with ground peanuts, a green chili, a shot of lime juice, and fish sauce. You can also vary the oils that you use—for an Asian-inspired taste use peanut oil and a little sesame oil. Or try a pesto made with avocado or walnut oil.

Savory Rhubarb Sauce

Serve a dab of this savory sauce on liver pâté or foie gras. It also tastes great with grilled chicken or fish, and makes a nice spring appetizer on melba toast with some pâté from the deli. Or give jars away for gifts—she'll be impressed.

1 lemon
¼ cup (60 mL) balsamic vinegar
½ cup (125 mL) sugar
1 clove garlic, minced

½ cup (125 mL) minced red onion
1 Tbsp (15 mL) minced fresh ginger
3 cups (750 mL) young rhubarb, diced
  (the red parts)

1 Remove the zest from the lemon and mince. Juice the lemon—you should have about 3 to 4 Tbsp (45 to 60 mL) of juice.

2 Combine the lemon juice, vinegar, sugar, garlic, onion, and ginger in a non-reactive saucepan (stainless steel is the best) and bring to a boil. Add the rhubarb, reduce the heat to low, and simmer uncovered for 15 minutes, until the sauce is thick. Cool. Makes 2 cups (500 mL).

Blender Mayonnaise

Choose a light olive or canola oil, as most extra virgin olive oil is too strong in flavor for mayonnaise (if you use a strong flavoured olive oil, it's aioli). Remember, mayonnaise contains raw eggs (a potential health risk to young children or the elderly, or anyone with a weakened immune system) so use the freshest eggs you can find.

1 large egg
¼ tsp (1 mL) salt
1 tsp (5 mL) Dijon mustard

1 Tbsp (15 mL) fresh lemon juice
1 cup (250 mL) light olive or canola oil

1 In a blender, whirl the egg for 2 to 3 seconds. Add the salt, mustard, and lemon juice and blend to combine. With the machine running, slowly drizzle the olive oil through the feed tube. The mayonnaise should emulsify. Pour into a jar and refrigerate. It will keep several days in the fridge. Makes ¾ cup (175 mL).

WISE GUY: For a classic aioli, mince 2 to 3 cloves of garlic with the salt in the blender, before adding the egg, mustard, and lemon juice. Slowly add flavorful olive oil and voilà—aioli!

Basic Vinaigrette

Use on all green salads. Vary the flavors by adding chopped fresh herbs like dill, oregano, or basil. Get creative and add lemon zest, chopped sun-dried tomatoes, or chopped roasted peppers.

½ cup (125 mL) extra virgin olive oil
2 Tbsp (30 mL) balsamic vinegar or freshly
   squeezed lemon juice

1 clove garlic, pressed in a garlic press
   or minced
1 Tbsp (15 mL) Dijon mustard
salt and freshly ground black pepper

1 Combine all the ingredients in a blender, food processor, or glass jar and whirl or shake until combined. Refrigerate up to three days. Makes ¾ cup (175 mL).

Speedy Caesar Salad Dressing

The Guy likes to add a little kick to his Caesar salads with a chipotle chili—but it's strictly non-conventional and optional.

1 cup (250 mL) mayonnaise
2 tsp (10 mL) anchovy paste or Asian fish sauce
1 Tbsp (15 mL) garlic, puréed in a press
3 Tbsp (45 mL) freshly squeezed lemon juice

2 tsp (10 mL) Dijon mustard
⅓ cup (75 mL) extra virgin olive oil
1 chipotle chili, in adobo (optional)
1 cup (250 mL) finely grated Parmesan

1 In a food processor, whirl together the mayonnaise, anchovy paste, garlic, lemon juice, mustard, olive oil, and chili (if using). Purée. Add the Parmesan and pulse to combine. Toss with chopped romaine hearts and croutons. Makes about 2 cups (500 mL).

Salsa

Sure, the supermarkets are full of commercial salsas—but nothing beats the intense flavors of this homemade salsa, something you can proudly serve as an appetizer with tortilla chips or haul along to a party as a thank-you gift. Make it in September, when the farmers' market is overflowing with cheap and delicious flats of ripe Roma tomatoes and multicolored hot and sweet peppers. It's worth the work.

8 cups (2 L) chopped plum (a.k.a. Roma) tomatoes, about 3 lb (1.5 kg)

4 cups (1 L) chopped banana peppers (medium-hot), seeds removed

1 cup (250 mL) chopped jalapeño or serrano peppers (hot), seeds removed

2 cups (500 mL) chopped onions

1 cup (250 mL) apple cider vinegar

½ cup (125 mL) chopped red bell pepper

½ cup (125 mL) chopped yellow bell pepper

4 cloves garlic, minced

one 5 ½-oz (156-mL) can tomato paste

2 Tbsp (30 mL) granulated sugar

1 Tbsp (15 mL) salt

2 tsp (10 mL) Hungarian paprika

2 tsp (10 mL) dried oregano

½ cup (125 mL) chopped fresh cilantro

2 tsp (10 mL) Asian chili paste, or to taste

1 Dice all the vegetables into relatively uniform chunks (¼ inch/6 mm). Wear surgical gloves while chopping the hot peppers and make sure you don't touch your face or eyes—these babies burn!

2 In a large, non-reactive pot (stainless steel is the best), combine the tomatoes, banana peppers, jalapeño peppers, onions, vinegar, bell peppers, garlic, tomato paste, sugar, salt, paprika, and oregano. Bring to a boil over medium-high heat, stirring often to prevent the salsa from sticking and burning on the bottom. When the pot boils, reduce the heat to medium-low. Continue to simmer for 1 to 2 hours, until the salsa is thickened to your liking. Remember, you want it to be scoopable, not runny.

3 Remove the pot from the heat and stir in the chopped cilantro. Add enough Asian chili paste to make the salsa as hot as you like. The Guy's recipe changes from year to year, as the hot peppers have different levels of heat depending on how they have been grown.

4 When you're satisfied with the flavor and texture, prepare the jars. Use the canning jars with two-part metal lids (the only kind that truly seal and preserve your efforts). Wash the jars and lids well and rinse in boiling water.

5 Using a wide-mouthed funnel to guide you, ladle the salsa into 1-cup (250 mL) jars, leaving ¼ inch (6 mm) of head space at the top to allow for expansion. Wipe the edges of the jars with a clean cloth, center the lids on top and tighten the screw bands. They should just be "finger tip" tight.

6 Place the jars in a canning kettle or very deep large pot filled with boiling water. The water must be a couple of inches above the tops of the jars. Return the water to a rolling boil and process the salsa (boil) for 20 minutes.

7 Lift the jars from the water using tongs and cool on a folded kitchen towel on the counter. The lids should pop and snap down as the salsa cools, indicating that the jars are properly sealed and safe. Your salsa will keep in a cool dark place for one year or more. Refrigerate it after opening. Makes about 8 cups (2 L) of salsa. You can easily double or triple the recipe.

Creamy Roasted Garlic Dressing

Roasted garlic has a buttery, nutty, sweet flavor—so you can use a lot without worry. It's right there in the fridge, right?

½ cup (125 mL) mayonnaise
6 to 8 cloves roasted garlic (see page 17)
2 tsp (10 mL) Dijon mustard

1 Tbsp (15 mL) freshly squeezed lemon juice
⅓ cup (75 mL) buttermilk
salt and freshly ground black pepper

1 In a blender, combine the mayonnaise, garlic, and mustard. Whirl together, then add the lemon juice, buttermilk, salt, and pepper. Blend until smooth.

2 Chill the dressing in the refrigerator for 30 minutes to blend the flavors. This is good all-purpose dressing for sturdy greens like romaine or wedges of iceberg lettuce. Add some freshly grated Parmesan cheese for a caesar-style salad. Makes 1 cup (250 mL).

Roasted Red Pepper Dressing

Drizzle this colorful dressing over salad greens or use it as a vegetable dip.

⅔ cup (150 mL) mayonnaise
⅓ cup (75 mL) sour cream or plain yogurt
3 cloves roasted garlic (see page 17)
1 roasted red bell pepper, from a jar (pat dry on a paper towel)
1 Tbsp (15 mL) lemon juice or balsamic vinegar

1 tsp (5 mL) Asian chili paste
1 green onion, minced
1 tsp (5 mL) minced fresh parsley
1 tsp (5 mL) cilantro
salt and freshly ground black pepper

1 In a blender, whirl together the mayonnaise, sour cream, roasted garlic, bell pepper, lemon juice, and chili paste until smooth. Stir in the green onion, parsley, and cilantro.

2 Season to taste with salt and pepper. Thin the dressing to your desired thickness with 1 to 2 Tbsp (15 to 30 mL) of milk or buttermilk. Makes 1½ cups (375 mL).

Blue Cheese Blender Dressing

Drizzle this over roast beef and caramelized onion sandwiches or toss with romaine salads and top with slivered red pears and chopped walnuts or pecans (or that leftover rare beef).

½ cup (125 mL) mayonnaise
¼ cup (60 mL) sour cream or yogurt
1 tsp (5 mL) white wine vinegar
¼ cup (60 mL) buttermilk

3 cloves roasted garlic
½ cup (125 mL) crumbled blue cheese
sea salt and freshly ground black pepper

1 In a blender, whirl together the mayonnaise, sour cream, vinegar, buttermilk, and roasted garlic until smooth. Using a fork, mash the blue cheese in a small bowl, then stir it into the mayonnaise mixture. Cover and refrigerate for up to 1 week. Thin with more buttermilk before serving over salad greens, if desired. Makes 1½ cups (375 mL).

Pear Mincemeat

This meatless mincemeat is amazing stuff—use it in tarts or pies, or simply spoon it over pound cake and ice cream for a speedy dessert. It's also something special to give away as a Christmas gift—your aunts and neighbors will think you're a star.

2 lb (1 kg) pears, peeled, cored, and chopped
1 green apple, peeled, cored, and chopped
grated rind and juice of 1 lemon
grated rind and juice of 1 orange
½ cup (125 mL) dried cranberries or currants
1 cup (250 mL) golden raisins
½ cup (125 mL) brown sugar

1 tsp (5 mL) cinnamon
1 tsp (5 mL) nutmeg
¼ tsp (1 mL) ground dried ginger
pinch of salt
½ cup (125 mL) chopped walnuts or pecans, toasted
½ cup (125 mL) cognac, Calvados, or pear brandy

1 Combine all the ingredients, except the walnuts and cognac, in a heavy pot. Bring to a boil. Cover, reduce heat, and simmer for 25 minutes, stirring occasionally.

2 Remove the cover and continue to simmer for 40 minutes, until the mixture is very thick. Stir in the walnuts and cognac and cook 5 minutes longer.

3 Spoon the mincemeat into hot, sterilized jars, leaving ½ inch (1 cm) head space. Seal the jars with 2-piece lids and process in a boiling water bath for 10 minutes. Makes 5 cups (1.25 L).

WISE GUY: Use a heavy, covered canner or stock pot for processing preserves. When submerged, boiling water should cover the jars by about 1 inch (2.5 cm). If you don't have a proper canner (with a wire lifting insert) place a metal rack in the bottom of the pot. Seal the filled jars with metal lids and rings, closing until just "finger tip" tight. Using a jar lifter, carefully lower the jars into the boiling water until they are all submerged in a single layer. Cover the pan. When water returns to a full, rolling boil start timing. Lift the processed jars from the water and set on a towel on the counter to cool. You will hear the lids pop down as the preserves cool—proof of a proper seal.

Crème Anglaise

A.k.a. vanilla custard (that oh-so-English sauce). Drizzling this slick sauce over and around most any dessert will take it up a notch. Great on plain pound cake, fruit, even pies and shortcakes. Learn to make it. Easy and impressive.

4 egg yolks, room temperature
¼ cup (60 mL) granulated sugar
1 tsp (5 mL) cornstarch

1½ cups (375 mL) milk
½ tsp (2 mL) vanilla extract

1 Find a metal bowl that fits into one of your saucepans. Put a few inches of water in the saucepan, bring it to a boil, and reduce the heat to simmer.

2 Put the egg yolks and sugar in the bowl and, using an electric mixer, beat until light, about 2 to 3 minutes.

3 Heat the milk, but don't boil it. Gradually add the hot milk to the eggs, while beating with the mixer. Immediately set the bowl over the simmering water in the saucepan and continue to stir (with a spoon or wire whisk) until the custard thickens slightly. The usual test is to dip a spoon in the custard, then run your finger down the back of the spoon—if the custard doesn't run quickly back together, it's thick enough.

4 Cool the custard quickly. Set the bowl in a sink or bowl filled with a few inches of ice water, then whisk. Stir in the vanilla, cover, and refrigerate. Keeps for up to 2 days. Serve cold.
Makes about 1½ cups (375 mL).

EGGS

Instant Pastry

The simplicity is stunning—mascarpone cheese (a super creamy Italian cheese available in tubs at the supermarket), flour, and sugar—and you have yourself some tender pastry. This is the crust to make for fresh fruit tarts, the kind you bake in advance, fill with custard, and top with sliced peaches, strawberries, or blueberries in the summer.

You can also use this pastry as the base for any single-shell baked tart. Just arrange concentric circles of cinnamon dusted apples or sliced red plums in crust and bake. Or roll it out, cut it into squares, and bake—layer with whipped cream and berries for a stylish Napoleon.

1½ cups (375 mL) mascarpone cheese
1½ cups (375 mL) all-purpose flour

2 Tbsp (30 mL) granulated sugar

1 Put everything into the food processor and pulse until it comes together in a ball.

2 Wrap in plastic. Chill for 1 to 2 hours.

3 Roll the pastry out on a floured surface and lay it into a shallow tart pan, with a removable bottom, pressing into the scalloped sides of the pan. Line with foil, fill with dried beans or pie weights, and bake at 425°F (220°C) for 8 minutes. Remove the foil and pie weights and brown for 5 minutes more.

4 If you're making Napoleons, roll the pastry to ¼-inch (6-mm) thickness and cut into equal-sized squares or rectangles (a size that would look nice in the middle of your favorite dessert plates). Line a baking sheet with parchment paper and place the squares on the parchment. Bake at 425°F (220°C) for 10 to 12 minutes or until golden.

WISE GUY: Fill your baked tart shell with cold custard cream (use a mix) and top with fresh fruit. A little apricot or red currant jelly (depending on the color of your fruit filling) can be melted in the microwave and brushed over the fruit for a shiny glaze.

For Napoleons, start with a square of baked pastry, top with some sweet whipped cream and berries, then another piece of pastry on top (make the pastry even or offset—your choice). Put a little icing sugar in a sieve or shaker and dust the desserts. Voilà!

Quickie Caramel Sauce

An old trick to make a creamy caramel sauce to drizzle over cakes, pancakes, and puddings.

one 10-oz (300-mL) can sweetened
  condensed milk
1 cup (250 mL) cereal cream

1 tsp (5 mL) vanilla extract
2 Tbsp (30 mL) unsalted butter

1 In a heavy saucepan, whisk together the condensed milk, cream, and vanilla. Add the butter and bring to a boil over medium heat. Simmer for 10 to 15 minutes, stirring frequently to prevent burning, until the sauce thickens and turns a nice deep caramel color. Serve warm. Makes 1½ cups (375 mL).

Cold Toddy

Other than Grandma's Chicken Soup—a.k.a. Jewish penicillin (see page 354)—The Guy's favorite "cure" for the common cold is lots of ginseng and this steamy lemon and honey toddy. You can just heat the ginger up in a pot with everything else, but if you make it in a thermos, you can have several cups without getting out of bed. It might not cure you overnight, but it can't hurt.

4 cups (1 L) boiling water
1-inch (2.5-cm) piece ginger, grated with a
  microplane grater

3 to 4 Tbsp (45 to 60 mL) natural honey
  (to taste)
juice and pulp of 1 lemon (about 4 to 5 Tbsp/
  60 to 75 mL)

1 Finely grate the ginger and put it into a four-cup thermos bottle with the honey and lemon juice (with pulp). Fill up the thermos with boiling water, screw on the lid and let the tea steep for 15 minutes. Take your thermos, and a mug, to bed and have some hot lemon tea. Makes 4 cups (1 L).

Croutons

You can't make a caesar salad without croutons, and why go to all that work with stale, store-bought croutons? Make these whenever you have a loaf of good French or sourdough bread that's too dry for sandwiches. The croutons will keep for a couple of weeks in a dry place.

4 cups (1 L) bread cubes (cut into ¾-inch/
  2-cm pieces)
2 to 3 Tbsp (30 to 45 mL) extra virgin olive oil

salt
dried herbs (oregano, thyme, basil, paprika, etc.)

1 Place the bread cubes in a bowl and drizzle with olive oil. Season with salt, pepper, and sprinkle with herbs. Toss together.

2 Spread the bread in a single layer on a baking pan and toast in a 400°F (200°C) oven for 10 to 15 minutes, until golden and crisp. Set aside to cool and store at room temperature.

The Tool Man

The Guy is a lover of gadgetry. He's always interested in using the right tool for the job—the more powerful the better. So he's smitten by the serious juicing machines, the simplicity of the bread machine, and the promise of an instant hit of caffeine every morning from his chic Italian espresso machine.

And while all kitchen tools are certainly not created equal—or are even necessary, for that matter—The Guy has had some success with machines in the kitchen, whether it's the food processor for a speedy spread or the bread machine for a quick pizza crust.

A good chef's knife is really the most important tool of all.

But there are special and useful tools for special jobs—from a reamer or citrus press to extract enough fresh juice from those sweet key limes for a proper margarita, to a tiny torch to instantly caramelize the topping on your crème brûlée.

An immersion blender is handy for creamy soups, and there would be no perfectly pink roast lamb without an instant-read meat thermometer.

So herewith, The Guy's primer for buying and using his favorite kitchen tools.

The Big Guns

Food Processor

The food processor is one tool The Guy cannot live without. Any soup or sauce comes together quickly when you use the processor to chop the onions, garlic, carrots, and celery. It's indispensable for purées—from creamy soups to dips and spreads. Buy one with a quiet motor and a big bowl. Not to drop names, but The Guy's Cuisinart is a quiet, reliable workhorse that's up to any job. Use the metal blade to chop and purée, the plastic dough blade for breads and pastries, and get a selection of grating blades (for grating all of those carrots and zucchinis for cakes or making an instant pile of grated cheese).

Blender

A blender with a glass jar is sturdy and serviceable. Make sure the blender you buy has the horsepower to grind ice (for slushy drinks) and will make breadcrumbs. A good blender is far more efficient than a food processor when you want something puréed perfectly smooth. But if you want to purée soups and sauces, nothing beats an immersion blender—no need to pour hot liquids out of a pot, just insert the blender and whizz away. Some of the newer models even have attachments to whisk, chop, and crush—it may be the only blender you need.

Juicer

The Guy's big, fancy centrifugal juicer makes any fruit or vegetable into instant juice (who knew you could squeeze juice from a stalk of celery?). It's a little noisy and difficult to clean, though. The real Cadillacs of the juice world are the masticating-type juicers like the Champion (the only kind to buy if you're into wheatgrass juice), but they tend to be extremely pricey. Still, do your research before buying a juicer. If you really plan to drink carrot juice every day, it's worth investing in a good machine. Expect to pay at least $200.

Hand-Held or Stand Mixer

A good hand-held mixer will do for whipping cream, beating egg whites, or making cakes, but a big stand mixer makes these tasks easier and is essential for kneading bread dough. Some stand mixers tilt back to let you change beaters while others have a mechanism to move the bowl up and down (eliminates smacking the head into overhead cabinets). If you plan to make bread with the mixer, make sure it has the power and capacity you need.

Bread Machine

While The Guy first thought a bread machine was the answer to his prayers, he soon learned that the kind of vertical, fluffy white bread his contraption created best was not really the kind of carb he wanted to consume on a regular basis. Anything interesting, from his favorite olive bread to the heavy rye and wholegrain breads that make the best sandwiches, failed to rise as promised and turned out dense and doughy.

But thankfully, before consigning the big white behemoth to the flea market, he discovered that the bread machine is a tool that can save time for mixing and proofing any bread. Just select the basic "dough" cycle and let the machine do the kneading and rising stages while you cook your main course. Then shape your own loaves and bake them in a hot oven (on a baking stone, if you have one) and you'll have artisan-style bread warm and fresh from the oven with half the effort and mess. It's also an easy way to make your pizza dough from scratch.

And now that the machine has found a home at the cottage, it does come in handy for baking up a batch of basic whole wheat, when The Guy forgets to bring the bread from the city, and the hammock is more alluring than the kitchen.

Coffee/Cappuccino Machine

If you want a cappuccino or espresso every morning before you leave the house, invest in a good cappuccino machine. Don't be lured by those that grind beans or require pre-ground pucks of coffee—just find a good machine, with a metal body and metal parts, that will make a good espresso and make enough hot steam to steam milk quickly. It doesn't take much time to learn how to properly tamp the coffee into the basket or steam the milk. Buy a metal steaming pot with a long handle and make sure you know how to use it before you leave the store.

Pressure Cooker

The pressure cooker is one of the best tools in The Guy's arsenal—a way to make slow foods (like stews, curries, stocks, and pot roasts) fast. The new generation of pressure cookers is unlike the scary, exploding versions of The Guy's youth. Now there are sleek stainless steel models with safety valves that release cool steam with the flick of a switch. You can literally pick up the ingredients for a beef stew on the way home from work and have it on the table in 30 minutes flat. A very cool tool for spontaneous, Old World–style dishes from lamb curry to osso buco. Saves precious fuel when cooking in the camper or on the boat, too.

Cool Small Tools

Quality Knives

You don't need to buy a "set" of knives but you will need several different knives for different jobs.

First and foremost, you need a wide-bladed chef's knife—the 8- or 10-inch (20- or 25-cm) knife is standard. The Guy is partial to his one-piece Furi East-West knife, sort of a combination between a chef's knife and a cleaver. Vital for any chopping knife is the rounded tip which makes the rocking motion of chopping and mincing easy.

You'll also need a long, serrated bread knife, a carving knife, and a 4-inch paring knife.

Buy quality. Go to a good culinary store and choose a knife that feels good in your hand—you'll be using it a lot. It's important that the tang (the extension of the blade) continues to the end of the handle and that the handle is riveted in place properly. The blade should be a carbon steel alloy.

Good knives will last forever if you look after them. Get them professionally sharpened from time to time and don't put them in the dishwasher. A wooden cutting board is best for your knives—avoid cutting directly on glass or granite.

Microplane Grater

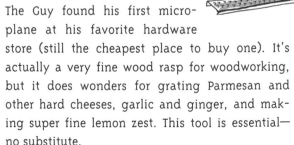

The Guy found his first microplane at his favorite hardware store (still the cheapest place to buy one). It's actually a very fine wood rasp for woodworking, but it does wonders for grating Parmesan and other hard cheeses, garlic and ginger, and making super fine lemon zest. This tool is essential—no substitute.

Instant-Read Thermometer

Whether you're cooking a pricey beef tenderloin to pink perfection, roasting the holiday turkey, or just making sure the internal temperature of your hamburger patty is up to snuff, nothing beats an instant-read, electronic meat thermometer. Get a good one and you'll never over- or under-cook the meat again.

Chefs' Tongs

Chefs use metal tongs for everything—turning meat in the pan, dunking things into batter or crumbs, moving things around on the grill. Good tongs keep your hands clean and the batter/crust on food intact. Buy a few.

Whisks, Spoons, and Spatulas

Make sure you have a good collection of spoons (wood and metal) and ladles for stirring and serving; metal whisks (large and small) for beating batters, eggs, and sauces; and spatulas (metal and plastic) for lifting cookies from baking sheets, flipping fish, and stir-frying. Most utensils are now offered in non-scratching, silicone versions—perfect for using in your nonstick cookware.

Kitchen Shears

Whether you use them to cut open a bag of pasta or chop up a chicken, good sharp kitchen shears are a necessity. The Guy's best pair have comfortable, rounded plastic handles, a sharp serrated blade, and are tough enough to cut through poultry bones, which is how they're often used. Also good for trimming fat and the pastry overhanging a pie plate, cut-ting pita breads into pieces for chips, snipping a whole can of tomatoes into slivers (while they're still in the can), chopping sticky dried fruit into bits, cutting parchment to line baking pans, etc.

Citrus Reamer

When you want to get the juice out of a lime for a mojito, you'll need a reamer. There are old-fashioned glass ones, with the pointy part set into the middle of a dish and a pouring spout, or hand-held wooden ones. You can also buy a simple hinged metal citrus press from Mexico to get the juice out of tiny key limes for drinks.

Mini Blowtorch (to Brûlée Desserts)

You'll find them in any kitchen store—tiny butane torches suitable for melting the sugar on top of your next crème brûlée or cheesecake. Refillable and inexpensive, this is a tool worth its weight in wow. A real conversation piece.

Kitchen Scale

Sometimes recipes call for a weighed amount of food. This is also a good tool if you want to know exactly how much of something you're consuming.

Waiter's Corkscrew

Learn how to use a simple waiter's corkscrew and you'll always be able to pull a cork stylishly. Buy a good one, with a rotary cutter at one end to help you quickly cut the foil from the top of the bottle.

Bowls

You can never have enough bowls. Big glass or ceramic bowls are good for mixing cookies and cakes, and stainless steel-bowls that fit inside your favorite pots make instant double boilers for melting chocolate or cooking custards. Buy bowls for serving cereal, soup, dessert, and salad. You'll also need lots of little glass bowls for measuring ingredients so you can assemble your meals à la minute like the best chefs. The Guy recently purchased a set of little nesting bowls labeled like measuring cups—very cool and useful to keep track of stuff while you're cooking.

Non-Stick Sauté Pan or Skillet

Today's non-stick stuff is tough, and The Guy cooks almost everything in his big 12-inch (30-cm) non-stick sauté pan. From fish and pork chops to sautés and pasta sauces, you can cook almost anything using far less fat. Look for a pan with an ovenproof handle and a heavy bottom. Use plastic or silicon utensils in your non-stick pans so you don't scratch them. Get a small, slope-sided non-stick pan for eggs and omelets.

Cookware

Saucepan

This is the pot you'll grab every day for steaming potatoes, cooking rice, and making sauces. Get something heavy—stainless interior with a sandwiched copper or aluminum base for even heat distribution. Make sure the handle is comfortable and stays cool. You need two saucepans—a medium or large one, and a slightly smaller one.

Stock Pot

 You'll need a big deep pot—at least 8-quart (9-L) capacity—to cook stocks, soups, pasta, lobster, corn, and tall stuff (like asparagus). Make sure the handles are comfortable (not sharp) as this pot is heavy when loaded full.

Dutch Oven

This is the heavy pot you need for braising pot roasts and making big batches of beef stew or chili. The Guy has a heavy, enameled cast iron pot—perfect for browning that pot roast on top of the stove and heavy enough to stay in a 275°F (140°C) oven all day—and a lighter stainless-steel Dutch oven for everyday soups and stews.

Wok

This is the specialized vessel you need for stir-frying (the deep sloped sides let you move things around quickly over high heat without tossing them all over the kitchen). The Guy survived quite well with an inexpensive carbon steel wok from Chinatown for years (make sure it comes with a lid), but now has a swankier anodized aluminum version that really keeps the heat even.

Roasting Pan

Make sure you have a couple of oblong pans that go into the oven for roasting meats and making casseroles like lasagna or moussaka. The Guy likes his big, heavy anodized aluminum roaster (big enough for most turkeys) and his ceramic oblong and oval bakers that go from the oven to the table, whether he's serving mac and cheese or apple crisp.

Bakeware

The good news is there's tons of wonderful nonstick bakeware on the market, from muffin tins to Bundt pans. Buy the heaviest gauge. You'll need muffin pans (mini and large); at least two baking sheets; round, square, and oblong cake pans; loaf pans; and bread pans. Silicon bakeware is nifty for the kind of things that tend to get stuck in the pan—mini-frittatas, muffins, and cakes brown perfectly and pop out like ice cubes.

Mix and Match Menus

Put together a party with these festive menu combos.

The Brunch Party

Guys (and girls) know that the best way to entertain (especially relatives or friends with kids) is during the day. Sunday lunch or brunch is perfect. Start at 11:00, end at 2:00, and you'll still have a good chunk of Sunday afternoon ahead of you.

Brunch for Adults
Champagne and Orange Juice
Sliced Melon
Eggs Bennie on Crab Cakes (page 59)
Almond Apricot Scones (page 66)
or Boozy Bread Pudding with Whisky Sauce (page 364)
Cappuccino

Family Brunch
Orange Juice
Cornmeal Hotcakes with Fresh Berries (page 62)
or Banana Pancakes (page 63)
Maple Syrup
Orange Wedges
Fruit Crisp

Doing Dim Sum

Dim sum is the other kind of Sunday brunch party to throw—for your sophisticated city friends. Get up early and buy some barbecue pork buns at the Chinese bakery and barbecue duck at the butcher, then simply augment with these home-cooked noshes.

Green Tea
Mu Shu Duck (page 106)
Asian Eggplant (page 288)
Prawn and Sweet Bell Pepper Bites (page 302)
Pan-Fried Shrimp and Scallop Dumplings with
    Spicy Dipping Sauce (page 306)
Chocolate Ginger Mousse (page 320)

Summer Solstice

Longest day on the deck—need I say more? This is a menu to enjoy with some crisp and fruity white wine, whether it's champagne, Frascati, or Riesling. And you can make it all in advance.

Crudités
Cool Tomato and Cucumber Soup (page 415)
Deviled Eggs on Baby Arugula (page 400)
Marinated Seafood Salad (page 419)
Simple Strawberry Trifle (page 321)

Mardis Gras Menu

A Cajun feast is always fun in February, especially when The Guy's resolved to give up rich food the day after Fat Tuesday and get into shape for spring. For a casual party, have the gumbo with dirty rice and pecan pie.

Southern Crab Cakes (page 304)
Chicken, Shrimp, and Sausage Gumbo (page 48)
Deep Dish Chocolate Pecan Pie (page 324)

Retro Schmooze

Take me back to those halcyon days of Mrs. Robinson, Woodstock, and big fat steak house dinners. Remember when steak was the only meal you went out to eat? Really—it once was the case.

Shrimp Cocktail
French Onion Soup (page 233)
Steak with Creamy Black Peppercorn Sauce (page 231)
Stuffed Baked Potatoes (page 234)
Creamy Ricotta Cheesecake (page 332)
or Chocolate Espresso Cake (page 327)

Beach Blanket Barbie

Gather up the blankets and beach umbrellas and plan to start a bonfire on the beach for these easy seafood packages (that you can make at home and plunk on ice in the cooler).

Mojitos and Spicy Caesars (pages 276 and 278)
Chunky Smoked Salmon Spread (page 286)
White Bean Purée and Crostini Toasts (page 288)
Seafood Bake (page 376)
Sangria Ice (page 248)
Chocolate Cookies (page 468)

Family Picnic

Gather the clan in the park, haul along the baseball glove, Frisbee, and croquet, and spend the afternoon noshing on the lawn, under a big shady tree.

Southern Fried Chicken (page 418)
Classic Coleslaw (page 165)
Perfect Potato Salad (page 410)
Carrot Spice Cake (page 453)
Watermelon

Bohemian Bistro

You may not be in Paris this week, but you can eat like you are. Pour a little Beaujolais and try a casual bistro menu, straight from the Rue Saint-Germain.

Not Foie Gras Paté (page 287)
or Gougères (page 242)
Warm Bacon, Egg, and Spinach Salad (page 71)
or French Onion Soup (page 233)
Steak Frites (page 70)
French Apple Tart (page 176)

Valentine's Day

Go all out. Let her know you really care. Cook.

Tomato and Bocconcini Salad (page 254)
Shellfish Stew for Two with Saffron Risotto
   (page 196 and 203)
or Tenderloin for Two with
   Garlic Mashed Potatoes (page 195 and 156)
French Apple Tart (page 176)

That's Amore

When you want to cook something that's romantic there's nothing like putting on some Puccini and letting the evening unfold.

Supplis (page 301)
Chicken Saltimbocca with Saffron Risotto (page 202)
or Roasted Halibut Italian-Style (page 73)
Creamy Polenta (page 161)
Warm Poached Figs on Ice (page 206)

Texas Two-Step

Well guys, it's time to do some boot scootin'. Just spin some Willie and Waylon, shake up some Caesars (or crack a couple of long-neck beers), and we'll go honky tonkin' with this good ol' boy chuck. Yee haw!

Guacamole and Chips (page 269)
Spicy Black Bean Soup (page 97)
Chicken Fried Steak and Buttermilk Biscuits
   (pages 140 and 64)
or Monster Beef Ribs (page 138)
Butter Pecan Banana Sundaes (page 207)

Fall Feast

When the harvest is done and the markets are brimming with fall's bounty, it's time to gather with friends and family to enjoy this seasonal feast.

Sweet Potato, Parsnip, and Roasted Onion Soup
   (page 360)
Perfect Roast Chicken (page 355)
or Duck Breast with Fig Gratin (page 244)
Zucchini and Tomato Gratin (page 162)
Ginger Cake with Warm Apple Compote (page 456)

Christmas Eve with Family

A simple family meal, based on the classic French Canadian meat pie, traditionally served on Christmas Eve.

Crab and Artichoke Dip with Melba Toasts (page 282)
French Onion Soup (page 233)
Tourtière (page 133)
Sticky Toffee Puddings with Rum Sauce (page 330)

Christmas Morning Breakfast

After the presents have been opened, it's always fun to indulge in a big Eggs Benedict breakfast/brunch on Christmas morning.

Champagne and Orange Juice
Mixed Melon, Grape, and Pineapple Fruit Salad
Eggs Bennie with Smoked Salmon (page 59)
Apple Cranberry Crisp (page 326)

Fireside Winter Menu

Gather 'round the crackling fire after a day on the slopes with this warm, wintry menu. It can all be prepared in advance, to be popped in the oven when you return from your outing.

Oat Cakes and Smoked Salmon (page 359)
or Fireside Fondue (page 378)
Canadian Cassoulet (page 390)
Carrot Spice Cake (page 453)
Blueberry Tea (page 277)

Family Movie (or Games) Night

Sometimes you just want to gather around the TV (or the dining room table) with the kids to spend some quality time. Of course, you've gotta eat, too, so it might as well be fun.

Cheesy Potato Skins (page 114)
or Guacamole and Chips (page 269)
Chicken Chili Wraps (page 120)
or Chili Con Carne Tostadas (page 371)
One, Two, Three-Bite Brownies (page 123)
Popcorn (page 369)

Memories of Athens

The tavernas of Athens hold wonderful memories for The Guy—the kind of places where people laugh, sing, and dance together spontaneously! When you want desperately to go back, and just can't afford the fare, pop a bottle of Greco di Tufo, get out the ouzo and dance.

Zorba's Mussels (page 219)
Classic Greek Salad (page 224)

Lamb Moussaka or Souvlakia Skewers
   (pages 394 and 264)
Wilted Spinach with Rice (page 163)
Peeled and Sliced Oranges, Drizzled with Honey
   and Cinnamon

Middle Eastern Menu

Stop at the shwarma shop down the street and pick up some fresh pita bread and grape-leaf dolmades to round out this feast.

Cilantro Hummus and Pita Chips (page 283)
Lemony Lentil and Tabbouleh Salad (page 407)
Falafel Sandwiches (page 31)
or Braised Lamb with Chickpeas (page 391)
Roasted Potatoes (page 223)
Honey and Walnut Baklava (page 225)

Goan Guy

The Guy has always been smitten by the Indian subcontinent. It's big, exotic, and chaotic—and the spicy cuisine is equally exciting and eclectic. So make your own exploratory trip to the local Indian grocery for exotic spices, and plan an evening of spicy food and colorful culture—Bollywood style. Chill some light lager or pour a Riesling or Gewürztraminer to match this aromatic menu.

Crispy Dal Fritters with Onion Chutney (page 290)
Masala Prawns (page 291)
Butter Chicken (page 92)
Tandoori Lamb Skewers (page 265)
Basmati Rice
Sliced Mangoes

Bangkok Nights

Thai food is another one of the world's hot cuisines—both literally and figuratively—and that always makes The Guy's palate happy. Make this simple but spicy meal to conjure the exotic sights and smells of Southeast Asia.

Satay Sticks with Peanut Sauce (page 305)
Thai-Style Coconut Curry Noodle Soup (page 82)
Grilled Salmon with Mango Salsa (page 438)
Basmati Rice
Spears of Fresh Pineapple, Mango,
   and Asian Pears

Latin Lover

You can woo her with this menu from points south. From plantains to Pisco, this is a meal for the Americas.

Pisco Sours (page 275)
or Mojitos (page 276)
Orange Scallop Ceviche (page 268)
Argentinian-Style Steak with Chimichurri Sauce (page 230)
Tostones and Red Beans (page 349)
Orange Crème Brûlée (page 322)

Nothing but Nibblies

Just the kind of stuff for grazing, when what you want is a cocktail party for two.

Martinis (page 275)
Sesame Ginger Chicken (page 89)
Hot Crab and Artichoke Dip with Pita Chips (page 282)
Asian Eggplant (page 288)
One, Two, Three-Bite Brownies (page 123)

An Intimate Holiday Dinner

Even a small holiday dinner for two can be festive and traditional—especially when you serve these chicken breasts with old-fashioned bread stuffing.

Creamy Sweet Potato, Parsnip, and Roasted Onion Soup (page 360)
All-Dressed Chicken Breasts (page 88)
Mashed Potatoes (page 155)
Green Salad (page 158)
Chocolate Lava Cakes with Crème Anglaise (page 328)
or Ginger Cake with Warm Apple Compote (page 456)

Old-Country Dining

The Guy likes to recall his grandmother's eastern European cooking—lots of sausage, noodles, dill, and paprika.

Sliced Garlic Sausage, Cheese, and Crackers
Grandma's Chicken Soup (page 354)
Hungarian Chicken and Dumplings in CreamyPaprika Sauce (page 90)
or Pork Goulash (page 393)
Cucumber Salad (page 165)
Apple Turnovers (a.k.a. Strudel) (page 217)

Birthday Bash

The gang's all arriving for a birthday party and you're in charge of the food. Make it easy on yourself. Let them eat tacos.

Chips and Dips (page 281)
Taco Buffet (page 182)
Lemony Yellow Pound Cake (page 451)
or The Guy's Chocolate Birthday Cake (page 452)

Asian Hot Pot

Plan a Chinese feast on a winter weekend around a pot of these savory short ribs.

Chow Cow Chips with Asian Eggplant (page 288)
Corn and Crabmeat Soup (page 311)
Mahogany-Glazed Short Ribs (page 141)
Spicy Szechuan Greens (page 317)
Rice
Tropical Fruit Brûlée (page 318)
Fortune Cookies

A Spanish Supper

Nibble on tapas, then make a communal paella filled with seafood.

Olives
Garlic Clams (page 297)
Potato and Spicy Sausage Frittata (cut into small squares for appetizers) (page 416)
A Party Paella (page 190)
Sangria Ice (page 248)

Guy Glossary

Wanna know more? Turn to this section—organized in alphabetical order—with all the details about unusual ingredients, basic equipment, and techniques. When you aren't clear about something, flip to this section to learn everything you ever wanted, or needed, to know.

These are the secret weapons of chefs and foodies—the tricks that make cooking easy, the ingredients and prepared foods that every good cooks uses to impress. While not an exhaustive glossary, it does cover many of the FAQ bases. Doesn't hurt to read through this stuff once in a while (great bedtime reading) to remind and inspire you.

Altitude

At high altitudes, The Guy's buns can be flat and unattractive. That's because altitude affects the way leavening agents like yeast, baking powder, and baking soda work to make things rise. Know the tricks and adjust your recipes accordingly.

For cakes that rise and fall, try reducing the baking powder or soda by ⅛ tsp (0.5 mL) per teaspoon called for in the recipe.

Moisture evaporates more quickly, so adjust your recipes with a little more liquid.

The higher the altitude, the lower the temperature of the food. Don't crank the heat but plan to bake things a little longer than specified.

Reduce the amount of sugar called for by about 1 tbsp (15 mL) per 1 cup (250 mL), since sugar can weaken the structure of baked goods.

Arborio Rice

This is the starchy, short-grain rice you use to make creamy risotto. Don't try to use regular or converted rice for this dish—you won't get the right texture. And don't be tempted to add the liquid all at once. The trick to making creamy risotto is in the stirring, adding hot liquid, ½ cup (125 mL) at a time, then stirring until enough liquid is absorbed to result in a soft but still slightly chewy grain. You'll need 3 to 4 cups (750 mL to 1 L) of liquid for every 1 cup (250 mL) of rice, and 30 minutes.

Asian Chili Paste

An essential secret weapon in The Guy's arsenal. Garlic chili paste (a.k.a. sambal oelek) is searingly hot, comes in jars at any Asian market, and is far better than the usual liquid hot sauces for adding a jolt of tangy heat to almost anything without adding excess acidity. Of course, a dollop is appropriate in any Szechuan stir-fry sauce, but you'll also use this paste in barbecue sauces and rubs and to add heat to soups, salad dressings, chili, or Italian puttanesca sauce. Use sparingly, but use it. You'll never chop another chili pepper.

Balsamic Vinegar

Real balsamic vinegar (balsamico) is made in and around Modena, Italy. The cheapest versions are just red wine vinegar with caramel flavoring and sugar added. The best are aged for decades in tiny wooden barrels until they're sweet, complex, and thick as molasses (sold in numbered bottles, vetted by the Italian consortzio and labeled "balsamico tradizionale"). You can pay anywhere from $5 for 4 cups (1 L) to $150 for ½ cup (125 mL) for balsamic vinegar. Try a few before you decide which to use on your salads. And here's a chef's trick—boil a bottle of inexpensive balsamic vinegar down until it's reduced to a thick glaze to use as a drizzling sauce.

Basmati Rice

This Indian rice has a perfumed, nutty flavor and delicate, long grains. The Guy buys a sack of top-quality basmati at an Indian grocery and uses it for all rice dishes (except sushi and risotto).

Beans

There's nothing wrong with using canned beans, especially when you're using them in soups or purées like bean dip. Canned beans are fast, convenient, and cheap. Just dump them into a colander and rinse under the tap to remove the starchy broth (it's high in sodium).

Chickpeas (a.k.a. garbanzo beans) are perfectly acceptable from the can, especially when they're going into hummus (puréed), but also for salads and soups.

If you're planning a special dish where a nice, toothsome bean is important (chili, baked beans, cassoulet, etc.), start from scratch with dried beans. Wash the beans well and soak them overnight in water. If you don't have that much time, put the dried beans in a pot and cover them with lots of cold water. Bring the beans to a boil, then cover the pot and remove from the heat. Let the beans soak for 1 hour before draining and starting your recipe.

Don't salt beans or try to cook them in an acidic sauce (like tomato sauce) or they will never soften properly. Cook them in lots of water first, then add your salty and acidic ingredients.

Remember, beans cook at different rates, depending on the type, size, and how fresh they are, so don't combine a bunch of different dried beans and expect them to be done at the same time.

Look for growers of unique heirloom beans at the local farmers' market—old varietals with an array of sizes, colors, and deliciously different flavors and textures. You'll fall in love with these luscious and lean legumes.

Blanch

This refers to quickly immersing food in boiling water to partially cook it. It's ideal for cooking tougher vegetables like broccoli or carrots before adding them to a stir-fry, or par-cooking beans to a bright green color for a salad. You can blanch your vegetables, chill them in ice water, drain, and refrigerate before a dinner party, then reheat them by sautéing in butter just before serving (this is what chefs do—the reheated veggies cook evenly and stay brightly colored this way). Vegetables are usually blanched before freezing. And you can use blanching to help you peel tomatoes or peaches—cut an x in the skin, dump into boiling water for a minute, then cool in ice water and slip off the skins.

Bok Choy et al.

Bok choy (a.k.a. pak choy or Chinese cabbage) is one of The Guy's favorite Asian vegetables—especially the mild baby bok choy, less than 5 inches (12 cm) long, that can be split lengthwise and braised or grilled as a side to almost any meal.

Bigger bok choy should be sliced and lightly stir-fried—the tougher ends added to the pan first, and the more delicate leafy parts stirred in at the end, just to wilt.

Bowls (see page 488)

Braise

Braising is the method of cooking something with liquid, usually with the lid on. You can braise in the oven or on top of the stove. You can braise with broth, wine, juice, cider, beer, or water. Braised meats are usually seared first in a little fat over medium-high heat to brown on all sides—this adds more of that yummy caramelized flavor to your braise. Then you lower the heat, add the liquid, clamp on the lid, and cook slowly for a long time. Braising is a tenderizing step. Braising is what makes beef stew, pot roast, and daube of lamb so darned delicious.

Broth

Canned broth is fine, but homemade is better. Save your scraps in the freezer (bones from chicken and pork; clean vegetable trimmings like leek and green onion tops, carrot peelings, etc.) And make stock from scratch, then freeze it in small containers. You can make stocks from chicken bones, meat bones, and fish bones. All benefit by the inclusion of aromatic vegetables like sliced onions, celery, carrots, garlic, and parsnips, and whole herbs and spices like black peppercorns, parsley, and bay leaves.

Just cover 4 to 5 lb (2 to 2.2 kg) of bones, vegetables, and flavorings with 12 to 16 cups (3 to 4 L) of cold water in a deep stock pot. Bring the stock to a boil over high heat, skim off any foam that rises to the top, then reduce the heat to medium-low and simmer the stock, uncovered, for 4 hours. Strain through a sieve that's been lined with cheesecloth. Discard the solids and then either chill the broth in the refrigerator or freeze. Season the broth to taste with salt before using in soups or other recipes.

Fish stock needs only about 30 minutes of simmering and benefits from the addition of some white wine. Use fish bones, heads, and tails but avoid salmon as the flavor is too strong.

Beef stock is best if it's simmered for 5 hours or more.

For more intense broths, start by roasting the bones and vegetables in the oven to brown before adding the water. This caramelizes the sugars and results in a broth with more color and flavor.

Butter

You can buy salted or unsalted butter, but purists usually reach for the unsalted kind, especially for baking. Salted butter keeps better (the salt is a preservative) but unsalted butter has a cleaner, purer flavor. Store it in the freezer if you don't plan to use it immediately.

Ghee is butter that is clarified—melted and separated from the milk solids and water until it is deep golden and slightly nutty in flavour. Ghee keeps well (up to 6 months in the refrigerator) and has a high enough smoke point for frying. It's the fat of choice for Indian cooking.

Cheese

Real cheese is never processed, it is a natural product. Try to buy good-quality, artisan cheese or at least authentic cheese made in countries like France and Italy where there are strict rules governing how cheeses are made. The industrial cheeses we've created in North America usually aren't anything like real cheese.

Every refrigerator should have some good cheese for eating and cooking. Buy a chunk of aged Parmigiano Reggiano or pecorino for grating, and a good artisan brie or Camembert for serving with wine. Have a nice Gouda, aged cheddar, fresh goat cheese, and blue cheese on hand. When you're making pizza, mozzarella or Friulano are good choices. Monterey Jack makes the best quesadillas.

Next time you have a party, buy three or four interesting cheeses and offer a cheese tray with bread and crackers. Instant appetizer.

Make a trip to a proper cheese store and begin sampling good-quality cheeses—you'll never go back.

Chili Paste (see Asian Chili Paste)

Chipotle Chilies

A chipotle is nothing more than a garden variety jalapeño with a little experience—a pepper that's been smoked over a wood fire. Find them dried in the supermarket produce section (soak to rehydrate) or, even better, buy them canned in adobo sauce from a Latin market. Once you open a can of chipotles, you can store any leftovers in a sealed container in the refrigerator for several months. Chipotles add a wonderful smoky sweet heat to chilies, soups, stews, dips, and rubs.

Coconut Milk

Coconut milk comes in a can, and can be found in well-stocked supermarkets or Asian groceries. Look for the unsweetened kind (the sweet stuff is only for desserts). Buy "lite" fat-reduced coconut milk, as the full-fat stuff is killer in the calorie department.

Coconut cream is a similar but more concentrated form of coconut milk. Neither is sweetened, so both are appropriate for soups, curries, and other savory dishes. But "cream of coconut" (used in desserts and cocktails) is a sweetened product so make sure you don't get the two confused.

Couscous

Technically, couscous is a very small pasta, made by rubbing semolina flour into tiny balls with water. The easiest couscous to use is the instant variety (this is also most commonly available). Look for it in the pasta sections of large supermarkets, in Middle Eastern groceries, and health-food stores.

For every 1 cup (250 mL) of couscous, you'll need about 1½ cups (375 mL) of boiling water or broth. Simply mix the dry couscous into the boiling liquid, cover, remove from the heat, and let it stand for about 10 minutes while the couscous hydrates. Fluff it with a fork to separate the grains and serve.

Think of couscous as a blank slate—traditionally, the broth used to cook it is flavored with saffron and then bits like raisins and fried onions are added. But couscous takes to all kinds of creative additions, from roasted peppers and chili powder, to dried fruits, chickpeas, and fresh herbs. Serve it hot with Moroccan stews or cold in potluck salads. A kind of tabbouleh can be made with couscous instead of bulgar (which is cracked and steamed whole wheat that cooks up about the same way), by combining cooked couscous with lots of chopped parsley, olive oil, tomatoes and cumin. Play with it. Experiment.

Israeli couscous is an entirely different animal—fat balls of semolina pasta with the look and texture of tapioca. Like the smaller version, Israeli couscous soaks up whatever flavor it's introduced to, and makes a toothsome side dish or salad.

Cream

Whipping cream, or "heavy cream," is highest in fat (36-40 percent butter fat) and can be whipped. It also instantly thickens a sauce when it's added at the end and reduced. Half-and-half, or "cereal cream," is a 50-50 combination of milk and cream—it won't whip but gives rich flavor to soups and sauces with fewer calories. For really low-fat cream soups, use condensed skim milk (canned) for a similar texture.

Crème Fraîche

This thickened sweet cream can go both ways—on a sweet dessert or swirled into a savory soup. Make it by mixing 2 cups (500 mL) of heavy whipping cream with ½ cup (125 mL) of sour cream. Whisk the mixture together in a bowl, cover with plastic wrap, and set aside at room temperature for 12 hours. When the crème fraîche is nicely thickened, store it in the refrigerator for up to 2 weeks. A nice option instead of sweetened cream on fruit desserts.

Curry Paste

This is another of The Guy's secret weapons. Indian curry pastes come in jars and are combinations of exotic spices like turmeric, coriander, fennel, cloves, chilies, and cardamom with ginger, garlic, and oil. There are mild and hot curry pastes for general cooking and pastes for specific Indian dishes like biryani, tandoori chicken, or rogan josh. Look for them at Indian groceries and stock a few. Curry pastes replace the old-fashioned curry powders—they're more intense, fresher, more convenient to use, and even shelf-stable at room temperature.

Thai curry pastes are essential to Thai cooking and are completely different from the Indian versions. While serious Thai chefs would grind their own pastes by hand with a mortar and pestle, you can save time by buying prepared pastes. Thai curry pastes come in two basic varieties: red curry paste and green curry paste. Both contain classic Southeast Asian flavorings like coriander seeds, lemon grass, galangal, shrimp paste, and kaffir lime zest, but the red paste is colored and flavored with dried red chilies, while the slightly milder green curry paste has fresh Thai or serrano peppers which give the paste its distinctive color. Find them in tubs or pouches in Asian markets. They should be refrigerated.

Stock both Indian and Thai curry pastes in your pantry for adding instant authentic flavor to stir-fries and other curry dishes, or for flavoring soups, dips, and sauces. Thai pastes are traditionally combined with coconut milk in curries and soups. Indian pastes do double duty as rubs for fish and chicken, to make a regular chicken and rice soup into an exotic mulligatawny, or to dress up side dishes of steamed potatoes and cauliflower.

Cut (Chop, Dice, Mince, Cube, Chiffonade, Julienne)

It seems every recipe asks for a different cut. If you're not familiar with these terms it can seem like recipes are written in a foreign language. But it pays to get a good knife and hone your knife knowledge. The best chefs have the best knife skills and can cut those beautiful even little cubes of red peppers or cucumbers by hand. It just takes practice.

Basic cuts range from coarse chopping and mincing to dicing, julienne, chiffonade, and diagonal or rolled cuts. Coarse chopping is used for vegetables that are used for flavoring and will eventually be strained out of the dish.

A regular "chop" or dice is cutting ¼- to ½-inch (6-mm to 1-cm) even cubes; a finer dice might be ¹⁄₁₆ to ⅛ inch (1.5 mm to 3 mm) in size. Mince means to chop very fine, almost purée. Julienne cuts are little sticks, batons, or almost shreds—which may be 2 inches (5 cm) long or so, chunky or very fine (nice in pasta dishes or salads).

To chop an onion, peel it, cut it in half lengthwise, then lay it flat on a cutting board. Cut even horizontal and vertical slices through the onion, all the way up to, but not through, the root end. Then slice across the onion, from the stem to the root end, to evenly dice.

Garlic, ginger, and herbs call for a finer cutting called mincing. After the food is coarsely chopped, gather it into a pile. Hold the tip of the knife on the board and, using a rocking motion, continue to chop over the pile until everything is finely minced. To prepare both garlic and ginger for quick mincing, place the flat blade of the chef's knife over the peeled vegetable and give it a firm whack with your fist. You can also get both garlic and ginger even finer in an instant by using a fine grater or pressing it through a garlic press (but then you have to clean another tool, which The Guy hates to do).

To evenly dice vegetables like carrots and potatoes, first peel and trim them into blocks (save trimmings for stock). Cut blocks into even strips (batonnets) or fine shreds (julienne). Stack strips and cut crosswise for perfect dice. A mandoline (see page 506) makes this easiest but you can do it by hand if you're accurate.

To make a chiffonade, roll leafy vegetables or herbs into tight cylinders like cigars and slice across the roll to form shreds.

The diagonal, or rolled, cut is used when you want to expose the most surface area to the heat and cook quickly—say in a stir-fry or stew. Cut even parallel cuts of celery, carrot, or parsnips on a sharp diagonal or make one diagonal, turn vegetable half a turn, then make a second diagonal cut and repeat. This gives you chunky pieces with two angled edges.

Edamame

These fresh green soy beans are the steamed, salty pods you get at the sushi bar. Buy them frozen, in bags, in the freezer section of your local Asian grocery and simply steam for 4 minutes in the microwave, douse with sea salt, and serve for snacking like they do in Japan. This may well be the coolest and easiest appetizer anywhere—and it's healthy.

The Guy also likes to buy the shelled soy beans at the market (same spot in the freezer department), steam them, and toss them with olive oil and garlic to serve as a side dish with almost anything. You'll see these electric green beans popping up on all of the best plates—they're rich tasting, incredibly easy to cook, and beautiful to behold.

Eggs

Use large eggs in all of these recipes—free range and farm fresh if possible. Bring them to room temperature before baking.

Fish Sauce

You may think you'll never use that big bottle of fish sauce (a.k.a. nam pla in Thailand or nuoc nam in Vietnam and shottsuru in Japan) but it's essential flavoring for Southeast Asian cooking. Don't smell or taste it straight—that strong, fermented fishy flavor will surely put you off, but use it when it's called for in an Asian recipe for authentic flavor.

Fish sauce, like soy sauce, has that elusive savory flavor that wine tasters call umami. It's a universally loved flavor sensation. So don't limit your fish sauce to Thai curries.

The Guy actually knows a chef who uses a dash of fish sauce to finish almost every soup and sauce he makes, whether it's French, Italian, or Japanese. The fish sauce adds that boost of je ne sais quoi that boosts the flavor of everything he cooks—think of it as liquid anchovies. It could become your own secret weapon.

Flour

When it comes to flour, The Guy uses less of the plain white stuff than the rest, but you should have a selection of flours in the pantry. For everyday flouring of meats and baking, the white flour of choice is unbleached, all-purpose wheat flour. Canadian brands have high gluten and are great for bread, but can be a little hard for delicate pastries—on these occasions, you'll want to buy a softer pastry flour. For most of his cooking and baking, The Guy reaches for wholegrain flours that have more nutrients and fibre intact, whether it's 100 percent whole wheat flour or barley flour. You can substitute wholegrain flour the white flour in many recipes—in baked goods, try using half whole wheat and half all-purpose flour to start. Barley flour can be substituted 1:1 for all-purpose flour.

In terms of nutrients, stone-ground flours are the healthiest of the bunch—there's less heat produced in the grinding process and the germ stays with the flour. This is the kind of flour you'll find at a health food store and the kind to store in the refrigerator or freezer as it will spoil and taste rancid faster than more highly processed flours.

Food Processor

The Guy would never give up his chef's knife or his other essential mincing and puréeing tool: the food processor.

Cuisinart is arguably the granddaddy of all food processors and a large, good-quality food processor will never let you down. Without it, you won't be able to make the simple dips, spreads, sauces, creamed soups, cheesecakes, and other dishes that rely on the puréeing power of the food processor. And, although you can always do it by hand, a food processor lets you mince the onions and garlic, and chop the carrots, mushrooms, and celery that you need to start soups, sauces, and stews almost instantly.

You can't do all of your mixing in a food processor (it's not great for whipping cream or beating egg whites and it makes horribly gluey puréed potatoes), but you can make bread or cracker crumbs, grate hard cheese, chop chocolate, grind nuts, purée whole tomatoes, chop spinach, and mix bread and pizza dough. If a recipe calls for chopped or ground ingredients, pulse them in the food processor using on and off bursts until the food is processed to your liking. Use the metal chopping blade for most jobs, the plastic blade for dough, and the special discs for shredding and slicing.

Always make sure the lid is securely in place before you turn the machine on (get a model that won't work unless the lid is attached) and always use the plastic pushing tool to feed foods into the shredding blades.

Garam Masala

This is a blend of Indian spices—a kind of chocolate brown curry powder that includes "hot" spices like cinnamon, cloves, black pepper, cardamom, fennel, mace, nutmeg, chilies, and cumin. Buy it at Indian groceries.

Garlic Press

This is a nifty gadget that turns a clove of garlic or a chunk of fresh ginger into the perfect pulpy consistency you need in sauces and salad dressings. Not essential, but handy. Get a good name brand version; the cheap ones are garage sale fodder.

Ginger

A fresh root with thin beige skin. The easiest way to peel a piece of ginger is by scraping away the skin with a spoon. Then you can lay the flat side of your chef's knife over the chunk of ginger and smash it with your fist—the result will be a pulpy mass that you can easily chop. Another good way to mince fresh ginger is to use your microplane grater or garlic press. Galangal is a type of mild Thai ginger—a pale yellow, pink-tinged relative.

Grains

Whole grains are healthier than processed white rice or flour.

Barley comes in two varieties: pearl barley or wholegrain pot barley. The latter is healthier but takes longer to cook. Cook 1 cup (250 mL) barley in 3 cups (750 mL) boiling water or stock for about 45 minutes.

Bulgar wheat is whole wheat that's been steamed, dried, and cracked. It cooks on its own (like couscous). Just pour 2 cups (500 mL) of boiling liquid over 1 cup (250 mL) of bulgar, cover, and let stand 20 minutes, or boil like rice.

Kasha is toasted buckwheat—a triangular little grain with a unique smoky flavor. To keep the cooked grains from sticking and to prevent mushy kasha, toast in a dry pan with a beaten egg for 5 minutes before adding 2½ cups (625 mL) of water

or stock for every 1 cup (250 mL) of kasha. Boil for 20 minutes.

Wild rice is not a rice but a long dark grain from a grass that grows in marshes and lakes throughout Canada and the northern U.S. Cook 1 cup (250 mL) of wild rice in 4 cups (1 L) of broth for 45 minutes until the grains split.

Grater

For hard cheese like Parmesan the only grater to use is the microplane grater, a slim steel grater with rows of tiny square teeth (see page 487).

A basic box grater (the stainless steel kind with different sized holes on each side) is cheap and useful for grating cheddar cheese, carrots, and onions for coleslaw and other such things. If you're grating a lot of stuff, get a grating blade for your food processor. It makes shavings of carrots, cabbage, and grated cheese in an instant.

Greens 101

The Guy likes salad, especially when the green stuff in the bowl tastes fresh, crunchy, and varied. Don't get stuck with limp lettuce or bland bowls of iceberg—experiment with new and eclectic greens for your salads and The Guy guarantees you'll be more likely to eat your greens.

You'll find an array of greens—from spinach and chard to gourmet salad mixes and kale—at most large supermarkets. For ethnic greens—bok choy, watercress, and mustard greens—check Asian markets. Italian markets often have fresh bunches of broccoli rabe, basil, and tight heads of crisp radicchio. You can count on local farmers to bring ultra fresh arugula, sorrel, dandelion, and other fresh greens to market. Or toss some seeds in a pot for your own supply of quick-growing arugula and salad herbs.

Here's a primer on what you'll get from your greens:

Arugula: this peppery green is a member of the mustard family and flourishes in cool climates. Also known as rocket, spicy arugula will perk up a regular salad. Or it can be sautéed with spinach and garlic, tossed with hot pasta, or stirred into a vegetable fritatta.

Basil: while basil is an herb, the large-leaf varieties add a lovely sweet anise and mint flavor to salads and combine well with other greens. Fresh basil makes a savory base or topping for a fresh tomato salad and is good in pasta sauces, on pizza, or stuffed into grilled vegetable sandwiches.

Sorrel: sorrel looks like spinach but belongs to the buckwheat family. It is a hardy perennial plant with a tart, lemony flavor. Shred it for a salad with a lemon vinaigrette, add it to lift a basic potato soup, purée it into mayonnaise, or add it to butter sauces for fish.

Watercress: The Guy loves these small peppery leaves with their radish-like flavor. Look for watercress with the parsley in supermarkets—Asian groceries usually have the freshest watercress. Serve it in elegant composed salads with pears and blue cheese, or use it instead of lettuce for crunchy flavor in sandwiches or wraps.

Edible flowers: please don't eat the daisies from the florist (they're probably sprayed) but many blooms that grow in The Guy's home garden are gorgeous as edible garnishes. Posies to pick for dinner include: bachelor buttons, pansies, violets, borage, carnations, daisies, chive blossoms, fuchsias, marigolds, nasturtiums, roses, and snap dragons.

Pea shoots: with the fresh, crisp flavor of garden peas, pea shoots are wonderful greens to add to salads. Try a tangle of pea shoots atop a piece of fish as an edible green garnish, or chop pea shoots and stir into your next risotto.

Mustard greens: called baby gai choy at Chinese markets, this chard-like leaf is tangy and peppery and makes excellent cooked greens. Baby bok choy is another great candidate for stir fries or to quickly grill or braise as a side dish.

Kale: kale is a tough customer and needs to be cooked or braised for a long time—great for soups. But curly green, purple, or ivory heads of flowering kale instantly decorate the buffet or salad station, and leaves are perfect for lining salad bowls or adding color to plates.

Chicory: if you like bitter greens, chicory is the one for you. Also called curly endive or frisée, this green has sharply cut and curled leaves .The youngest leaves are generally sweetest, but all have a bitter tinge.

Radicchio: this Italian form of chicory has small purple-and-white heads. Radicchio adds color to mixed salads, and a bittersweet flavor.

Spinach: spinach has medium-sized, arrow-shaped leaves and can be eaten raw or cooked. Blanch quickly or sauté, just until bright green, but don't use an aluminum pan—your spinach will turn grey and take on a metallic taste.

Chard: Swiss chard is a sweet-flavored green that anyone can grow. Look for colorful rainbow chard with red, yellow, and white stems. Substitute for spinach or beet greens.

Nasturtium leaves: The Guy always plants nasturtiums in his flower pots since they do double duty for entertaining. Not only are the plants and flowers beautiful—cascades of big round leaves and pretty red, orange, and gold blooms—but all parts of the plant are edible and add a unique peppery flavor to salads or garnishes.

Dandelion greens: keep the herbicides off your lawn, and harvest a spring crop of edible young dandelion greens for salads before the plants flower and go to seed. Dandelion greens are very nutritious. Eat cooked or in salads.

Grilling

The Guy does a lot of cooking on his gas grill—fast and fat free. You gotta like that.

Purists cook on charcoal (admittedly, it adds flavor) but speed demons go for gas (natural or propane). Instant on, instant off. When it's cold outside, instead of the outdoor grill, fire up the oven broiler or use an indoor grill to provide similar results.

The best things to grill are chicken, steaks, burgers, and fish steaks—anything thin enough to be nicely browned on the outside and cooked through at the same time. For bigger pieces of meat, you'll need to brown it on the grill first, then turn off one of the burners, move the meat to the unlit side, cover the barbecue and roast until done.

While we often say "barbecue" we really mean "grill"—barbecue is slow cooking, indirectly over smoky heat, the kind of cooking that gives you pulled pork and the best brisket.

Ground Beef

Not all ground beef (a.k.a. hamburger) is created equal, and you want to choose the right ground beef for your recipe.

Regular: with the most fat, this is the ground beef to choose when you're making something like spaghetti sauce or tacos—recipes where the beef is browned first, and the excess fat can be drained and rinsed off.

Medium: less fat and better for meatballs or hamburgers—recipes that allow you to drain off at least some of the fat. Still enough fat to keep foods juicy.

Lean or extra lean: choose this kind of ground beef for meat loaf, cabbage rolls, and dumplings—recipes that don't let you drain off any of the excess fat.

Remember, always cook ground beef (and chicken, pork, lamb, or any ground meat) until it's well done all the way through. The bacteria that are often found on the outer surfaces of whole cuts of raw meats are destroyed when that meat is seared on the outside, so a rare steak is fine. But when meat or poultry is ground, any surface contamination is mixed throughout the meat and you must get it all up to high temperatures to make sure it's safe.

Herbs

The Guy uses fresh herbs whenever possible. Do yourself a favor and plant a pot of basil, rosemary, mint, dill, cilantro, and Italian parsley this spring. All of them are easy to grow. Then, when you need a bit of fresh herbal flavor, you can just snip off what you need. Some of the woodier herbs, like thyme and sage, are perennials and if you plunk a plant in a sheltered spot in the flower garden, it will come back year after year.

In most cases, you want to use just the leaves and discard the stems as they can be coarse or downright woody. If you end up with a bumper crop of herbs, try making pestos by puréeing the herbs with olive oil in the food processor and freezing the pesto in ice cube trays. Pop them out, put them back in the freezer in plastic bags, and toss a cube into your next soup, stew, or dip for instant fresh herb flavor.

If you must substitute dried herbs remember that they are much stronger—use ⅓ to ½ the amount of dry herb when fresh herbs are called for in a recipe.

In winter months, The Guy always keeps a couple of jars in the fridge—Italian basil pesto and coriander chutney (an Indian pesto-like purée made with cilantro), perfect to add just the right flavor to Asian or Mexican dishes when fresh coriander (a.k.a. Cilantro) is hard to find.

Hoisin, Black Bean, Oyster, et al.

Who knows exactly what it is about these assertive Asian sauces—suffice to say every Chinese restaurant kitchen uses them and you should, too. Dark, thick, sweet, and spicy combinations of soy beans, chilies, sugar, and other exotic notes, they add that *je ne sais quoi* to every stir-fry and make it taste just right. Don't use too much—1 to 2 tbsp (15 to 30 mL) is always enough—but find a source of sauces and keep them in your refrigerator. Experiment when you're marinating chicken or pork for the grill, creating a new salad dressing, or just stir-frying seasonal veggies.

Jicama

Ever seen a round, beige veggie in the market, like a flattened turnip with a tan skin the color of ginger? That's a jicama—a crisp, juicy Latin vegetable that makes a lovely addition to a veggie tray and can be shredded with carrots into a refreshing slaw. You can also cube the white flesh and use it in stir-fries instead of fresh water chestnuts.

Kitchen shears (see page 487)

Knives (see page 487)

Lemongrass

Spot this lemony herb in an Asian market and you'll think you've come across a big, tough, dried-out green onion. Use in Thai cooking and curry pastes—but only the white bit at the bottom—the leaves are too chewy. And make sure to mince or purée it in a blender.

Lemon Reamer

This simple hand tool is indispensable for removing the juice from citrus fruits like lemons, limes, and oranges. The Guy's version is a plain wooden affair—like a ridged wooden top with a handle attached at the base, although old-fashioned reamers were usually made of glass, a small dish with the ridged reamer perched vertically in the center. Simply cut the lemon in half crosswise, insert the pointy end of the reamer into the center of the fruit, and twist (or press down over the point of the dish). You'll soon have all of the juice and luscious pulp in your bowl.

Lentils

Brown lentils are the little flat disc-shaped ones

that are most common, ranging in color from beige to khaki. They keep their shape when cooked and are often used for soups.

A similar and more rare lentil is the tiny French lentil, dark green to black in color. If you find them, they're worth buying for pilafs and warm lentil salads as they keep their shape and toothsome texture when cooked.

Tiny orange lentils disintegrate when cooked and turn a golden color—the basis for thick lentil soups and purées.

Mandoline

Not the musical variety, a cook's mandoline is a fancy slicer/dicer, the kind your mother probably bought from a huckster at the summer fair. It's a flat bed, with an adjustable ultra-sharp blade, which you slide the food across to cut it into perfect thin slices.

The mandoline is the secret weapon of the professional chef—used to cut perfect paper-thin potatoes or the finest julienne of carrots and cucumbers. Professional mandolines are lovely stainless steel affairs, but cost hundreds of dollars. You can find a very inexpensive and functional Japanese version at Asian houseware shops for about $40. Just be very careful and always use the plastic guard to hold the food while you're slicing—these babies are super sharp, and dangerous in the wrong hands.

Measuring Cups/Devices

The Guy will say this again—the glass measuring cups are for liquids, and the individually-sized metal or plastic cups (i.e., ¼ cup/60 mL, ½ cup/125 mL, etc.) are for dry ingredients. If you mix them up, your cakes, breads, and cookies won't work out right. Dry measures and measuring spoons should never be heaped—fill them, then use the back of a knife to scrape off any excess sugar or flour. Solid fats like butter, shredded cheese, or sour cream are also measured in dry measuring cups or spoons.

Get down at eye level to see how much liquid you have in a glass measuring cup.

It's really handy to have some big heatproof glass measuring cups, too—you can essentially mix batters right in the cup. A scale is also handy for weighing meats or following recipes that ask for a pound of onions or eggplant.

Mirin

This sweet rice wine is used in Japanese cooking. Also good in Asian sauces, glazes, and salad dressings.

Miso

This is a fermented Japanese soybean paste that adds salty flavor and substance to many Japanese dishes. The color ranges from a light golden color to a dark mahogany. Like wine, the lighter the color, the smoother and less complex the flavor. High in B vitamins and easy to digest, it's a very nutritious condiment. Use miso in soups, sauces, marinades, salad dressings, and dips. It comes refrigerated, or frozen, in tubs in Asian markets, and keeps well for several months in the refrigerator.

Mushrooms

Morels, chanterelles, shiitake—you can't know your mushrooms without a program. And you don't want to pick anything from the back forty to eat unless you know exactly what you're getting into—tie into the wrong fungus and you're no longer among us.

But commercial mushrooms are a different story and there's an amazing selection of delicious mushrooms on the market.

Standard white and brown mushrooms are always available. Portobellos are massive versions of your basic brown mushroom (sometimes growing 8 inches /20 cm across) and take well to baking and grilling—just brush with a little olive oil and sprinkle with herbs and seasoning. They make yummy appetizers, topped with things like sun-dried tomatoes and Parmesan cheese, then baked and cut into wedges. Or a whole portobello that's grilled can stand in for a meaty hamburger patty for vegetarians.

Morels are wonderful earthy mushrooms that you get in the springtime. The long, conical caps look like little black sponges and are perfect to add to pasta or risotto, along with asparagus and other seasonal ingredients.

Chanterelles are available at the other end of the season (fall). They are elegant orange mushrooms, vase shaped with a beautiful aroma.

Porcini are some of The Guy's favorite—a sweet mushroom that's perfect on all occasions. Porcini are from Italy and are most often sold dried.

Shiitakes are Asian mushrooms—sometime found fresh, but usually sold dried in bags at Chinese grocery stores.

Speaking of dried mushrooms, it is the most convenient way to buy exotic mushrooms and the best way to make sure that you always have some interesting mushrooms on hand. Morels, chanterelles, shiitakes, and porcini—all are available dried for rehydrating on a whim. To rehydrate, soak in warm water or simmer in a little white wine for a few minutes for added flavor. Asian mushrooms like shiitake can be simmered in water flavored with soy sauce to rehydrate.

Truffles are not exactly mushrooms, but they are in the fungus family. They're imported from France and Italy in the fall and winter where they are routed out of the ground by trained pigs and dogs. There are black truffles and rare white truffles, but both of these luxuries are ultra expensive and used sparingly. The Guy actually owns a tool designed to shave paper-thin slices from a truffle, although he has never had an actual specimen in his kitchen.

If you really want to impress someone, buy a tiny bottle of good-quality truffle oil at a gourmet shop and drizzle a few drops over a dish just before you serve it. The aroma of truffles is heavenly.

Mustard

Every culture enjoys the fiery flavor of good mustard. While most of the mustard seed that goes into the world's mustard is grown on the Canadian prairies, it's shipped around the globe to be ground and flavored to create spicy English mustards, grainy German mustards, smooth Dijon, fiery Chinese mustard, and oceans of American ballpark mustard for hot dogs. Buy a selection of different mustards for your pantry.

You can make your own mustards by combining dry mustard powder with cold water, vinegar, and flavorings, then letting it cure for a few weeks in the refrigerator. You can even tailor mustard to your personal taste—using fruit juices and special vinegars, sweetening your mustard with honey or maple syrup, or adding flavorings like chopped herbs and spices.

With oil and vinegar, a spoon of mustard is the

tie that binds a vinaigrette. Mustard adds zip and cuts the richness in a cheese sandwich. And cured meats like ham or sausages are always better with a dab of mustard.

Nuts

Nuts have a high oil content so can become rancid if not properly stored. Buy nuts in bulk from a busy natural foods store (where they turn over quickly) and use them up quickly. If you find yourself with too many nuts to use up, bag them and freeze them—they won't go rancid like they do at room temperature.

To get the best flavor from nuts, especially if you're using them in salads or as a garnish, toast them first. Spread the nuts in a single layer on a cookie sheet and toast them in a 375°F (190°C) oven for about 10 minutes. Cool the nuts before using.

The food processor is great for chopping or grinding nuts. Use on/off pulses until the nuts are chopped to your liking. If the nuts are destined for a cake or other recipe that includes sugar or flour, add a little sugar to the processor to prevent the nuts from turning into a paste.

Or make your own nut butters and spreads—whole toasted almonds, puréed in a food processor, melt into beautiful crunchy spreads in just a couple of minutes.

Olive Oil

If you don't believe there's a significant difference between inexpensive olive oil and pricey extra virgin, take The Guy's advice and do a taste test at home.

Go to a supermarket and to a good Italian grocery, and buy three bottles of olive oil. Ask the grocer to recommend an especially tasty oil for salads or dipping. Buy one marked "light olive oil," one marked "virgin olive oil," and one marked "extra virgin olive oil." Then taste them side by side to see the difference.

There are regulations that govern these terms—it has to do with the natural acidity of the oil. The best extra virgin olive oil from the first cold pressing of the fruit has less than 1 percent acidity, while virgin olive oil is of lesser quality and light olive oil is refined to remove much of the distinctive olive flavor and color (but none of the calories—it's exactly the same amount of fat, so don't be fooled). Make sure you see the words "cold pressed" on the label of your extra virgin oil, an indication of high-quality extraction methods.

Some olive oils are pale in color, some are deep golden, and others are brilliant green. Color is not an indication of flavor, so you have to try different brands, from different countries, to see what you like. Good oils are produced in many countries, from Spain and Italy to Greece—find one you like that's in your price range.

Some olive oils are sweet and fruity, others have a distinct peppery flavor. Each works differently with different foods. Find an inexpensive virgin or light olive oil for everyday cooking and frying. Use a neutral-flavored olive oil in baking. Save the more expensive extra virgin oils for drizzling over salads and cooked vegetables or g rilled fish.
Tasty extra virgin olive oil is also delicious served with good bread for dipping—serve two of your favorites drizzled on plates or shallow bowls to start a meal. It will stimulate both the appetite and the conversation.

Parchment Paper

This non-stick paper is a miracle when you're baking—you'll never have a cookie stick or have to scrub burned bits from your sheet pans again. Use it to line baking pans whenever you make cookies or squares (easy release and clean up), cake pans (ditto), or whenever you're baking chicken or fish. The paper is perfect for cooking packets of lean meats like chicken breasts or fish fillets with vegetables. They steam and brown at the same time. Just place the meat/fish on a piece of parchment, add chopped veggies (bell peppers, pea pods, onions, green beans, etc.), a drizzle of olive oil or white wine, some herbs and seasoning, then fold to seal, forming a neat square or oval. Place the packets on a baking sheet and bake at 400°F (200°C) for 10 minutes. The packets will brown and puff up. Cut the packets open with kitchen shears to let the steamy aromas out—eat right from the paper packets. Very fast and delicious, especially for fish and seafood.

Parmesan

Just to reiterate, nothing will save a pasta dish faster than a grating of real Parmesan cheese—that's the Parmigiano Reggiano cheese from the Parma/Modena region of Italy, aged a minimum of 18 months (by law) and up to 4 years for the finest cheeses. You can tell if it's real Parmigiano Reggiano—the name is stamped right into the rind of the cheese. There is no substitute for the real thing when it comes to Parmesan cheese. Never buy the fake, dried stuff in the can (you already know that, I'm sure) and resist the urge to purchase cheaper Parmesan-style cheeses made elsewhere. Parmigiano Reggiano is expensive but because it's so flavorful, you don't need to use much and a chunk will keep for a month or two in the refrigerator. Grate this hard, granular cheese with a microplane grater for the finest shreds, and serve it on the cheese platter in a full piece, with a short-bladed knife to pry off small chunks for eating.

Parsley

There's a big difference in the taste of curly parsley and flat-leafed Italian parsley—the latter has a much more assertive flavor. Buy it whenever you can and keep it wrapped in a moist paper towel in a plastic bag in the crisper. You can also keep it standing upright like a bouquet in a jam jar of water in the refrigerator. Make sure you always have a herb like parsley around. Chop it up and scatter it over any soup or stew and it will look—and taste—better.

Pasta and Noodles

Good pasta has a nice bite when it's cooked, while bargain pasta is soft and mushy. Make sure to look for a good semolina-based pasta—usually a brand imported from Italy is best. Whole wheat or spinach pastas are interchangeable for most dishes, except those with delicate cream sauces. Multi-colored pastas should be flavored naturally (with beets, spinach, carrots, etc.), and are pretty in cold pasta salads.

Make sure to buy a selection of pastas—different sizes and shapes. Long pasta like spaghetti and linguine work best with smooth and creamy sauces. Short pasta like rotini and penne are better for chunky sauces as they grab and hold bits of vegetables, olives, and meat. Orzo is a small pasta, shaped like grains of rice, and is good cold in salads.

Small egg noodles (shaped like tiny diamonds) are also a staple in The Guy's kitchen. He dumps them into chicken broth for instant chicken soup.

Asian noodles include Japanese soba (buckwheat noodles sold in bundles of 6-inch/15-cm sticks), ramen (dry Japanese instant noodles), and Chinese noodles (dry instant noodles or steamed fresh noodles sold in the produce sections of many supermarkets). The Guy likes to buy the fresh steamed noodles to serve beneath everyday stir-fries, instead of rice, or for Asian noodle soups, or cold noodle salads. They need less than five minutes of cooking.

Rice noodles are another type of Asian noodle. They are translucent white noodles, sold dry or fresh, and used in salad rolls. Rice noodles can be rehydrated without cooking, usually in about 15 minutes in a bowl of warm water. Cellophane or bean thread noodles are made from mung bean starch and can be added to soups or deep-fried.

Pesto

Pesto is an important Italian condiment made with fresh herbs, olive oil, and garlic. Basil pesto is the traditional combination of ground fresh basil leaves, pine nuts, garlic, and olive oil. Make it in the fall when basil is inexpensive, freeze it in ice cube trays, then pop out the cubes and keep them in a bag in the freezer to add instant fresh basil flavor to tomato sauce, soups, and stews. Or find a commercial brand that you like and keep a jar of basil pesto on hand as a pantry staple. Basil pesto is also nice to slather over a thin crust pizza (instead of tomato sauce), to stir into chopped fresh tomatoes for bruschetta, or to add to sour cream and mayo for a fast dip.

 Sun-dried tomato pesto is another great ingredient to keep in the refrigerator. Slather it on toasts for an appetizer, toss it with noodles for an instant pasta side dish, or mix it into dips and tomato sauces for a boost of flavor.

Coriander chutney is an equally useful condiment (sort of an Indian version of pesto, using ground fresh coriander, a.k.a. cilantro). The Guy always has a jar in the fridge to stir into anything that calls for cilantro, from Mexican salsas to Thai curries.

Potatoes

The Guy is a sucker for any spud, but you should be sure to choose the right potato for the job. Some potatoes are perfect for mashing as they disintegrate and nearly mash themselves when cooked, while others are waxy in texture and retain their shape perfectly in dishes like potato salad and fried potatoes.

Red-skinned potatoes are usually waxy and best for boiling, while yellow-fleshed varieties like Yukon Gold have a lovely flavor and color for mashing. Large white potatoes, like russets, are best for french fries and baked potatoes.

Gourmet potatoes add instant cachet to a special meal. Look for tiny yellow fingerling potatoes to boil in their skins and serve alongside grilled meats or fish. Blue potatoes, an heirloom variety from South America, are a deep purplish-blue all the way through, even when cooked, and make deliciously striking navy blue mashed potatoes.

New potatoes, freshly dug, can be scrubbed and boiled in their skins. Many chefs swear by boiling all potatoes in their skins, even potatoes destined for mashing—the skins come off quite easily after they're cooked, although it's hot work, and this way the flesh never gets waterlogged, keeping its true potato flavor.

When potatoes are new and skins are thin, The Guy likes to make rustic mashes of roasted garlic, caramelized onions, and potatoes in their skins. You don't lose any of the healthy fiber and vitamin C. Or try this yummy combo: regular potatoes and sweet potatoes, mashed with cooked carrots and/or parsnips, then seasoned with onions and ginger that have been fried in butter until golden. This delicious mash takes potatoes into a brand new realm—and makes a colorful statement on any plate!

Pots and Pans

Do not get sucked in by the marketers and buy a complete set of matching pots and pans. You'll end up with pans you don't need and will find some important ones are missing. The Guy's workhorse cooking vessels are industrial heavy spun aluminum frying pans, coated with a good non-stick coating. Chefs use small ones to cook individual portions à la minute—you'll do best with a large 12-inch (30-cm) model that will hold anything from pancakes to a batch of tomato sauce and a smaller 8- or 10-inch (20- or 23-cm) pan for crêpes and omelets. Make sure they have lids and ovenproof handles (no plastic) so you can finish cooking something you sear on the stove (like a beef tenderloin or a chicken breast) in the oven.

You'll also need a covered Dutch oven, a good heavy wok, one small and one medium covered saucepan, a large, deep stock pot (with a pasta strainer insert), a heavy roasting pan for meats and turkeys, two heavy rimmed baking sheets, a soufflé dish, a large covered baking dish, a shallow oval baking dish, and an assortment of loaf and cake pans, including a 9-inch (2.5-L) springform pan, a square pan, muffin tin, and a tart pan with a removable bottom.

Prep

Cook like a chef. Always read the recipe through before you start and get everything out to make sure you have all of the ingredients on hand. When you're cooking for a crowd, it's best to pre-chop, measure, and portion ingredients for your recipes (in little bowls, plastic container, or zippered plastic bags) and label them, so you can cook quickly at the last minute when there are other pressures and distractions.

Always preheat the oven before baking or roasting.

Pressure cooker (see page 486)

Rice

There are many different types of rice, from short and starchy Japanese sushi rice and arborio rice for creamy risotto (see page 146) to long-grain rice, brown rice, and converted rice. The latter is pre-steamed and dried, to infuse the kernel with some of the nutrients from the bran and to help it stay fluffy when cooked. It's a good, no-fail white rice. But The Guy likes the aromatic nutty flavor in white or brown basmati rice, another long-grain rice that steams up beautifully.

You don't need to buy a rice cooker to make perfect rice. It's the basic 2:1 rule—twice as much liquid as rice. Just boil the water with some salt, say, 2 cups (500 mL) water with ½ tsp (2 mL) salt. When the water boils, stir in 1 cup (250 mL) rice, cover the pot, reduce the heat to low and simmer for 20-30 minutes, until you can see little craters forming on top. Remove from heat, cover and set aside to steam for 5 minutes, fluff, and serve with butter.

Brown rice has more nutty flavor along with more fiber, because all of the bran is intact. Wholegrain brown rice will take longer to cook than white rice, up to 40 minutes, and may also need a little more liquid.

The Guy once watched a chef add a tea bag to the pot when he boiled his brown rice, then season it with a splash of orange juice and a little butter before serving. The tea adds a little color and an exotic aroma—perfect for pairing with fish.

For an herbed rice pilaf, start by sautéeing some onion and garlic in olive oil or butter, then simmer the rice in chicken broth or tomato juice and stir in some fresh herbs. For coconut rice—perfect with Asian food—use half water and half canned coconut milk. Or just stir a spoon of basil pesto or curry paste into a pot of hot cooked rice, to match whatever you're planning to serve it with.

Rice Paper

This is the thin white dough they use in Vietnamese restaurants to make the fresh salad rolls for appetizers. The rice paper is sold in round flat sheets, flat packages of 10-inch (25-cm) dried, translucent wafers in Asian grocery stores. Just dip each sheet in a big bowl of warm water for about 5 seconds, then lay on a clean towel for a minute until it's soft, pliable, and ready to fill with things like shredded lettuce, mint, cilantro, carrots, and cooked shrimp.

The dough is stretchy and sticks to itself to seal the rolls—it's easy to work with once you get the hang of it. Cover the rolls well with plastic wrap until serving so the delicate rice paper doesn't dry out.

Salad spinner

This is an important tool for whipping the water out of freshly washed salad greens. If you don't have one, loosely wrap your washed lettuce in a kitchen towel, gather it up like a sack, and go outside into the garden. Whip or whirl the towel around until all of the water is gone. Really, it works.

A salad spinner is also essential for drying fresh herbs, especially leafy ones like cilantro and parsley, after they're washed.

Once you have washed and dried your greens in a spinner, wrap them loosely in a paper towel, then seal them in a plastic bag—they'll keep in the fridge for several days.

Salt

There are too many salts in the sea these days, but sea salt is the only kind to buy. Get rid of any iodized salt (the garden variety table salt made from mined salts) and replace it with sea salt (made from sea water that's evaporated). Sea salts from different parts of the world have different flavors—some of minerals, some even sweet.

Kosher salt has large flakes and dissolves more easily than regular salt. It's also nice for finishing dishes. The hand-harvested sel gris and fleur de sel, gathered off the coasts of France, have a moist consistency.

Keep a small bowl of salt nearby when you're cooking, to add a pinch by hand. Salt should heighten the flavor of whatever you're cooking. If you can taste the salt, you've added too much. In a soup or stew, add a whole potato that you can remove later, to absorb excess salt.

Sauté (or Stir-Fry)

Don't we always say sauté when we really just mean fry? Well, sort of. When you sauté, you heat the food in a shallow pan (a sauté pan or a frying pan), usually with a little butter or olive oil, over fairly high heat, and stir it around until it's just starting to brown. This step is the basic beginning to every good sauce. Don't skip it.

You can also sauté meat and fish as a searing step or to cook thin, tender cuts like minute steaks, pork medallions, or turkey cutlets.

Stir-frying is basically sautéing in a wok. It's faster, because you use higher heat, and the shape of the wok prevents the food from burning while you're constantly moving everything around. A traditional wok is round, and sits on a wok ring over the burner, but an easier pan to handle at home has a small flattened bottom and a single long handle. You can't get the real flavor of restaurant stir-fries at home unless you have a professional gas stove (with big BTUs). The basic Asian drill: heat the wok and oil on high; add the onion, ginger, and garlic for 20 seconds; add the small pieces of meat and veggies and stir-fry until almost tender; add the sauce ingredients; cover for 1 minute to steam; thicken with cornstarch (see cornstarch solution page 104); and serve.

Sesame Oil

Buy this nutty, amber oil at any well-stocked supermarket. Not only is it wonderful in Asian cooking, it makes a lovely addition to salad dressings.

Use sesame oil at the end of cooking to add flavor to a dish like a stir-fry—not as a cooking oil. Refrigerate after opening (the oil will get cloudy and coagulate when cold, but it will return to liquid as it warms to room temperature).

Silicon

No, not the valley or the implants—silicon has gone high-tech in the kitchen. You may have heard of the Silpat, a rubbery-looking silicon mat that you can use to line your baking sheets. Nothing sticks to this stuff. On this miracle mat you can make lacy tuile cookies, spectacular caramel decorations to crown your desserts, and potato pavés just like the world's greatest chefs. A great, great toy.

But there's more. Now they're making spatulas out of silicon. They look just like the old rubber spatulas that are so handy for folding cake and cookie batters, but these new units are heat-proof, too—you can use them when you're sautéing or stirring stuff in your expensive non-stick cookware.

But The Guy's absolute favorite silicon stuff is the bakeware—Indian rubber red cake pans that go into the oven and withstand up to 450°F (230°C). You can literally turn the pan inside out to clean or to pop out that sticky carrot cake like an ice cube. The Bundt is brilliant—no more cakes that end up stuck in the pan. This is a lot more expensive than the usual tin cake tin, but you'll never go back. And there are little tart pan molds for mini quiche, even tiny pyramids that shape perfect frozen desserts, or little terrines, and tiny cakes.

Soy Sauce

Keep your wits about you in the soy sauce aisle of the Chinese grocery. There are several kinds of soy, and they're not all created equal.

The Guy favors Japanese tamari, a naturally fermented soy sauce with lots of rich, dark flavor. But a light Chinese soy sauce is also handy to have on the counter—it's light in color (like a white wine versus a red) and won't add an unwanted darkness to delicate sauces for vegetables or seafood.

Indonesian soy sauce (a.k.a. kecap manis) is a sweetened soy sauce, thick like molasses. If you don't have it, combine equal parts of dark soy and liquid honey or corn syrup—not exactly the same, but okay in a pinch.

Springform Pan

These are the round, straight-sided baking pans that come apart into two pieces—a flat bottom and an outer ring that springs open when you flip a latch on the side. This makes it easy to unmold cheesecakes, savory polenta tortes, layered and baked vegetable terrines, and even carrot cakes and steamed puddings. The Guy loves his non-stick springforms. A 9-inch (2.5-L) is standard, but buy a few other sizes as well. A bigger 10-inch (3-L) pan is always useful, as is the deep tiny one that fits neatly inside his pressure cooker and makes moist and speedy "pressure-baked" sweet and savory cheesecakes.

Steamer Basket

This is a collapsible metal gizmo that fits into any saucepan to hold vegetables and other foods above simmering water for steaming. Cheap and useful.

If you want to steam a whole fish or a batch of Chinese egg tarts, go to Chinatown and buy a bamboo steamer (looks like a flat basket with a tightly woven domed lid). This fits right into your wok, above steaming water, and will hold a red snapper or a plate of steamed buns.

In a pinch, cut the bottom and top off of a tuna can to elevate any heatproof plate above the water in a wok or covered sauté pan for steaming.

Stir-Fry (see Sauté)

Substitutions and Equivalents

Remember, most recipes are infinitely adaptable so you can be creative. Here are some simple substitutions that will work on most occasions:

1 Tbsp (15 mL) Dijon = 1 tsp (5 mL) dry mustard powder

Large-flake oats = quick-cooking oats (not instant)

1 cup (250 mL) white sugar = 1 cup (250 mL) brown sugar

1 cup (250 mL) cream cheese = 1 cup (250 mL) puréed cottage cheese + ¼ cup (60 mL) butter (for cheesecakes)

1 Tbsp (15 mL) worcestershire sauce = 1 tbsp (15 mL) soy sauce + a dash of lemon, hot sauce, and sugar

Hoisin sauce = oyster sauce

1 cup (250 mL) self-rising flour = 1 cup (250 mL) all-purpose flour + 1 tsp (5 mL) baking powder + pinch of salt

1 tsp (5 mL) baking powder = ¼ tsp (1 mL) baking soda + ½ tsp (2 mL) cream of tartar

1 cup (250 mL) sour cream or buttermilk = 1 cup (250 mL) plain yogurt

1 cup (250 mL) tomato sauce = ½ cup (125 mL) tomato paste + ½ cup (125 mL) water

1 Tbsp (15 mL) chopped fresh herbs = 1 tsp (5 mL) dried herbs (not always a good substitute)

1 lemon = ¼ cup (60 mL) juice and 1 tbsp (15 mL) zest

1 tsp (5 mL) lemon juice = ½ tsp (2 mL) vinegar

1 clove garlic = ¼ tsp (1 mL) garlic powder

Sun-Dried Tomatoes

In danger of becoming an '80s California cliché, sun-dried tomatoes are nonetheless delicious and great to have in the pantry. Keep a few small jars packed in oil (never discard the flavorful oil, add it to salad dressings) and some dried and ready for rehydrating. The oil-packed dried tomatoes are sweet and chewy, adding instant flavor to dips, salads, and pizza. The dried versions can be kept in a dark, dry place for months, then rehydrated in hot water to use like oil-packed tomatoes. Or simply crush the dry tomatoes to a powder that adds intensive tomato flavor to sauces and dips.

Today's "fresh" alternative is the "oven-roasted tomato"—peeled tomatoes (even canned) that are cut in half, seeded, drizzled with olive oil and fresh herbs, and then roasted on a parchment-lined baking sheet for about 1½ hours in a 300°F (150°C) oven. They provide chewy, concentrated tomato flavor for soups, sauces, and sandwiches. Keep them in the fridge.

Tahini

Tahini is a delicious paste made of ground sesame seeds—like peanut butter with intense sesame flavor. It's essential for Middle Eastern foods like hummus. Find it in Middle Eastern groceries or most supermarkets. In a pinch, substitute natural peanut butter and a little sesame oil.

Tapenade

This condiment made with finely chopped black olives, olive oil, garlic, and herbs is another of The Guy's pantry staples. Not only is tapenade an instant appetizer when smeared on toasts, it can be used on pizza, added to salad dressings and tomato sauces, or tossed with pasta—anywhere you'd use olives, tapenade offers an instant jolt of flavor. Buy it in specialty stores or make your own (see page 21).

Thaw

Thaw meats and poultry in the refrigerator overnight before cooking, on the bottom shelf, on a plate, so that raw juices don't drip down and contaminate other food. You'll need five hours to thaw every 1 lb (500 g) of food, especially large cuts like roasts and turkeys.

You can use low power in the microwave to thaw, but you risk cooking the meat on the outside while the inside remains frozen (and then undercooking the product).

Timing

Timing is everything, as they say, but it's never an exact science when it comes to cooking. You'll learn to tell when a cake is done, how the cookies smell when they're ready to come out of the oven, and when it's time to take a steak off the grill. There are always other issues that affect timing, too—the thickness of your pan, the calibration of your oven, whether you're cooking on a professional gas or aging electric stove, and if you're grilling in Alaska or Alabama. Even the food itself can have a bearing on its perfect preparation—some beans are older and drier than others and may take an extra hour in the pot; a really fresh cob of corn only needs a few minutes to heat through. Don't cook by the clock. Taste and try things while you cook. They're done when you say they are.

Tomatoes

When The Guy says canned tomatoes in a recipe, he means plum or Roma tomatoes, which tend to be meatier, sweeter, and less watery than other tomatoes. The best way to pick your favorite brand is to buy one of each, open the cans and taste them. Some canned tomatoes are more acidic than others, some have a tinny taste. Be brand savvy. You don't have to buy imported tomatoes to get good plum tomatoes—most domestically canned tomatoes are Romas, too.

If you have the good fortune to come upon a case of beautiful, ripe plum tomatoes in the fall, buy them and can or freeze the lot. Canning tomatoes is a bit of work but the results are great. Get a good canning book and make sure you process them properly so that they're well sealed and safe. Or simply wash them, dry them, use a paring knife to cut out the cores, and pop them whole into zippered plastic bags, then right into the freezer. When you need a tomato or two in the winter for a sauce, just run the rock-hard orbs under hot tap water. The skin will pop off and you can chop your romas or plunk them directly into the sauce or stew where they'll disintegrate nicely.

In tomato season, search for fresh heirloom tomatoes at the farmers' markets for salads. These heirloom varieties are the old-fashioned flavorful tomatoes that people used to plant before some greedy Guy decided it was more economical to ship tomatoes all over the planet and grow the cheap, watery ones that travel well but taste like nothing. Heirloom tomatoes are erratic, eclectic, and beautiful—different sizes and colors like little pear-shaped yellow tomatoes, electric green and sweet zebra tomatoes, tomatoes with black and purple stripes, and just amazing-tasting big red beefsteaks. Buy them and try them—so you know what a real tomato is supposed to taste like.

Wasabi

Wasabi is the bright green horseradish paste that you get alongside your sushi at a Japanese restaurant. Buy it at Asian grocery stores in tubes (like toothpaste) that you can keep in the fridge, or in little tins (dried wasabi powder that you mix with water). It's great for adding instant authentic flavor to Asian soups, salad dressings, and sauces. No wasabi in the house? Substitute a touch of Dijon or hot dry mustard powder to taste.

Whisk

A balloon whisk is handy for keeping lumps out of your sauces. Get a medium-sized fairly stiff version and whisk away.

Zest

This is the colored portion of a citrus fruit, whether it's a lemon, lime, orange, or grapefruit. The best way to remove the zest (and not the bitter white pith) is with a zester, a little hand tool with a perforated, triangular metal end that strips the zest off any citrus fruit in long, thin strips.

Index

About the Author

After 20 years in the journalism trenches Cinda Chavich is sure of one thing: you can't beat the food and wine beat.

Writing about food is about more than regurgitating recipes or recommending a nice bottle to buy. It's about helping families and friends enjoy the communal experience of creating and sharing a wonderful meal together. It's about telling stories—stories about passionate people and unique places, culture and history, environmental and health issues related to food. And it's one of the warmest spots in the reporting world—because people who love food and wine, love life.

Cinda makes her living as a food and wine journalist, traveling the world and poking into kitchens wherever she goes. Every adventure is a new inspiration, a new chance to explore a regional cuisine, a unique ingredient, a particular chef or winemaker's passion. Dining with an extended family in the mountains of southern Greece, slurping spicy hot pots in Sichuan, following the southern barbecue trail in North Carolina or exploring the plight of the wild Pacific salmon are topics that have taken Cinda around the globe.

Her food, wine and travel stories have appeared in newspapers and magazines across North America—from the *Globe and Mail* and CBC Radio to *Cooking Light*, *Wine Access*, *Health*, *Avenue*, *Wine Spectator* and *Chatelaine*. She has written several cookbooks. *High Plains*, which focuses on the regional cuisine from her home on the Canadian prairies, won two gold medals from Cuisine Canada, including the top Canadian Food and Culture Award.

Cinda loves to share food in her own home and created The Guy (and The Girl before him) to speak to those who love good food but haven't had the chances she has had to learn about this fascinating topic from the experts. After years of writing, traveling, creating recipes, food styling, broadcasting and hanging around in the world's best kitchens, she's developed a cooking style that's easy but eclectic, and filled with the tricks that the best cooks use to make fabulous food.

Her husband Delbert is one happy beneficiary of this cumulative knowledge and the muse for this book designed to get more guys into the kitchen, more often. They spend quality time together hiking, cycling and relaxing at their cabin—and eating well!

About the Illustrator

Kirsten Horel is an illustrator and lettering artist. She brought The Girl to life in *The Girl Can't Cook* and now she's back with more sparkle and whimsy to bring us The Guy! Kirsten creates The Guy with pen on paper and then he jumps into her computer for fine tuning and coloring. What Kirsten loves about digital art is that when she makes a mark she wants to change, "delete" doesn't make any eraser crumbs. Kirsten spends way more time making art than food, so she's looking forward to more kitchen help from both The Girl and The Guy. Kirsten lives with her husband and kids in Calgary, Alberta.